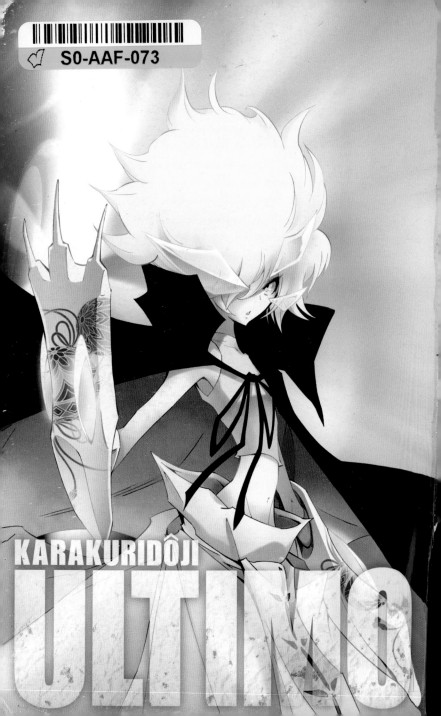

KARAKURIDÔJI
ULTIMO

ULTIMO
KARAKURI DÔJI

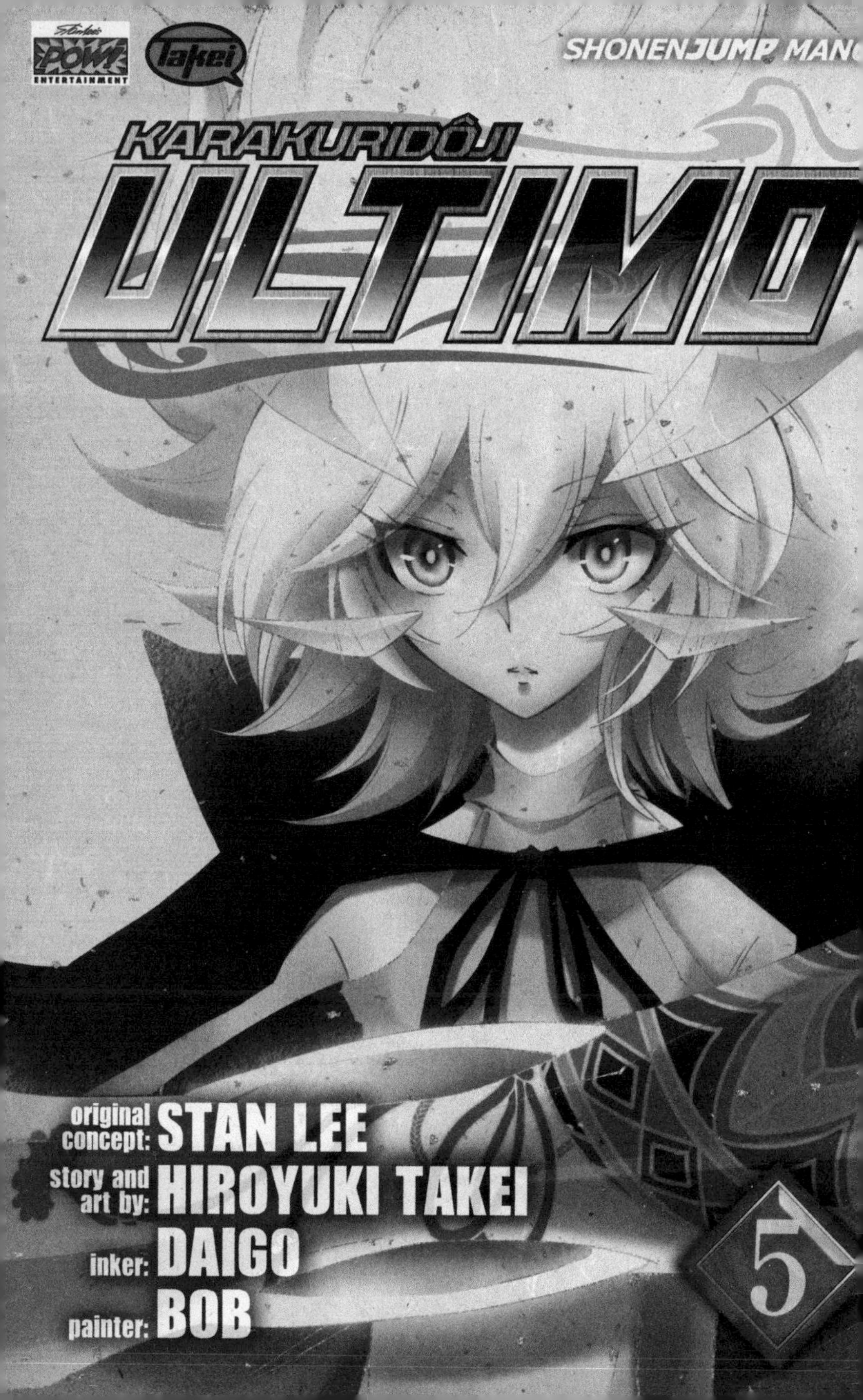
Stan Lee's POW! ENTERTAINMENT
Takei
SHONENJUMP MANG
KARAKURIDÔJI
ULTIMO
original concept: STAN LEE
story and art by: HIROYUKI TAKEI
inker: DAIGO
painter: BOB
5

Karakuri Dôji Ultimo

Characters

Ultimo

Agari Yamato

Sayama Makoto

Oume Hibari

Matsumoto Kiyose

Otake Akitsu

The Story Thus Far

Kyoto in the 12th century. A bandit named Yamato encounters a mysterious man named Dunstan and two Karakuri Dôji, dolls who embody good and evil.

West Tokyo in the 21st Century. Yamato is reborn and reencounters the good dôji Ultimo. When his good friend Rune becomes master to the evil dôji Jealousy, the two clash and the Hundred Machine Funeral—the ultimate battle between good and evil that Dunstan has been plotting—erupts. Yamato turns back time to the day he met Ultimo so he can fix everything that went wrong, and then, in order to know more about Iruma's past, he jumps even further into the past...

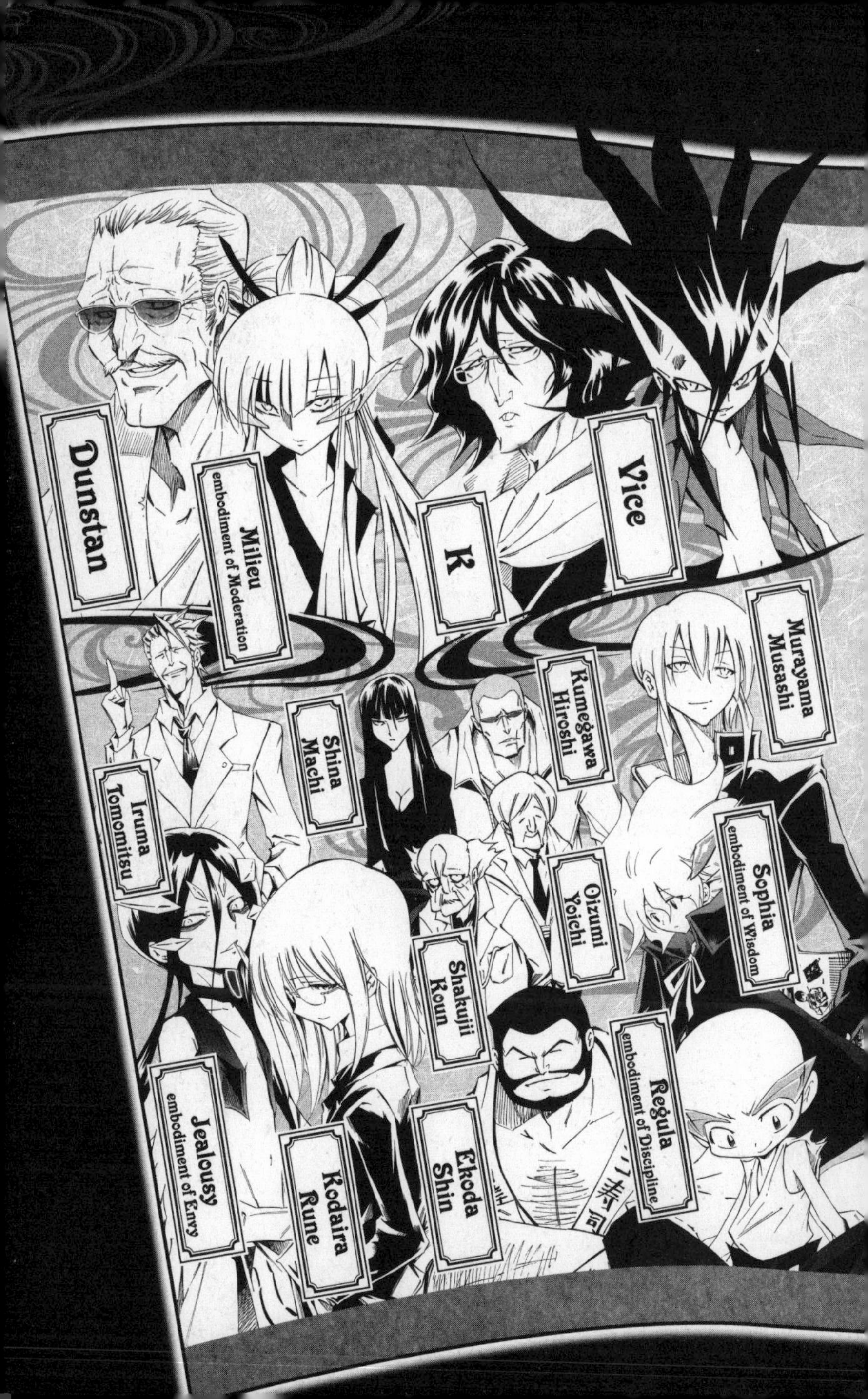
Vice
K^2
Milieu embodiment of Moderation
Dunstan
Murayama Musashi
Kumegawa Hiroshi
Shina Machi
Iruma Tomomitsu
Sophia embodiment of Wisdom
Oizumi Yoichi
Shakujii Koun
Regula embodiment of Discipline
Ekoda Shin
Kodaira Rune
Jealousy embodiment of Envy

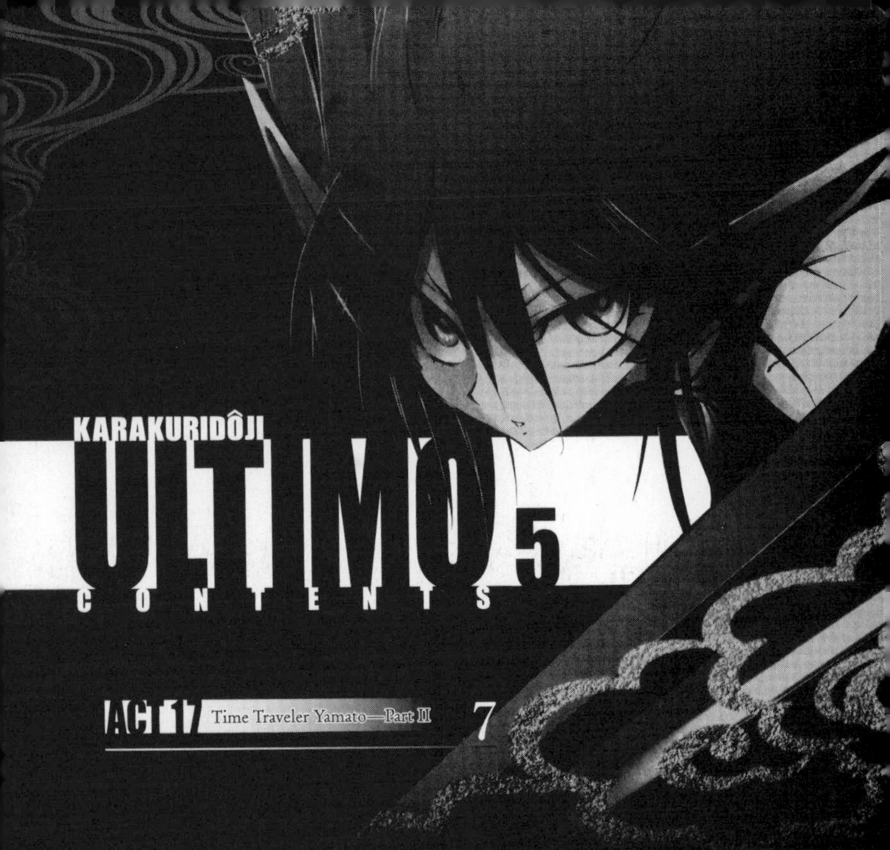

KARAKURIDÔJI

ULTIMO 5

CONTENTS

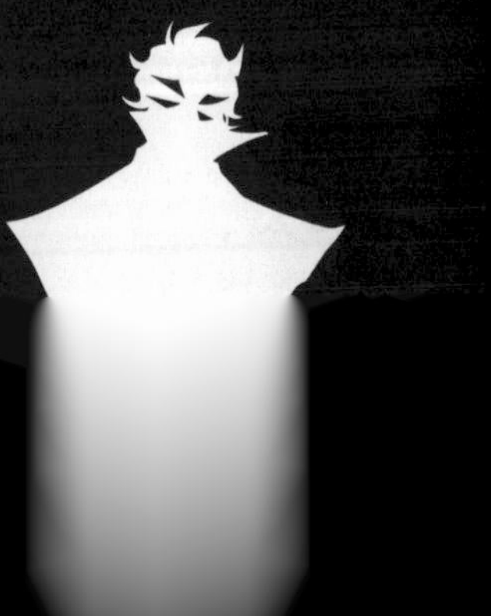

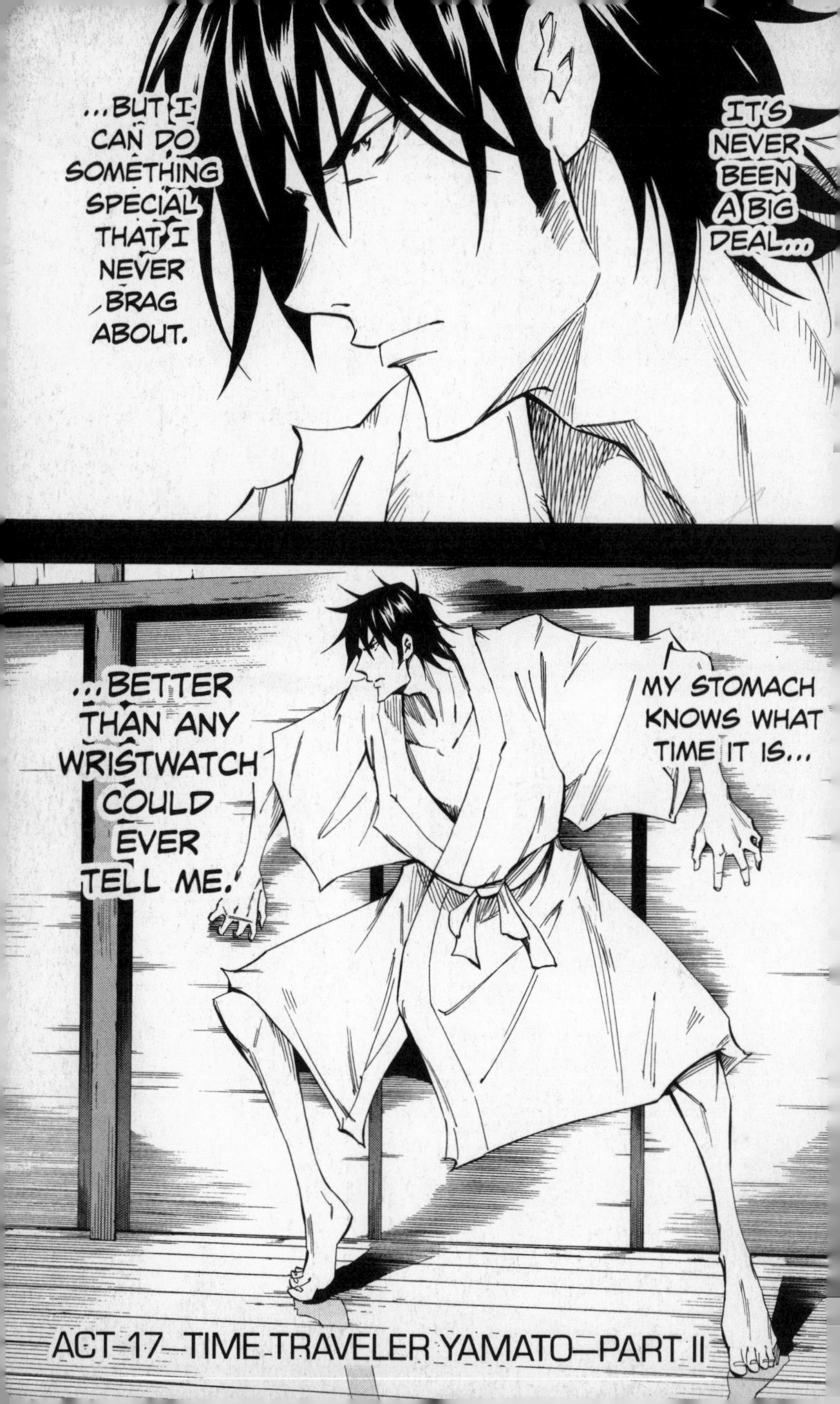
IT'S NEVER BEEN A BIG DEAL...
...BUT I CAN DO SOMETHING SPECIAL THAT I NEVER BRAG ABOUT.
MY STOMACH KNOWS WHAT TIME IT IS...
...BETTER THAN ANY WRISTWATCH COULD EVER TELL ME.
ACT 17 TIME TRAVELER YAMATO—PART II

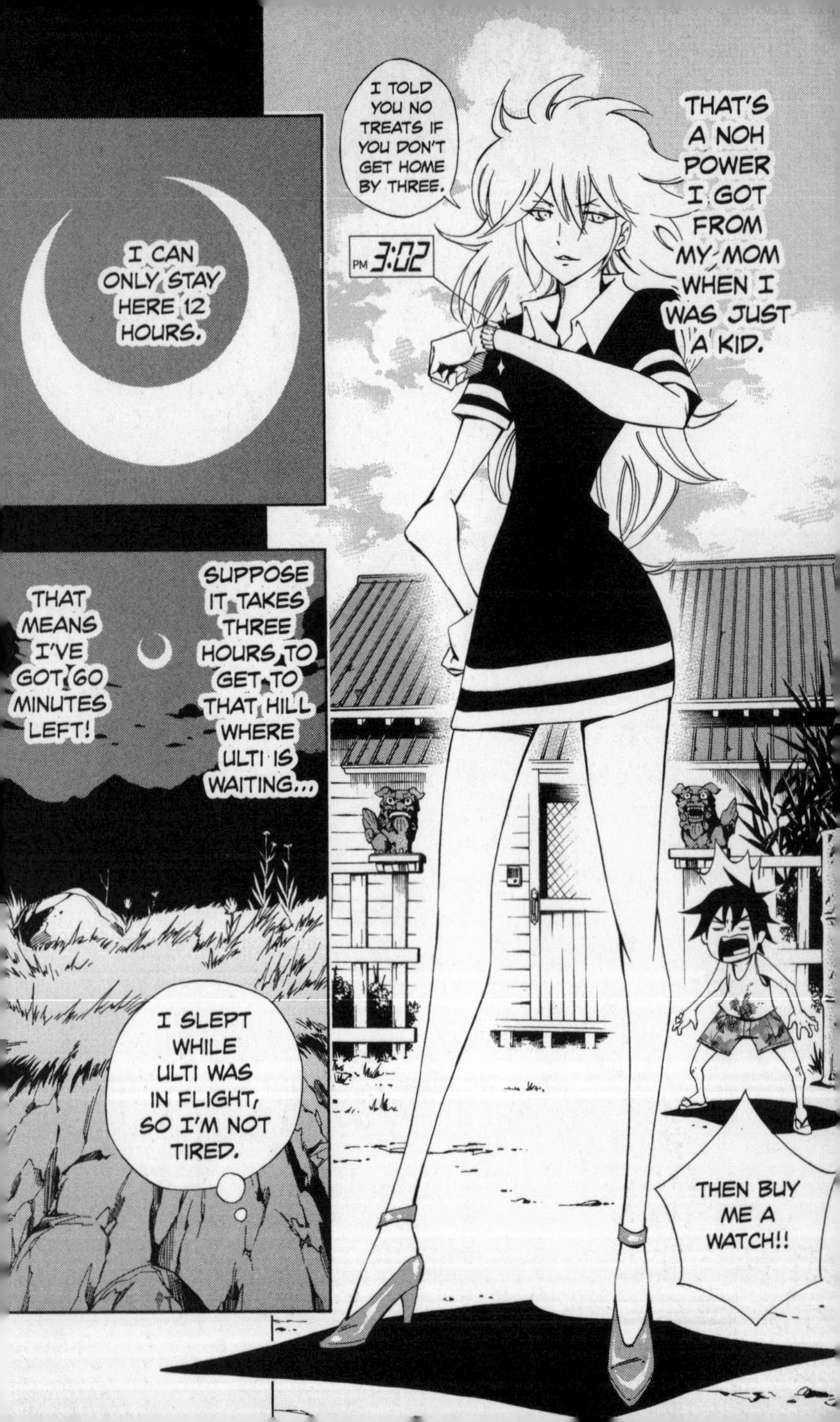
THAT'S A NOH POWER I GOT FROM MY MOM WHEN I WAS JUST A KID.
I TOLD YOU NO TREATS IF YOU DON'T GET HOME BY THREE.
PM 3:02
THEN BUY ME A WATCH!!
I CAN ONLY STAY HERE 12 HOURS.
SUPPOSE IT TAKES THREE HOURS TO GET TO THAT HILL WHERE ULTI IS WAITING...
THAT MEANS I'VE GOT 60 MINUTES LEFT!
I SLEPT WHILE ULTI WAS IN FLIGHT, SO I'M NOT TIRED.

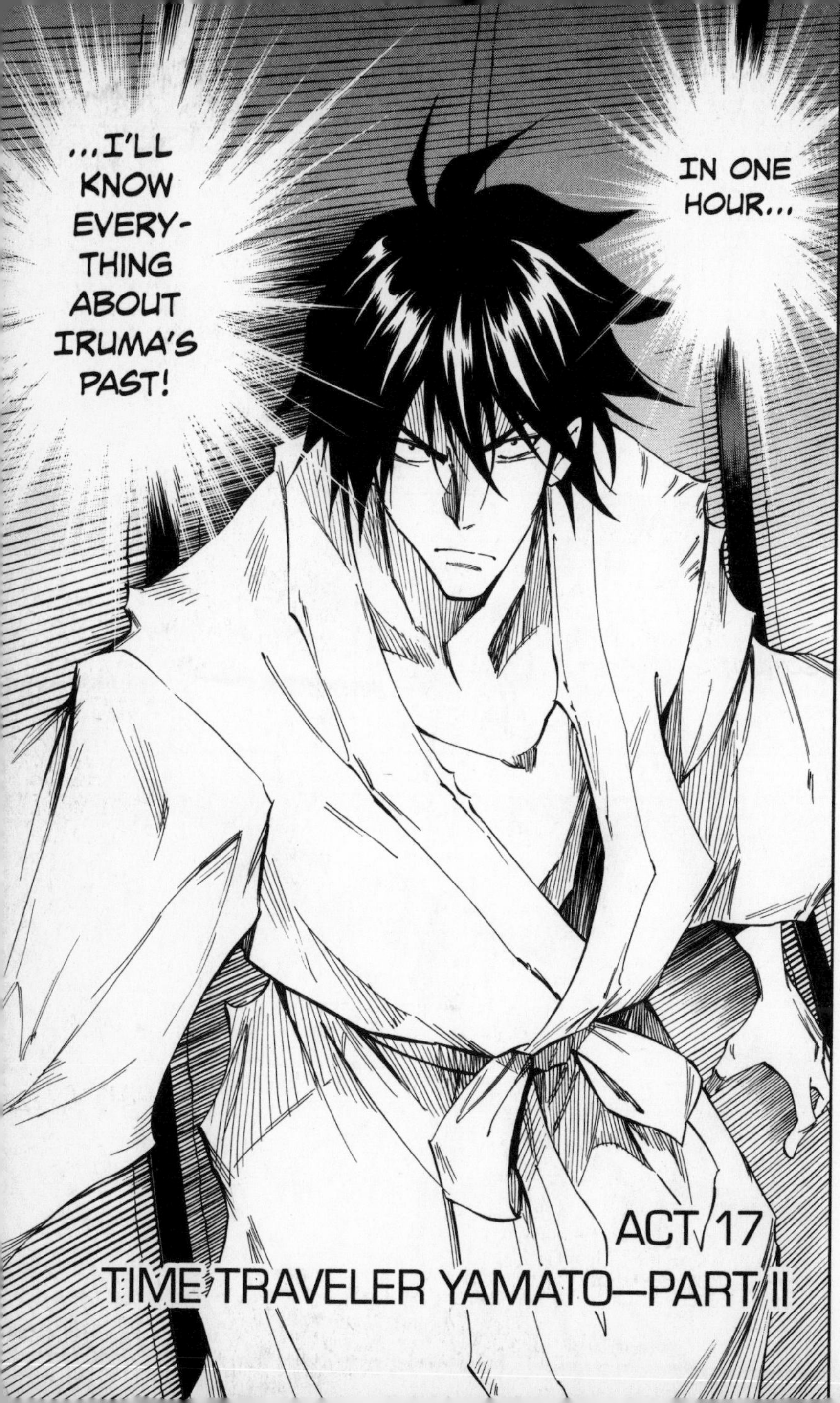
IN ONE HOUR...
...I'LL KNOW EVERYTHING ABOUT IRUMA'S PAST!
ACT 17
TIME TRAVELER YAMATO—PART II

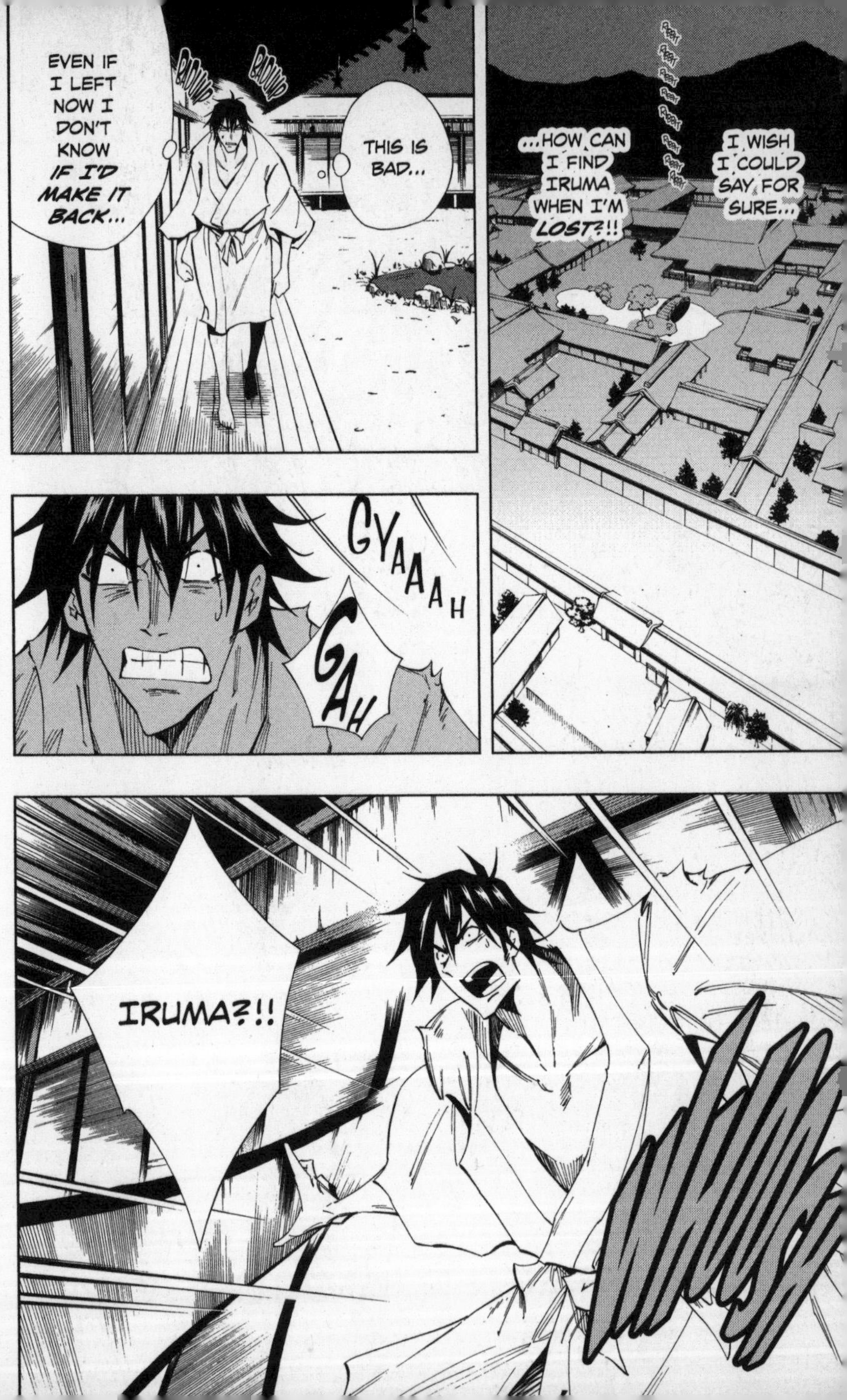

I WISH I COULD SAY FOR SURE...
...HOW CAN I FIND IRUMA WHEN I'M LOST?!!
THIS IS BAD...
BADUMP
BADUMP
EVEN IF I LEFT NOW I DON'T KNOW IF I'D MAKE IT BACK...
GYAAAAH
GAH
IRUMA?!!

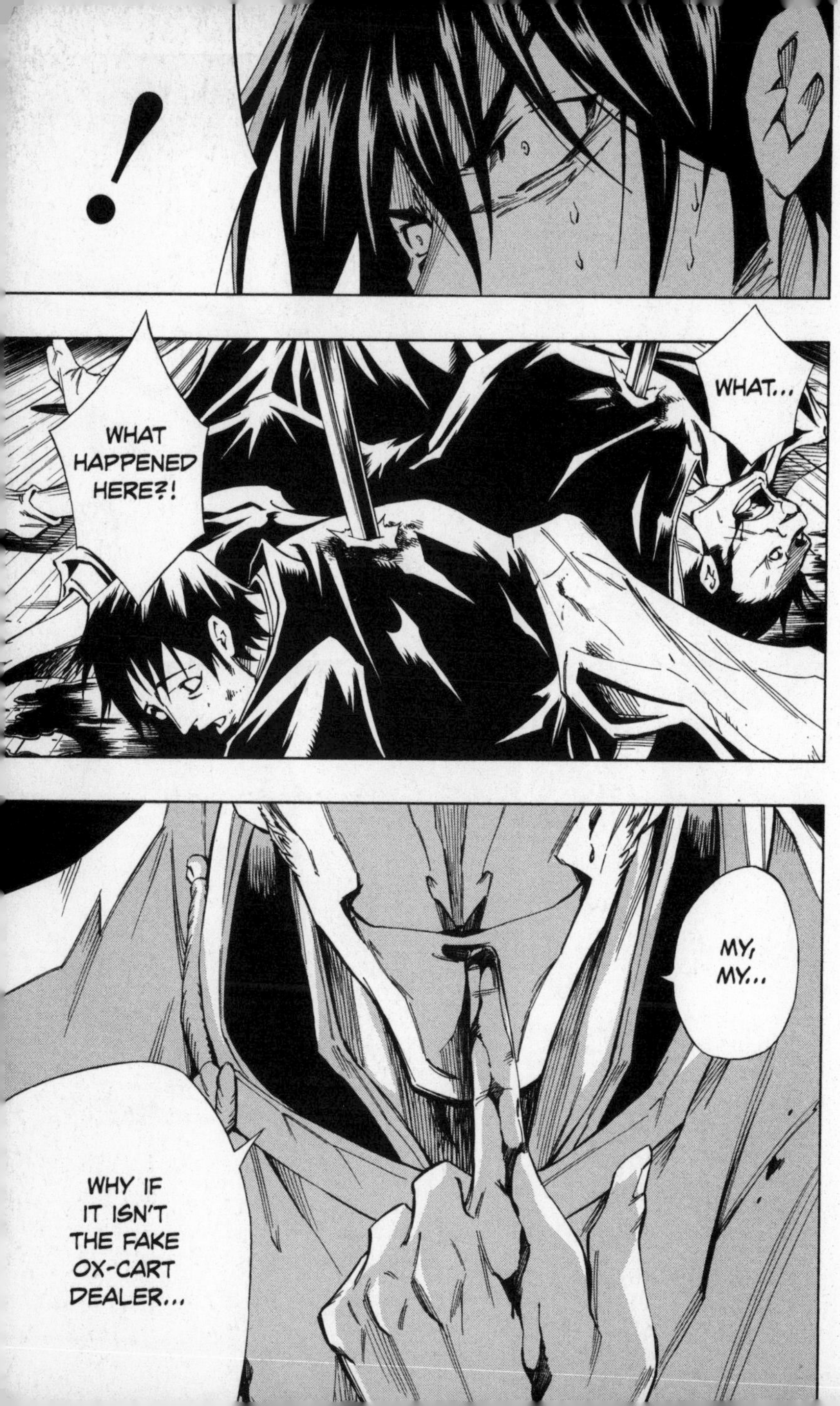
!
WHAT...
WHAT HAPPENED HERE?!
MY, MY...
WHY IF IT ISN'T THE FAKE OX-CART DEALER...

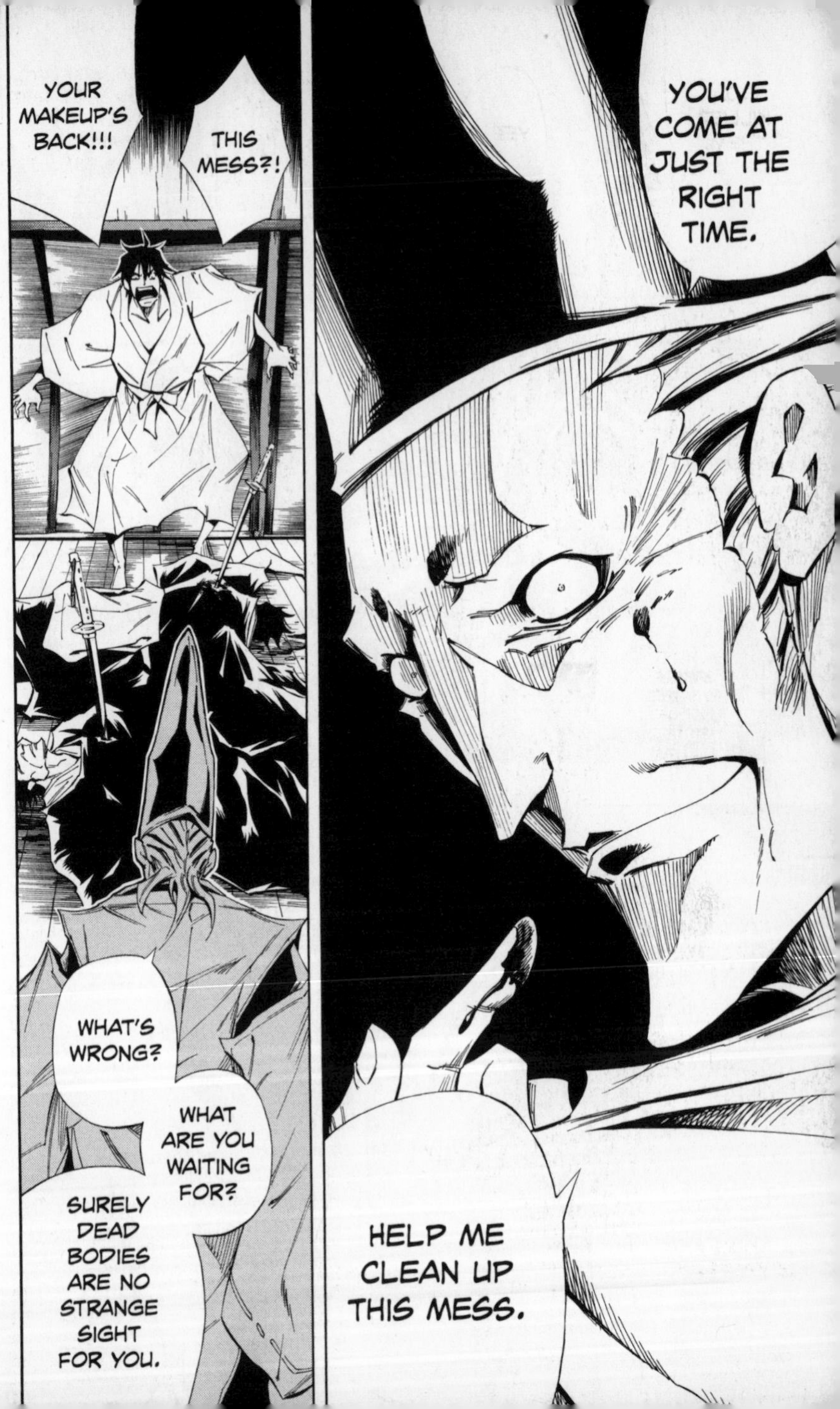
YOU'VE COME AT JUST THE RIGHT TIME.
HELP ME CLEAN UP THIS MESS.
THIS MESS?!
YOUR MAKEUP'S BACK!!!
WHAT'S WRONG?
WHAT ARE YOU WAITING FOR?
SURELY DEAD BODIES ARE NO STRANGE SIGHT FOR YOU.

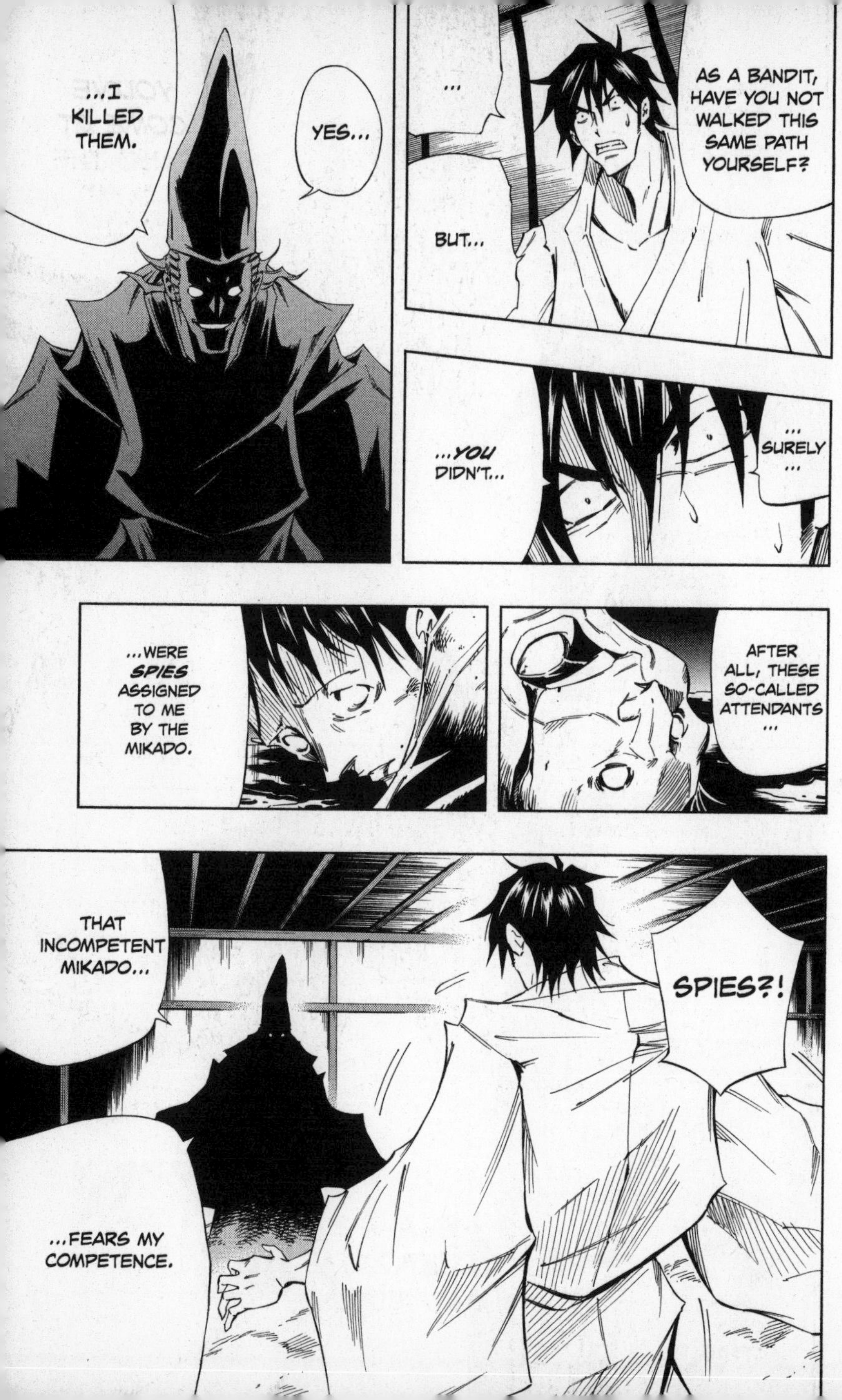
AS A BANDIT, HAVE YOU NOT WALKED THIS SAME PATH YOURSELF?
...
BUT...
... SURELY ...
...YOU DIDN'T...
YES...
...I KILLED THEM.
AFTER ALL, THESE SO-CALLED ATTENDANTS ...
...WERE SPIES ASSIGNED TO ME BY THE MIKADO.
SPIES?!
THAT INCOMPETENT MIKADO...
...FEARS MY COMPETENCE.

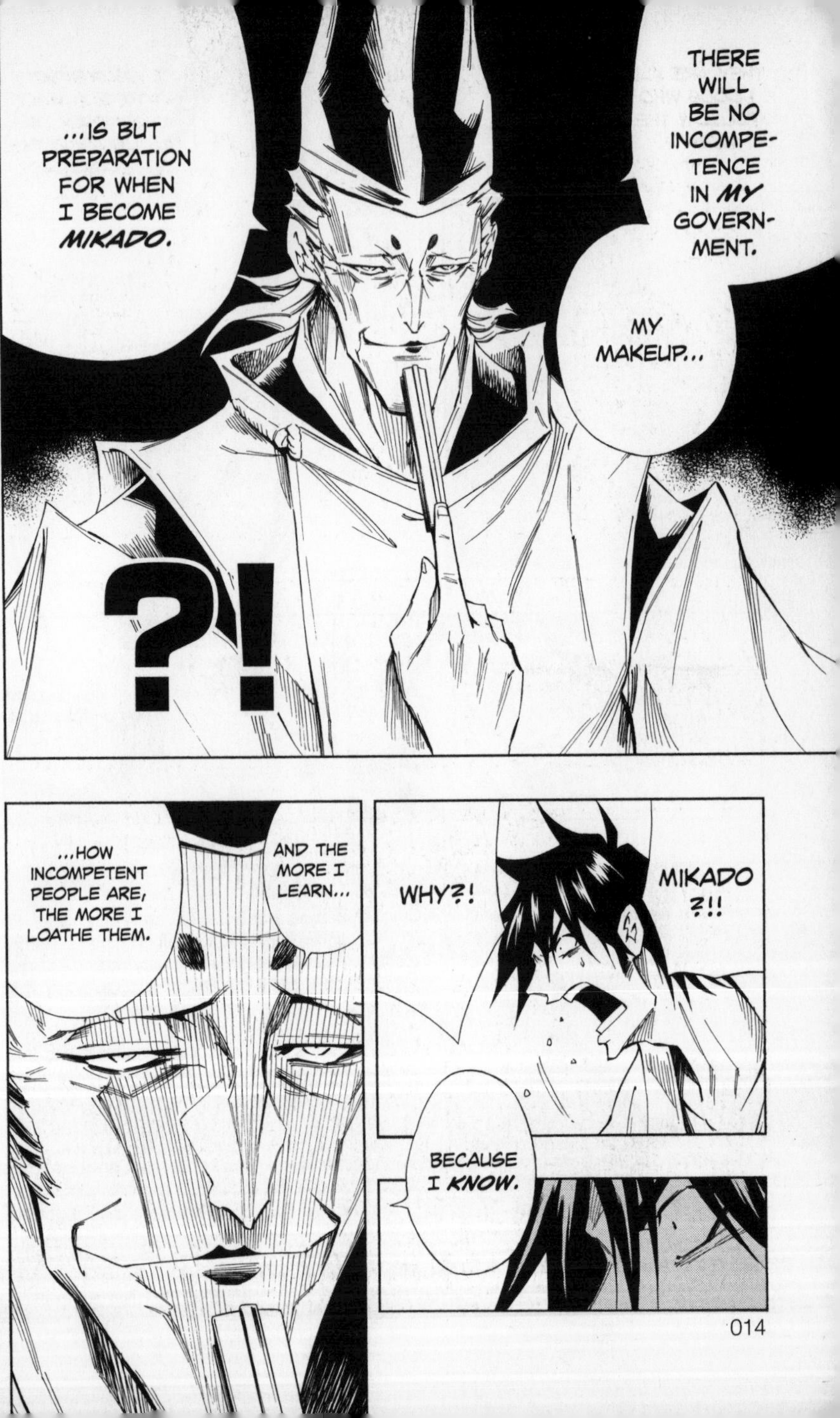
THERE WILL BE NO INCOMPETENCE IN *MY* GOVERNMENT.
MY MAKEUP...
...IS BUT PREPARATION FOR WHEN I BECOME *MIKADO*.
?!
MIKADO ?!!
WHY?!
BECAUSE I *KNOW*.
AND THE MORE I LEARN...
...HOW INCOMPETENT PEOPLE ARE, THE MORE I LOATHE THEM.

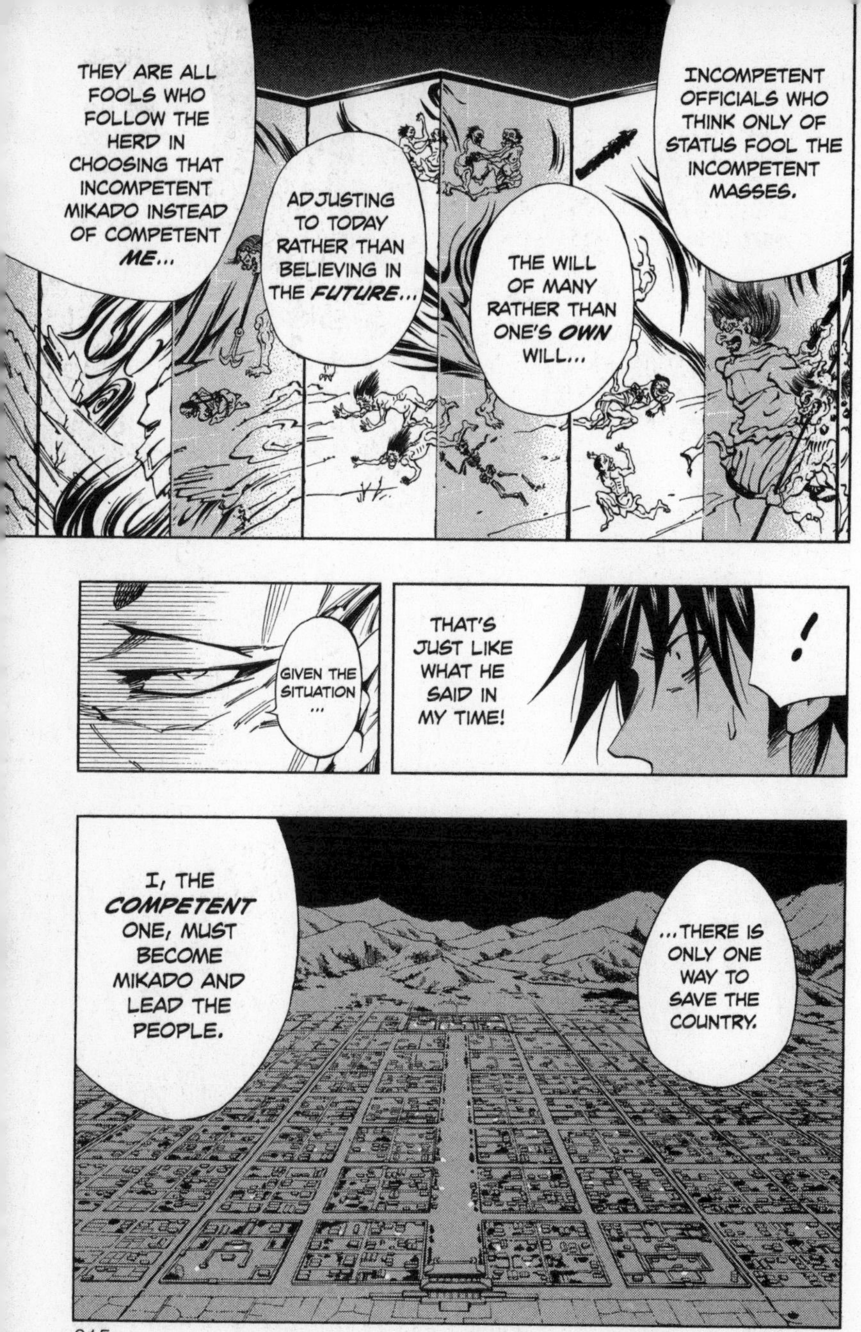

INCOMPETENT OFFICIALS WHO THINK ONLY OF STATUS FOOL THE INCOMPETENT MASSES.
THE WILL OF MANY RATHER THAN ONE'S OWN WILL...
ADJUSTING TO TODAY RATHER THAN BELIEVING IN THE FUTURE...
THEY ARE ALL FOOLS WHO FOLLOW THE HERD IN CHOOSING THAT INCOMPETENT MIKADO INSTEAD OF COMPETENT ME...
!
THAT'S JUST LIKE WHAT HE SAID IN MY TIME!
GIVEN THE SITUATION ...
...THERE IS ONLY ONE WAY TO SAVE THE COUNTRY.
I, THE COMPETENT ONE, MUST BECOME MIKADO AND LEAD THE PEOPLE.

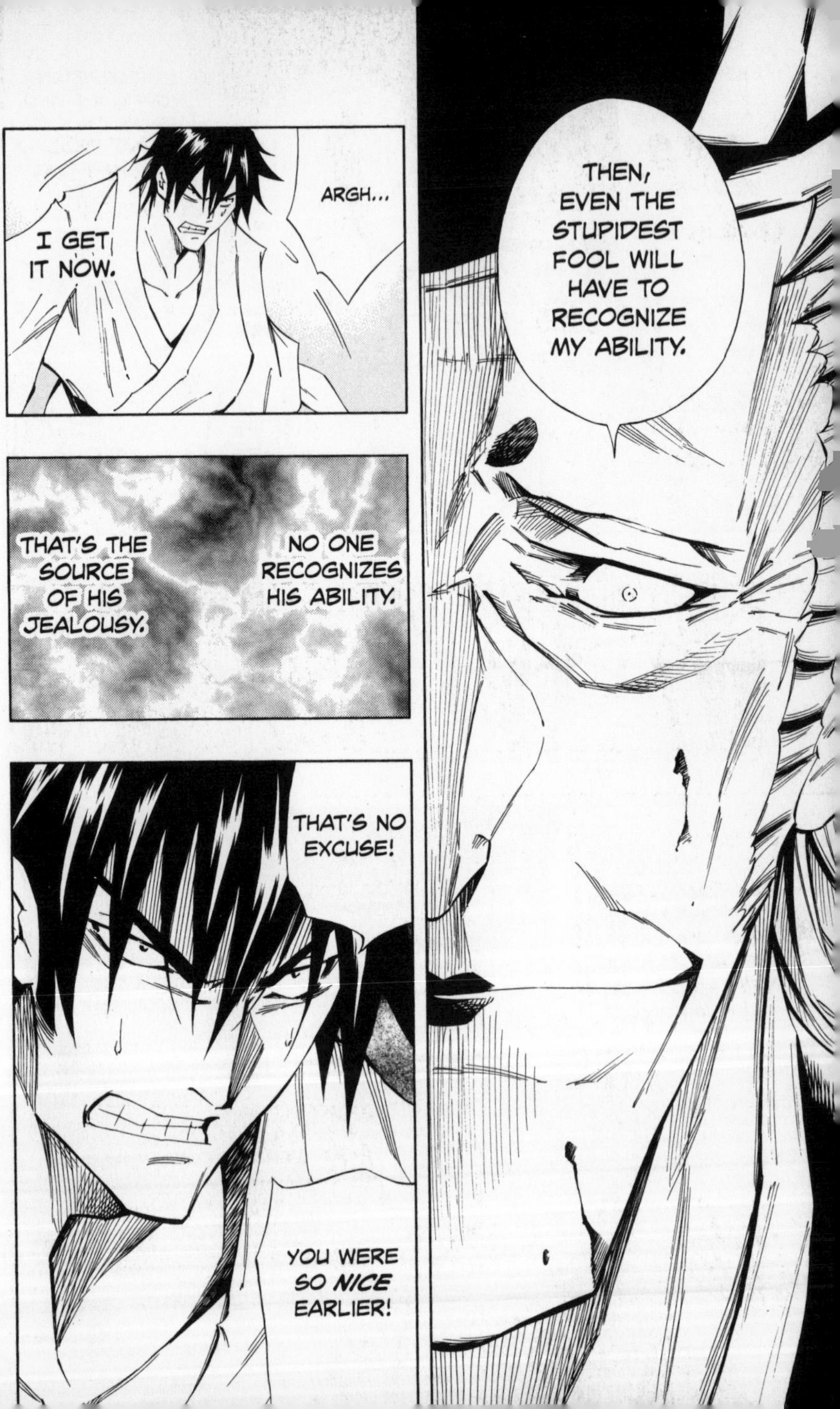
THEN, EVEN THE STUPIDEST FOOL WILL HAVE TO RECOGNIZE MY ABILITY.
ARGH...
I GET IT NOW.
NO ONE RECOGNIZES HIS ABILITY.
THAT'S THE SOURCE OF HIS JEALOUSY.
THAT'S NO EXCUSE!
YOU WERE SO *NICE* EARLIER!

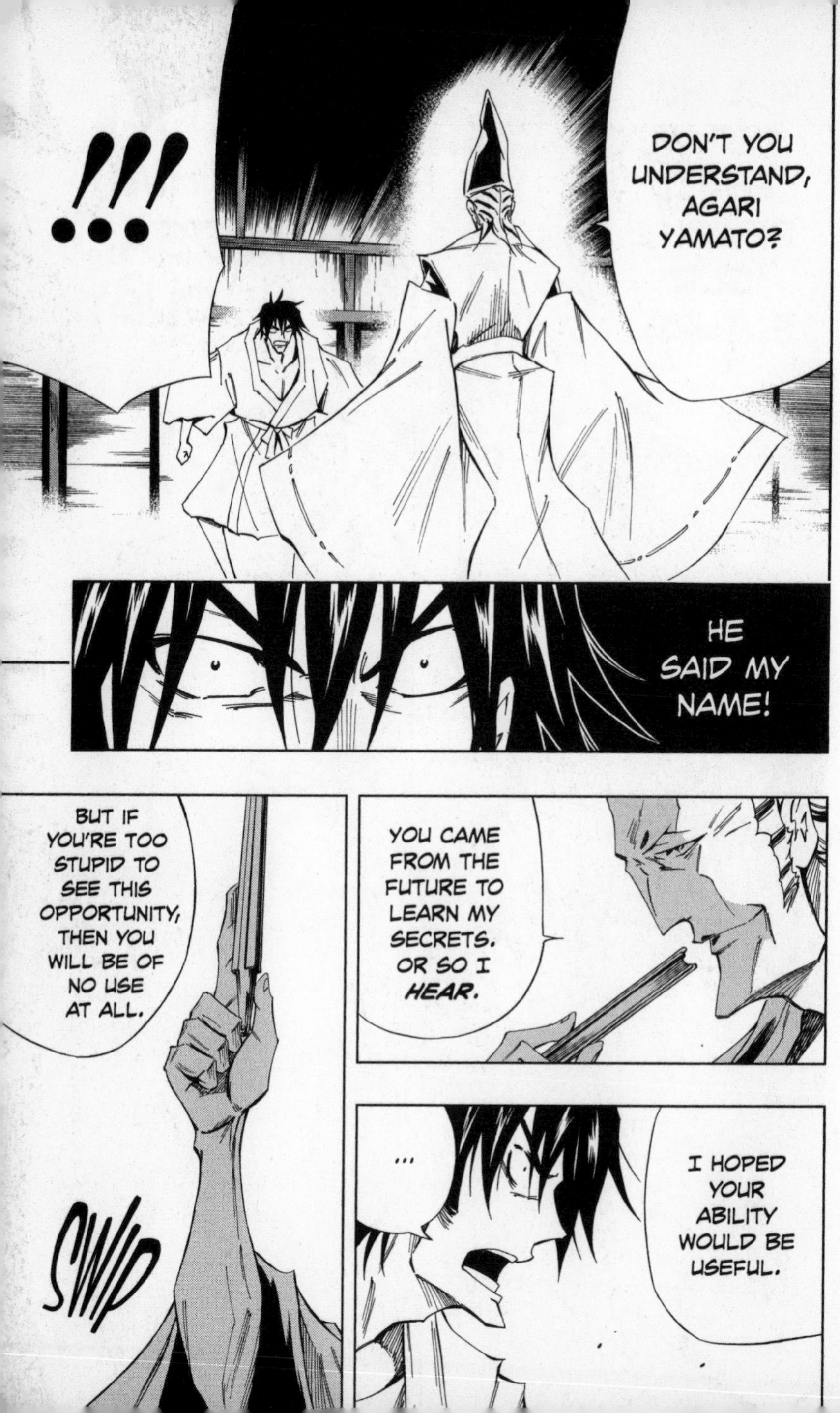
DON'T YOU UNDERSTAND, AGARI YAMATO?
!!!
HE SAID MY NAME!
YOU CAME FROM THE FUTURE TO LEARN MY SECRETS. OR SO I *HEAR*.
I HOPED YOUR ABILITY WOULD BE USEFUL.
...
BUT IF YOU'RE TOO STUPID TO SEE THIS OPPORTUNITY, THEN YOU WILL BE OF NO USE AT ALL.
SWIP

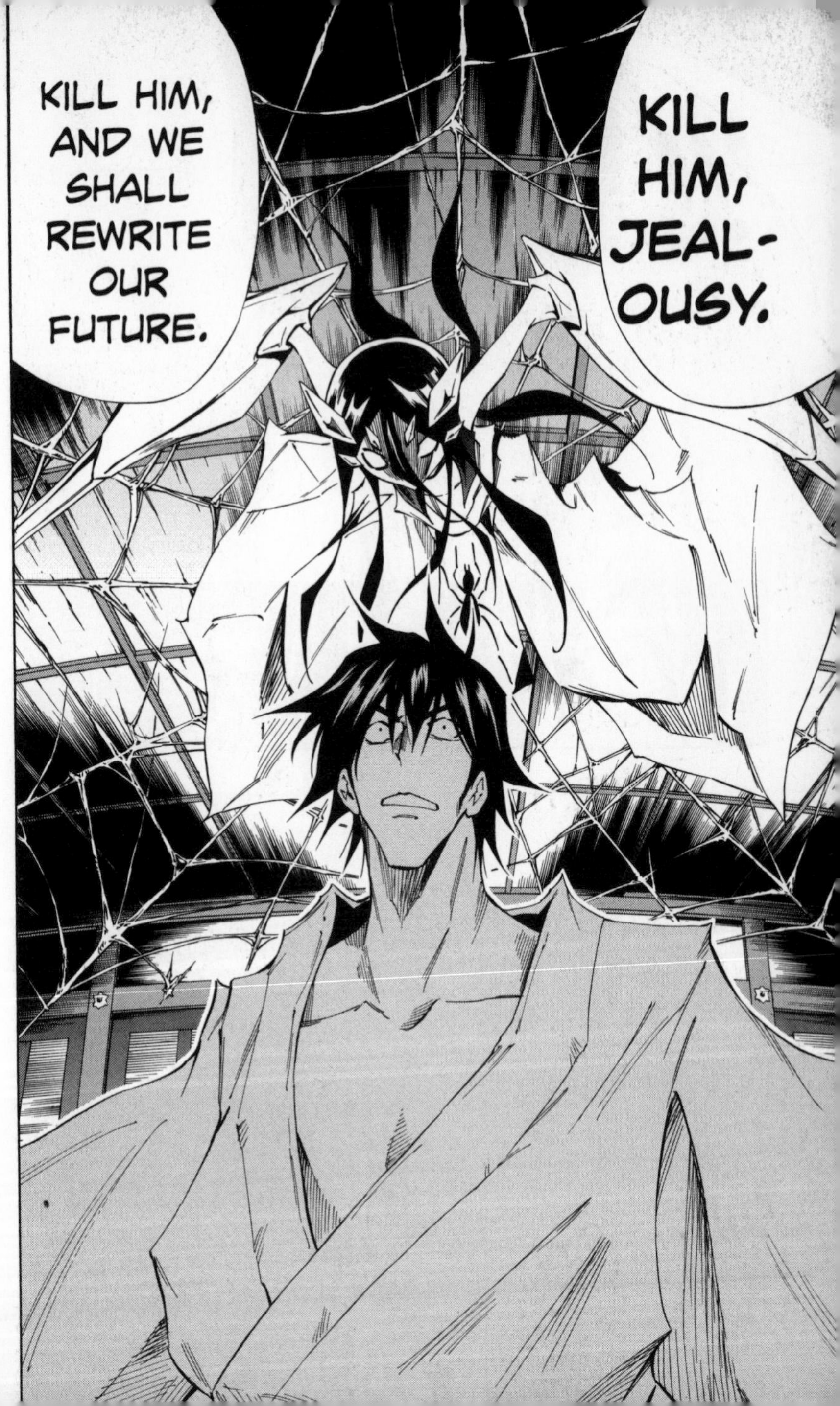
KILL HIM, JEAL-OUSY.
KILL HIM, AND WE SHALL REWRITE OUR FUTURE.

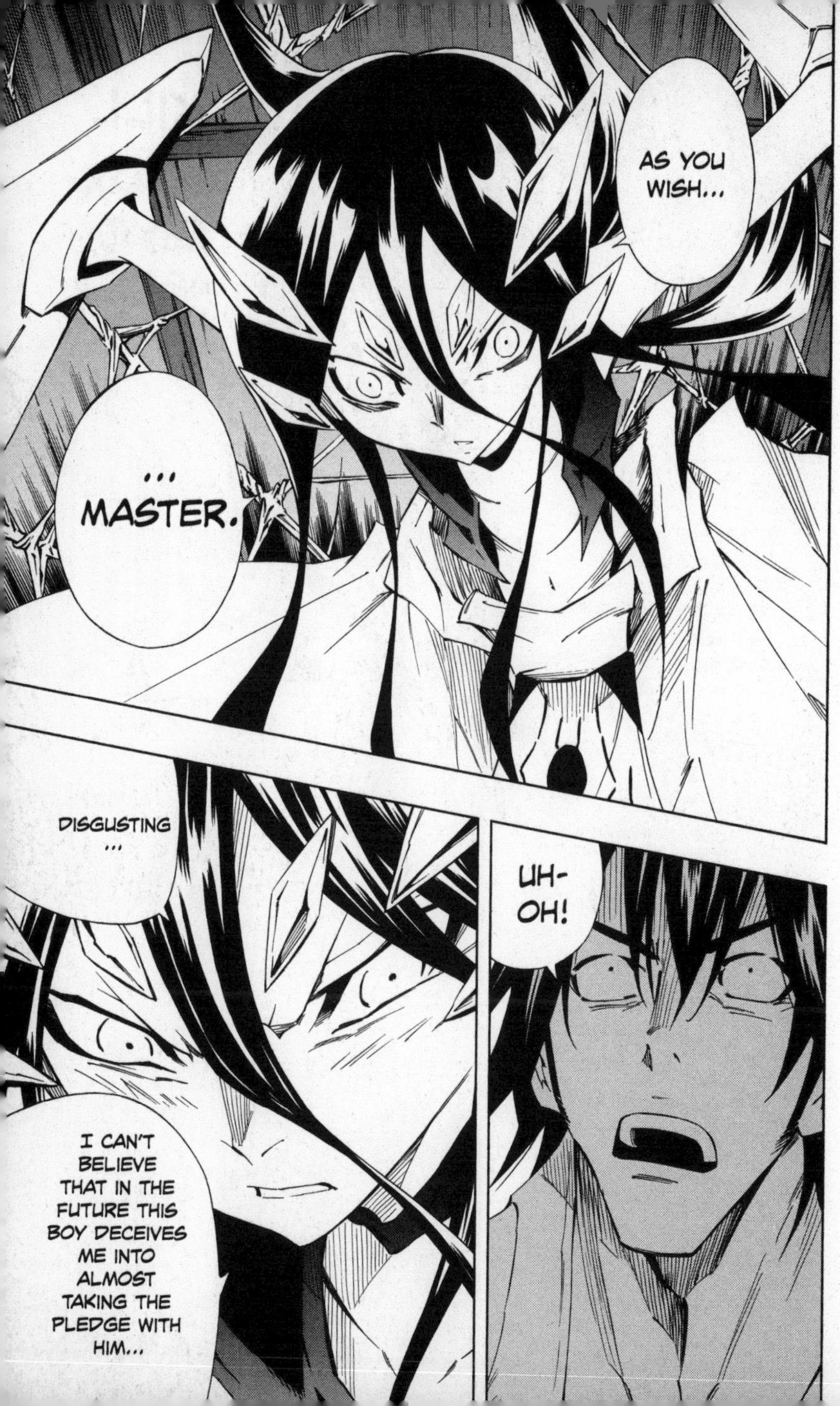
AS YOU WISH...
... MASTER.
UH-OH!
DISGUSTING ...
I CAN'T BELIEVE THAT IN THE FUTURE THIS BOY DECEIVES ME INTO ALMOST TAKING THE PLEDGE WITH HIM...

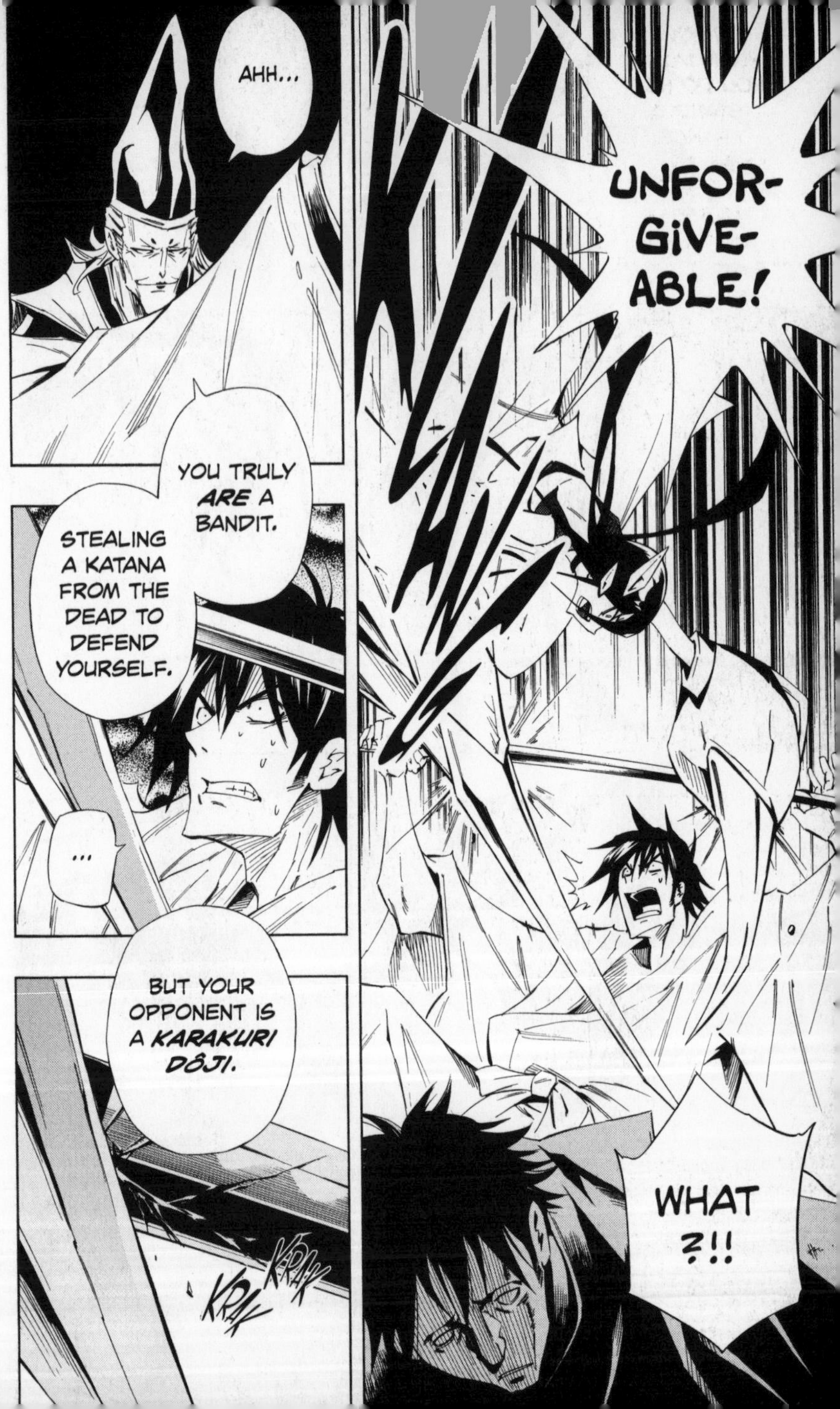
UNFOR-GIVE-ABLE!
WHAT?!!
AHH...
YOU TRULY *ARE* A BANDIT.
STEALING A KATANA FROM THE DEAD TO DEFEND YOURSELF.
...
BUT YOUR OPPONENT IS A *KARAKURI DÔJI*.
K-RAK
KRAK

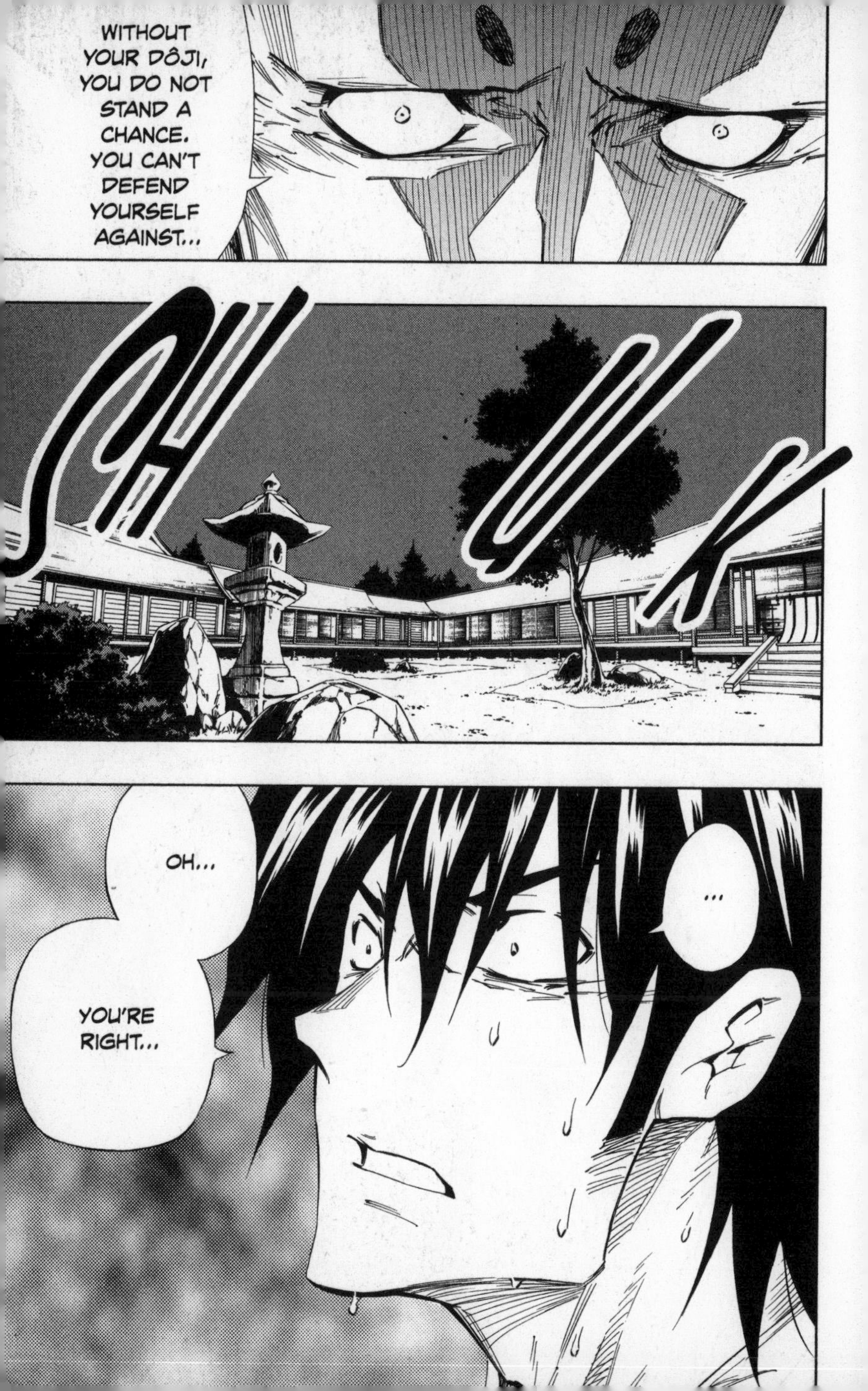
WITHOUT YOUR DÔJI, YOU DO NOT STAND A CHANCE. YOU CAN'T DEFEND YOURSELF AGAINST...
SCHUNK
...
OH...
YOU'RE RIGHT...

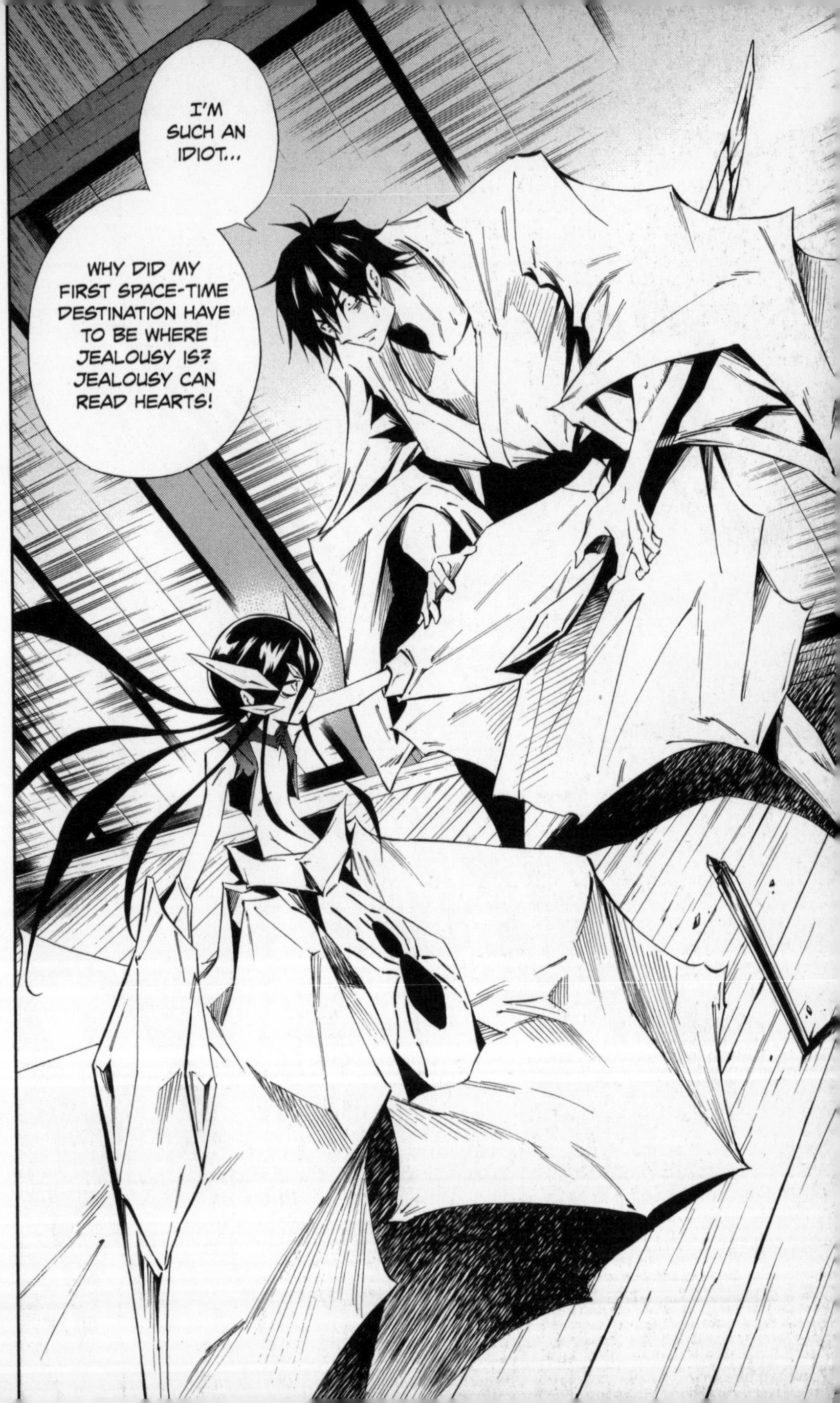
I'M SUCH AN IDIOT...
WHY DID MY FIRST SPACE-TIME DESTINATION HAVE TO BE WHERE JEALOUSY IS? JEALOUSY CAN READ HEARTS!

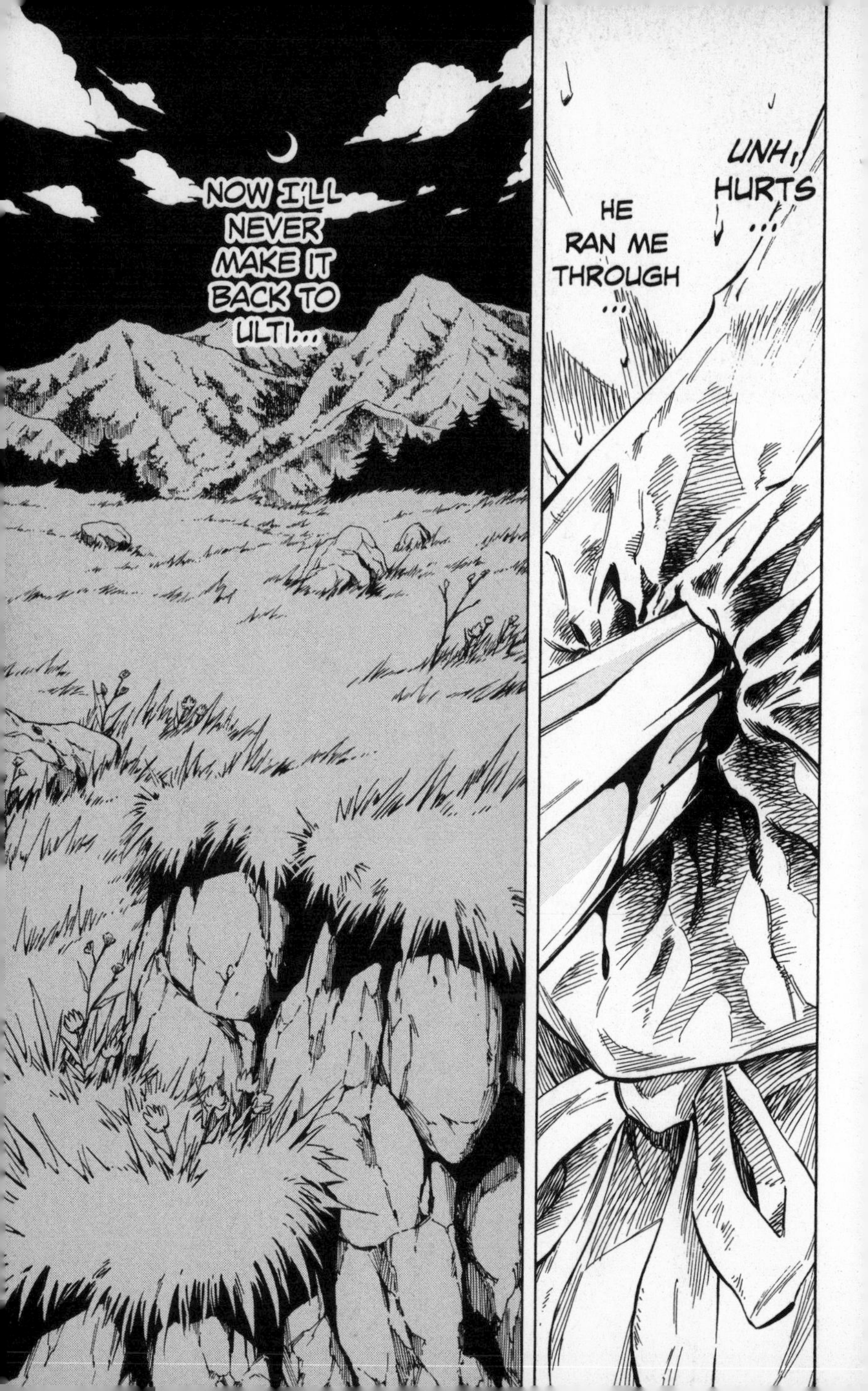
UNH, HURTS...
HE RAN ME THROUGH...
NOW I'LL NEVER MAKE IT BACK TO ULTI...

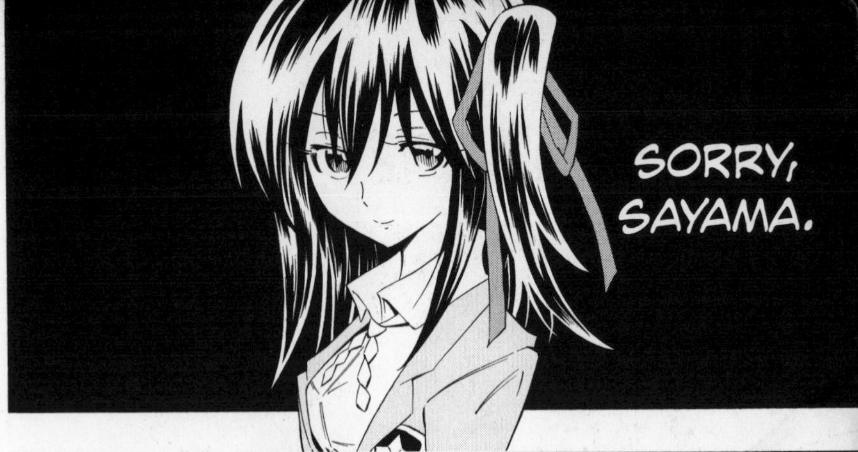
SORRY, SAYAMA.

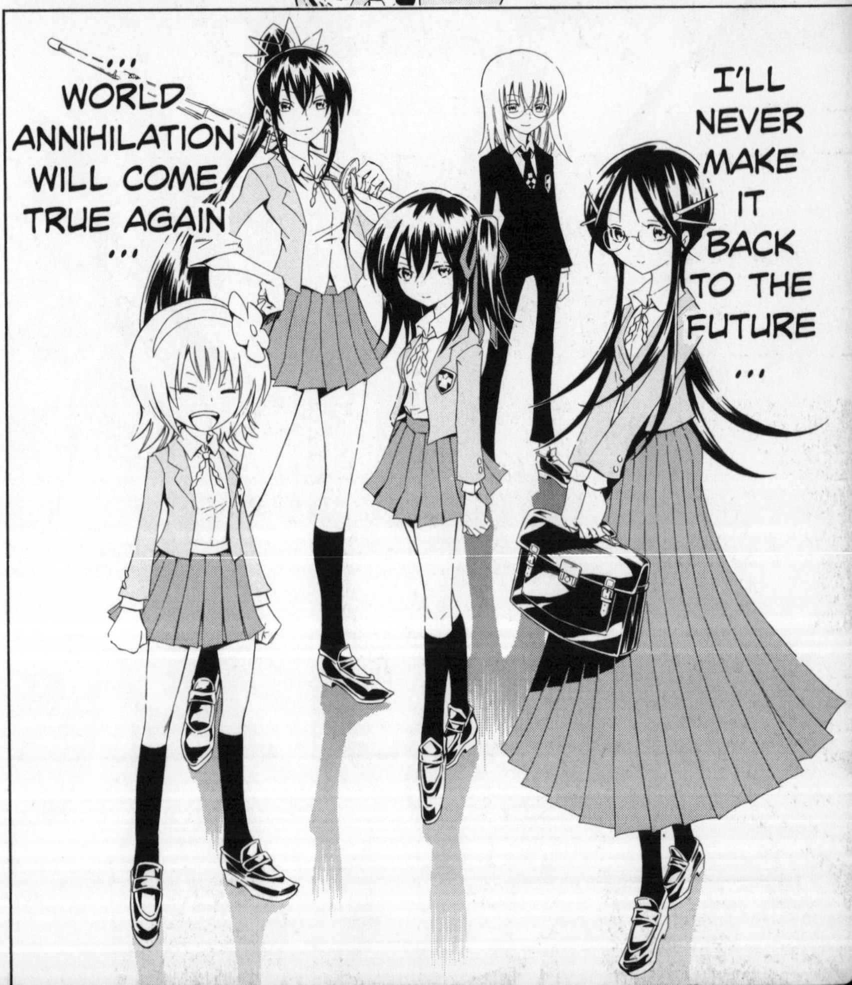
I'LL NEVER MAKE IT BACK TO THE FUTURE ...
... WORLD ANNIHILATION WILL COME TRUE AGAIN ...

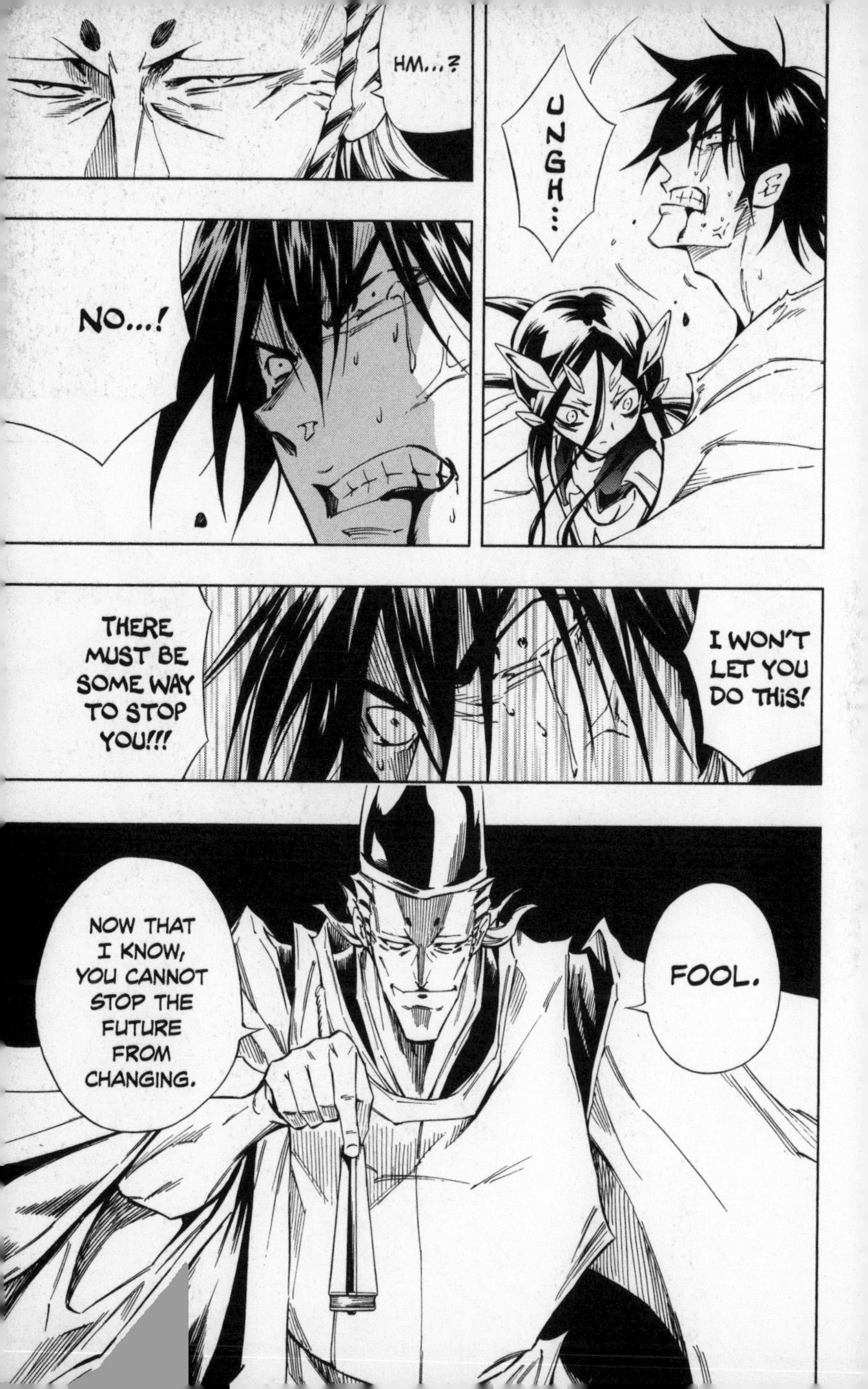
UNGH...
HM...?
NO...!
I WON'T LET YOU DO THIS!
THERE MUST BE SOME WAY TO STOP YOU!!!
FOOL.
NOW THAT I KNOW, YOU CANNOT STOP THE FUTURE FROM CHANGING.

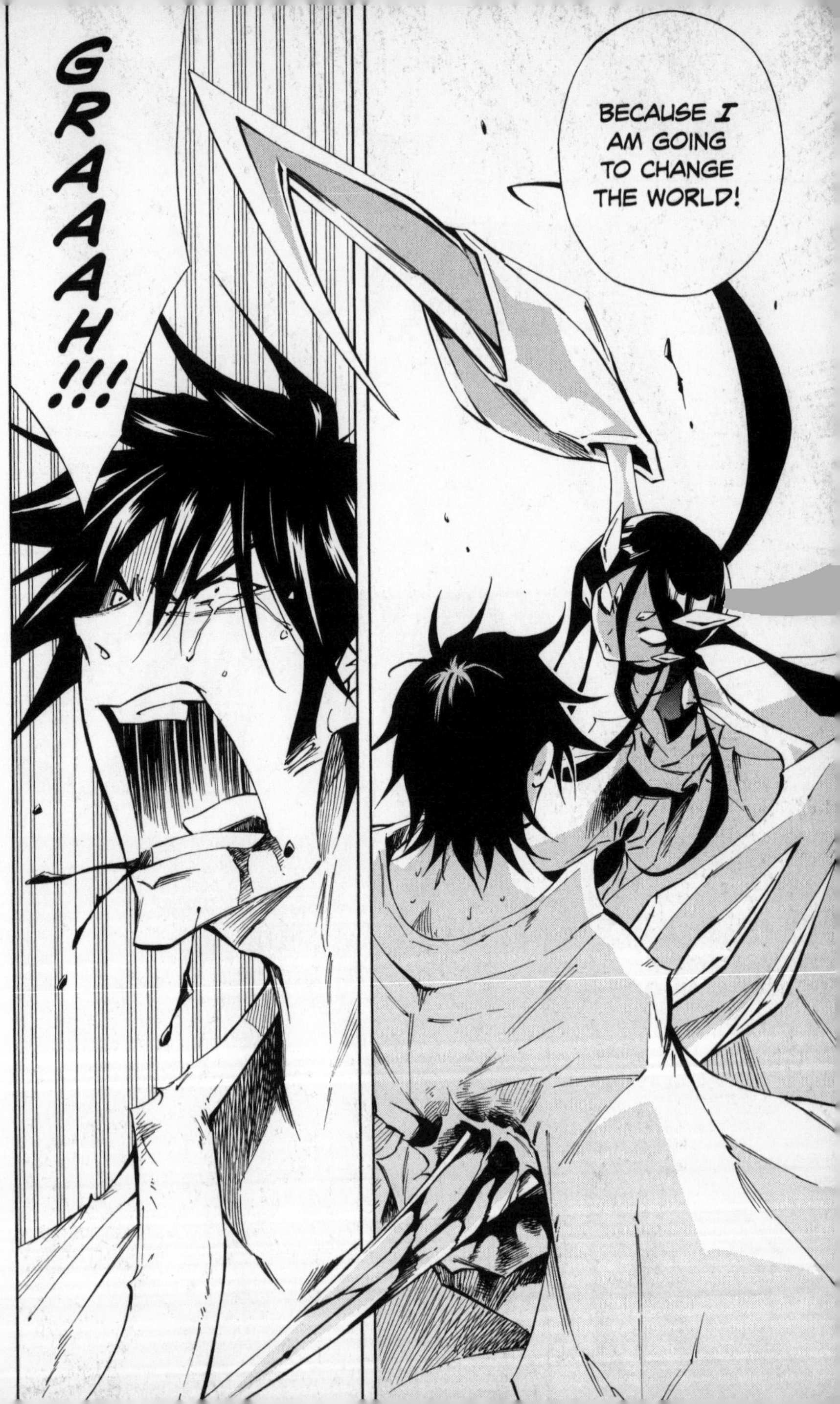
BECAUSE I AM GOING TO CHANGE THE WORLD!
GRAAAAH!!!

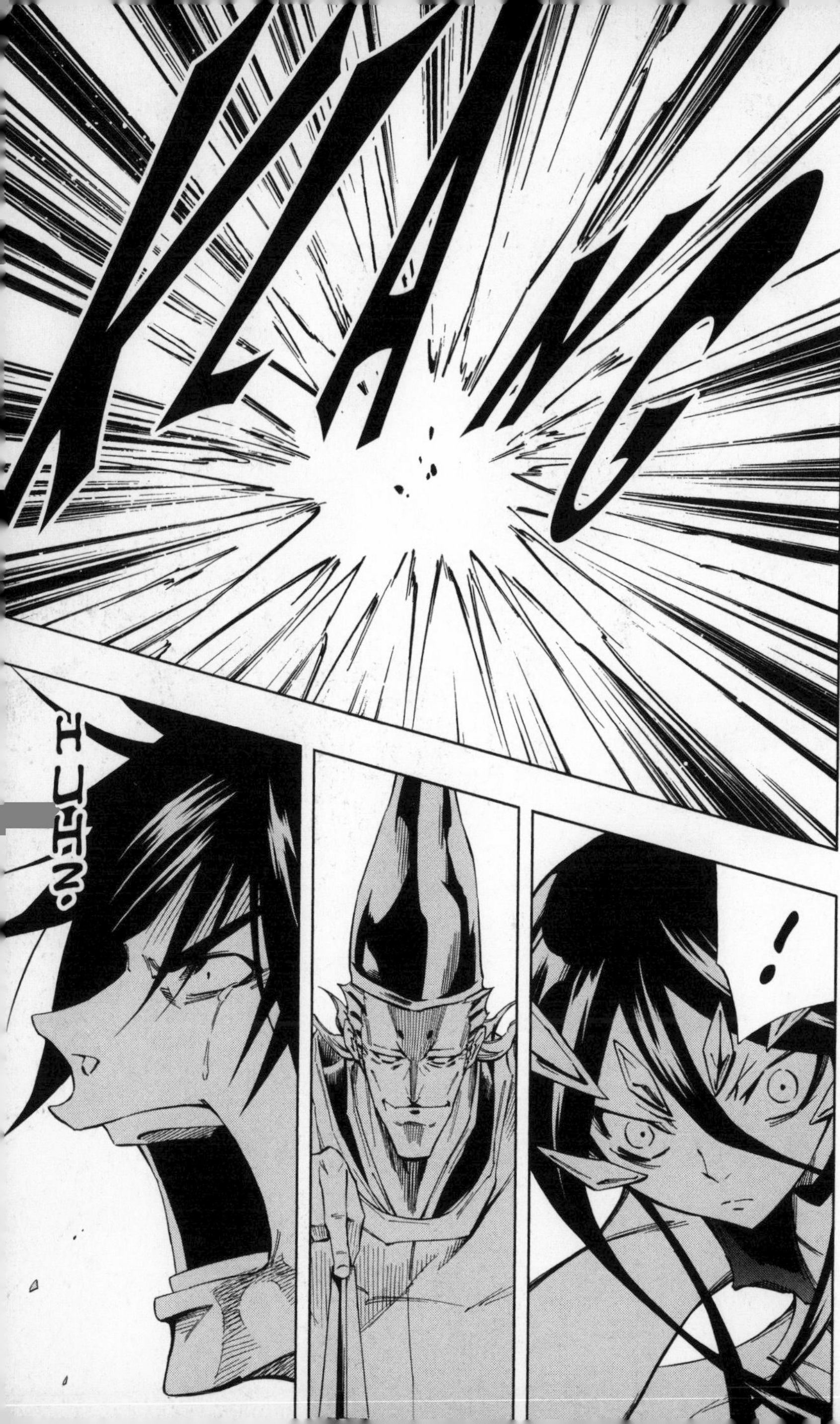
KLANG
!
HUH?

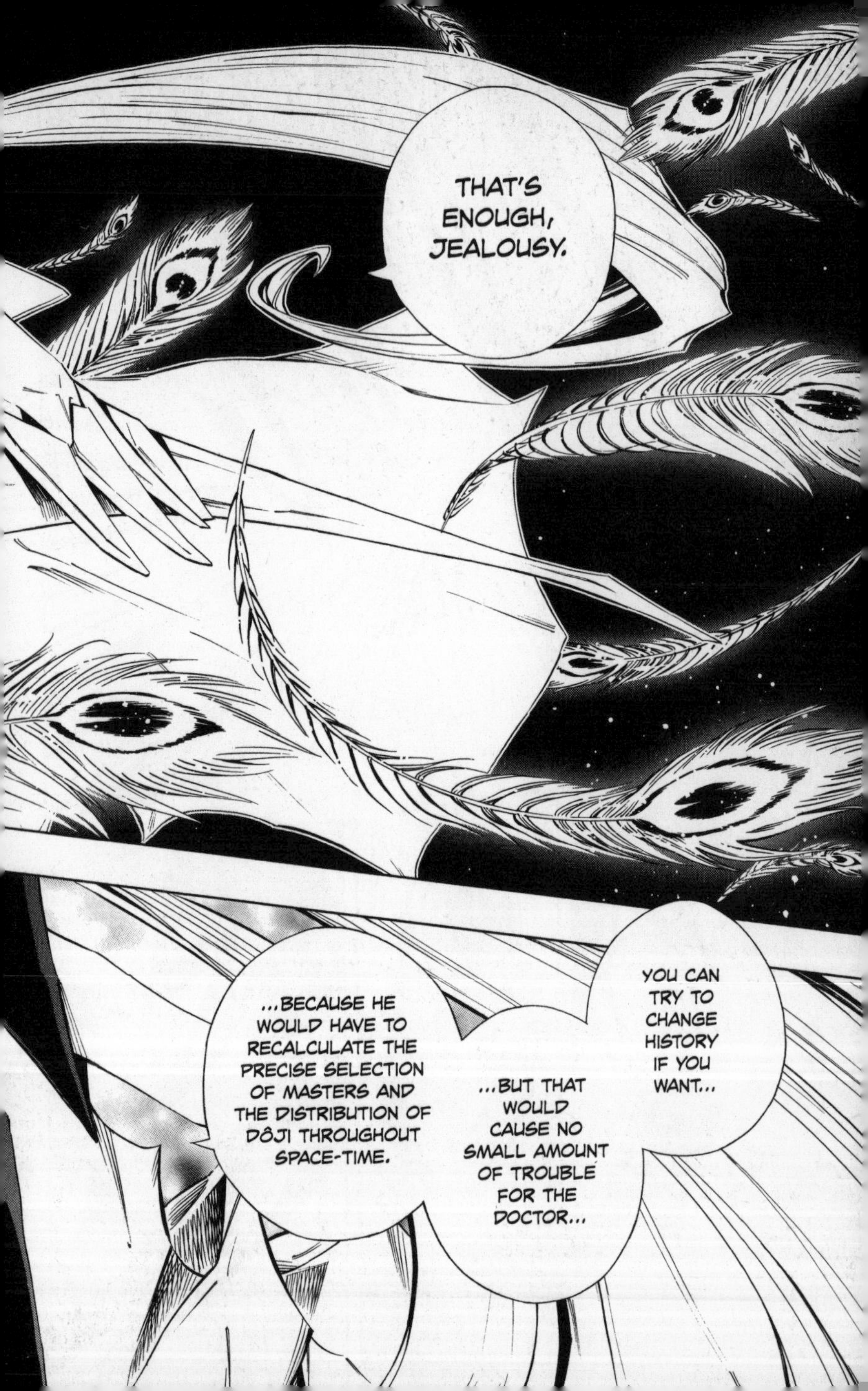
THAT'S ENOUGH, JEALOUSY.
YOU CAN TRY TO CHANGE HISTORY IF YOU WANT...
...BUT THAT WOULD CAUSE NO SMALL AMOUNT OF TROUBLE FOR THE DOCTOR...
...BECAUSE HE WOULD HAVE TO RECALCULATE THE PRECISE SELECTION OF MASTERS AND THE DISTRIBUTION OF DÔJI THROUGHOUT SPACE-TIME.

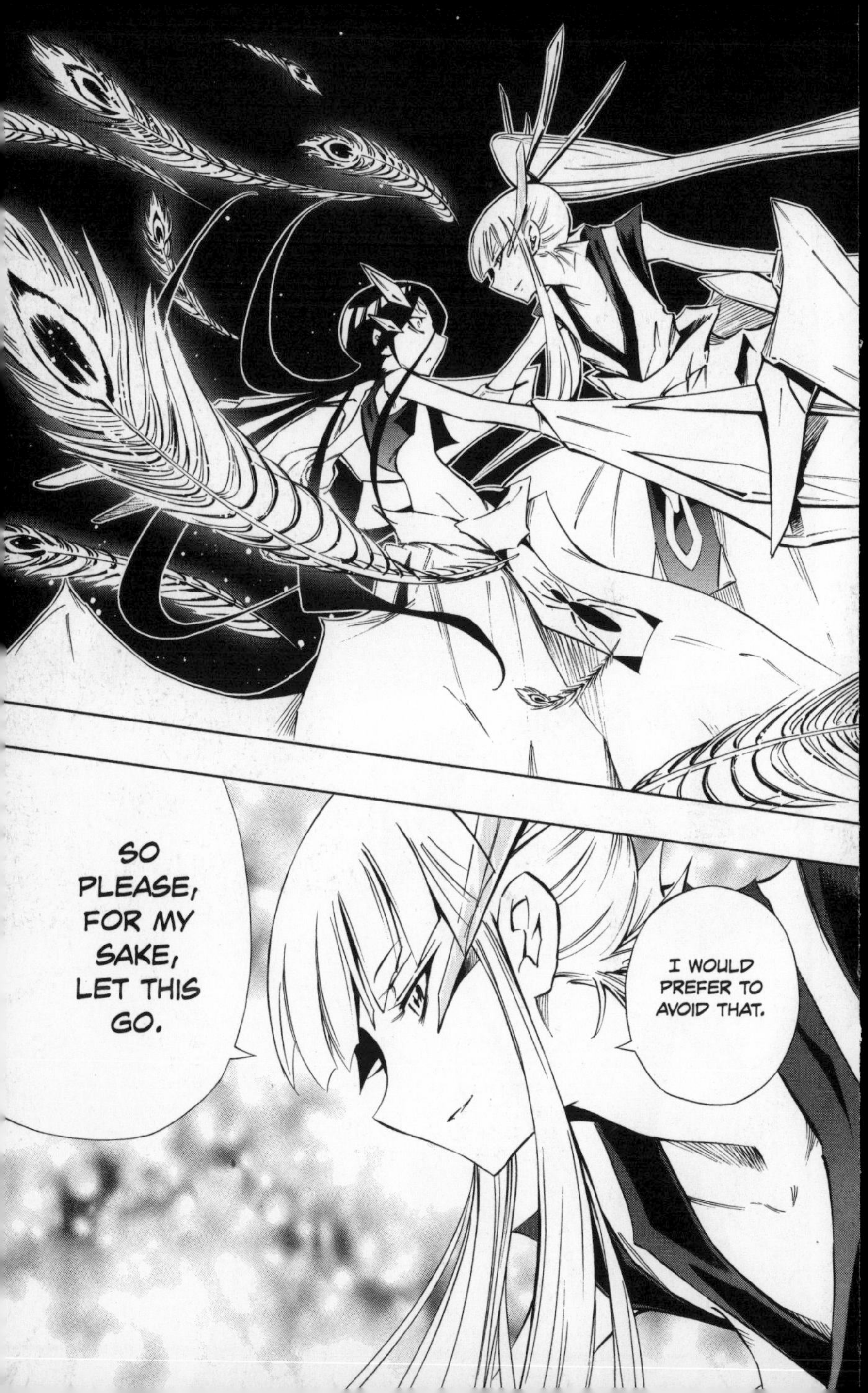
I WOULD PREFER TO AVOID THAT.
SO PLEASE, FOR MY SAKE, LET THIS GO.

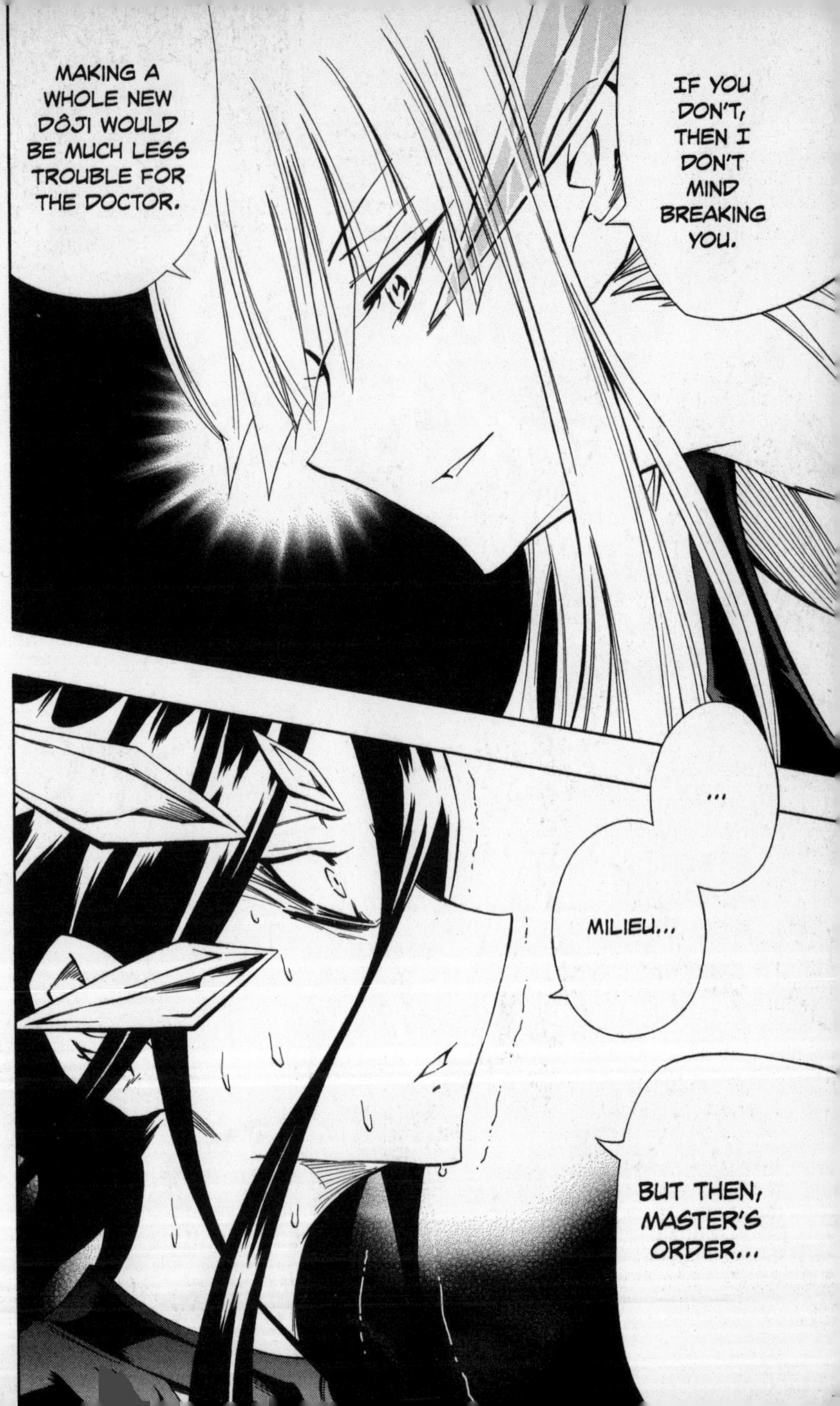
IF YOU DON'T, THEN I DON'T MIND BREAKING YOU.
MAKING A WHOLE NEW DÔJI WOULD BE MUCH LESS TROUBLE FOR THE DOCTOR.
...
MILIEU...
BUT THEN, MASTER'S ORDER...

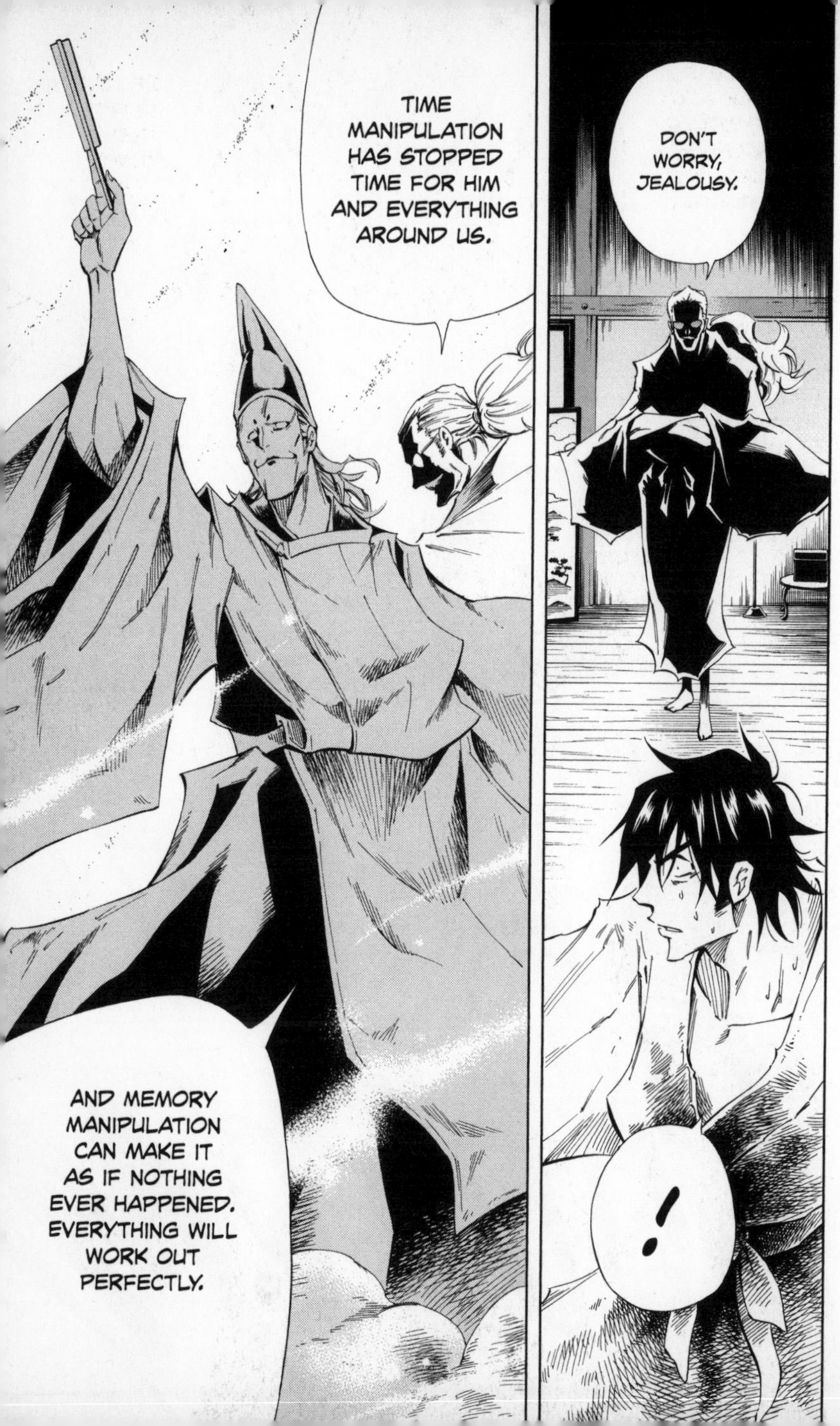
DON'T WORRY, JEALOUSY.
!
TIME MANIPULATION HAS STOPPED TIME FOR HIM AND EVERYTHING AROUND US.
AND MEMORY MANIPULATION CAN MAKE IT AS IF NOTHING EVER HAPPENED. EVERYTHING WILL WORK OUT PERFECTLY.

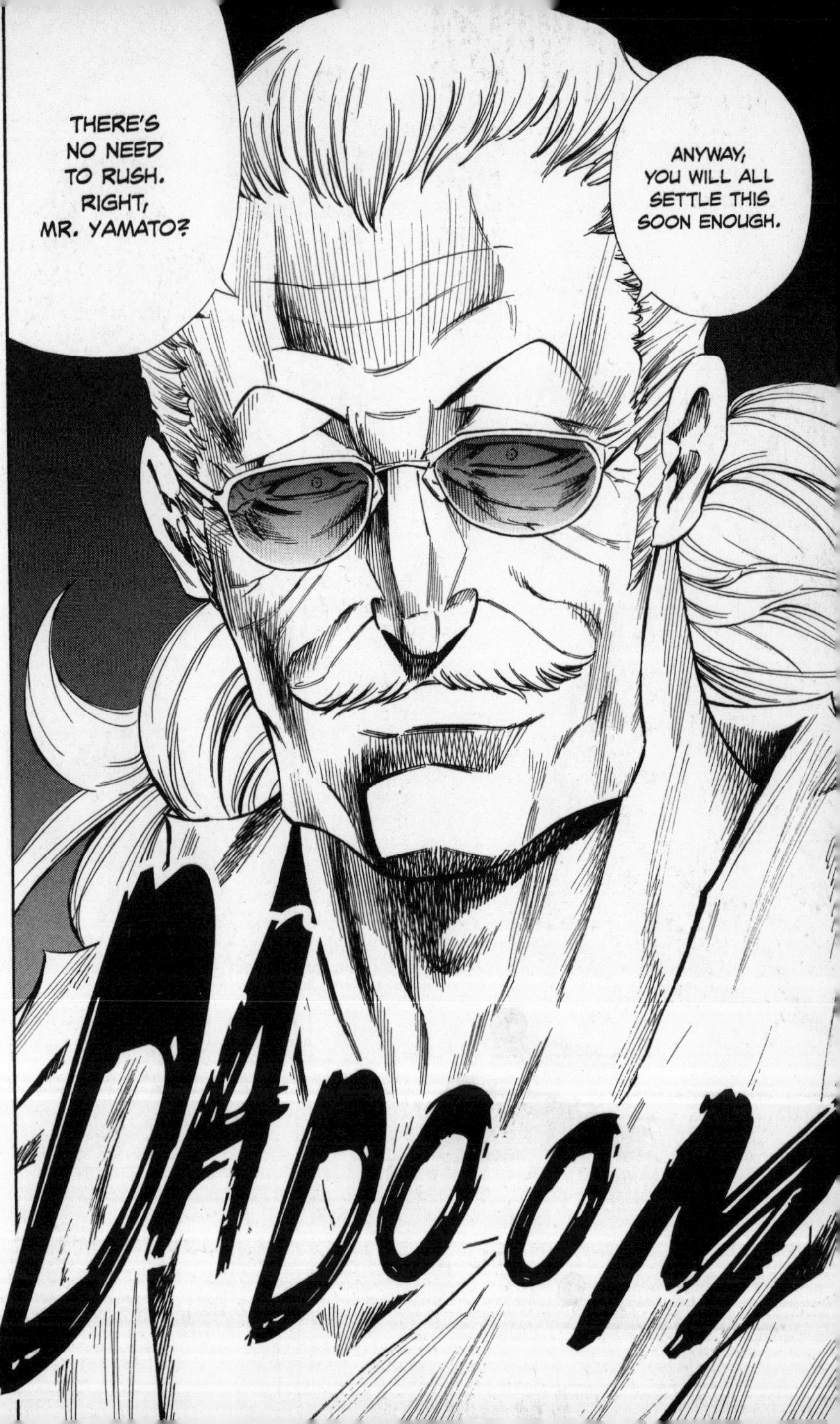
ANYWAY, YOU WILL ALL SETTLE THIS SOON ENOUGH.
THERE'S NO NEED TO RUSH. RIGHT, MR. YAMATO?
DADOOM

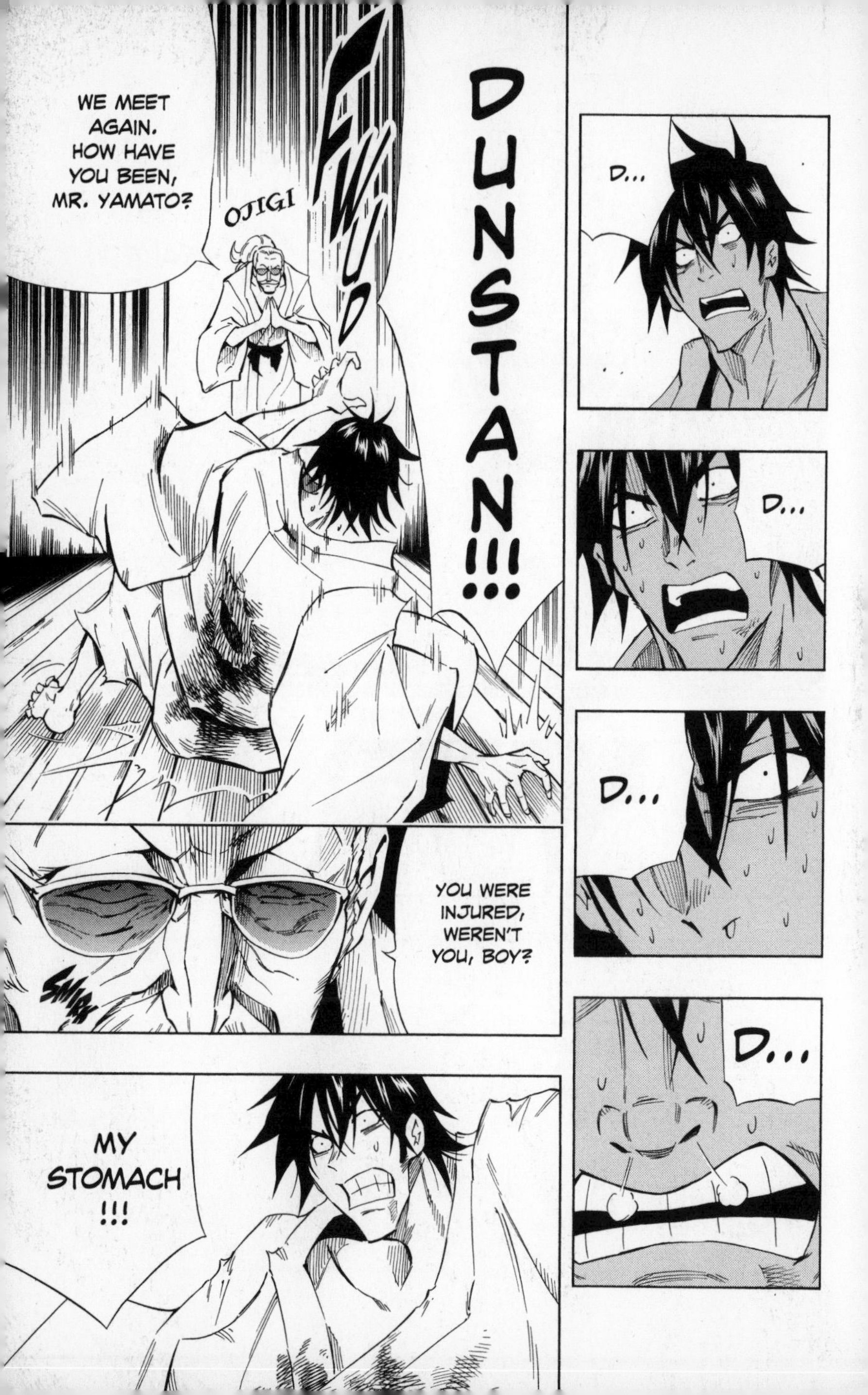
D...
D...
D...
D...
DUNSTAN!!!
WE MEET AGAIN. HOW HAVE YOU BEEN, MR. YAMATO?
OJIGI
YOU WERE INJURED, WEREN'T YOU, BOY?
MY STOMACH!!!

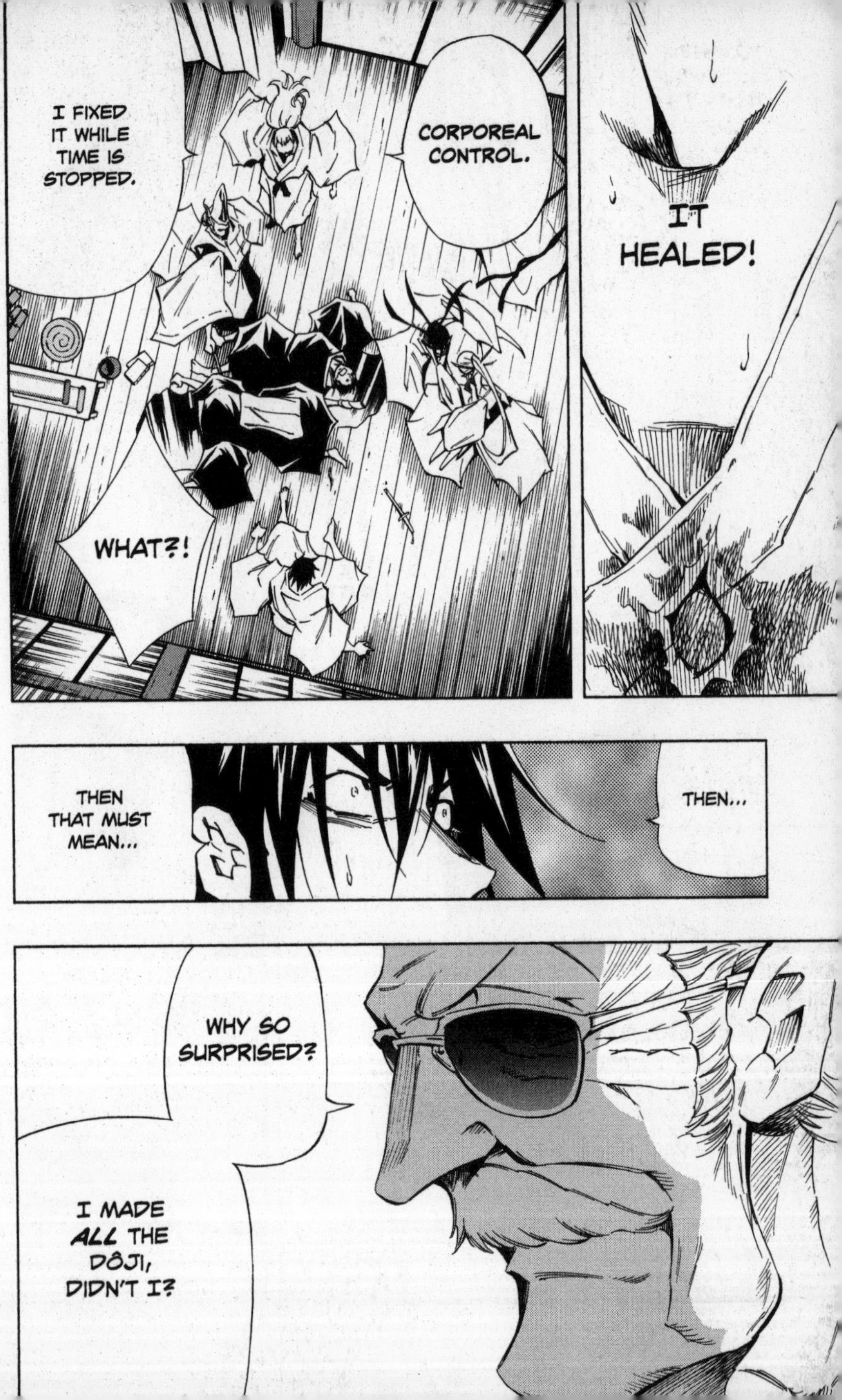
IT HEALED!
CORPOREAL CONTROL.
I FIXED IT WHILE TIME IS STOPPED.
WHAT?!
THEN...
THEN THAT MUST MEAN...
WHY SO SURPRISED?
I MADE *ALL* THE DÔJI, DIDN'T I?

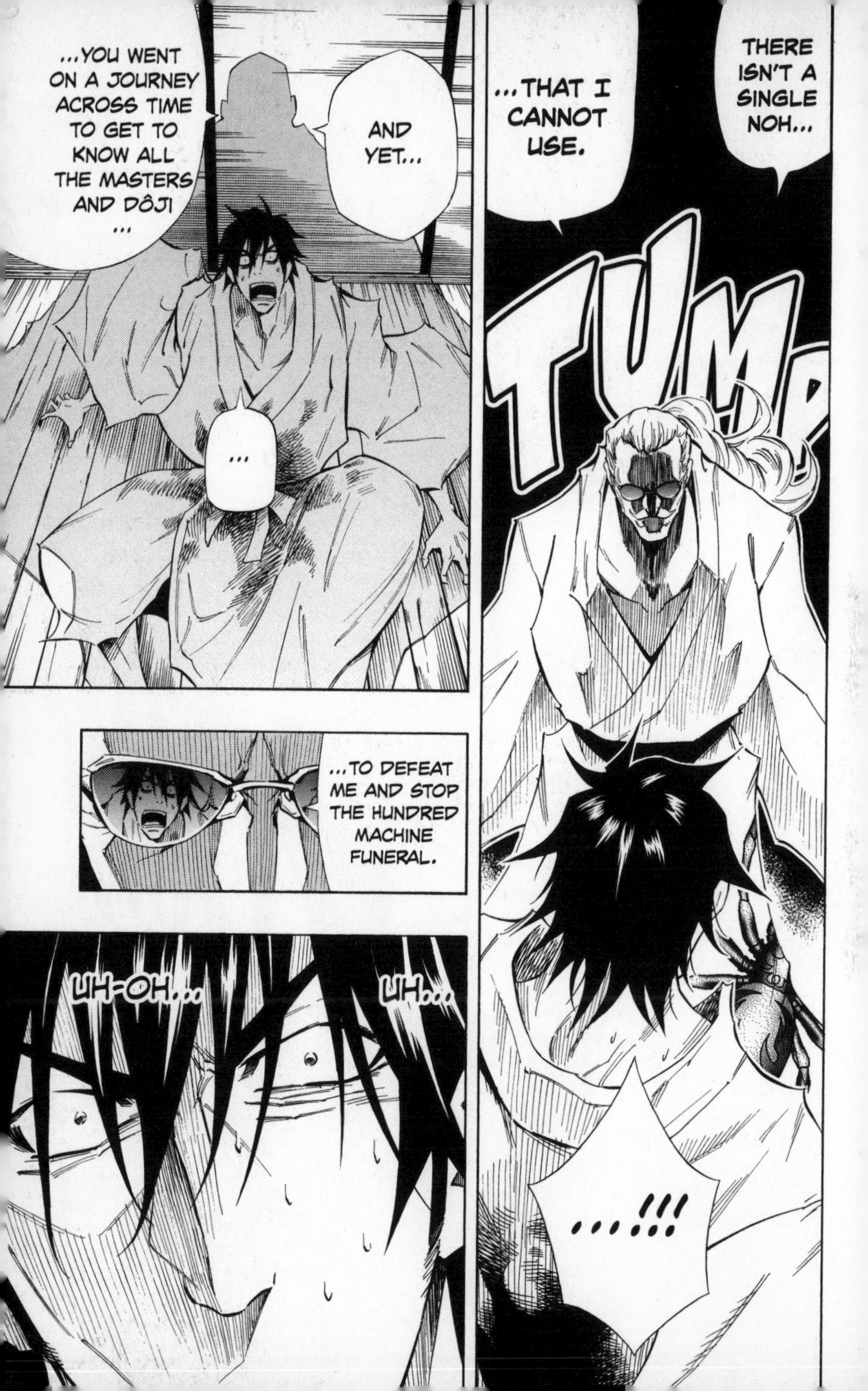
THERE ISN'T A SINGLE NOH...
...THAT I CANNOT USE.
TUMP
...!!!
...YOU WENT ON A JOURNEY ACROSS TIME TO GET TO KNOW ALL THE MASTERS AND DÔJI ...
AND YET...
...
...TO DEFEAT ME AND STOP THE HUNDRED MACHINE FUNERAL.
UH...
UH-OH...

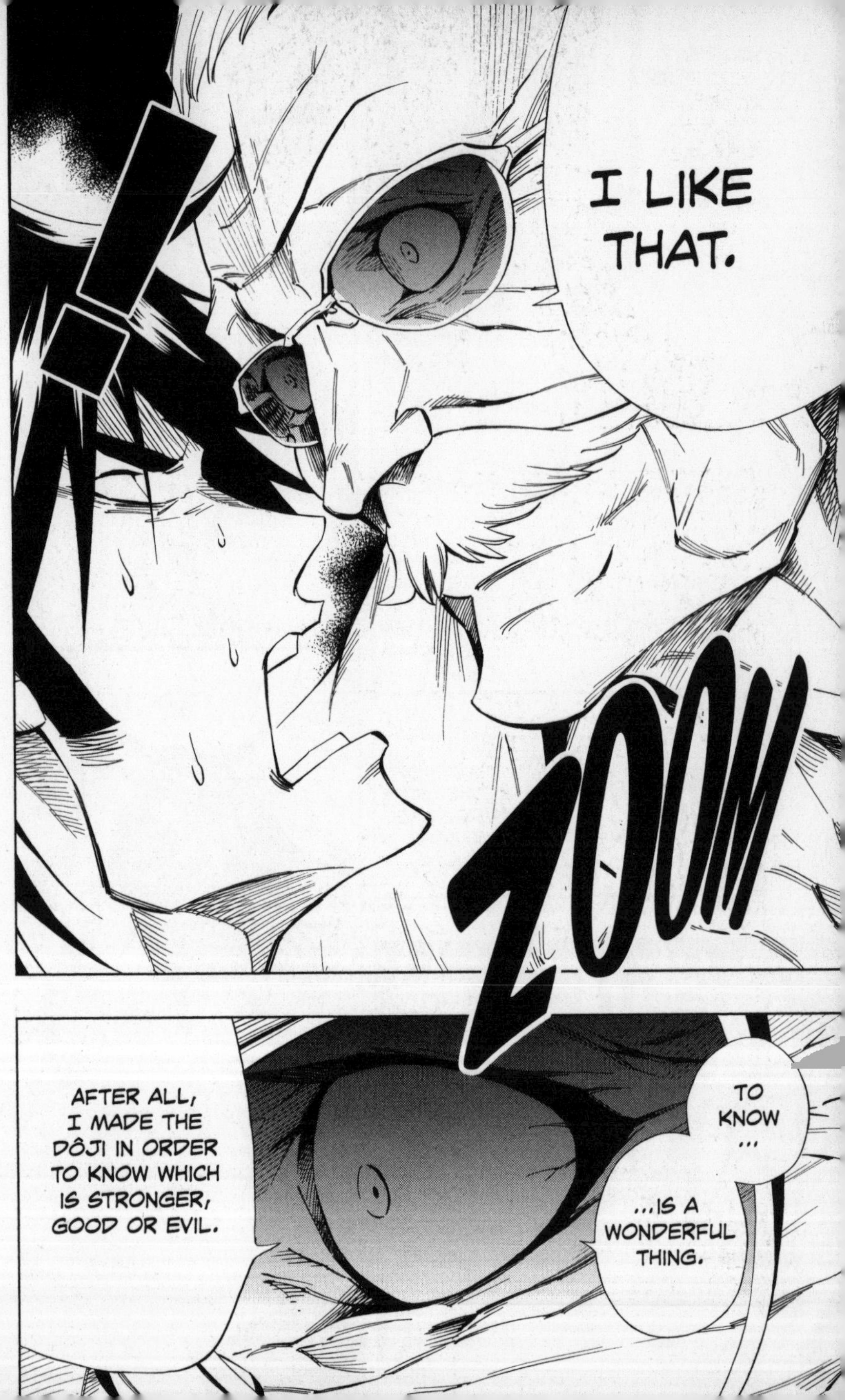
!!
I LIKE THAT.
ZOOM
TO KNOW ...
...IS A WONDERFUL THING.
AFTER ALL, I MADE THE DÔJI IN ORDER TO KNOW WHICH IS STRONGER, GOOD OR EVIL.

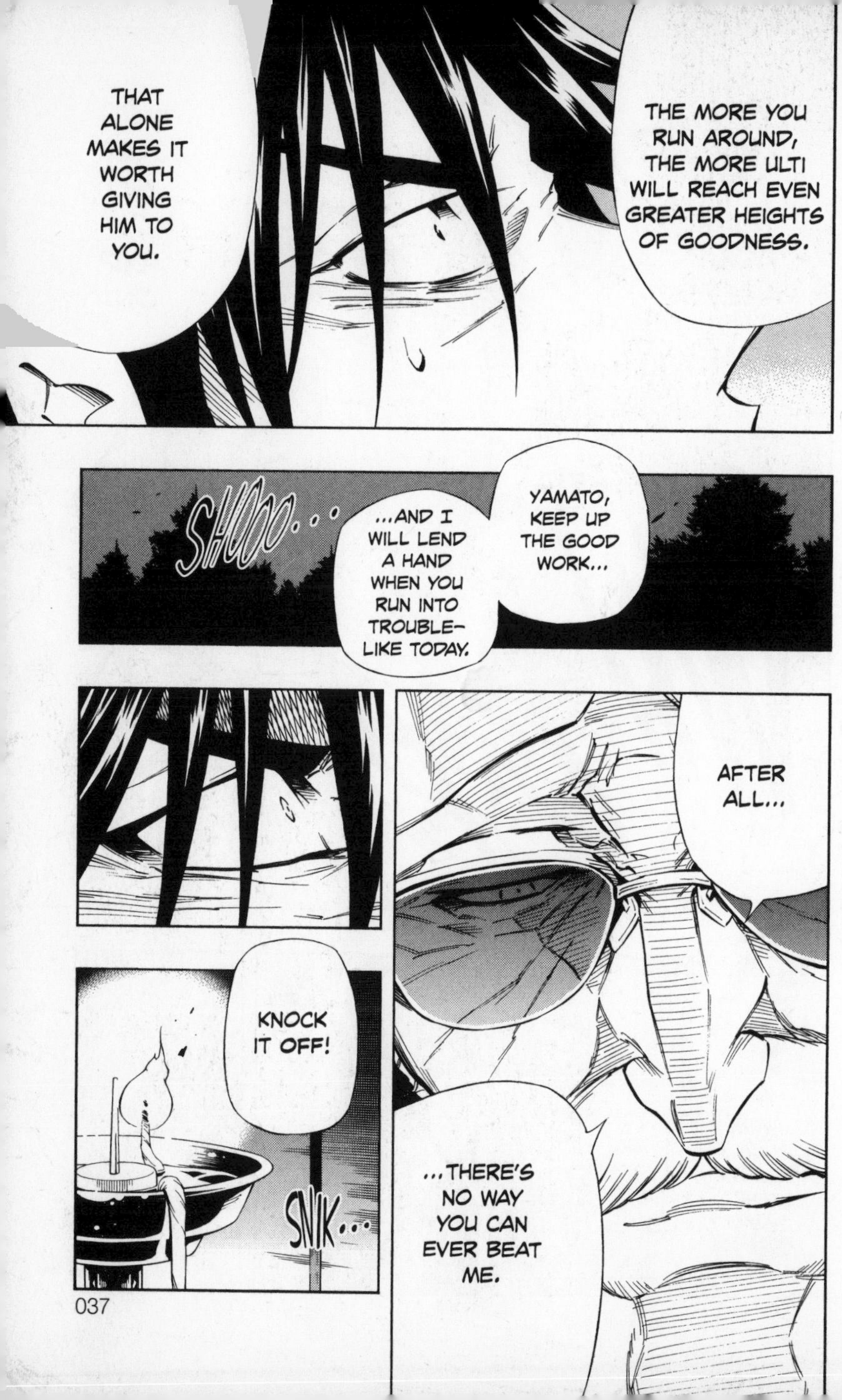
THE MORE YOU RUN AROUND, THE MORE ULTI WILL REACH EVEN GREATER HEIGHTS OF GOODNESS.
THAT ALONE MAKES IT WORTH GIVING HIM TO YOU.
YAMATO, KEEP UP THE GOOD WORK...
...AND I WILL LEND A HAND WHEN YOU RUN INTO TROUBLE-LIKE TODAY.
SHUOOO...
AFTER ALL...
...THERE'S NO WAY YOU CAN EVER BEAT ME.
KNOCK IT OFF!
SNIK...

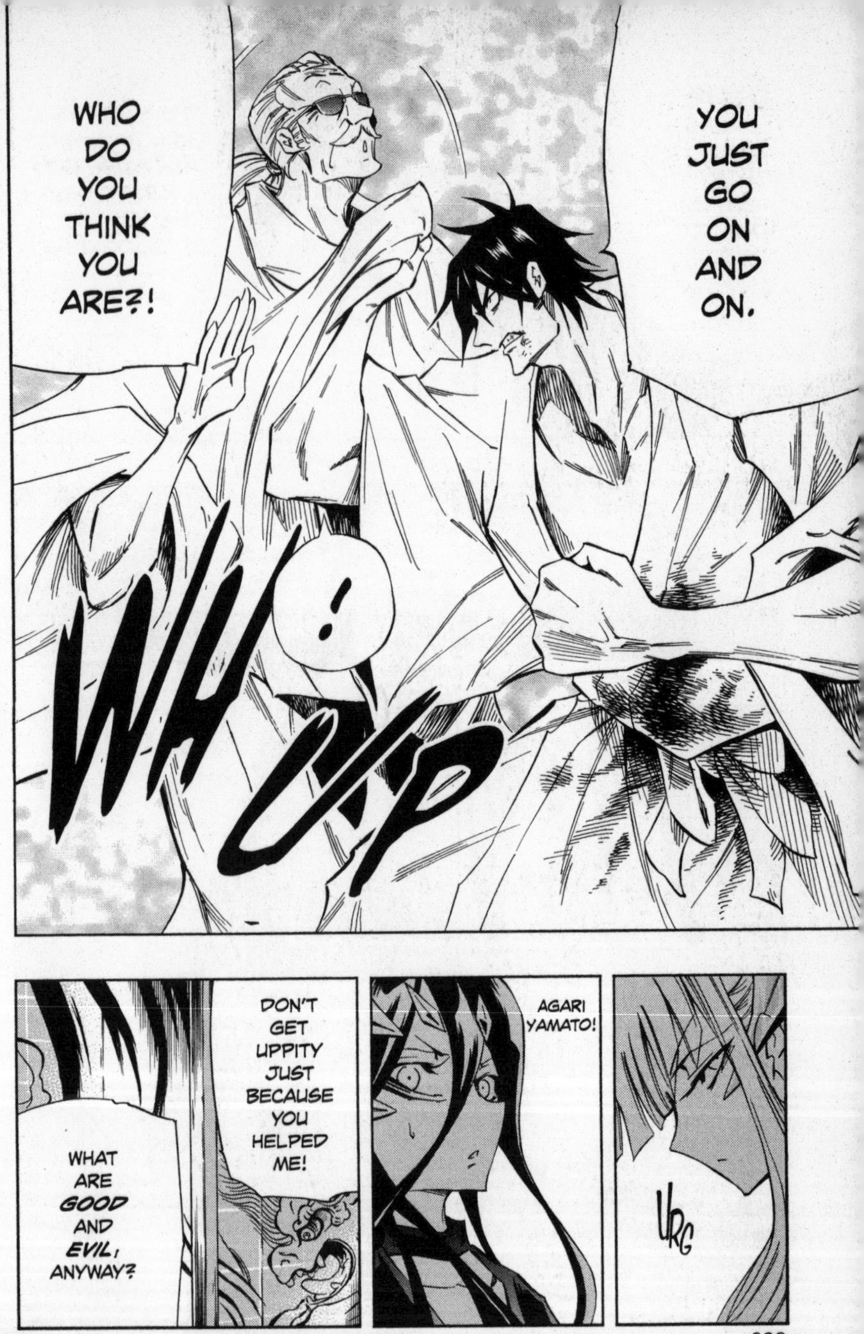
YOU JUST GO ON AND ON.
WHO DO YOU THINK YOU ARE?!
!
WHUP
URG
AGARI YAMATO!
DON'T GET UPPITY JUST BECAUSE YOU HELPED ME!
WHAT ARE *GOOD* AND *EVIL*, ANYWAY?

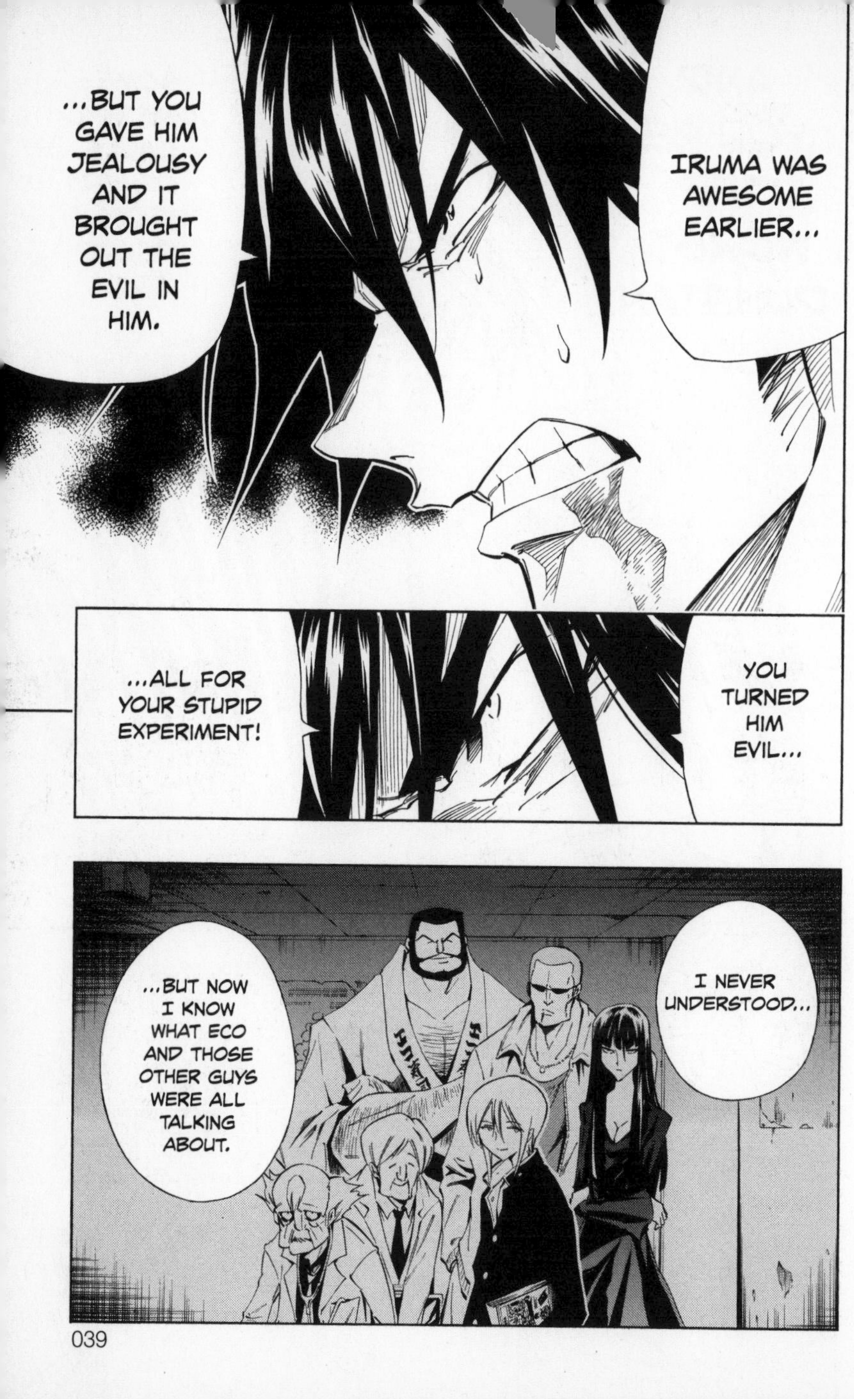
IRUMA WAS AWESOME EARLIER...
...BUT YOU GAVE HIM JEALOUSY AND IT BROUGHT OUT THE EVIL IN HIM.
YOU TURNED HIM EVIL...
...ALL FOR YOUR STUPID EXPERIMENT!
I NEVER UNDERSTOOD...
...BUT NOW I KNOW WHAT ECO AND THOSE OTHER GUYS WERE ALL TALKING ABOUT.

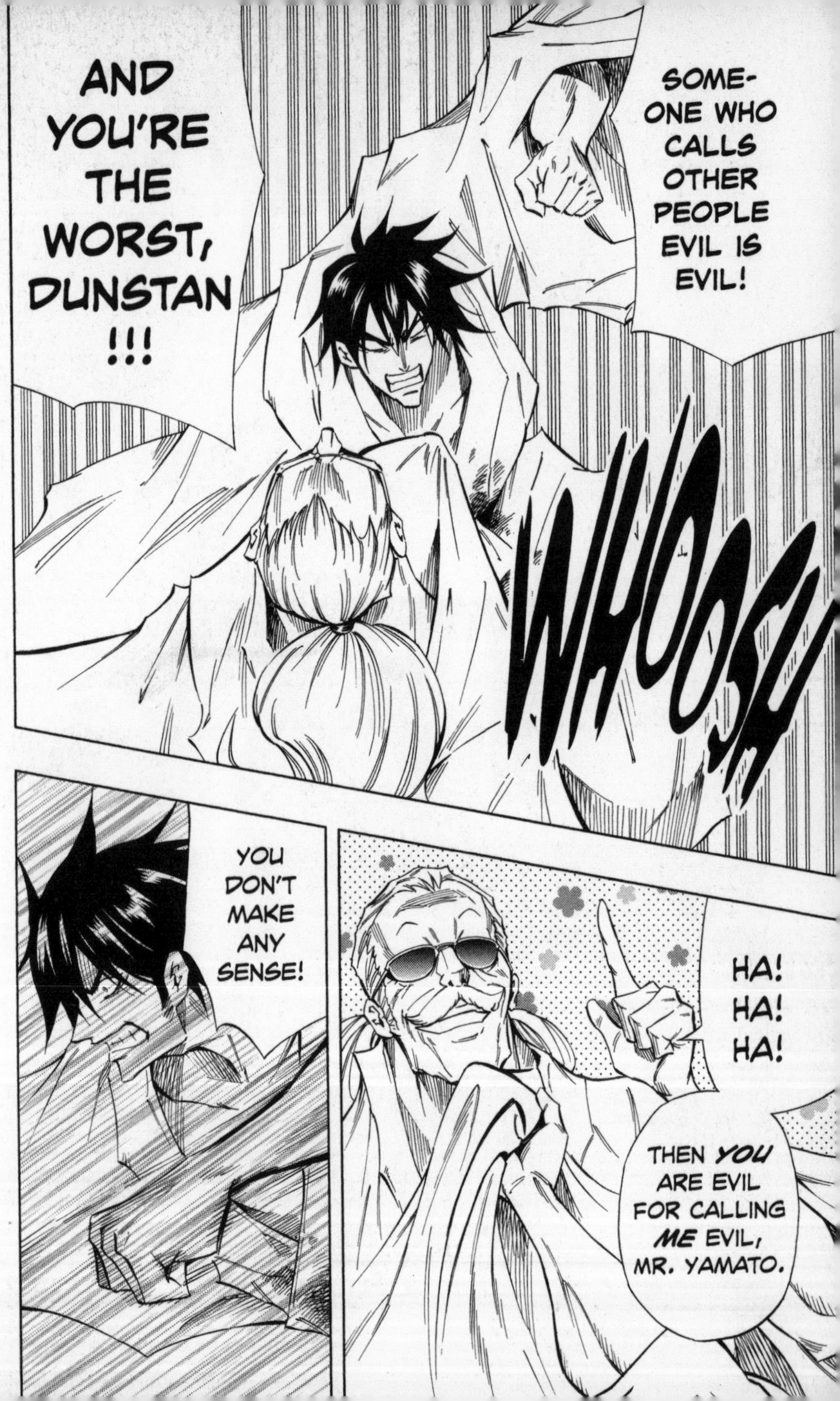
SOME-ONE WHO CALLS OTHER PEOPLE EVIL IS EVIL!
AND YOU'RE THE WORST, DUNSTAN!!!
WHOOSH
HA! HA! HA!
THEN *YOU* ARE EVIL FOR CALLING *ME* EVIL, MR. YAMATO.
YOU DON'T MAKE ANY SENSE!

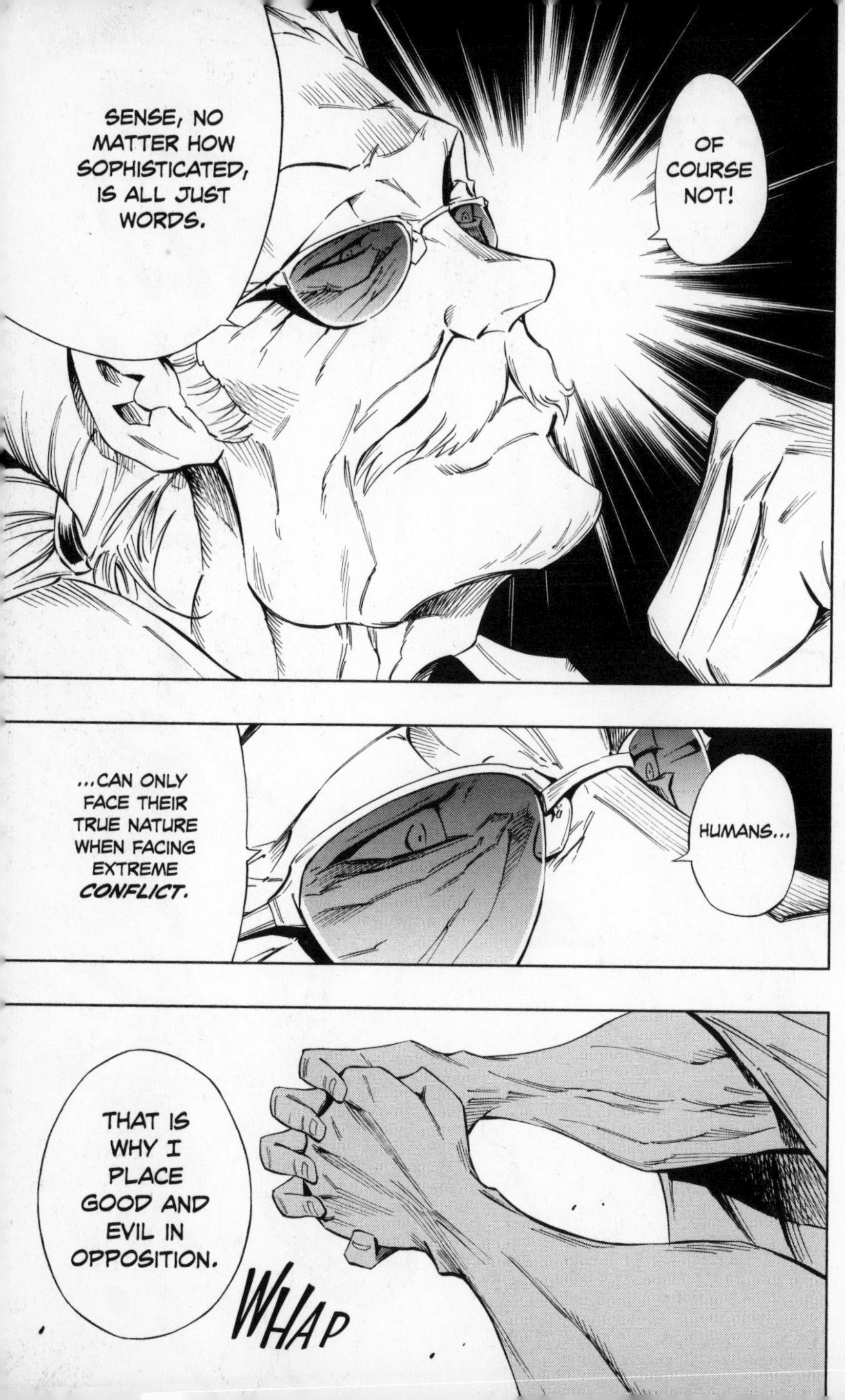
OF COURSE NOT!
SENSE, NO MATTER HOW SOPHISTICATED, IS ALL JUST WORDS.
HUMANS...
...CAN ONLY FACE THEIR TRUE NATURE WHEN FACING EXTREME CONFLICT.
THAT IS WHY I PLACE GOOD AND EVIL IN OPPOSITION.
WHAP

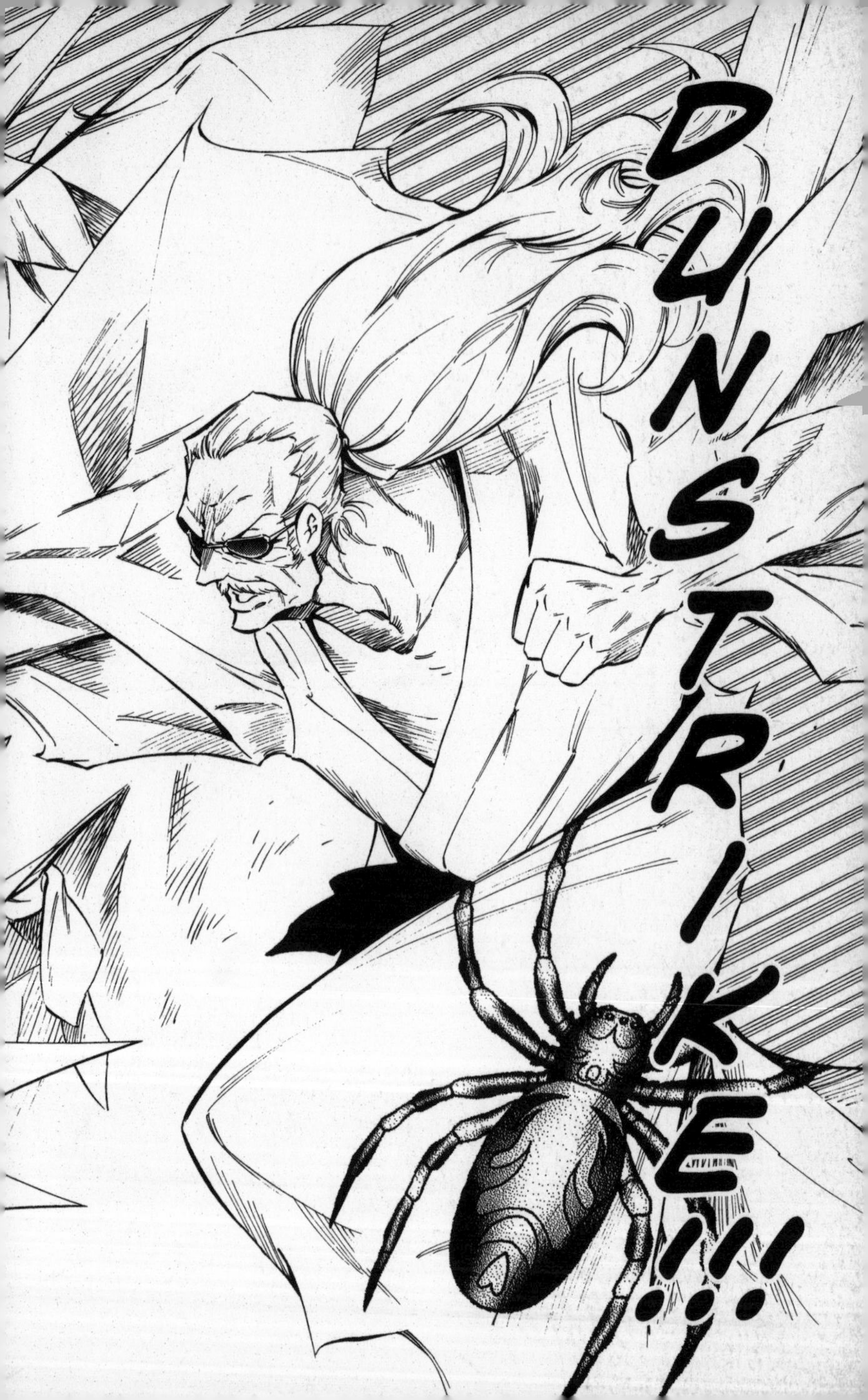
DUNSTRIKE!!!

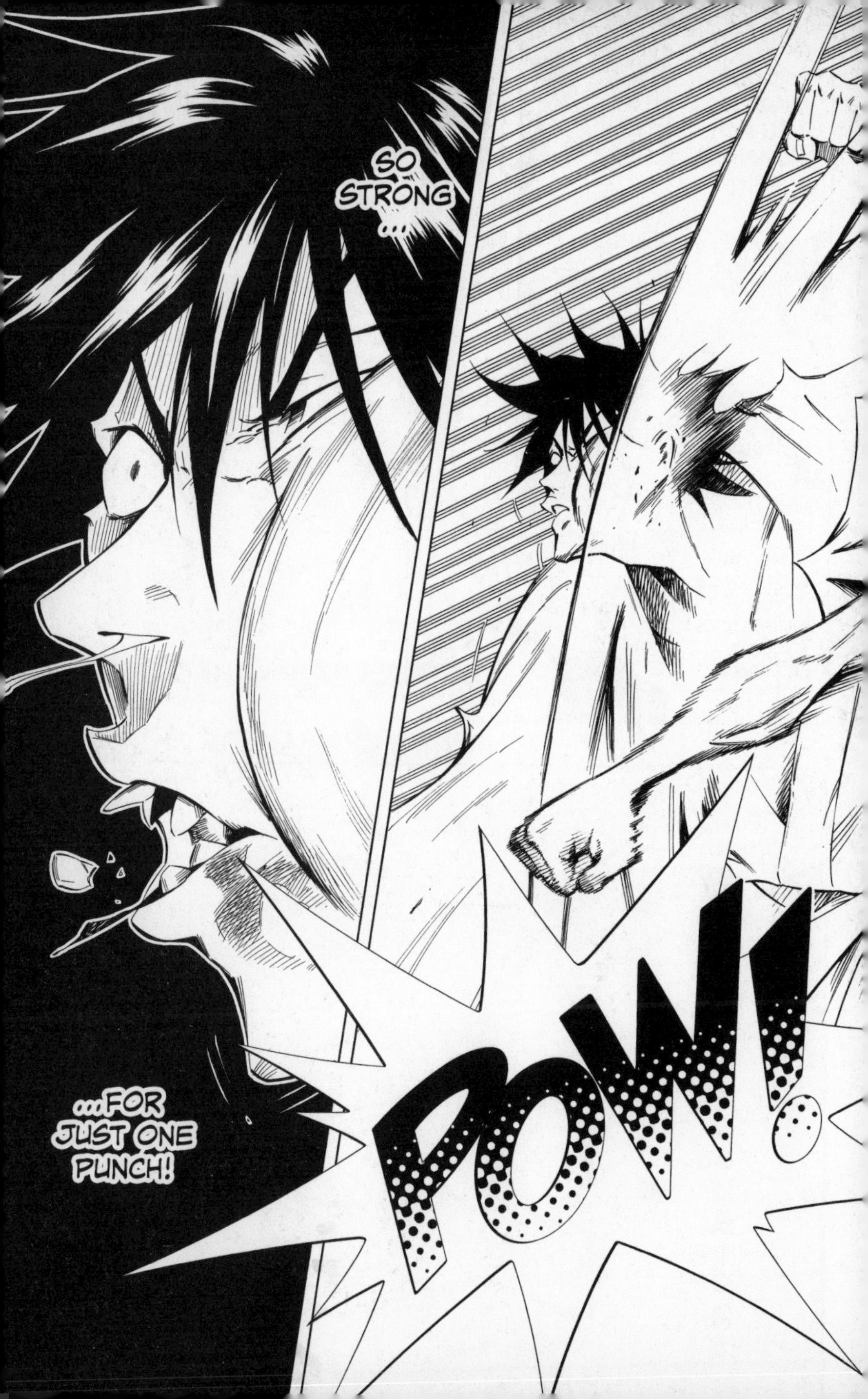
SO STRONG ...
...FOR JUST ONE PUNCH!
POW!!

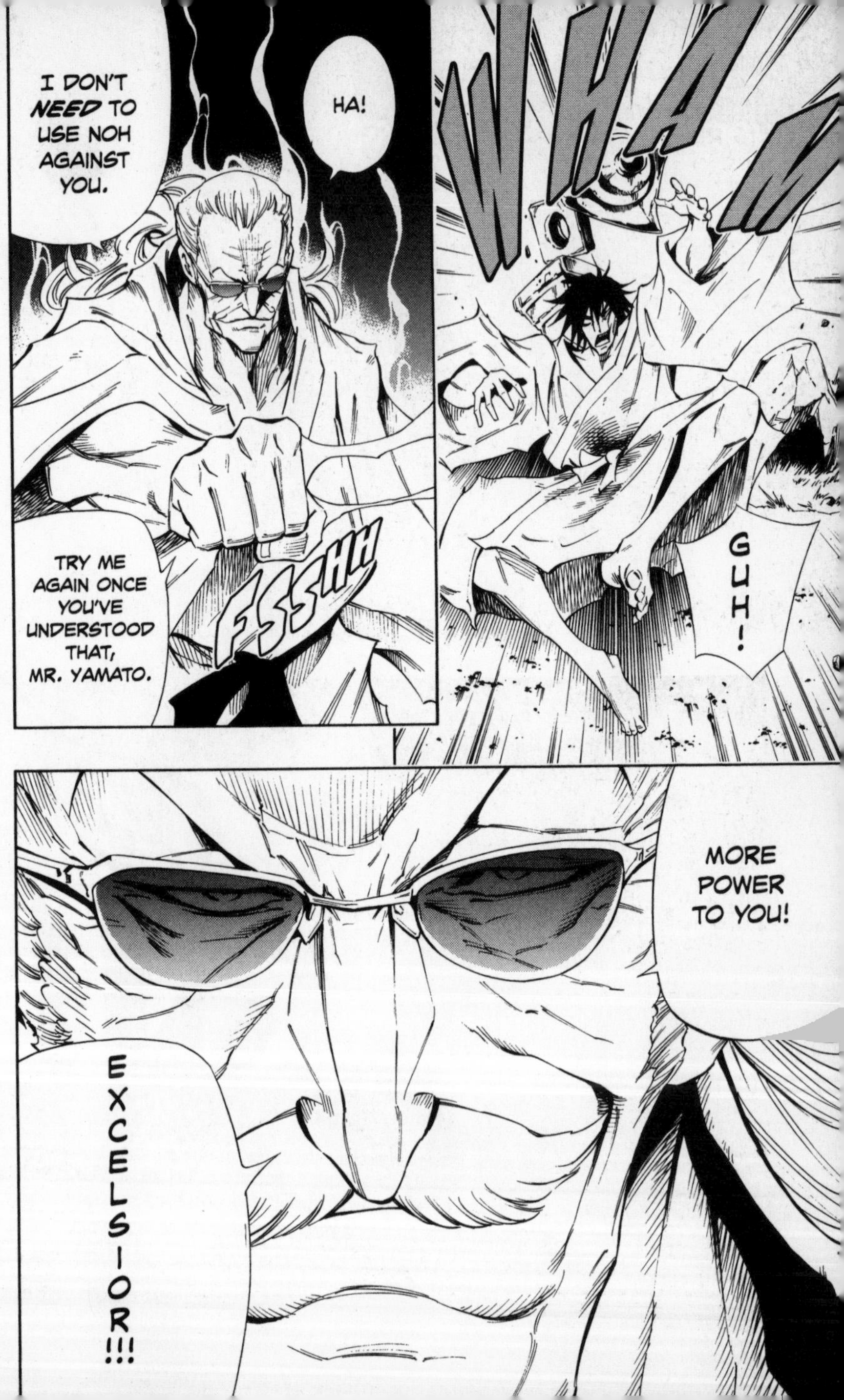
WHAM
GUH!
I DON'T NEED TO USE NOH AGAINST YOU.
HA!
FSSHH
TRY ME AGAIN ONCE YOU'VE UNDERSTOOD THAT, MR. YAMATO.
MORE POWER TO YOU!
EXCELSIOR!!!

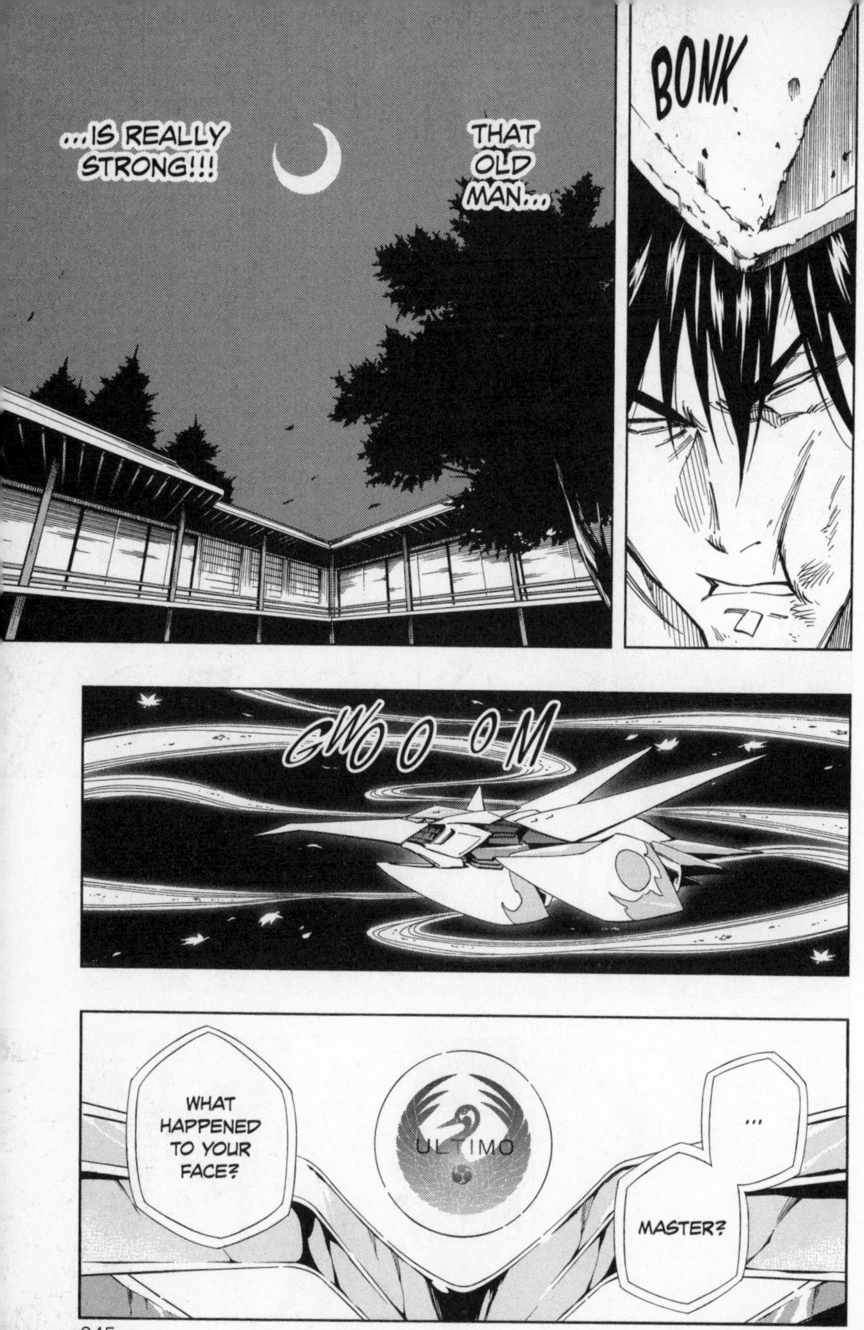
BONK
THAT OLD MAN...
...IS REALLY STRONG!!!
...
MASTER?
ULTIMO
WHAT HAPPENED TO YOUR FACE?

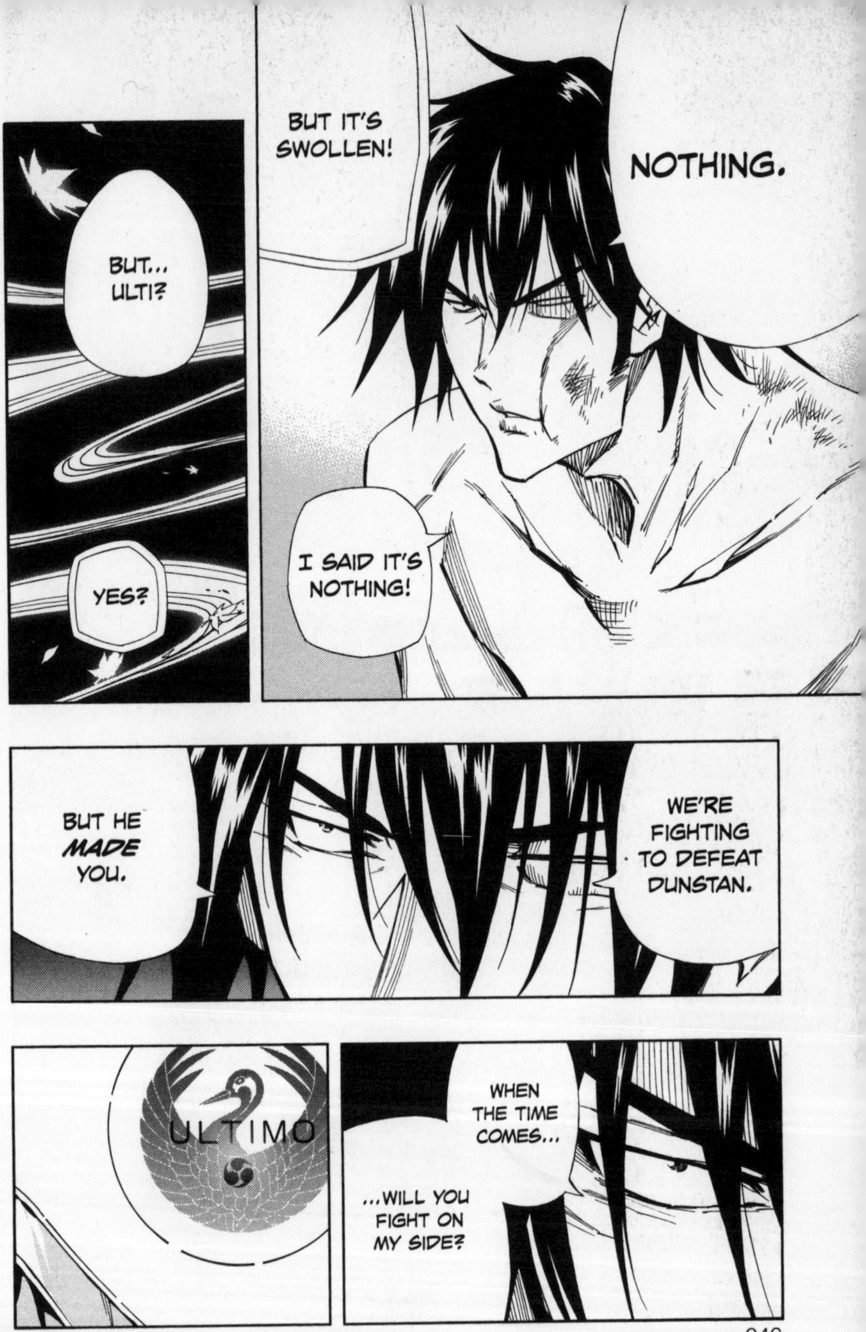
NOTHING.
BUT IT'S SWOLLEN!
I SAID IT'S NOTHING!
BUT... ULTI?
YES?
WE'RE FIGHTING TO DEFEAT DUNSTAN.
BUT HE *MADE* YOU.
WHEN THE TIME COMES...
...WILL YOU FIGHT ON MY SIDE?
ULTIMO

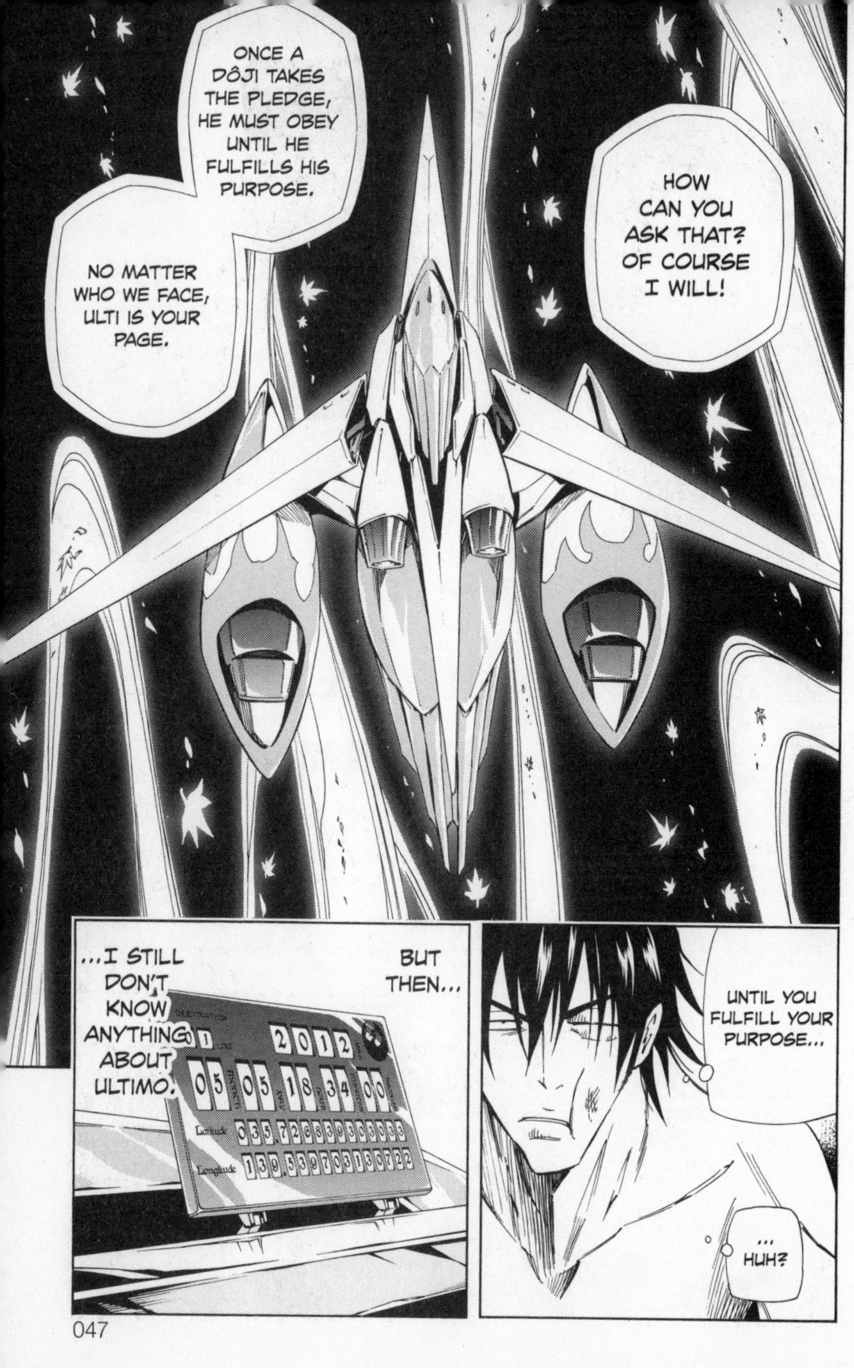
ONCE A DÔJI TAKES THE PLEDGE, HE MUST OBEY UNTIL HE FULFILLS HIS PURPOSE.
NO MATTER WHO WE FACE, ULTI IS YOUR PAGE.
HOW CAN YOU ASK THAT? OF COURSE I WILL!
UNTIL YOU FULFILL YOUR PURPOSE...
... HUH?
BUT THEN...
...I STILL DON'T KNOW ANYTHING ABOUT ULTIMO.
1
2012
05 05 18 34 00
Latitude 035.7268393033033
Longitude 139.5397031307 22

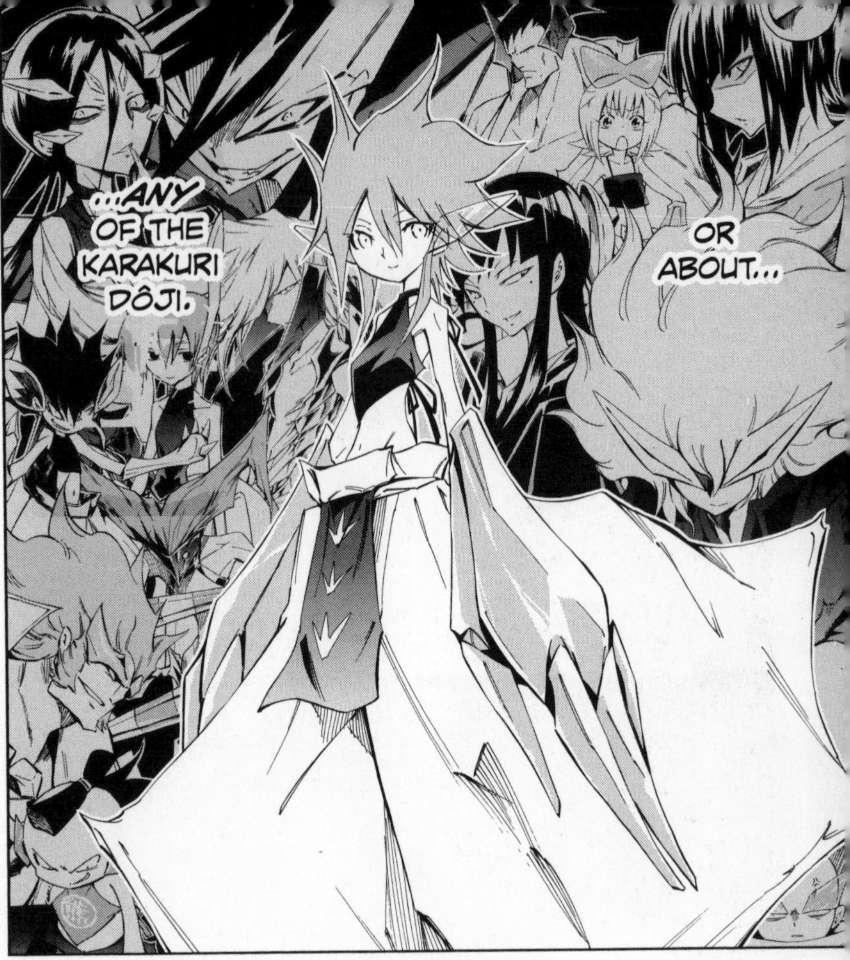
OR ABOUT...
...ANY OF THE KARAKURI DÔJI.

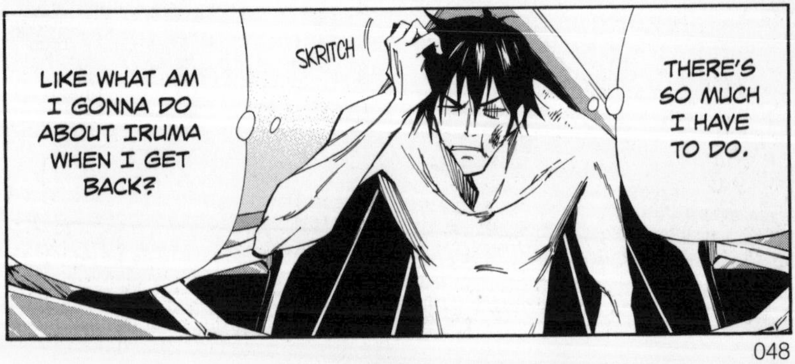
THERE'S SO MUCH I HAVE TO DO.
SKRITCH
LIKE WHAT AM I GONNA DO ABOUT IRUMA WHEN I GET BACK?

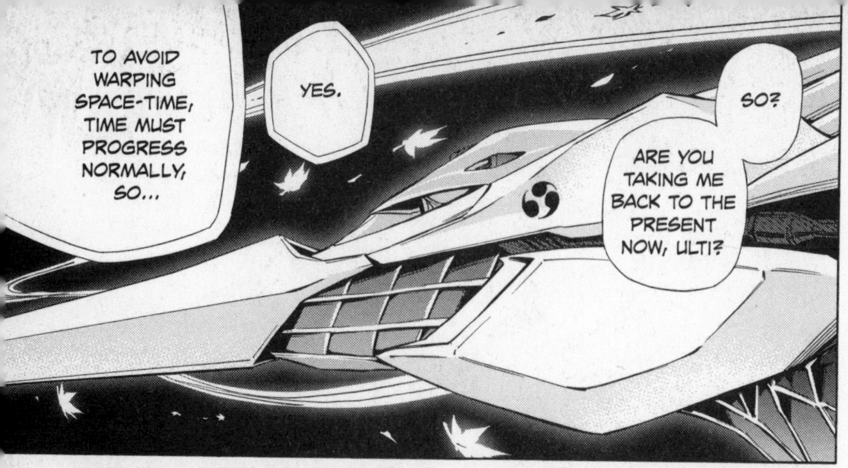
SO?
ARE YOU TAKING ME BACK TO THE PRESENT NOW, ULTI?
YES.
TO AVOID WARPING SPACE-TIME, TIME MUST PROGRESS NORMALLY, SO...

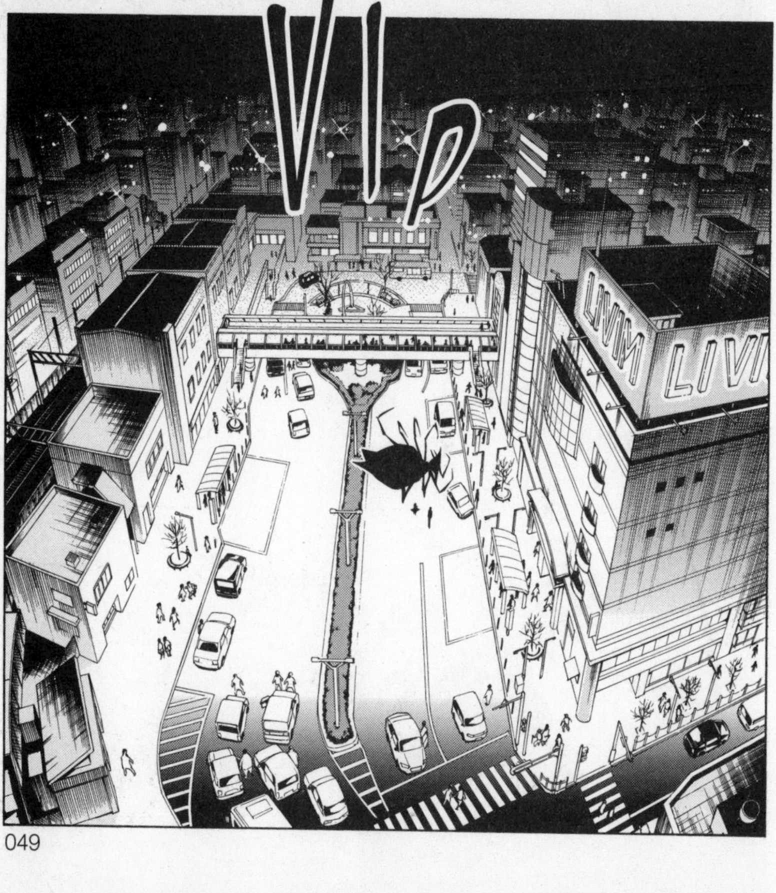
VIP
LIVIM

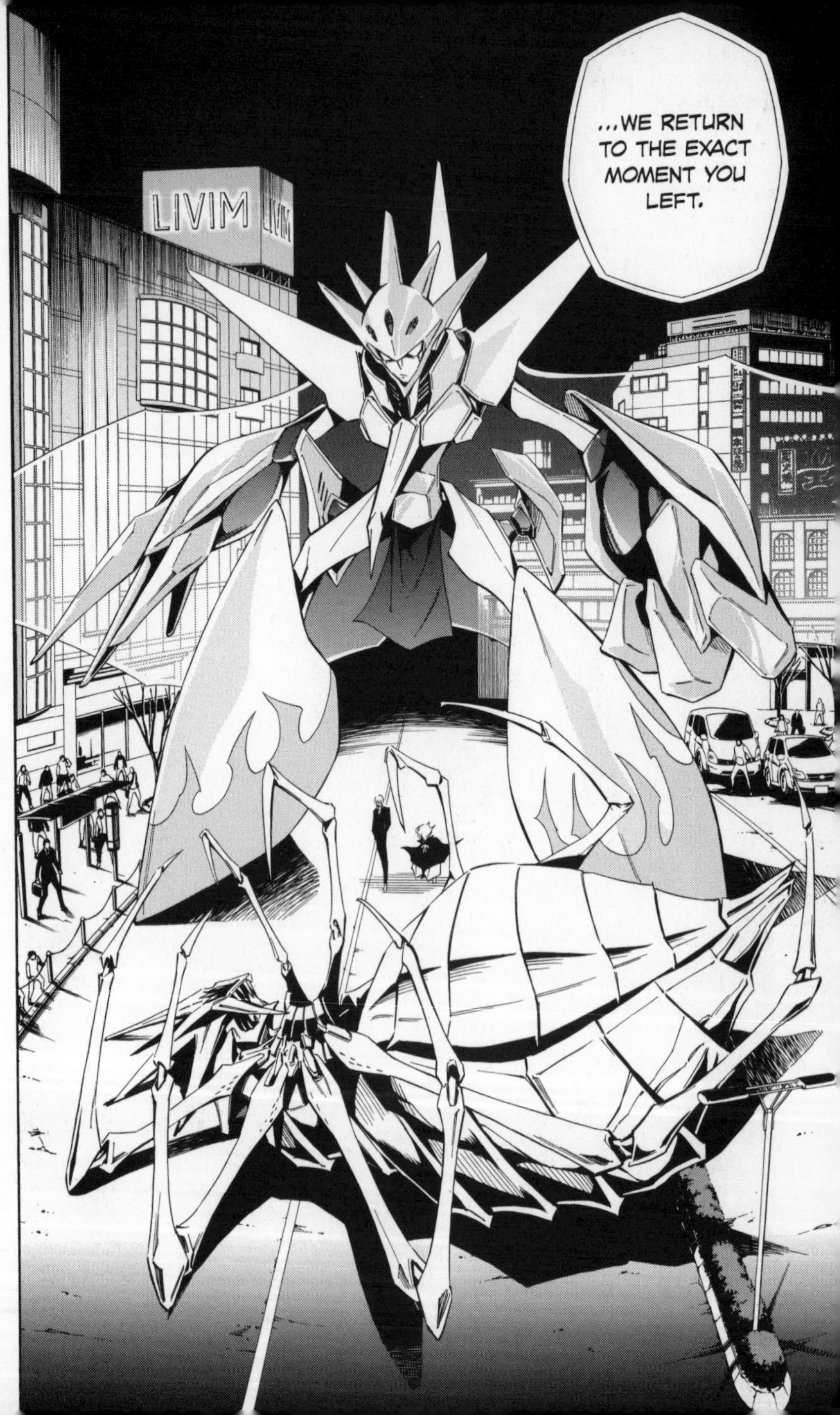
...WE RETURN TO THE EXACT MOMENT YOU LEFT.
LIVIM
LIVIM

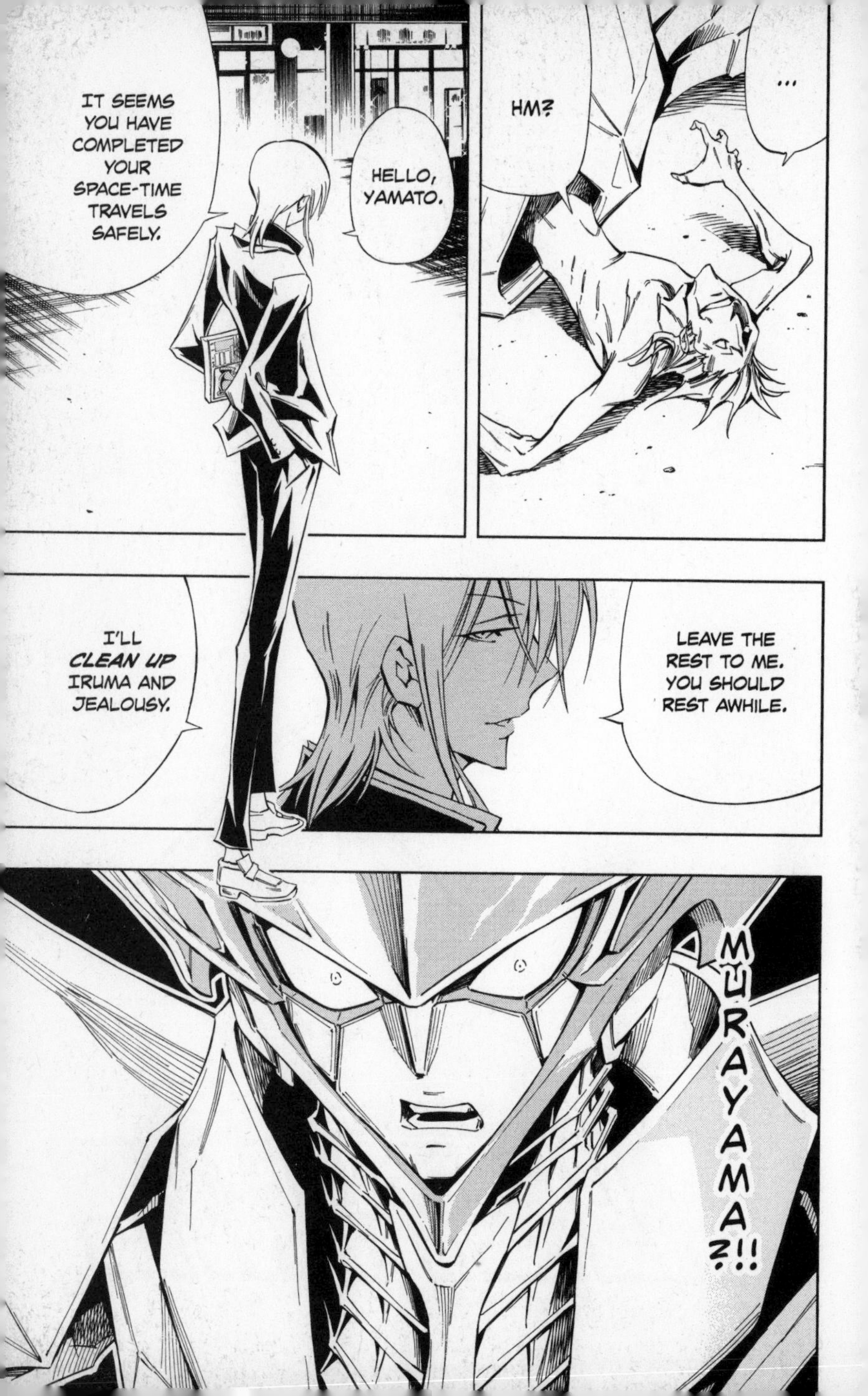
...
HM?
HELLO, YAMATO.
IT SEEMS YOU HAVE COMPLETED YOUR SPACE-TIME TRAVELS SAFELY.
LEAVE THE REST TO ME. YOU SHOULD REST AWHILE.
I'LL *CLEAN UP* IRUMA AND JEALOUSY.
MURAYAMA?!!

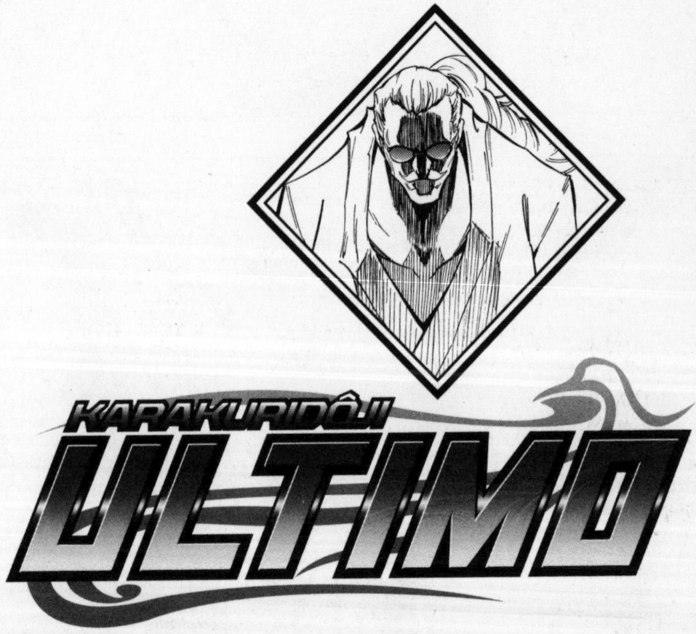

KARAKURIDÔJI
ULTIMO

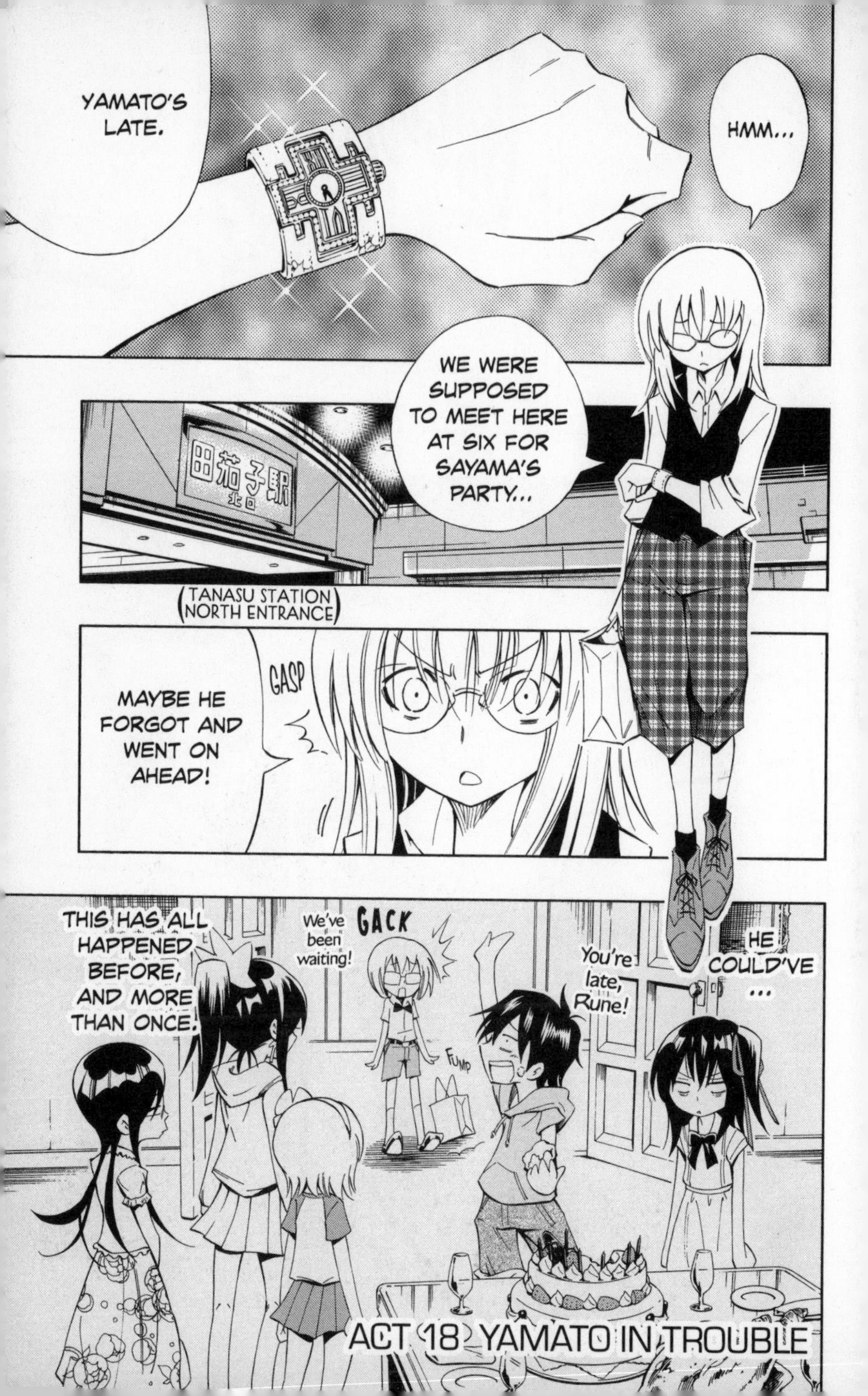
HMM...
YAMATO'S LATE.
WE WERE SUPPOSED TO MEET HERE AT SIX FOR SAYAMA'S PARTY...
田茄子駅
北口
(TANASU STATION NORTH ENTRANCE)
GASP
MAYBE HE FORGOT AND WENT ON AHEAD!
HE COULD'VE ...
You're late, Rune!
GACK
We've been waiting!
FUMP
THIS HAS ALL HAPPENED BEFORE, AND MORE THAN ONCE.
ACT 18 YAMATO IN TROUBLE

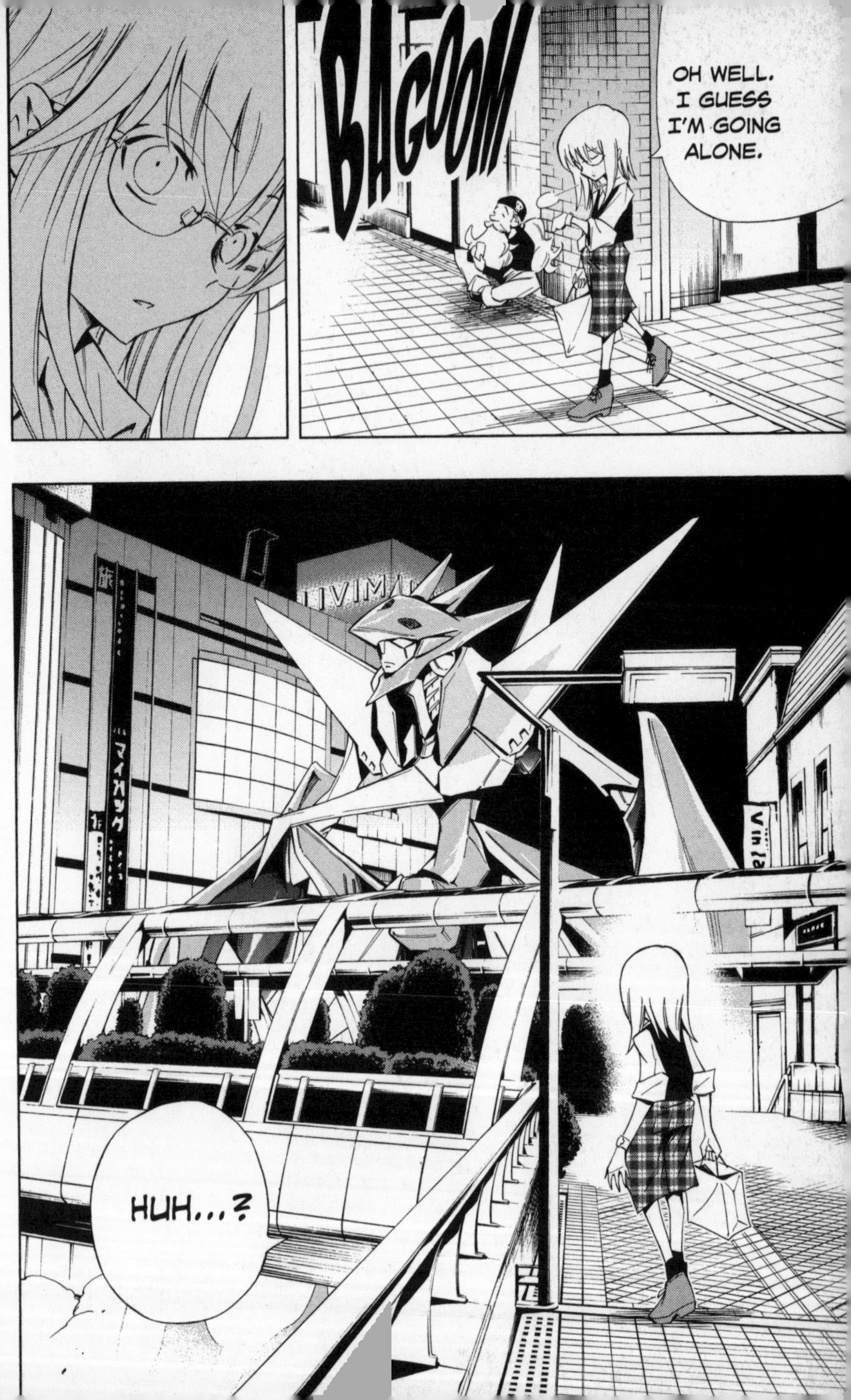
OH WELL. I GUESS I'M GOING ALONE.
BAGOOM
HUH...?

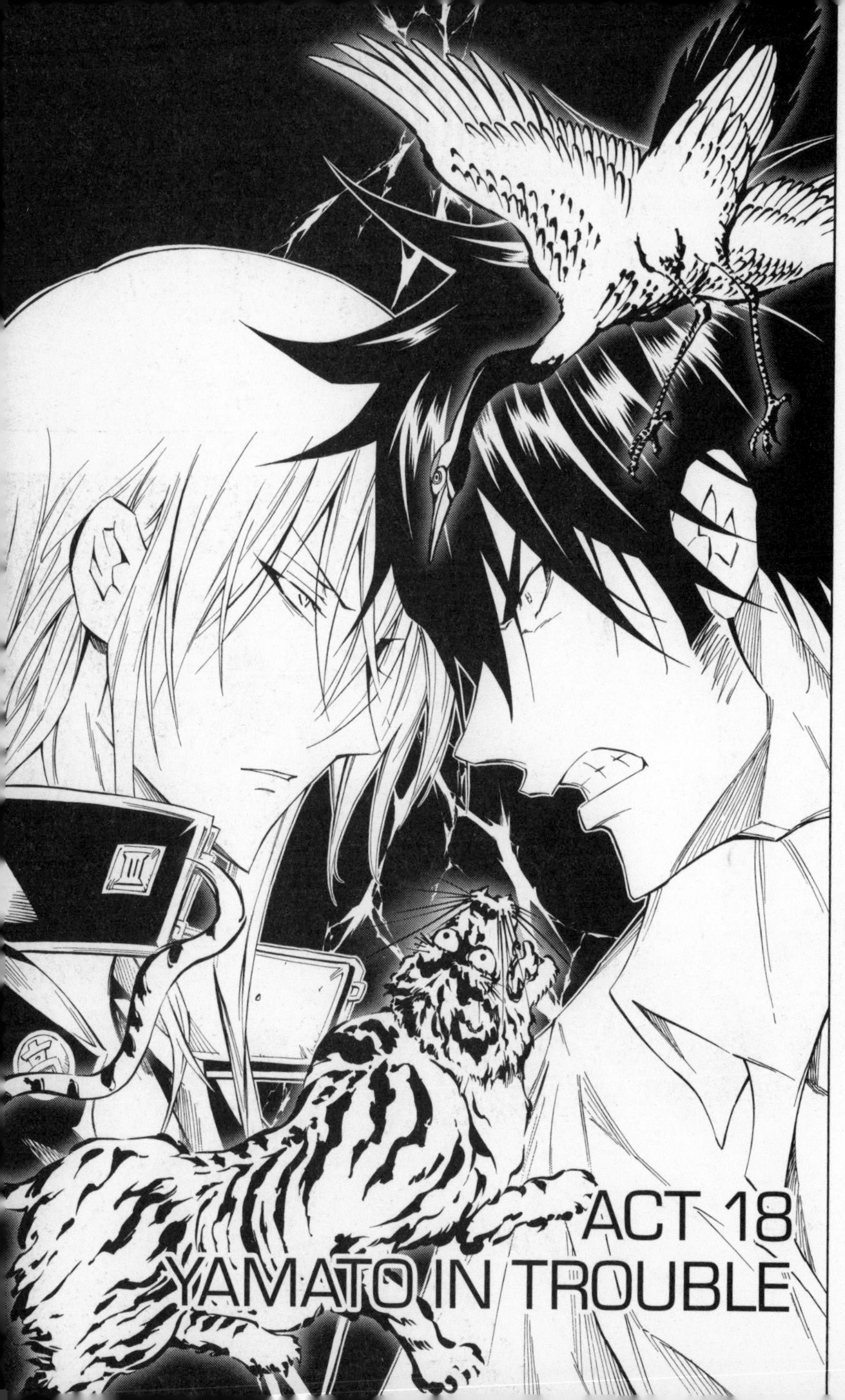
ACT 18
YAMATO IN TROUBLE

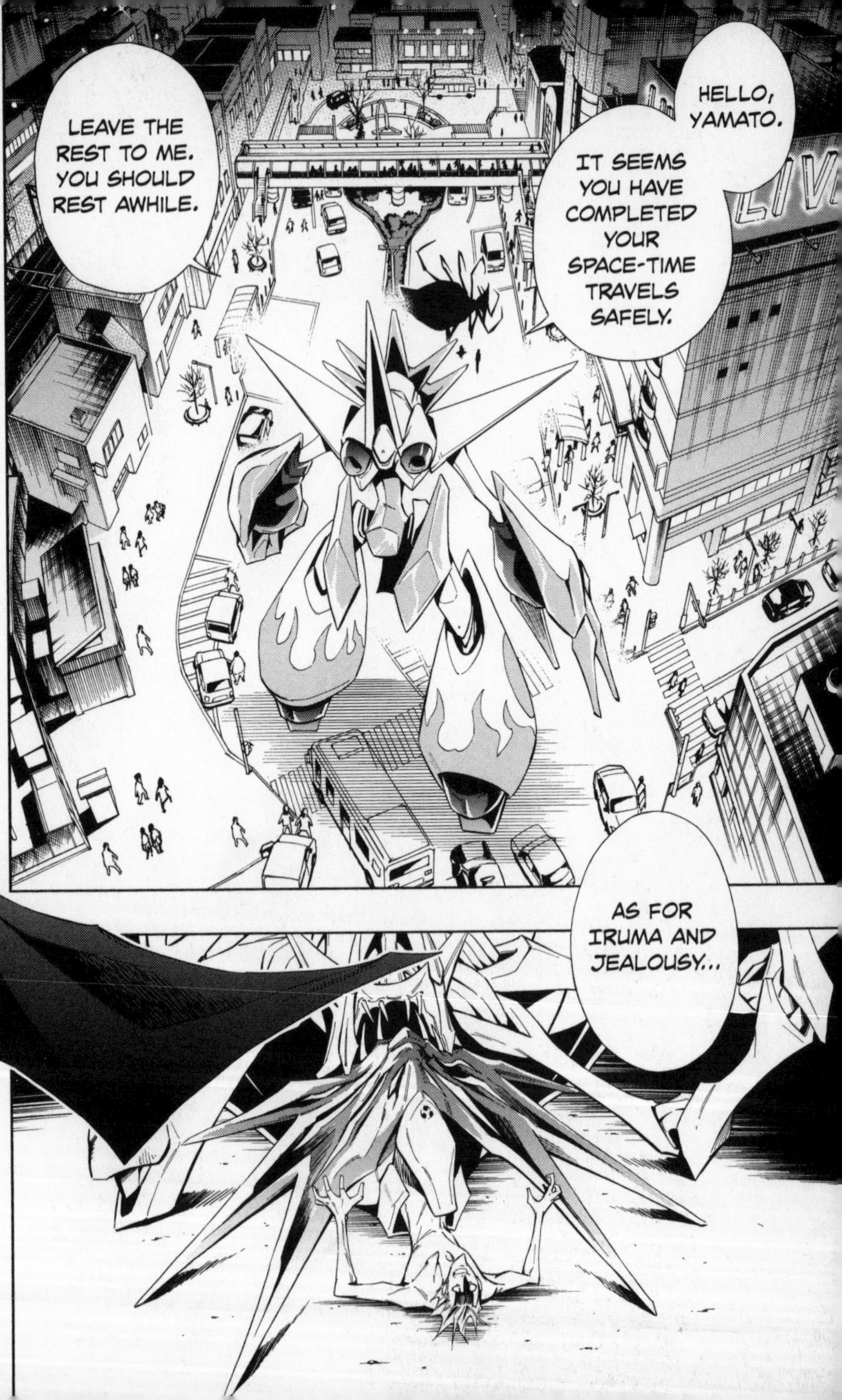
HELLO, YAMATO.
IT SEEMS YOU HAVE COMPLETED YOUR SPACE-TIME TRAVELS SAFELY.
AS FOR IRUMA AND JEALOUSY...
LEAVE THE REST TO ME. YOU SHOULD REST AWHILE.

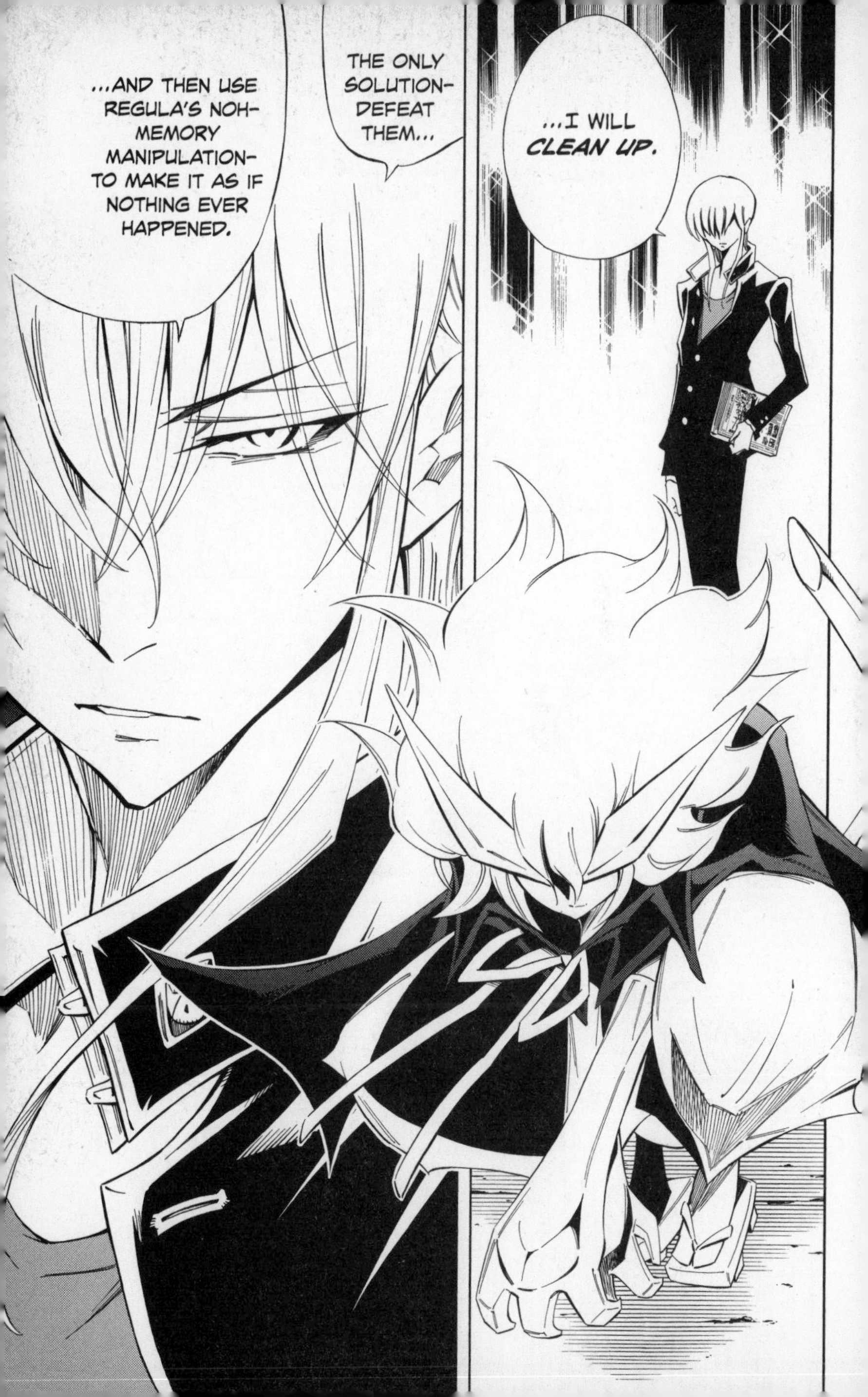
...I WILL CLEAN UP.
THE ONLY SOLUTION- DEFEAT THEM...
...AND THEN USE REGULA'S NOH- MEMORY MANIPULATION- TO MAKE IT AS IF NOTHING EVER HAPPENED.

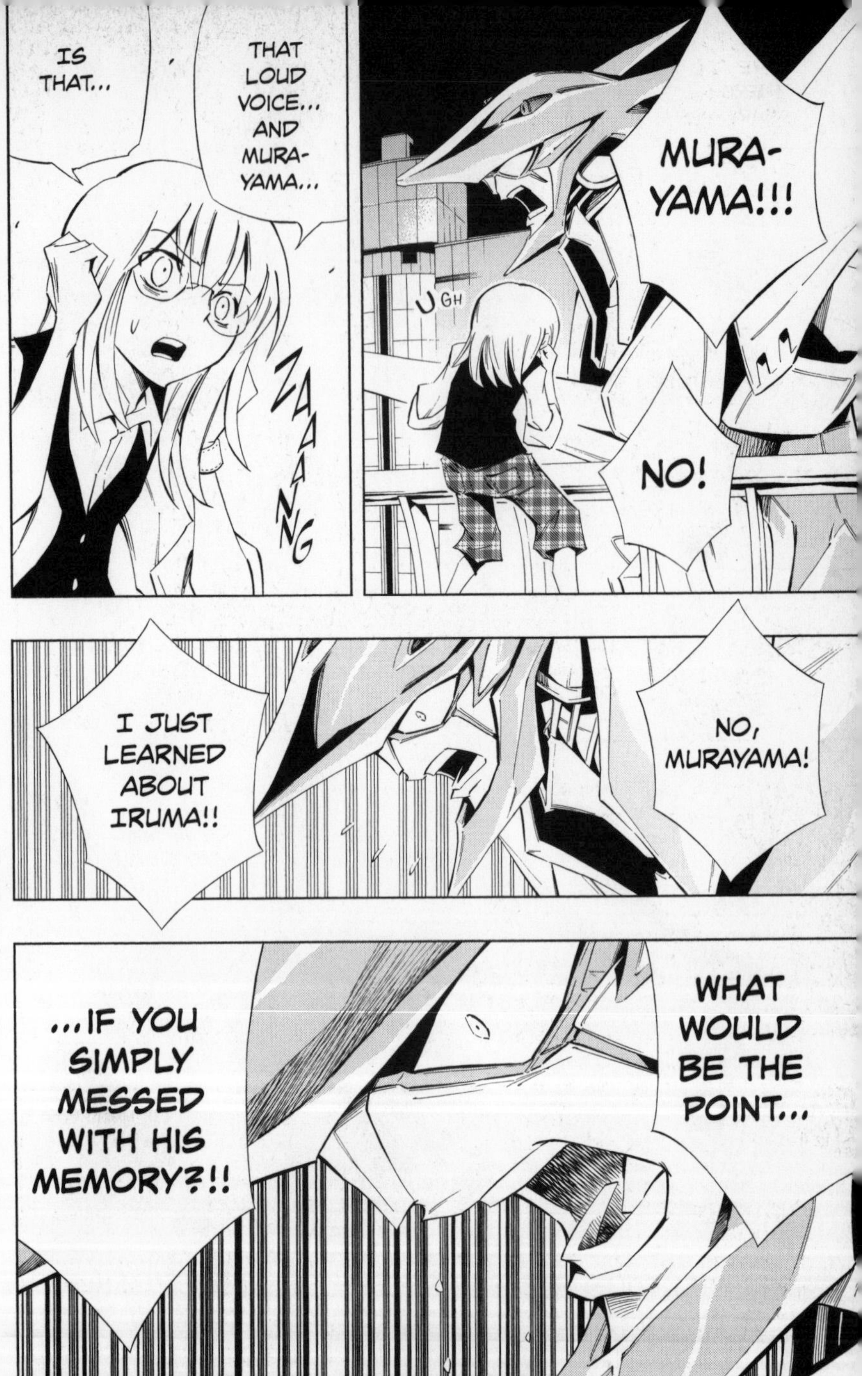
MURA-
YAMA!!!
UGH
NO!
THAT LOUD VOICE... AND MURA-
YAMA...
IS THAT...
ZAAAANG
NO, MURAYAMA!
I JUST LEARNED ABOUT IRUMA!!
WHAT WOULD BE THE POINT...
...IF YOU SIMPLY MESSED WITH HIS MEMORY?!!

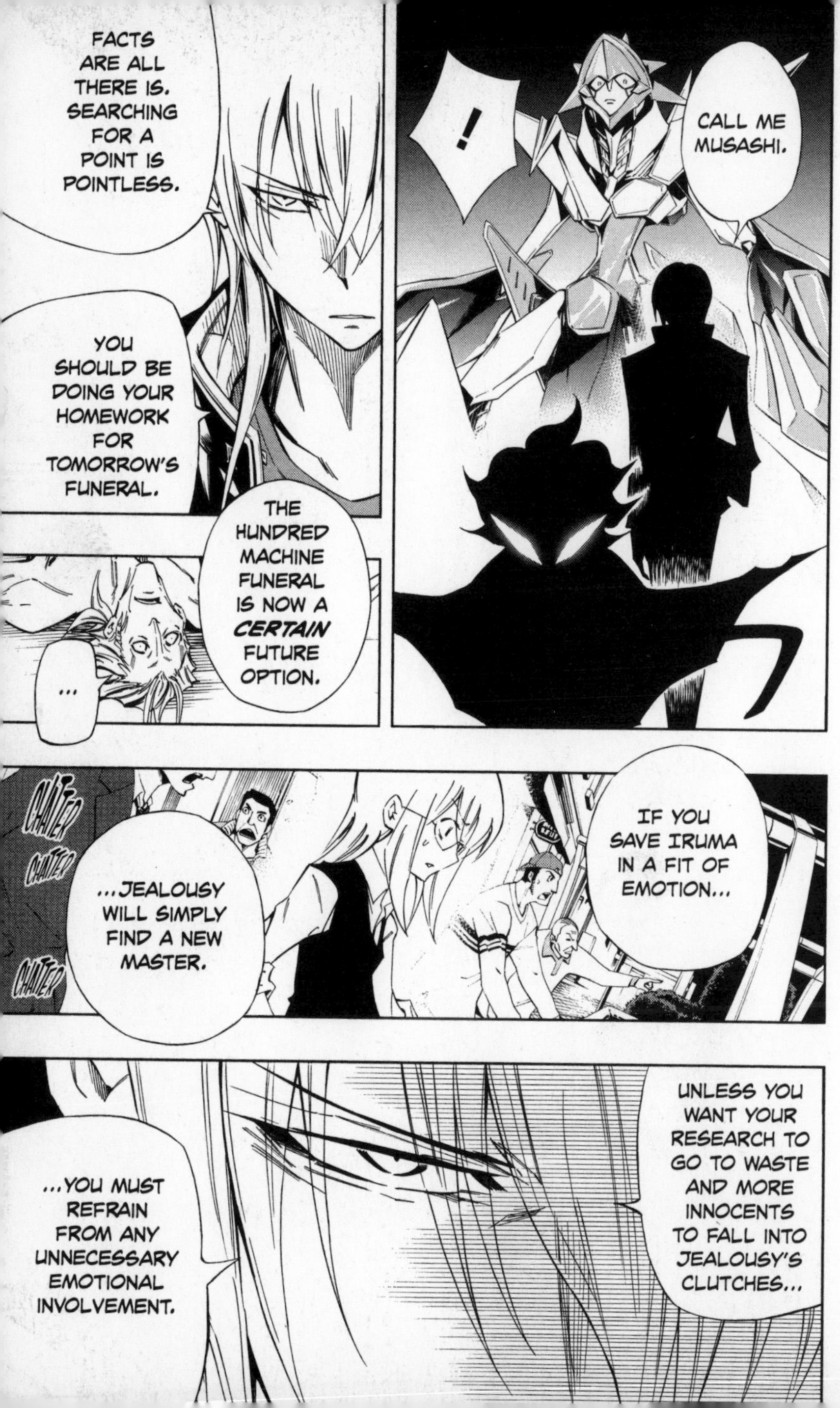
CALL ME MUSASHI.
!
FACTS ARE ALL THERE IS. SEARCHING FOR A POINT IS POINTLESS.
YOU SHOULD BE DOING YOUR HOMEWORK FOR TOMORROW'S FUNERAL.
THE HUNDRED MACHINE FUNERAL IS NOW A *CERTAIN* FUTURE OPTION.
...
IF YOU SAVE IRUMA IN A FIT OF EMOTION...
...JEALOUSY WILL SIMPLY FIND A NEW MASTER.
CHATTER
CHATTER
CHATTER
UNLESS YOU WANT YOUR RESEARCH TO GO TO WASTE AND MORE INNOCENTS TO FALL INTO JEALOUSY'S CLUTCHES...
...YOU MUST REFRAIN FROM ANY UNNECESSARY EMOTIONAL INVOLVEMENT.

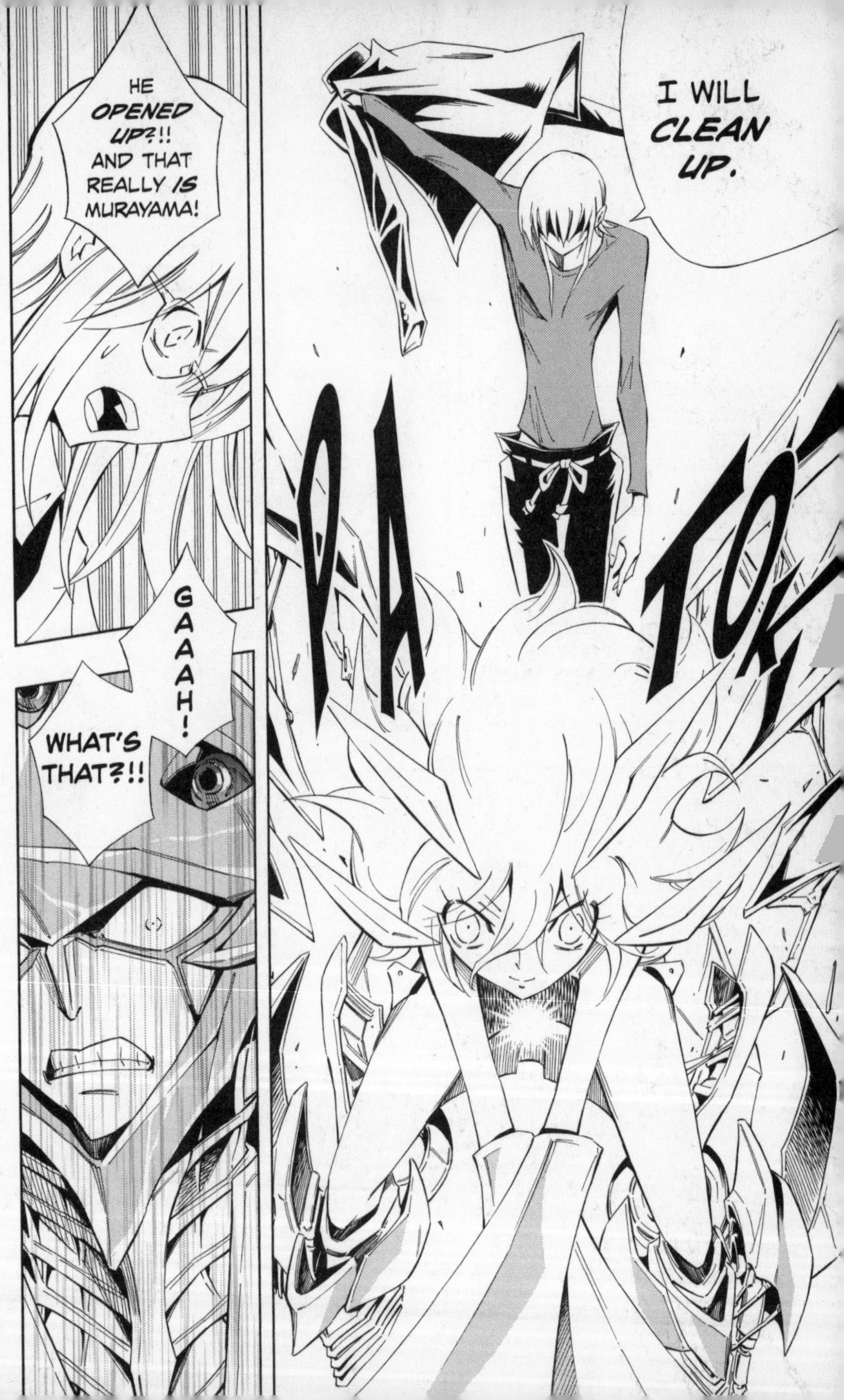
I WILL CLEAN UP.
PA
TO
HE OPENED UP?!! AND THAT REALLY IS MURAYAMA!
GAAAAH!
WHAT'S THAT?!!

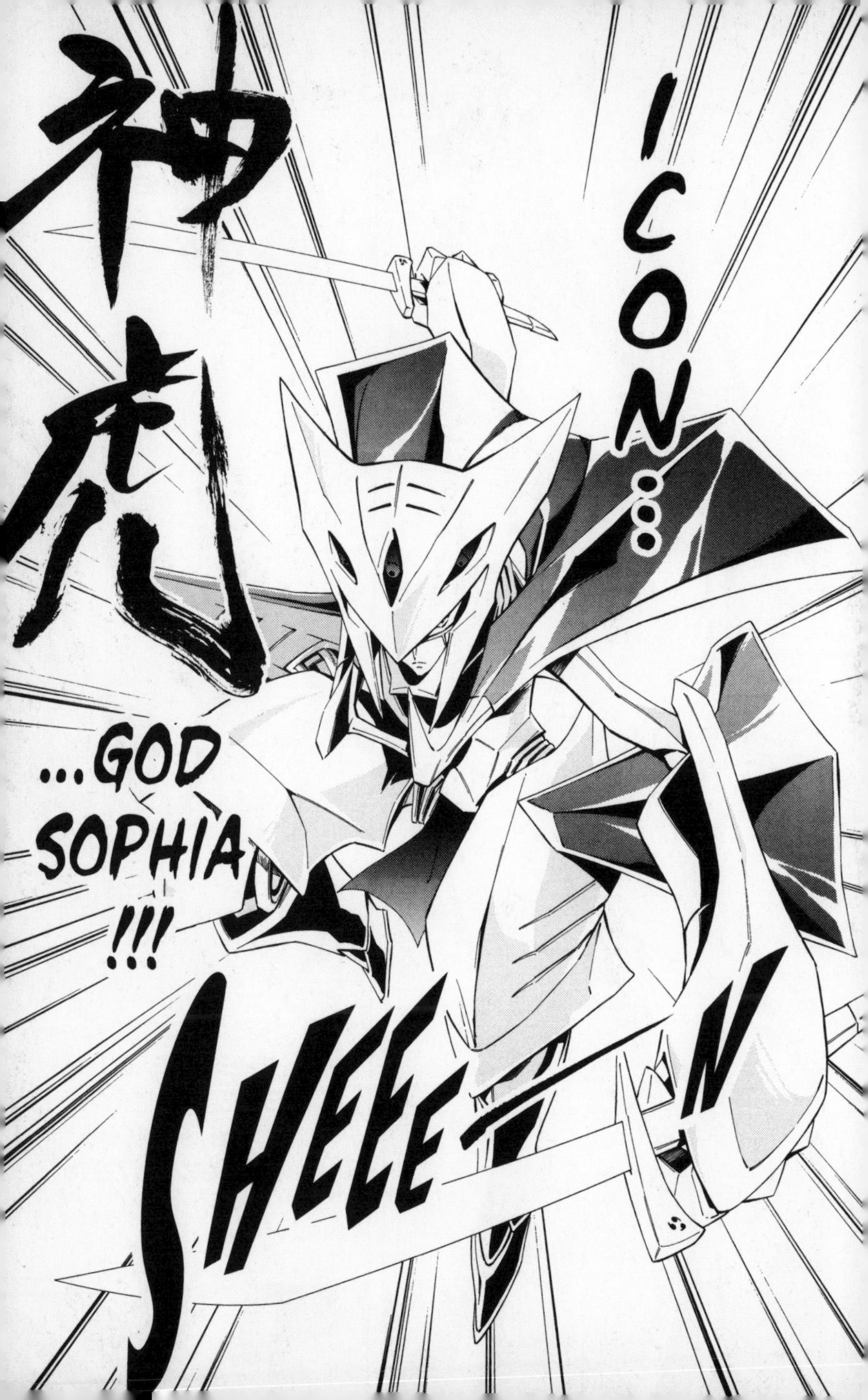
ICON...
...GOD SOPHIA!!!
SHEEE—N

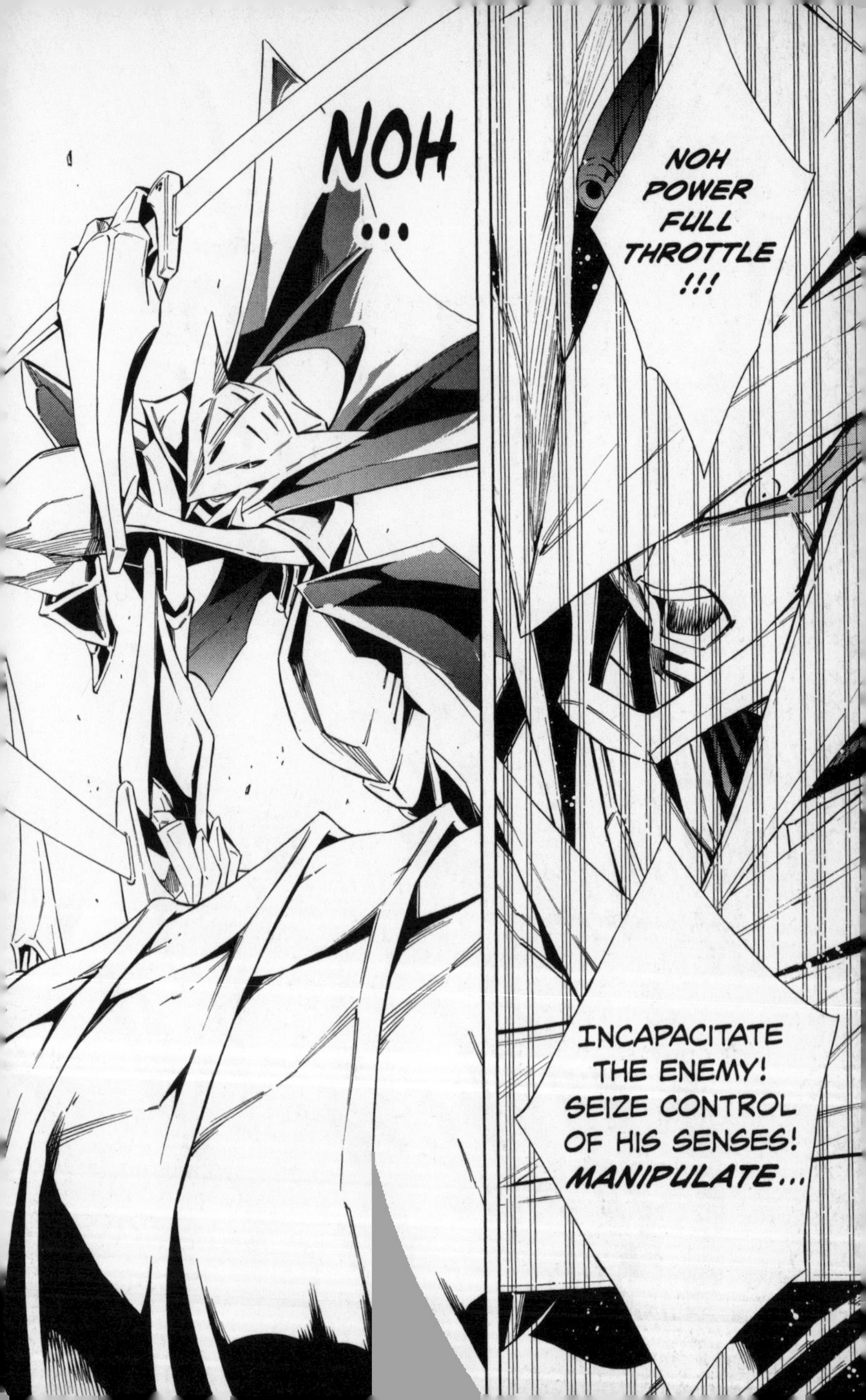
NOH POWER FULL THROTTLE !!!
INCAPACITATE THE ENEMY! SEIZE CONTROL OF HIS SENSES! *MANIPULATE...*
NOH
...

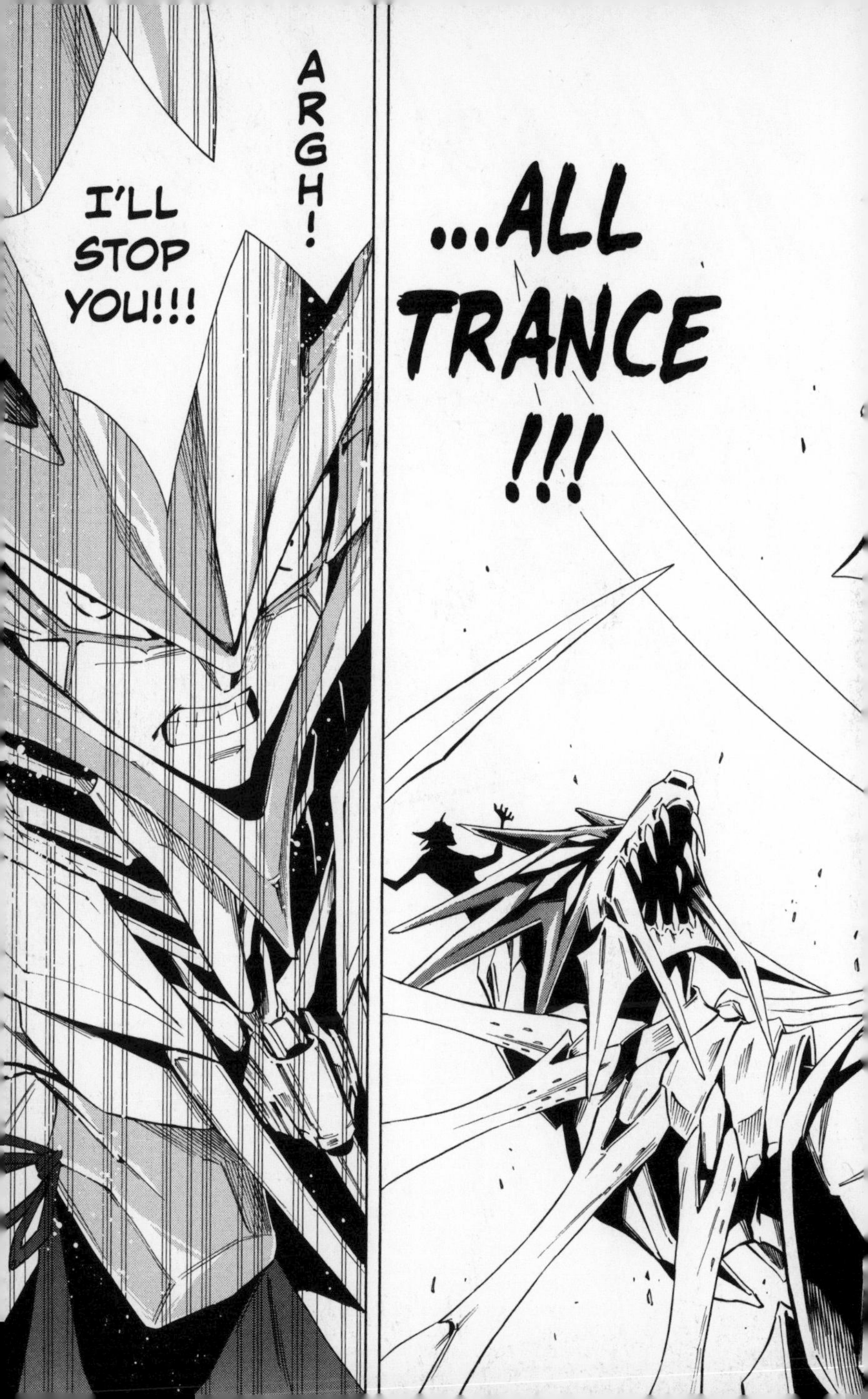
...ALL TRANCE!!!
ARGH!
I'LL STOP YOU!!!

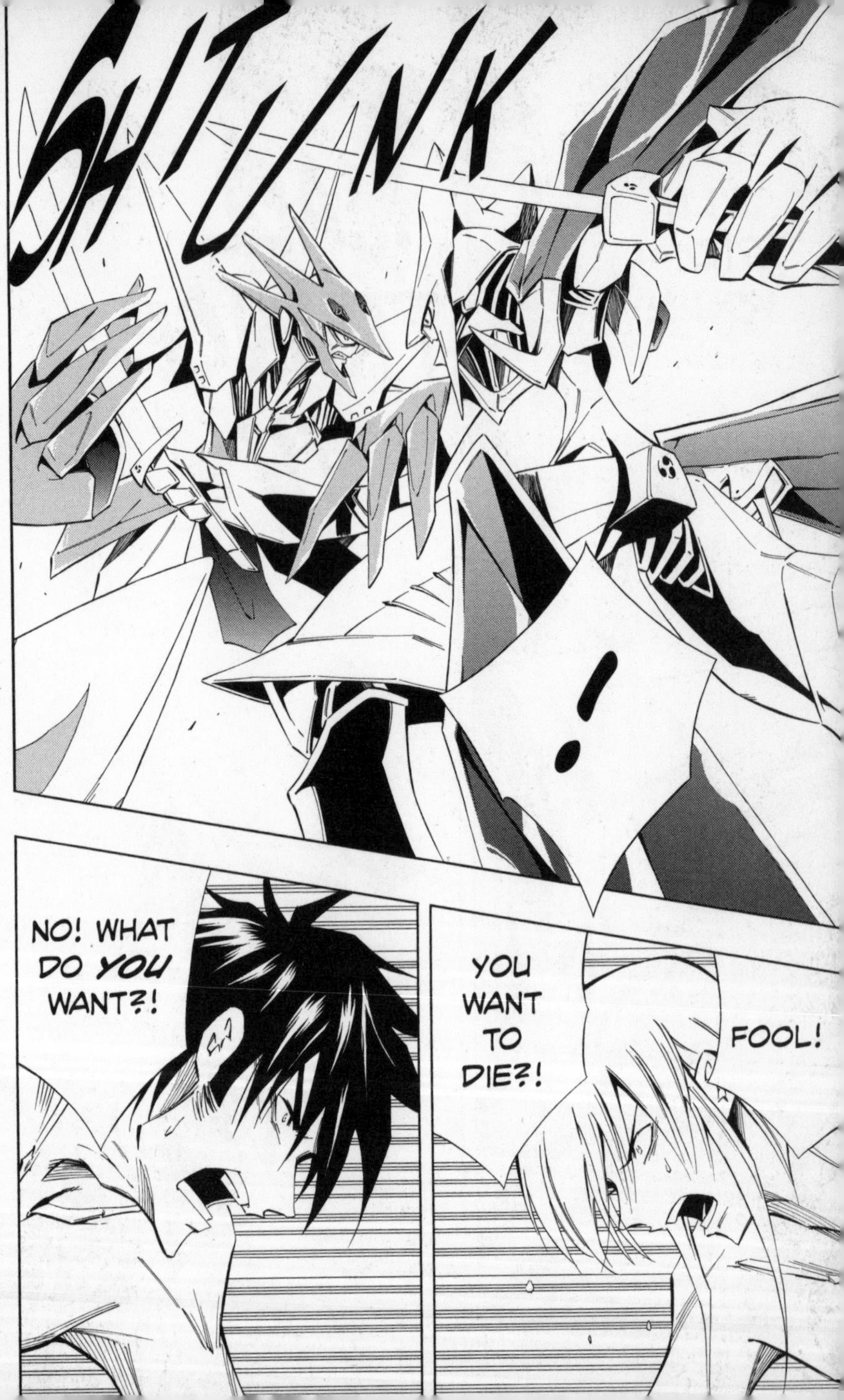
SHUNK!
!
FOOL!
YOU WANT TO DIE?!
NO! WHAT DO *YOU* WANT?!

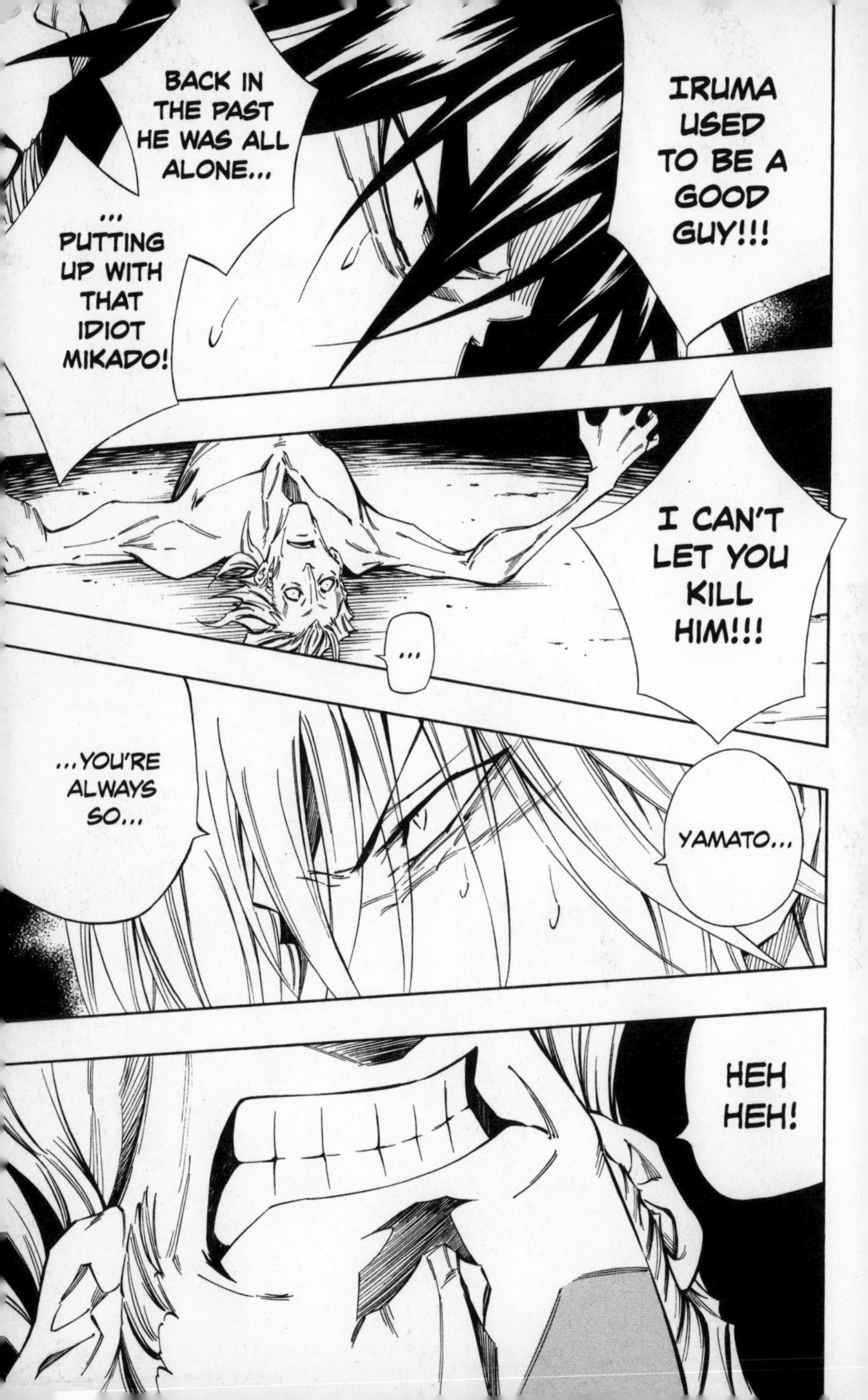
IRUMA USED TO BE A GOOD GUY!!!
BACK IN THE PAST HE WAS ALL ALONE...
... PUTTING UP WITH THAT IDIOT MIKADO!
I CAN'T LET YOU KILL HIM!!!
...
YAMATO...
...YOU'RE ALWAYS SO...
HEH HEH!

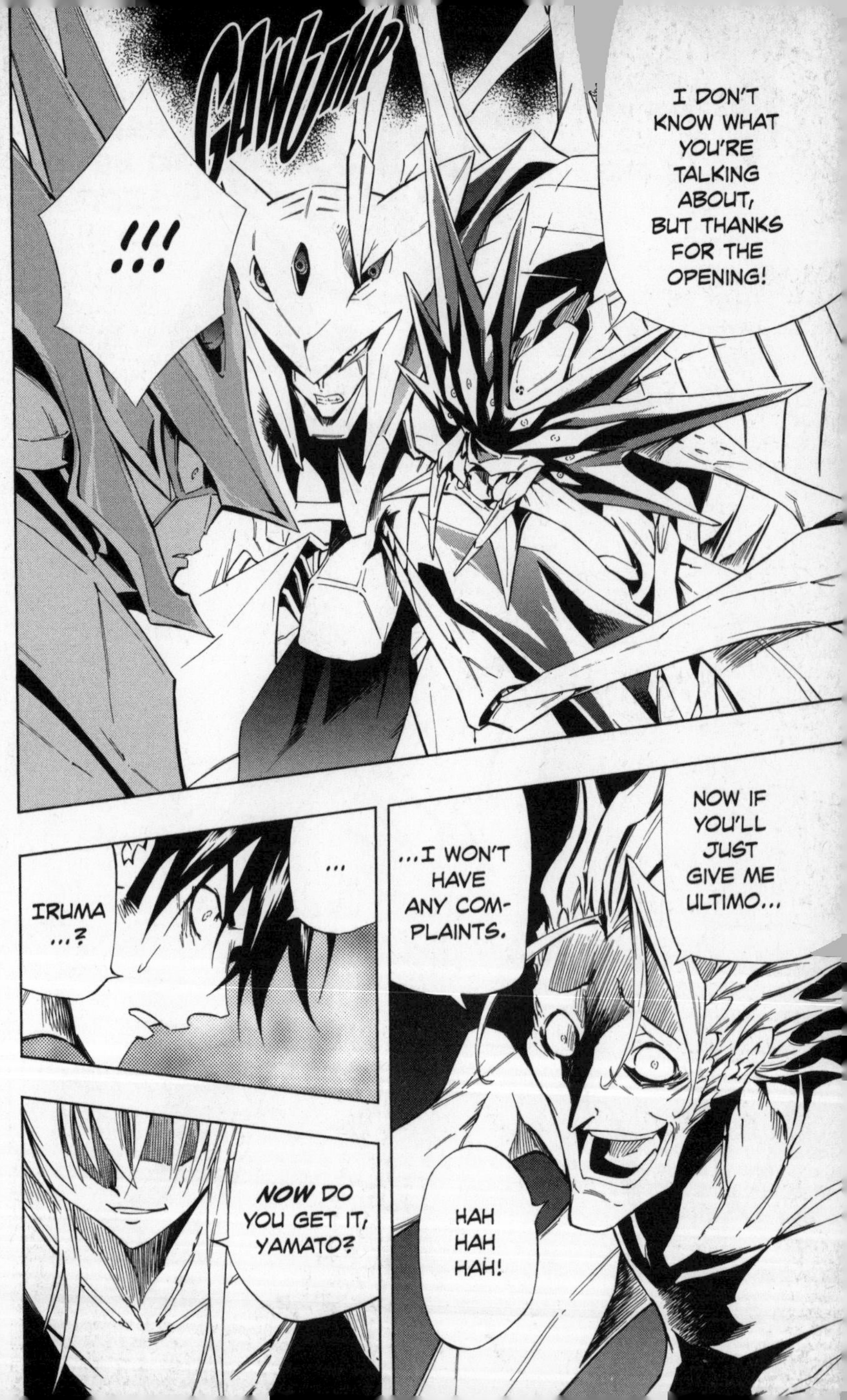
I DON'T KNOW WHAT YOU'RE TALKING ABOUT, BUT THANKS FOR THE OPENING!
!!!
NOW IF YOU'LL JUST GIVE ME ULTIMO...
...I WON'T HAVE ANY COM-PLAINTS.
HAH HAH HAH!
...
IRUMA ...?
NOW DO YOU GET IT, YAMATO?

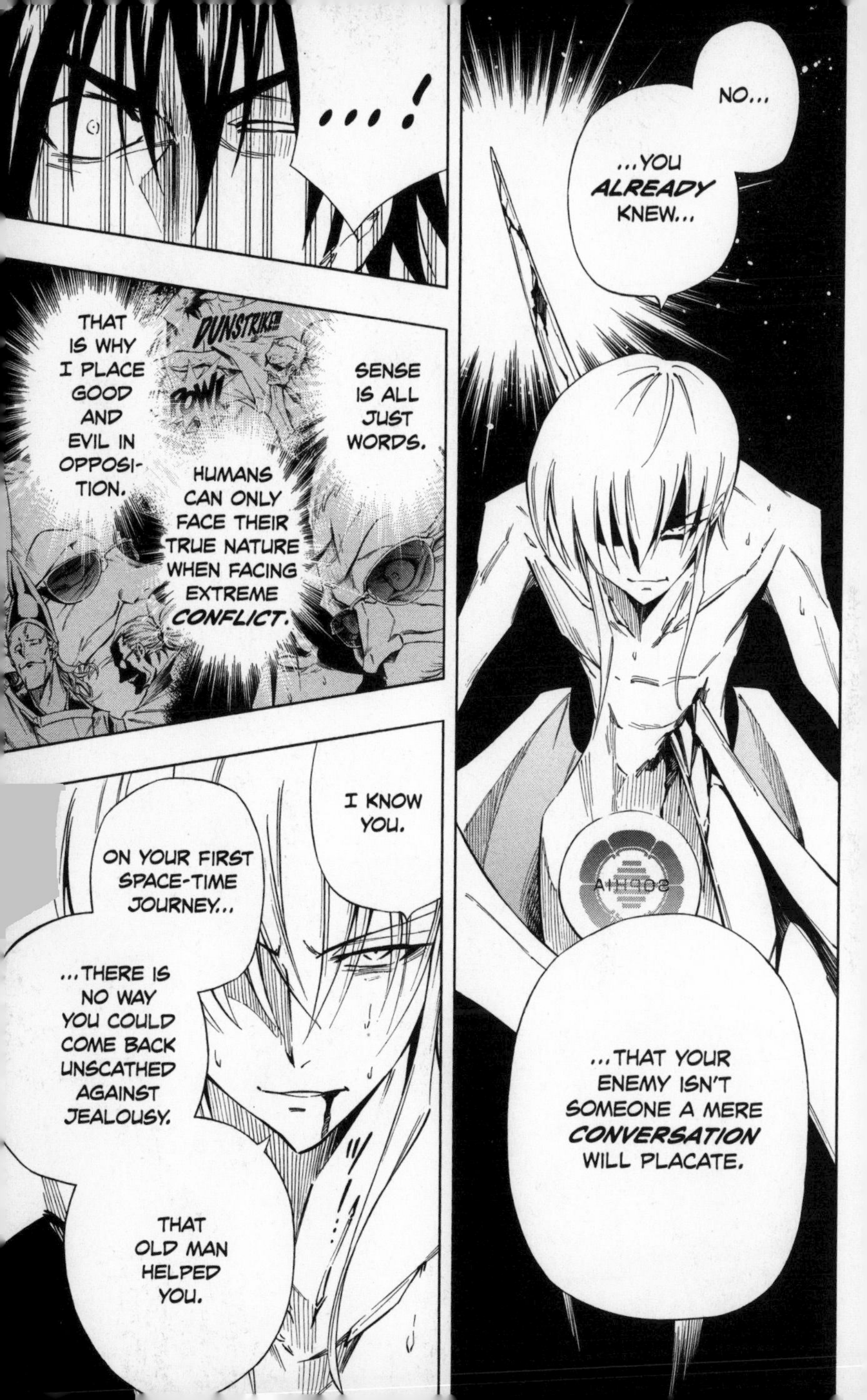
NO...
...YOU ALREADY KNEW...
...THAT YOUR ENEMY ISN'T SOMEONE A MERE CONVERSATION WILL PLACATE.
...!
SENSE IS ALL JUST WORDS.
HUMANS CAN ONLY FACE THEIR TRUE NATURE WHEN FACING EXTREME CONFLICT.
DUNSTRIK!!!
BOW!
THAT IS WHY I PLACE GOOD AND EVIL IN OPPOSITION.
I KNOW YOU.
ON YOUR FIRST SPACE-TIME JOURNEY...
...THERE IS NO WAY YOU COULD COME BACK UNSCATHED AGAINST JEALOUSY.
THAT OLD MAN HELPED YOU.

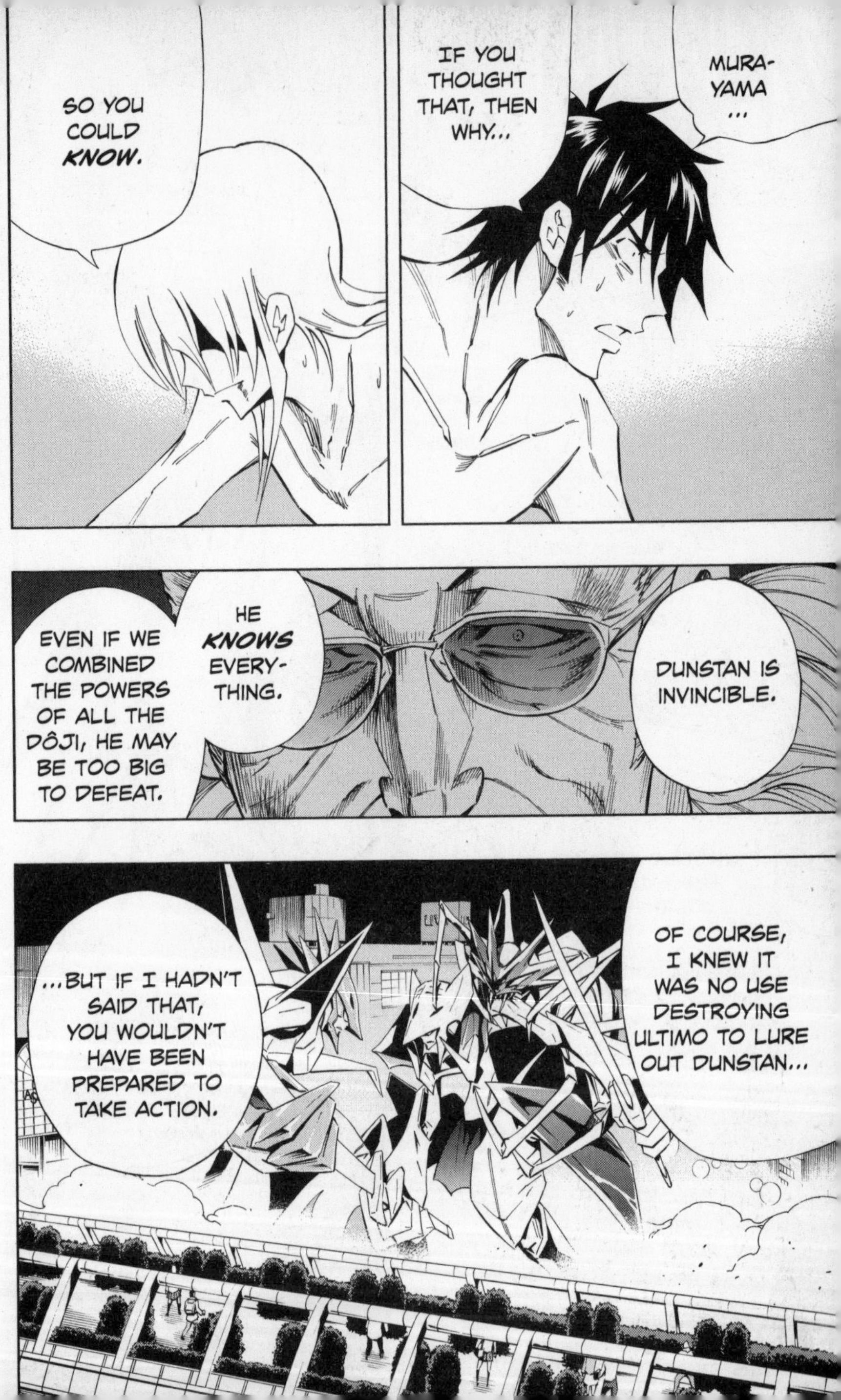
MURA-YAMA ...
IF YOU THOUGHT THAT, THEN WHY...
SO YOU COULD *KNOW*.
DUNSTAN IS INVINCIBLE.
HE *KNOWS* EVERY-THING.
EVEN IF WE COMBINED THE POWERS OF ALL THE DÔJI, HE MAY BE TOO BIG TO DEFEAT.
OF COURSE, I KNEW IT WAS NO USE DESTROYING ULTIMO TO LURE OUT DUNSTAN...
...BUT IF I HADN'T SAID THAT, YOU WOULDN'T HAVE BEEN PREPARED TO TAKE ACTION.

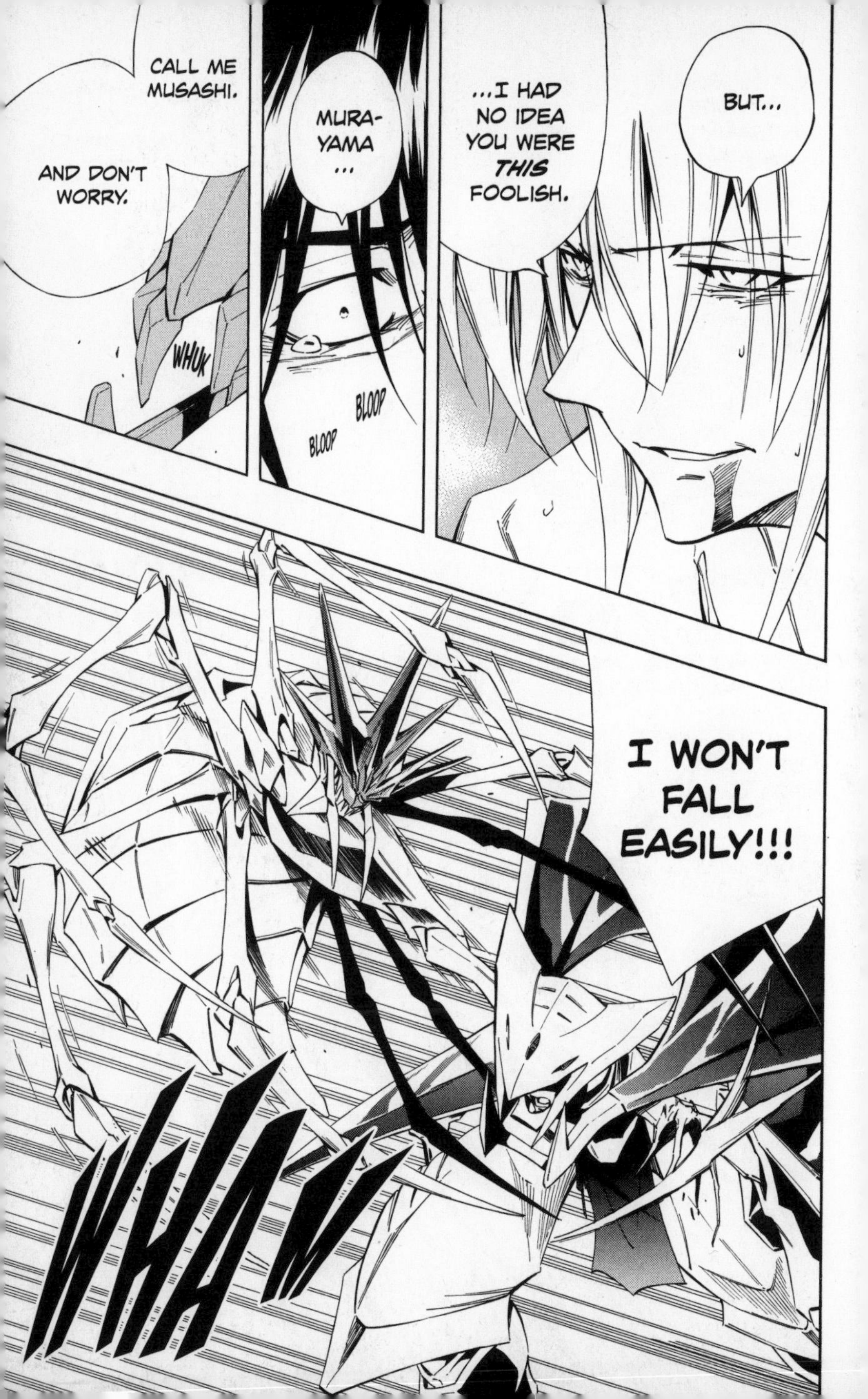
BUT...
...I HAD NO IDEA YOU WERE THIS FOOLISH.
MURA-YAMA ...
BLOOP
BLOOP
CALL ME MUSASHI.
AND DON'T WORRY.
WHUK
I WON'T FALL EASILY!!!
WHAM

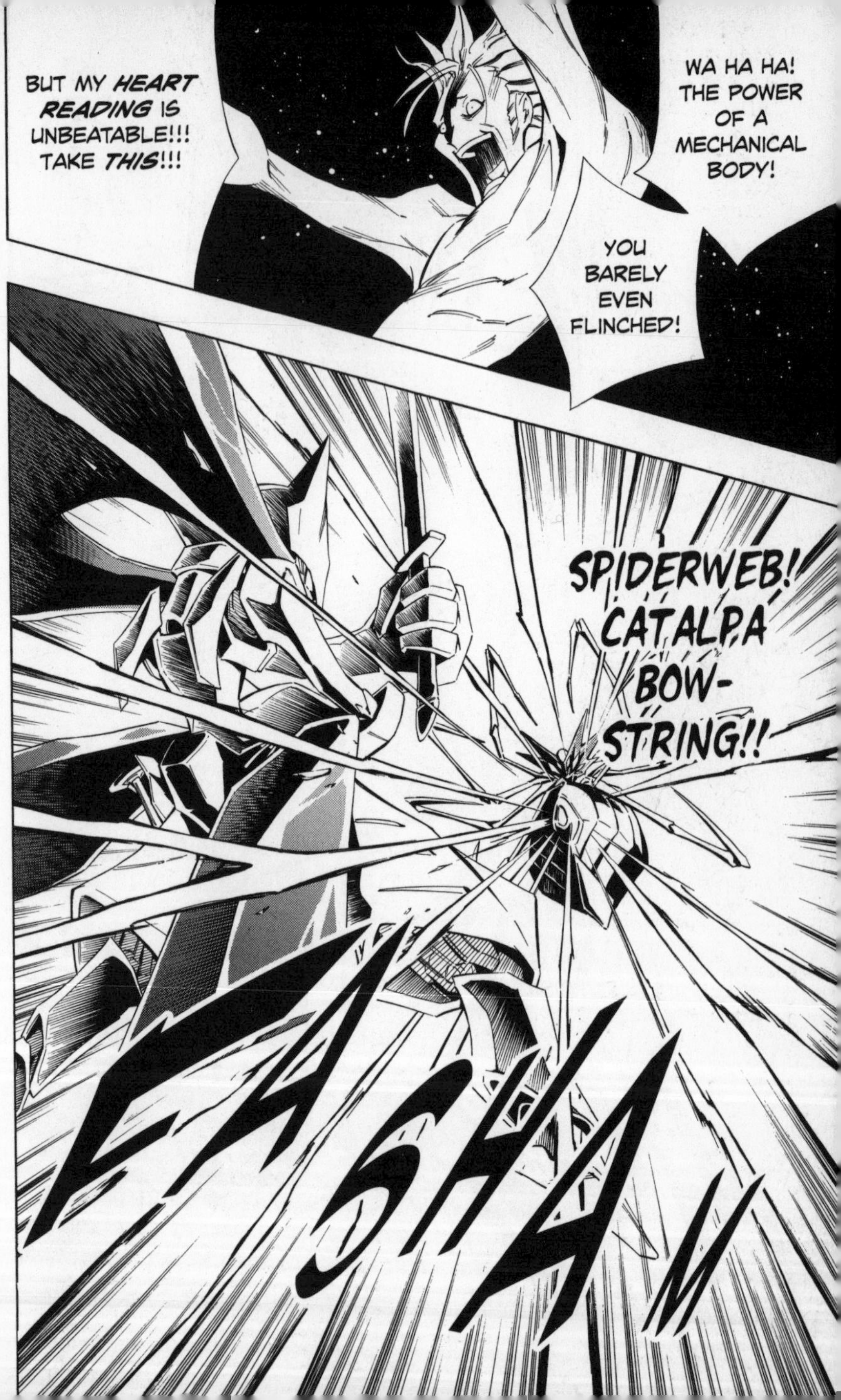
WA HA HA! THE POWER OF A MECHANICAL BODY!
YOU BARELY EVEN FLINCHED!
BUT MY *HEART READING* IS UNBEATABLE!!! TAKE *THIS*!!!
SPIDERWEB! CATALPA BOW-STRING!!
ZASHAN

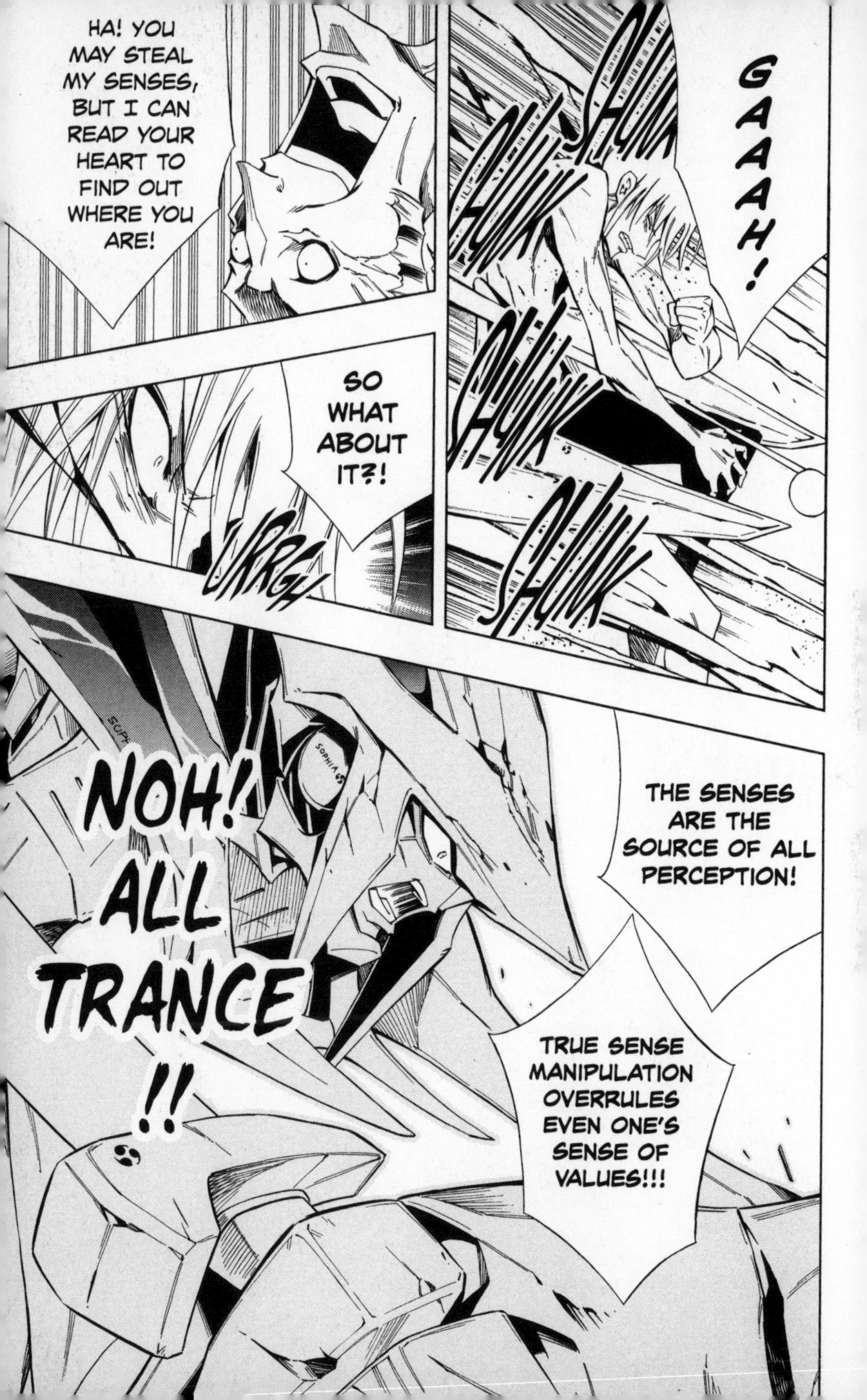
GAAAAH!
SHUNK
SHUNK
SHUNK
SHUNK
HA! YOU MAY STEAL MY SENSES, BUT I CAN READ YOUR HEART TO FIND OUT WHERE YOU ARE!
SO WHAT ABOUT IT?!
URRGH
THE SENSES ARE THE SOURCE OF ALL PERCEPTION!
TRUE SENSE MANIPULATION OVERRULES EVEN ONE'S SENSE OF VALUES!!!
NOH! ALL TRANCE!!

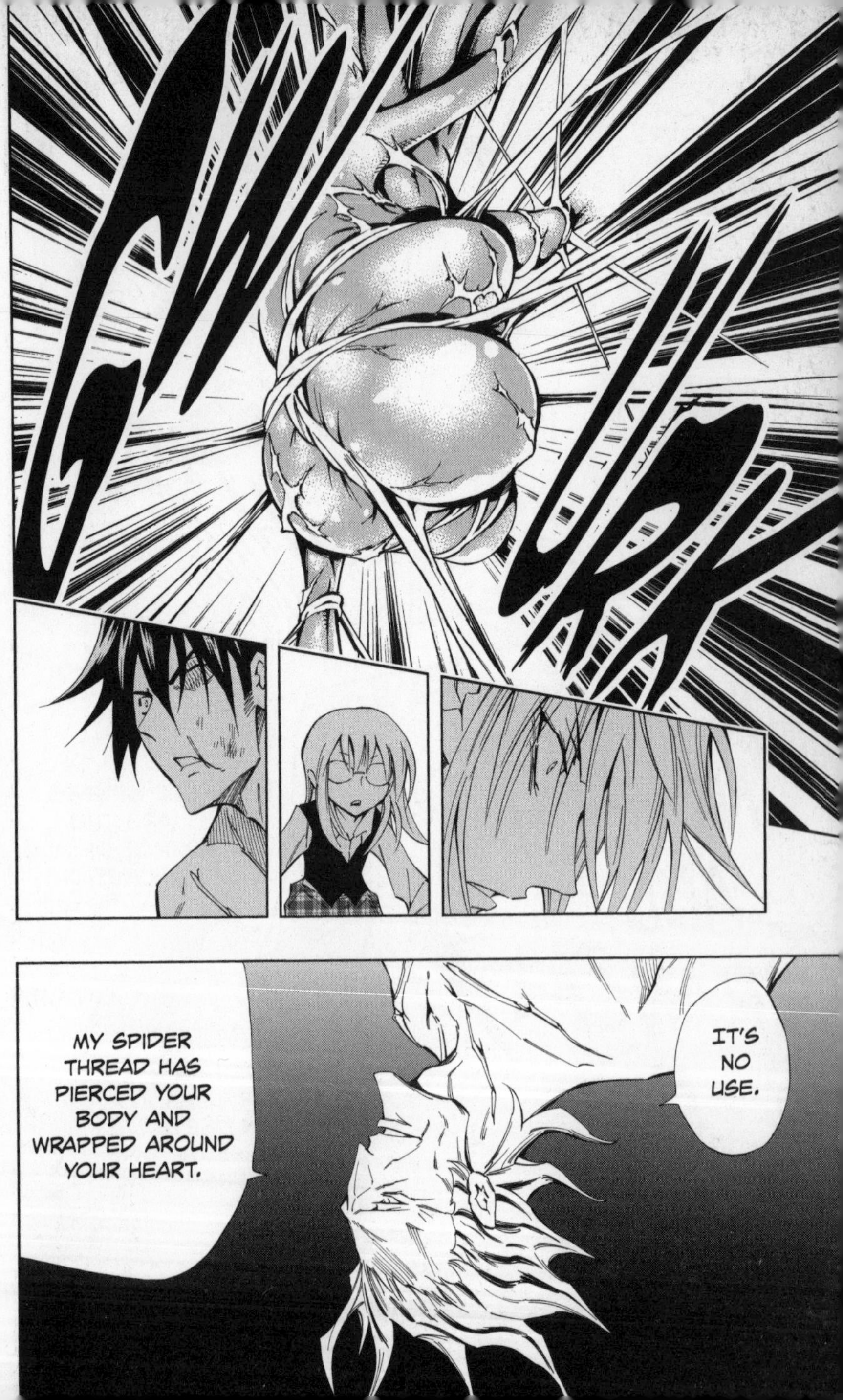
IT'S NO USE.
MY SPIDER THREAD HAS PIERCED YOUR BODY AND WRAPPED AROUND YOUR HEART.

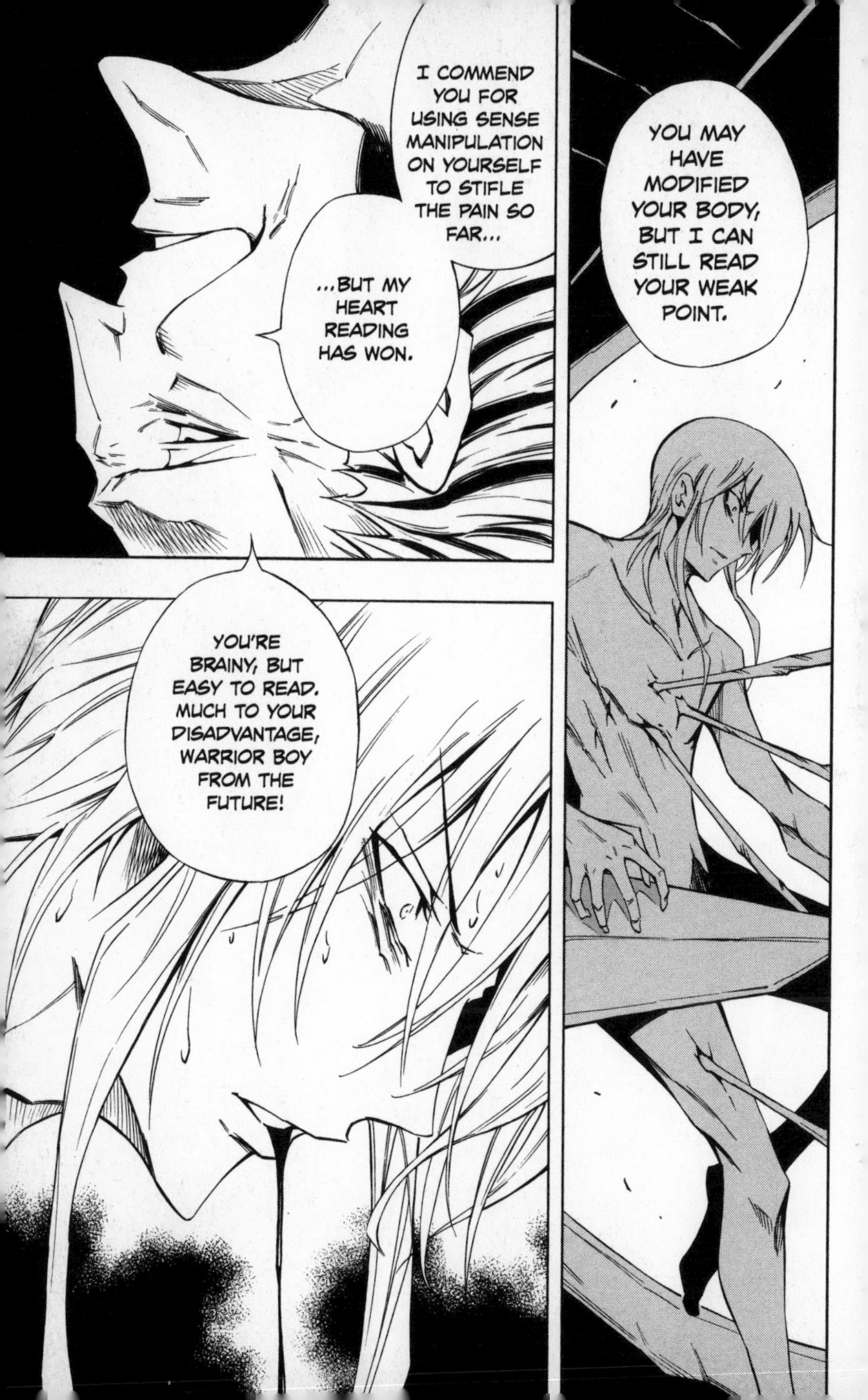
YOU MAY HAVE MODIFIED YOUR BODY, BUT I CAN STILL READ YOUR WEAK POINT.
I COMMEND YOU FOR USING SENSE MANIPULATION ON YOURSELF TO STIFLE THE PAIN SO FAR...
...BUT MY HEART READING HAS WON.
YOU'RE BRAINY, BUT EASY TO READ. MUCH TO YOUR DISADVANTAGE, WARRIOR BOY FROM THE FUTURE!

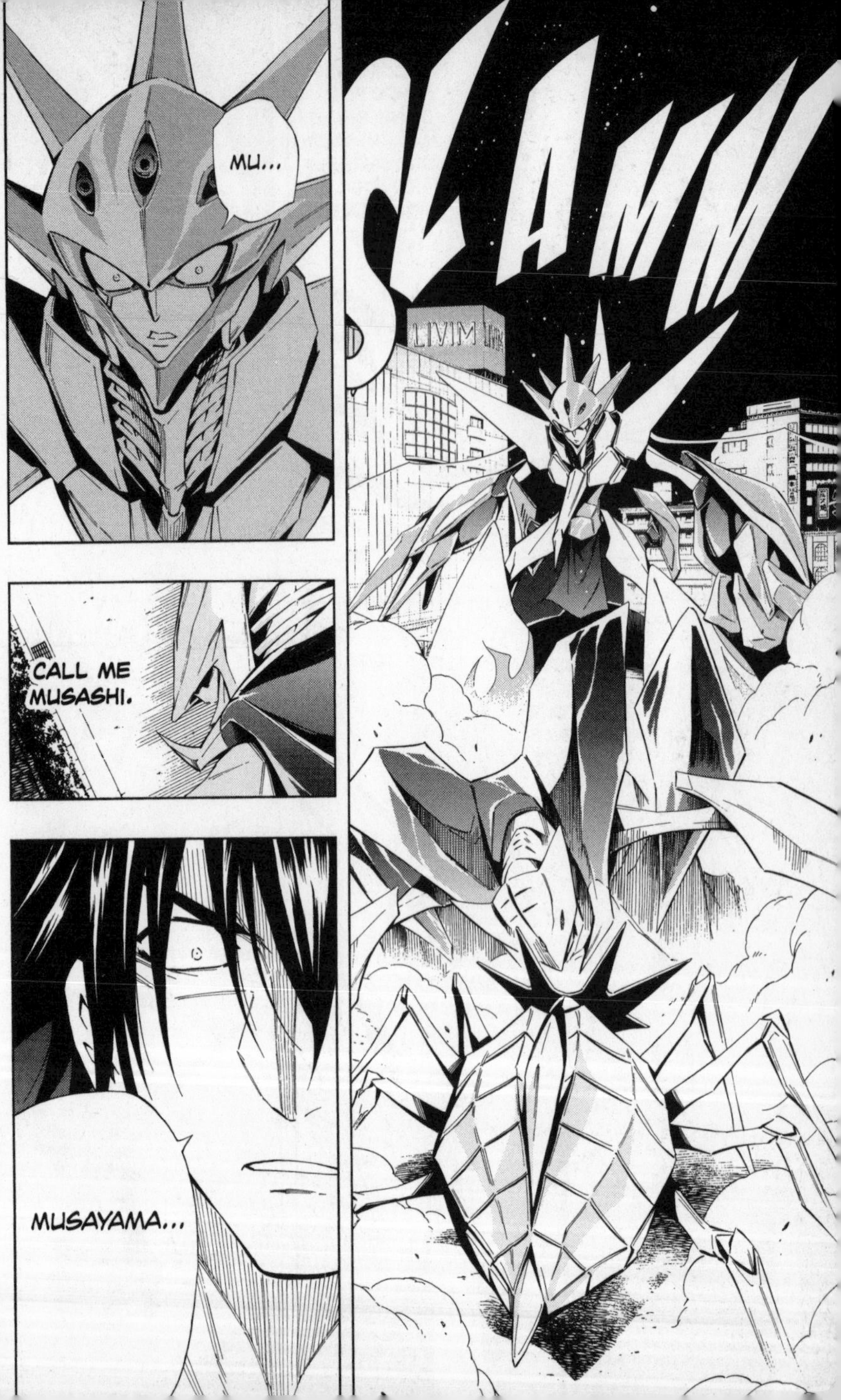
SLAMM
LIVIM
MU...
CALL ME MUSASHI.
MUSAYAMA...

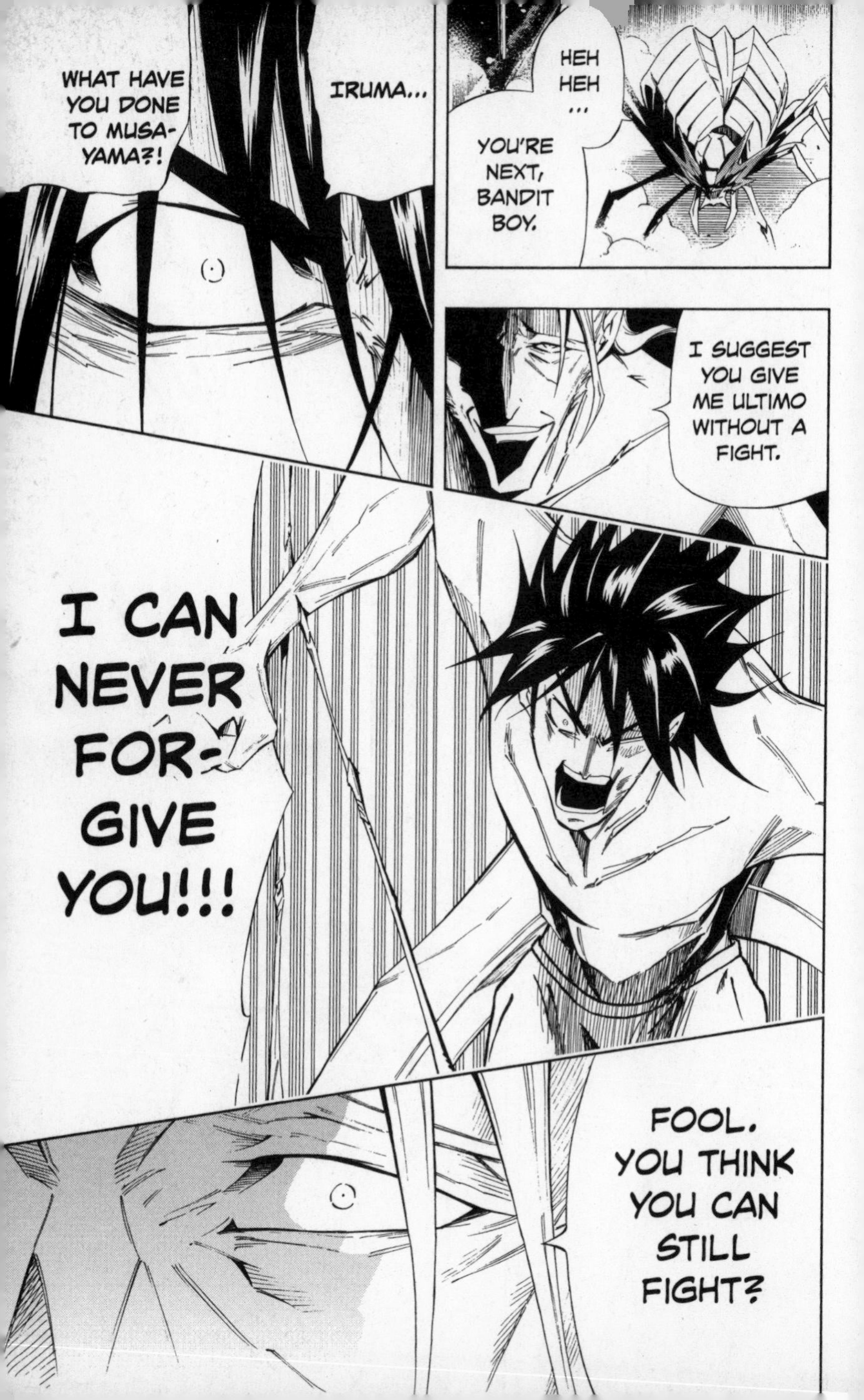
HEH HEH ...
YOU'RE NEXT, BANDIT BOY.
I SUGGEST YOU GIVE ME ULTIMO WITHOUT A FIGHT.
IRUMA...
WHAT HAVE YOU DONE TO MUSA-YAMA?!
I CAN NEVER FOR-GIVE YOU!!!
FOOL. YOU THINK YOU CAN STILL FIGHT?

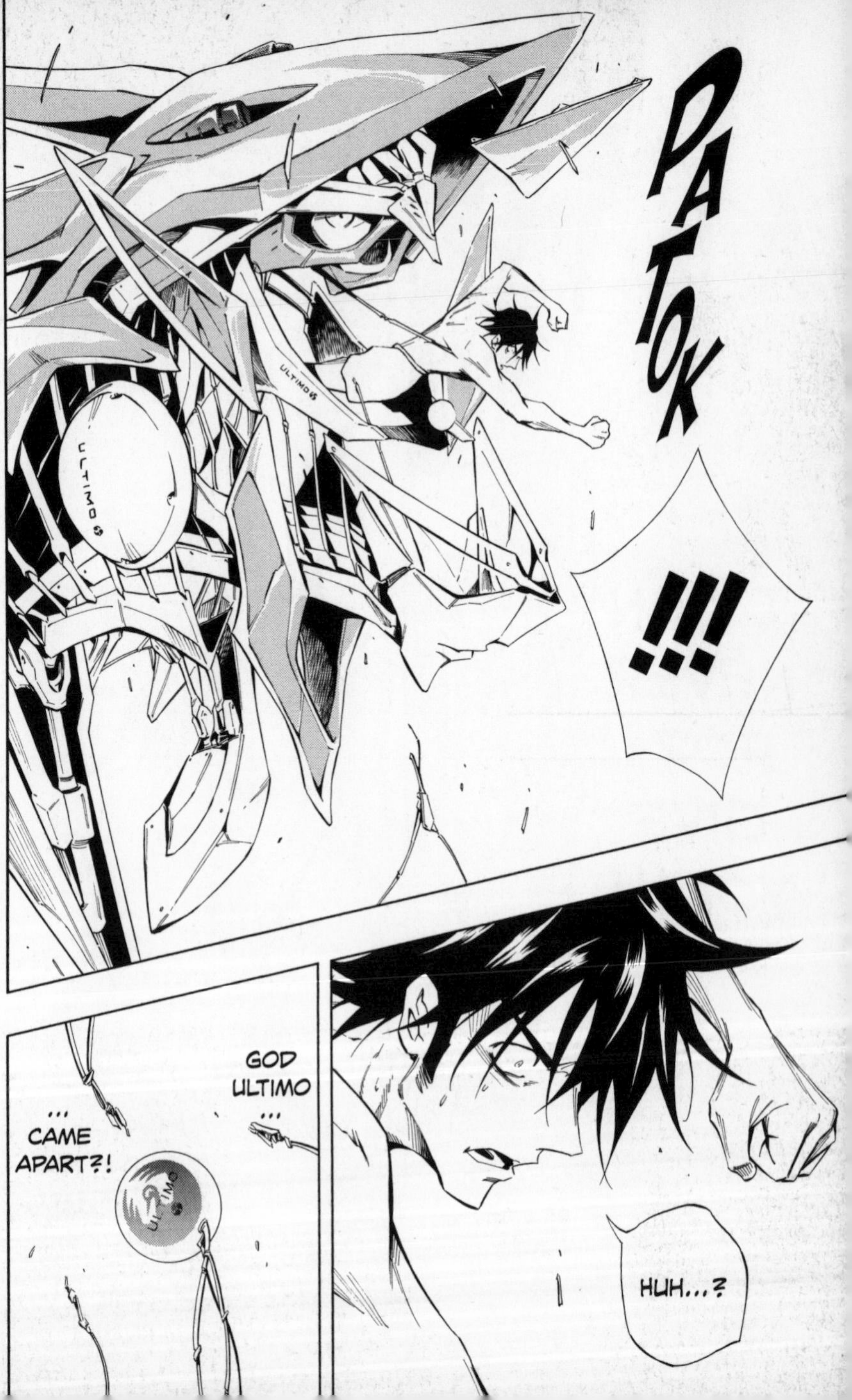
DATOK
!!!
HUH...?
GOD ULTIMO ...
... CAME APART?!

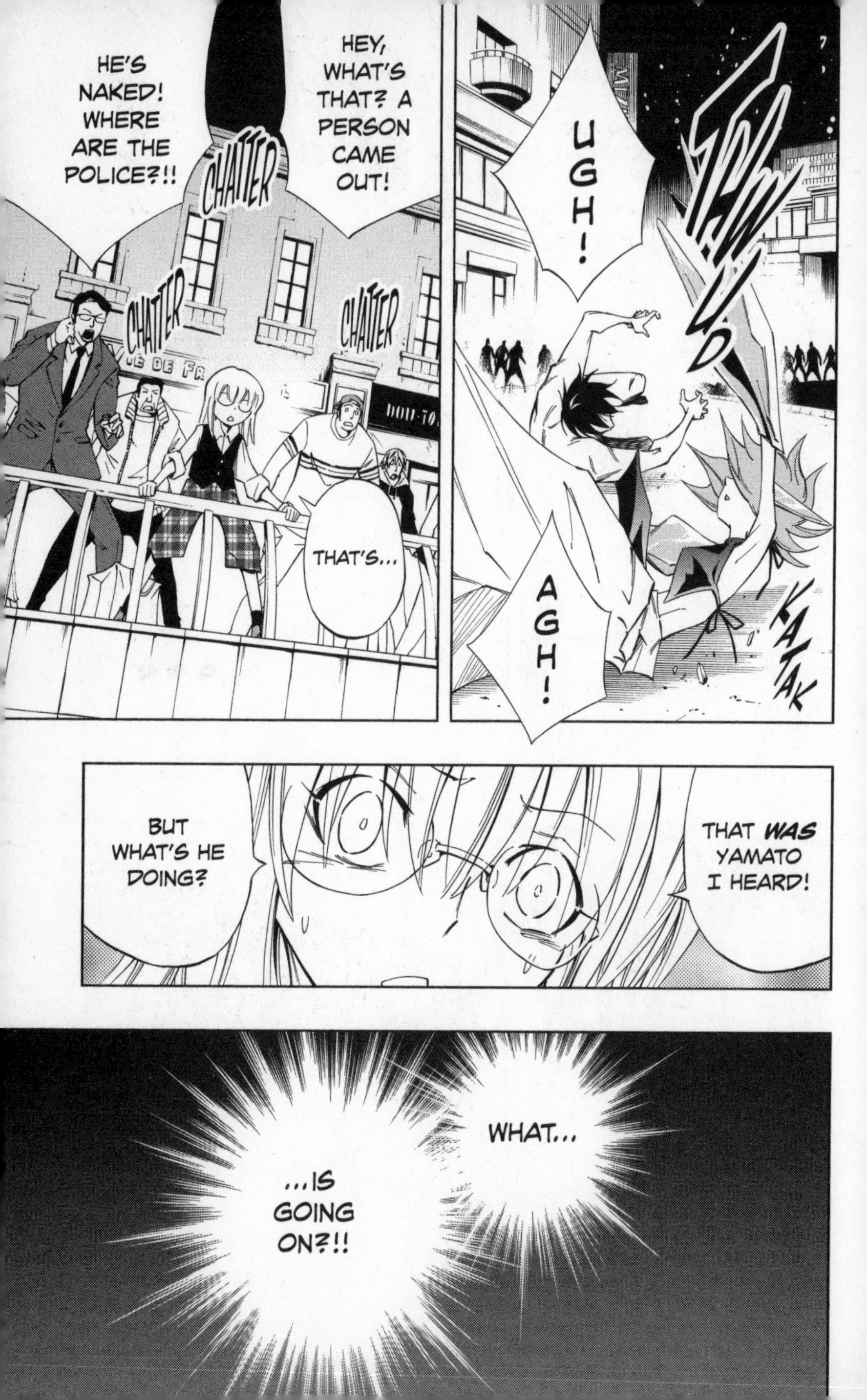
UGH!
AGH!
KLAKAK
HEY, WHAT'S THAT? A PERSON CAME OUT!
HE'S NAKED! WHERE ARE THE POLICE?!!
CHATTER
CHATTER
CHATTER
THAT'S...
THAT *WAS* YAMATO I HEARD!
BUT WHAT'S HE DOING?
WHAT...
...IS GOING ON?!!

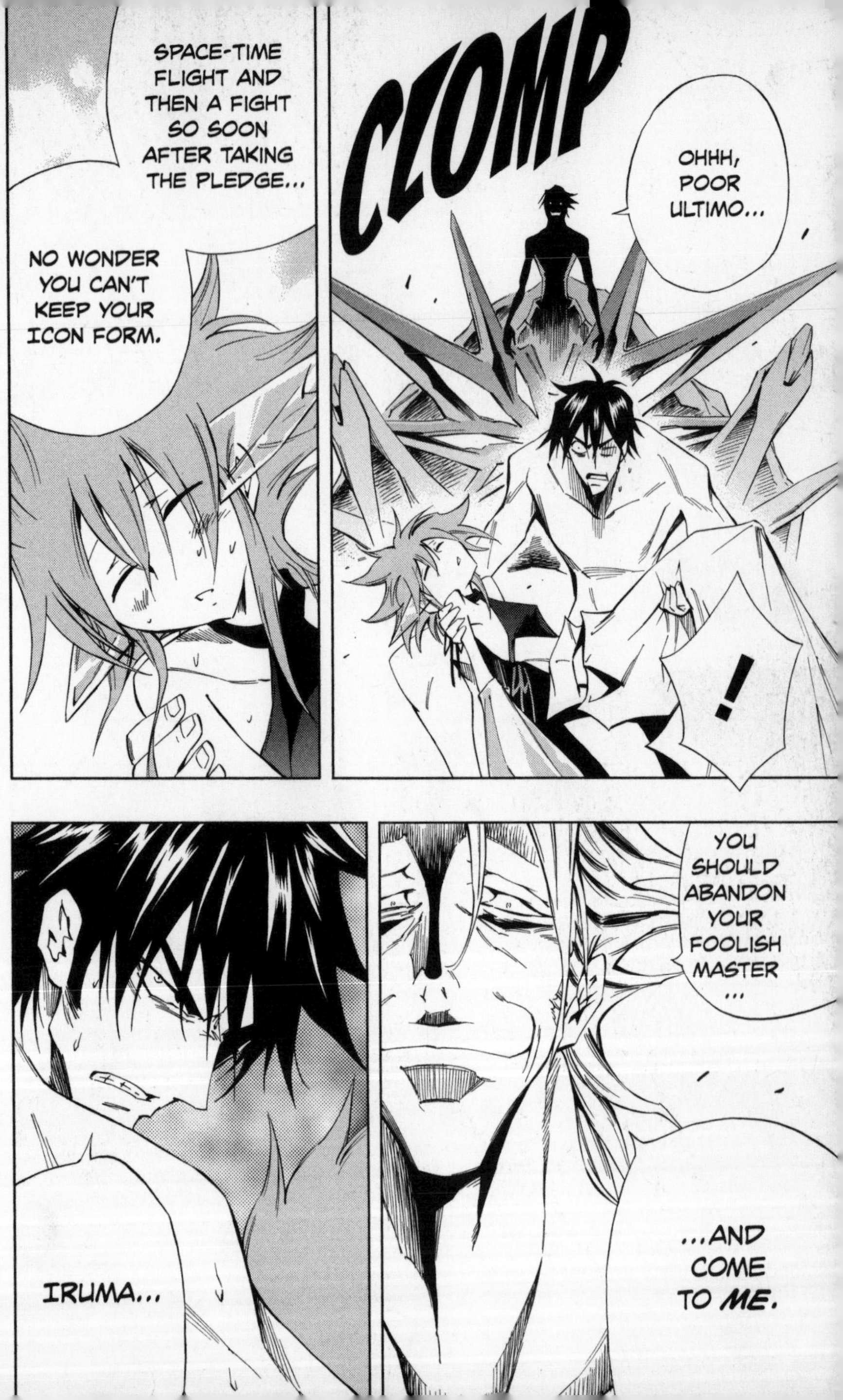
CLOMP
OHHH, POOR ULTIMO...
!
SPACE-TIME FLIGHT AND THEN A FIGHT SO SOON AFTER TAKING THE PLEDGE...
NO WONDER YOU CAN'T KEEP YOUR ICON FORM.
YOU SHOULD ABANDON YOUR FOOLISH MASTER...
...AND COME TO *ME*.
IRUMA...

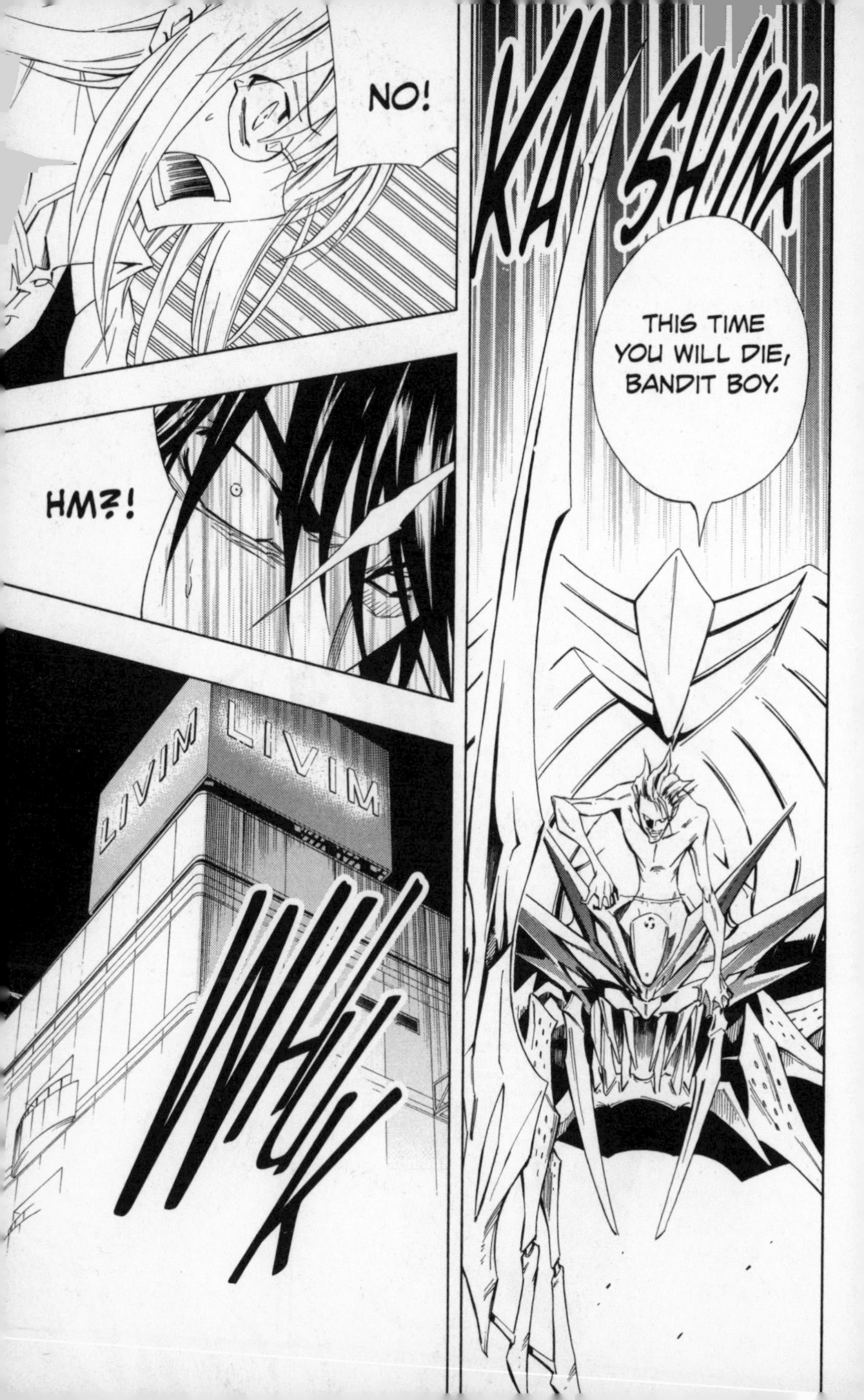
KA SHINK
THIS TIME YOU WILL DIE, BANDIT BOY.
NO!
HM?!
LIVIM
LIVIM
WHUK

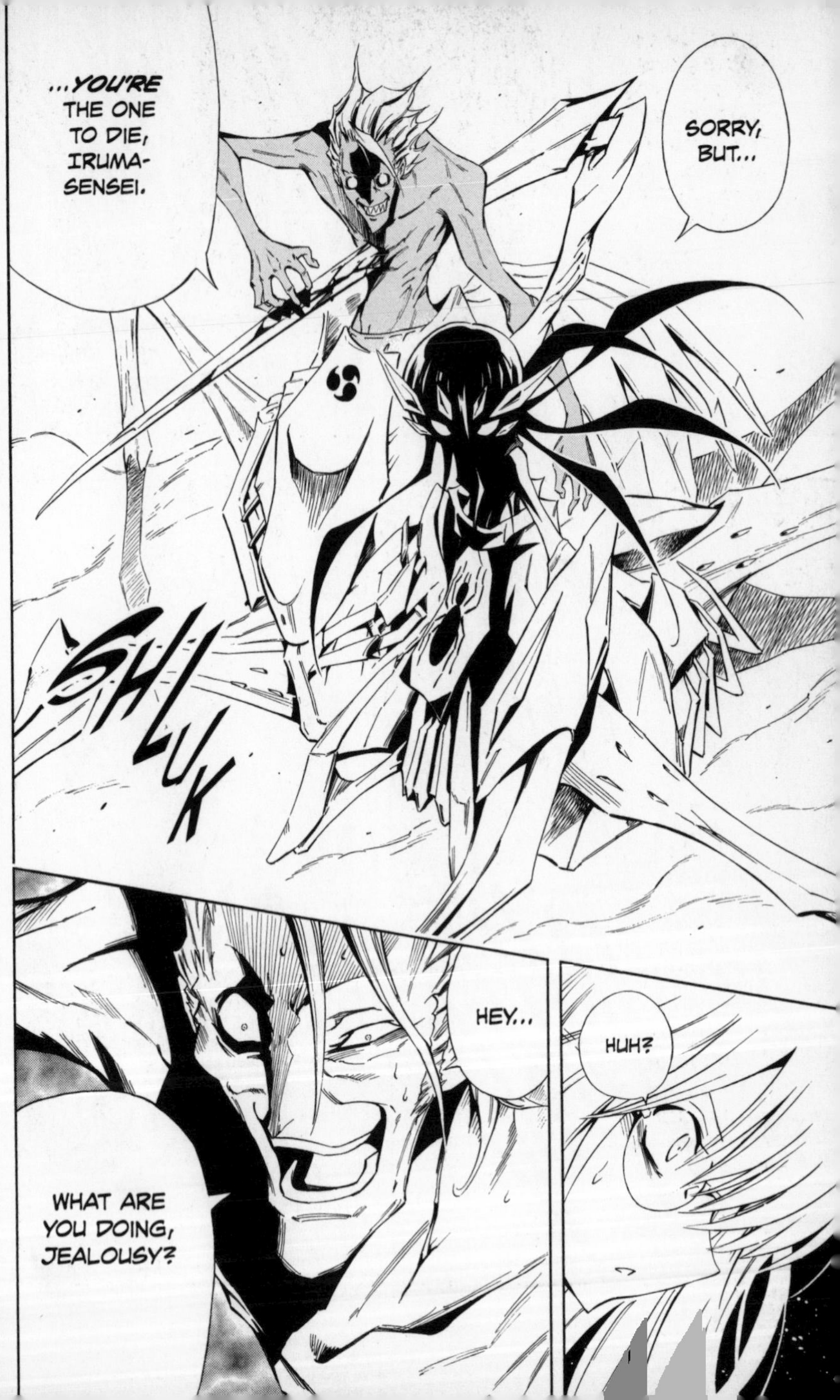
SORRY, BUT...
...YOU'RE THE ONE TO DIE, IRUMA-SENSEI.
SHLUK
HUH?
HEY...
WHAT ARE YOU DOING, JEALOUSY?

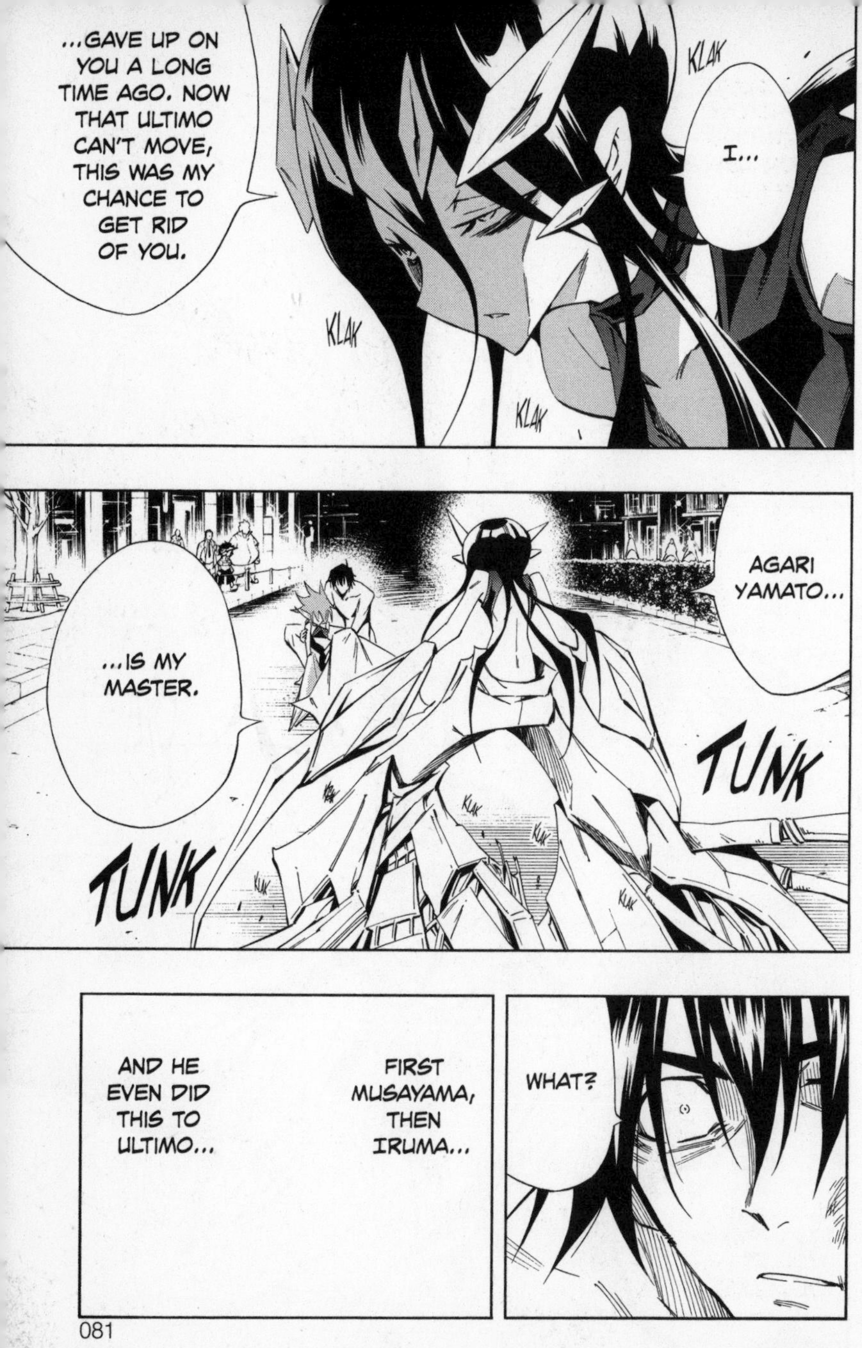
KLAK
I...
...GAVE UP ON YOU A LONG TIME AGO. NOW THAT ULTIMO CAN'T MOVE, THIS WAS MY CHANCE TO GET RID OF YOU.
KLAK
KLAK
AGARI YAMATO...
TUNK
...IS MY MASTER.
TUNK
WHAT?
FIRST MUSAYAMA, THEN IRUMA...
AND HE EVEN DID THIS TO ULTIMO...

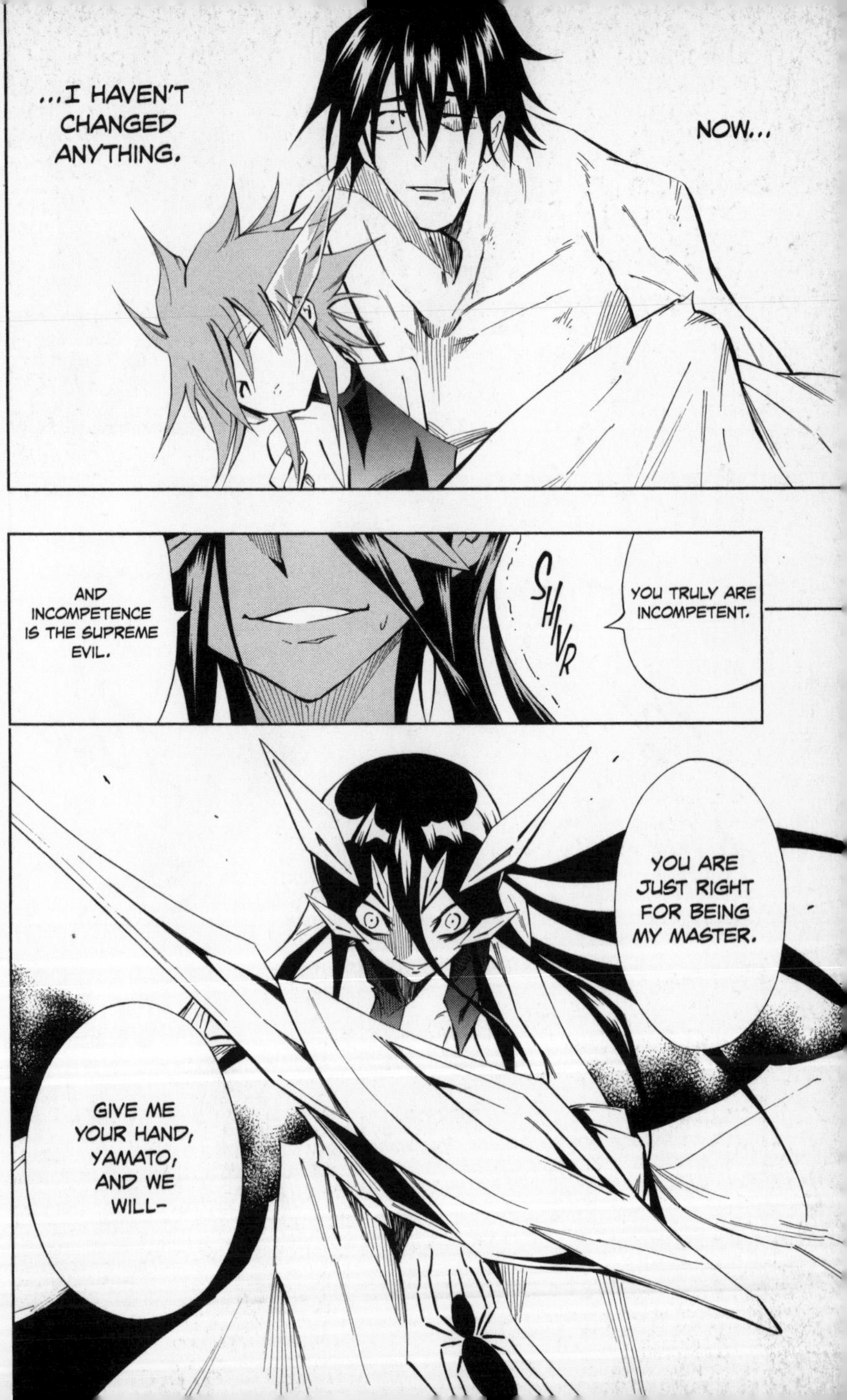
NOW...
...I HAVEN'T CHANGED ANYTHING.
YOU TRULY ARE INCOMPETENT.
SHIVR
AND INCOMPETENCE IS THE SUPREME EVIL.
YOU ARE JUST RIGHT FOR BEING MY MASTER.
GIVE ME YOUR HAND, YAMATO, AND WE WILL-

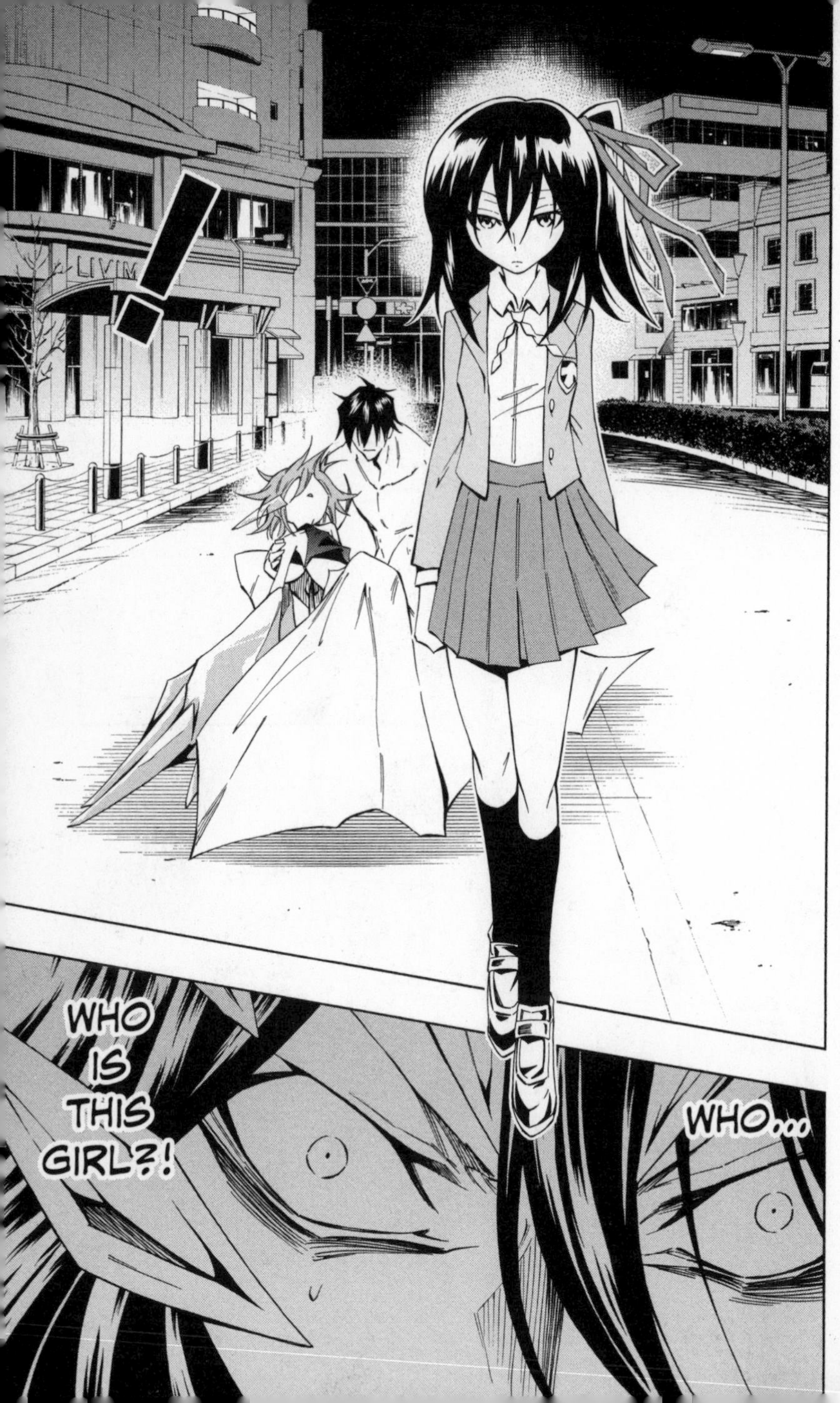
!
WHO...
WHO IS THIS GIRL?!

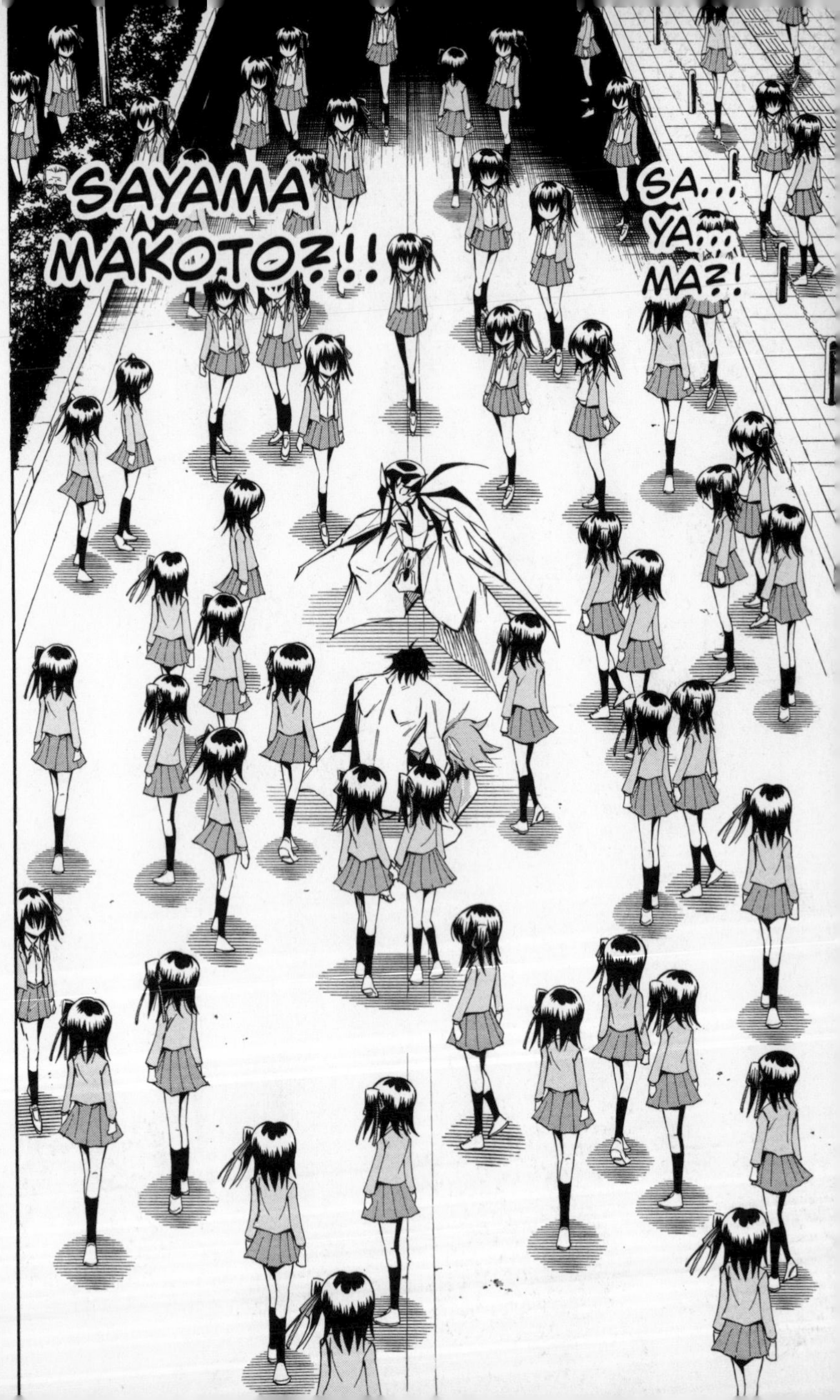
SA...
YA...
MA?!
SAYAMA MAKOTO?!!

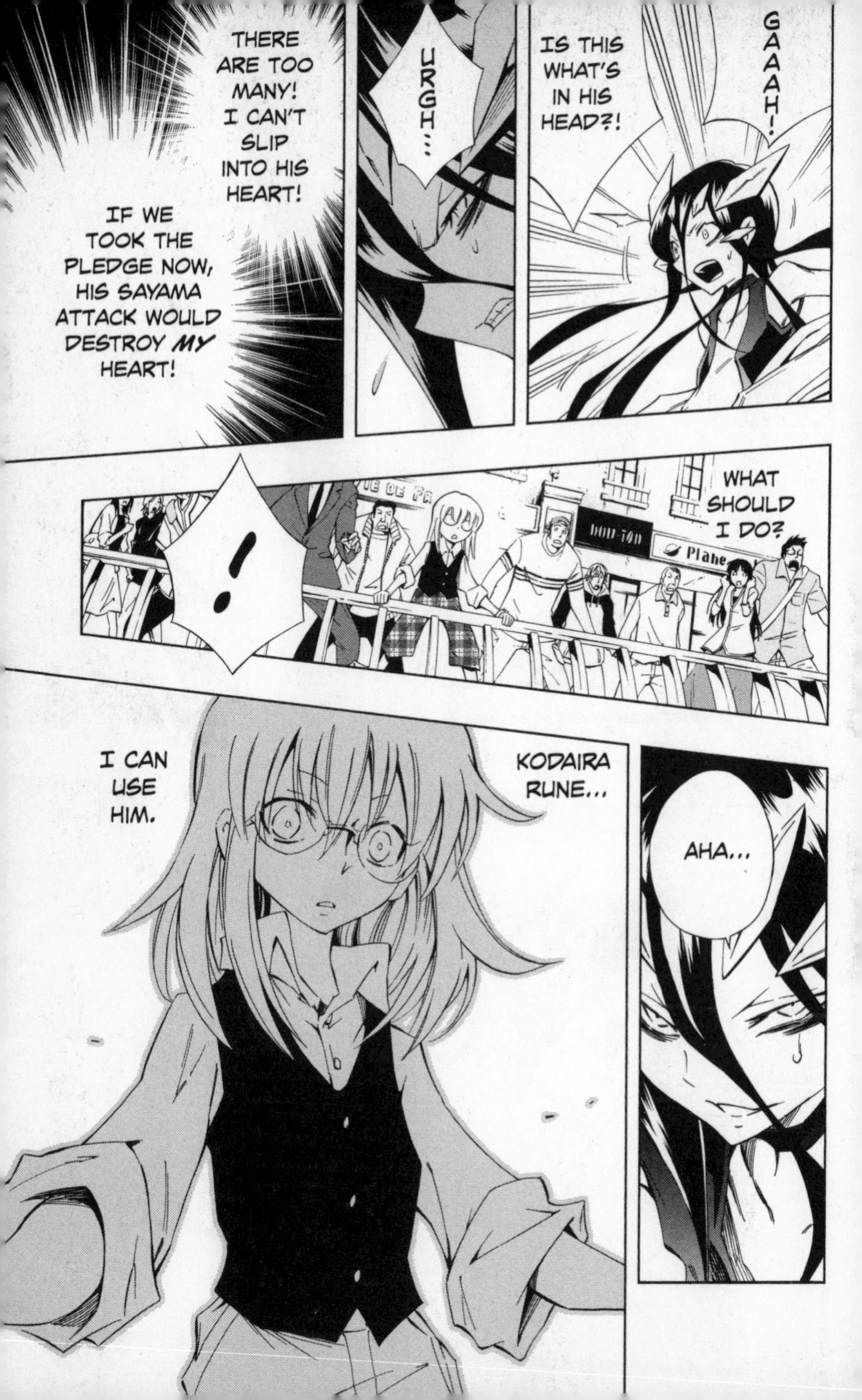
GAAAH!
IS THIS WHAT'S IN HIS HEAD?!
URGH...
THERE ARE TOO MANY! I CAN'T SLIP INTO HIS HEART!
IF WE TOOK THE PLEDGE NOW, HIS SAYAMA ATTACK WOULD DESTROY *MY* HEART!
WHAT SHOULD I DO?
!
AHA...
KODAIRA RUNE...
I CAN USE HIM.

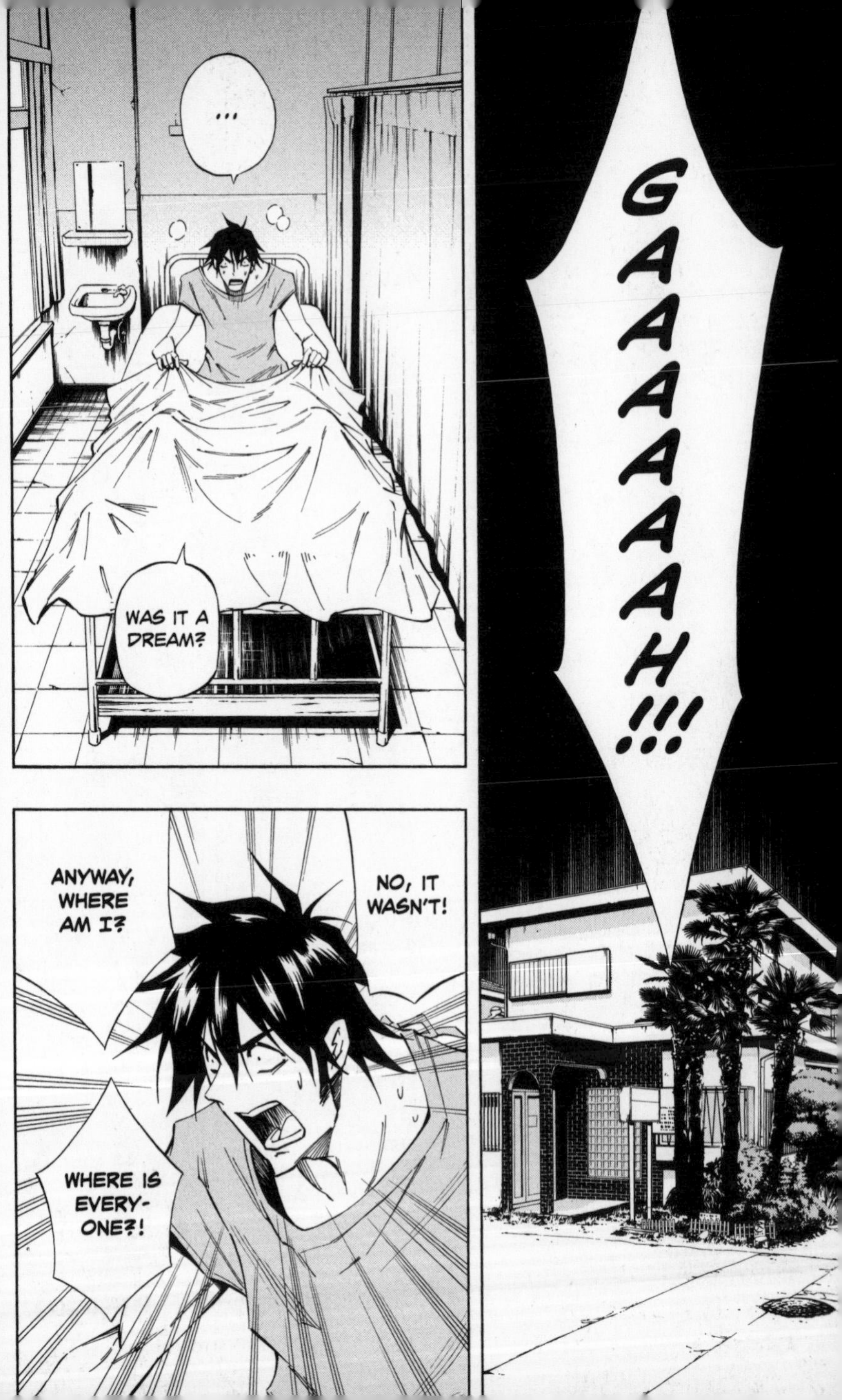
GAAAAAAH!!!
...
WAS IT A DREAM?
NO, IT WASN'T!
ANYWAY, WHERE AM I?
WHERE IS EVERY-ONE?!

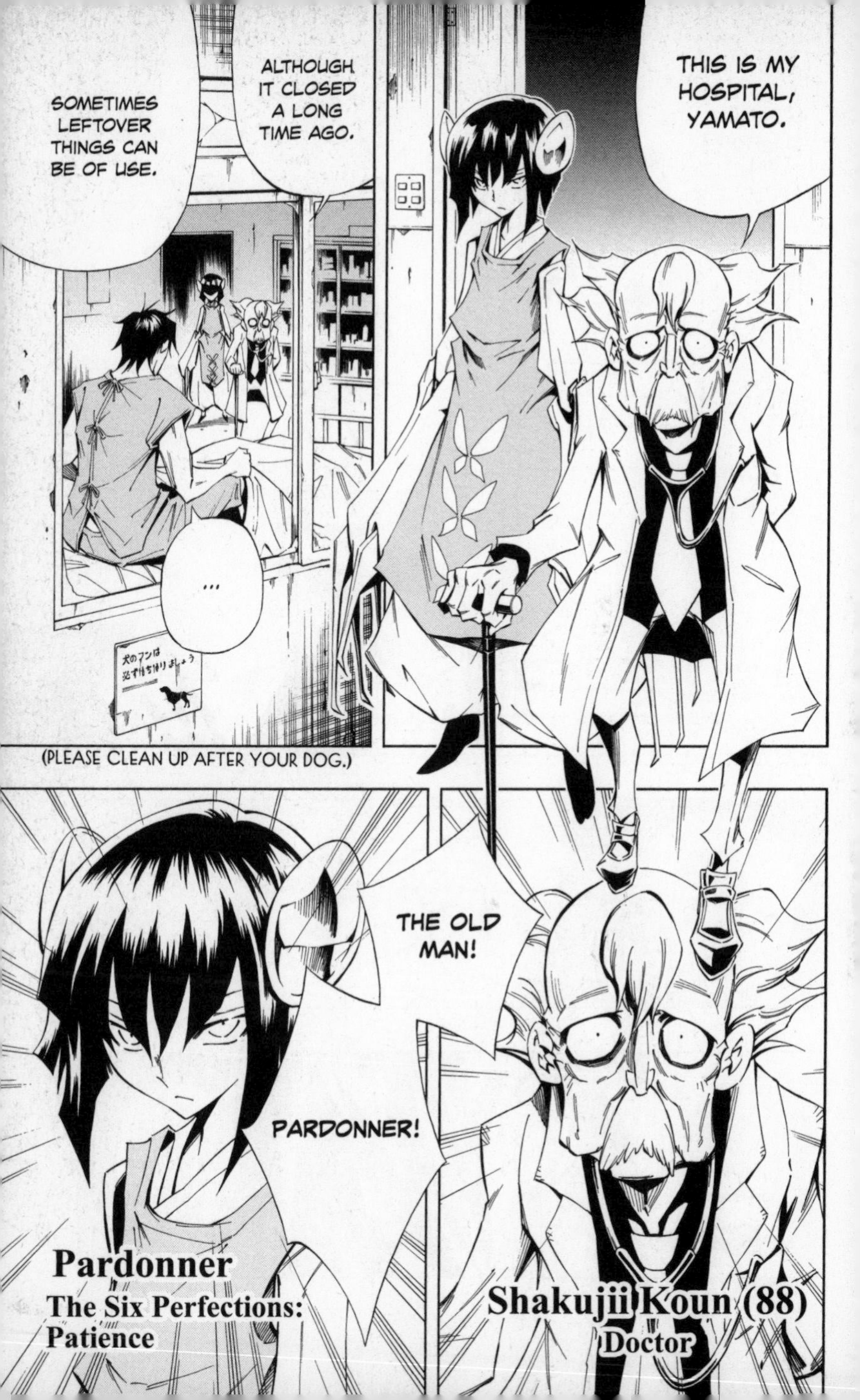
THIS IS MY HOSPITAL, YAMATO.
ALTHOUGH IT CLOSED A LONG TIME AGO.
SOMETIMES LEFTOVER THINGS CAN BE OF USE.
...
犬のフンは必ず持ち帰りましょう
(PLEASE CLEAN UP AFTER YOUR DOG.)
THE OLD MAN!
Shakujii Koun (88)
Doctor
PARDONNER!
Pardonner
The Six Perfections: Patience

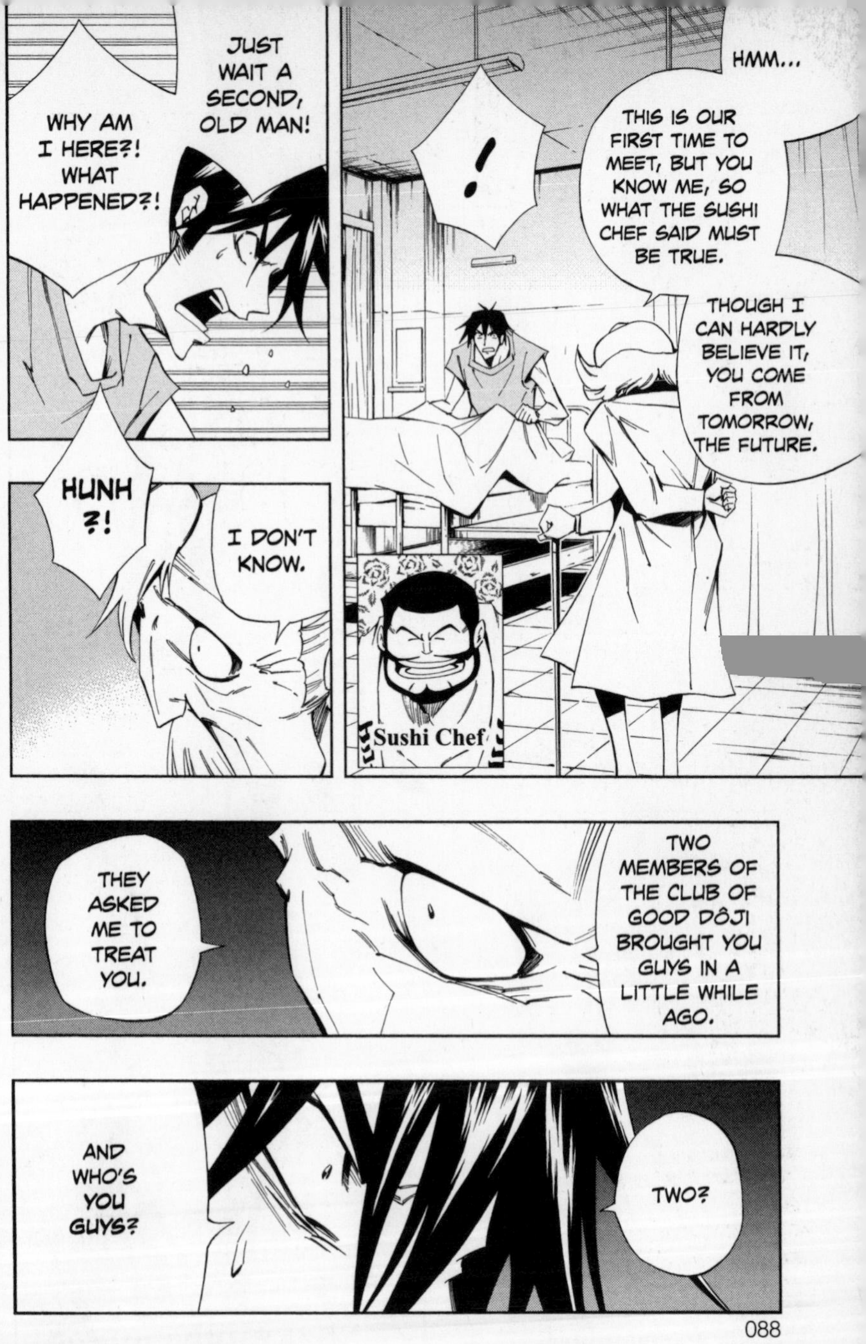
HMM...
THIS IS OUR FIRST TIME TO MEET, BUT YOU KNOW ME, SO WHAT THE SUSHI CHEF SAID MUST BE TRUE.
!
THOUGH I CAN HARDLY BELIEVE IT, YOU COME FROM TOMORROW, THE FUTURE.
Sushi Chef
JUST WAIT A SECOND, OLD MAN!
WHY AM I HERE?! WHAT HAPPENED?!
I DON'T KNOW.
HUNH ?!
TWO MEMBERS OF THE CLUB OF GOOD DÔJI BROUGHT YOU GUYS IN A LITTLE WHILE AGO.
THEY ASKED ME TO TREAT YOU.
TWO?
AND WHO'S YOU GUYS?

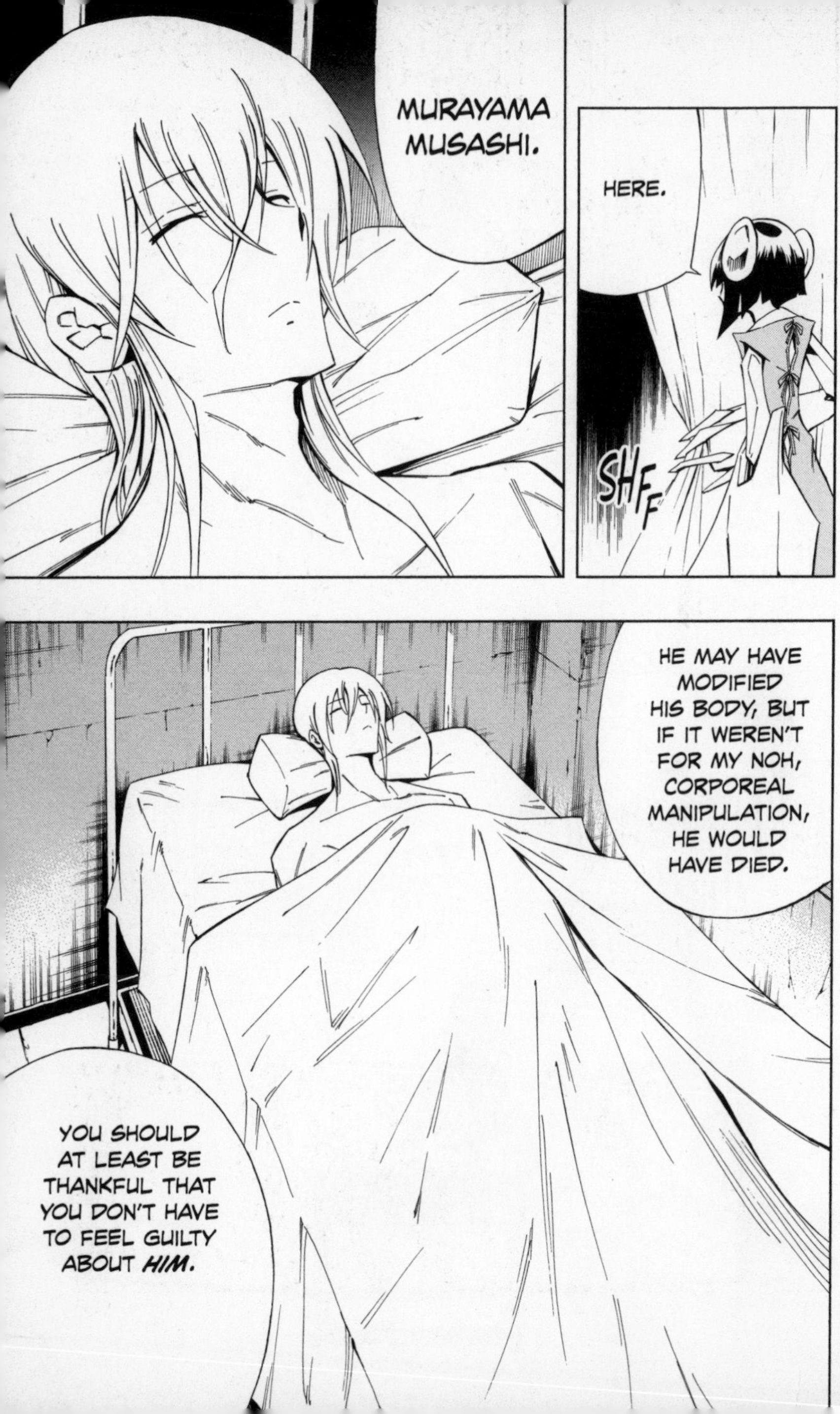
MURAYAMA MUSASHI.
HERE.
SHFF
HE MAY HAVE MODIFIED HIS BODY, BUT IF IT WEREN'T FOR MY NOH, CORPOREAL MANIPULATION, HE WOULD HAVE DIED.
YOU SHOULD AT LEAST BE THANKFUL THAT YOU DON'T HAVE TO FEEL GUILTY ABOUT *HIM*.

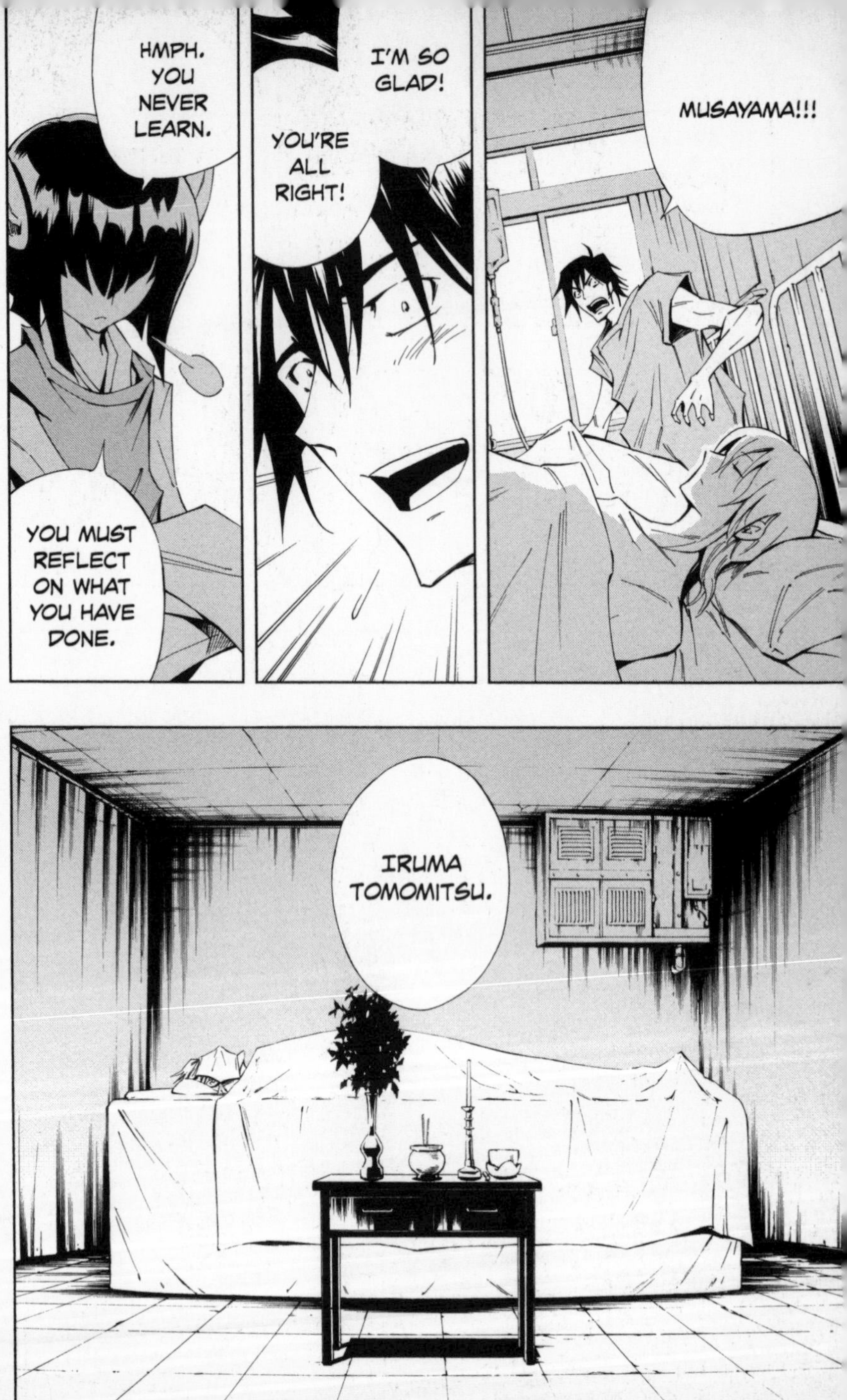
MUSAYAMA!!!
I'M SO GLAD!
YOU'RE ALL RIGHT!
HMPH. YOU NEVER LEARN.
YOU MUST REFLECT ON WHAT YOU HAVE DONE.
IRUMA TOMOMITSU.

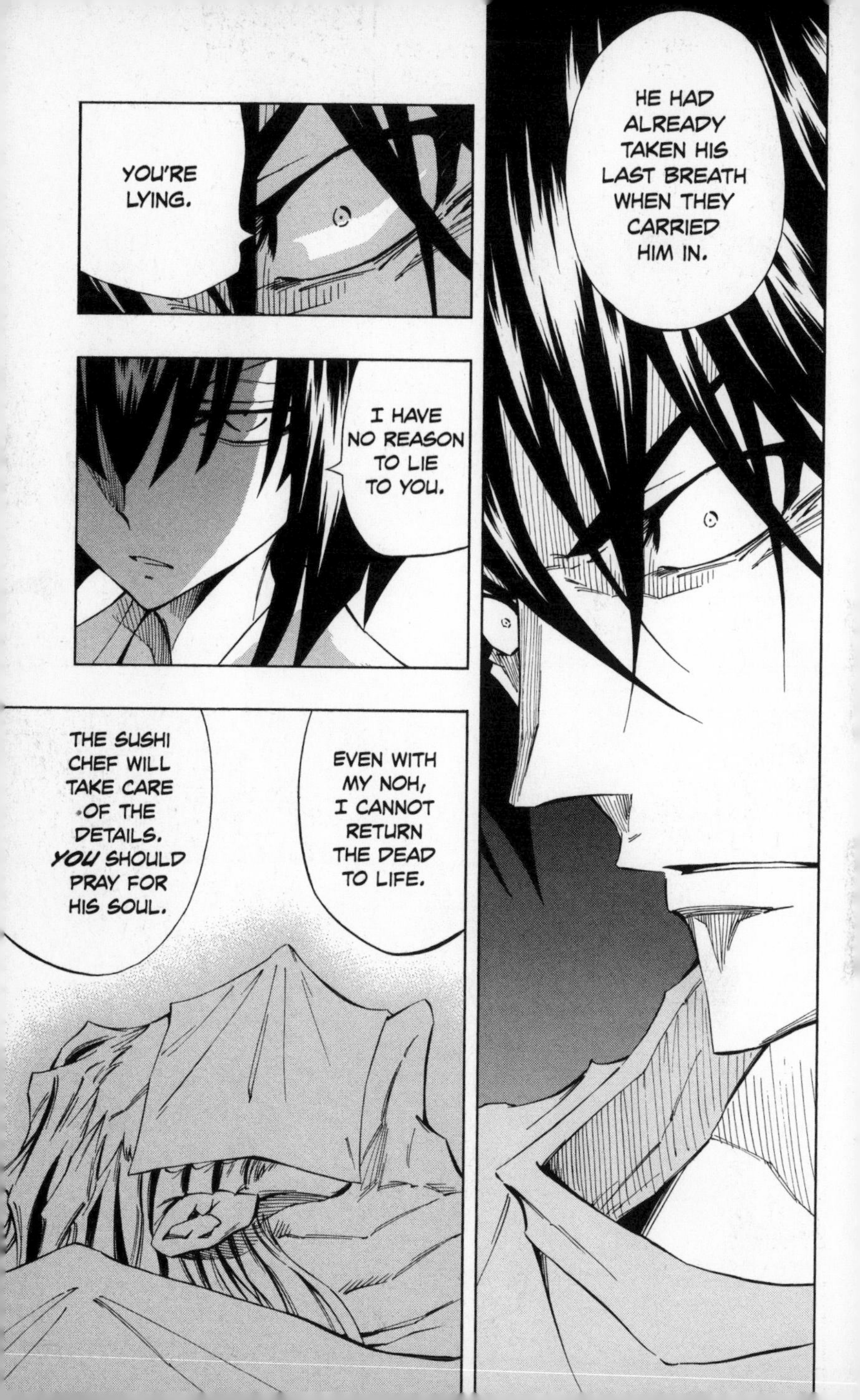
HE HAD ALREADY TAKEN HIS LAST BREATH WHEN THEY CARRIED HIM IN.
YOU'RE LYING.
I HAVE NO REASON TO LIE TO YOU.
EVEN WITH MY NOH, I CANNOT RETURN THE DEAD TO LIFE.
THE SUSHI CHEF WILL TAKE CARE OF THE DETAILS. ***YOU*** SHOULD PRAY FOR HIS SOUL.

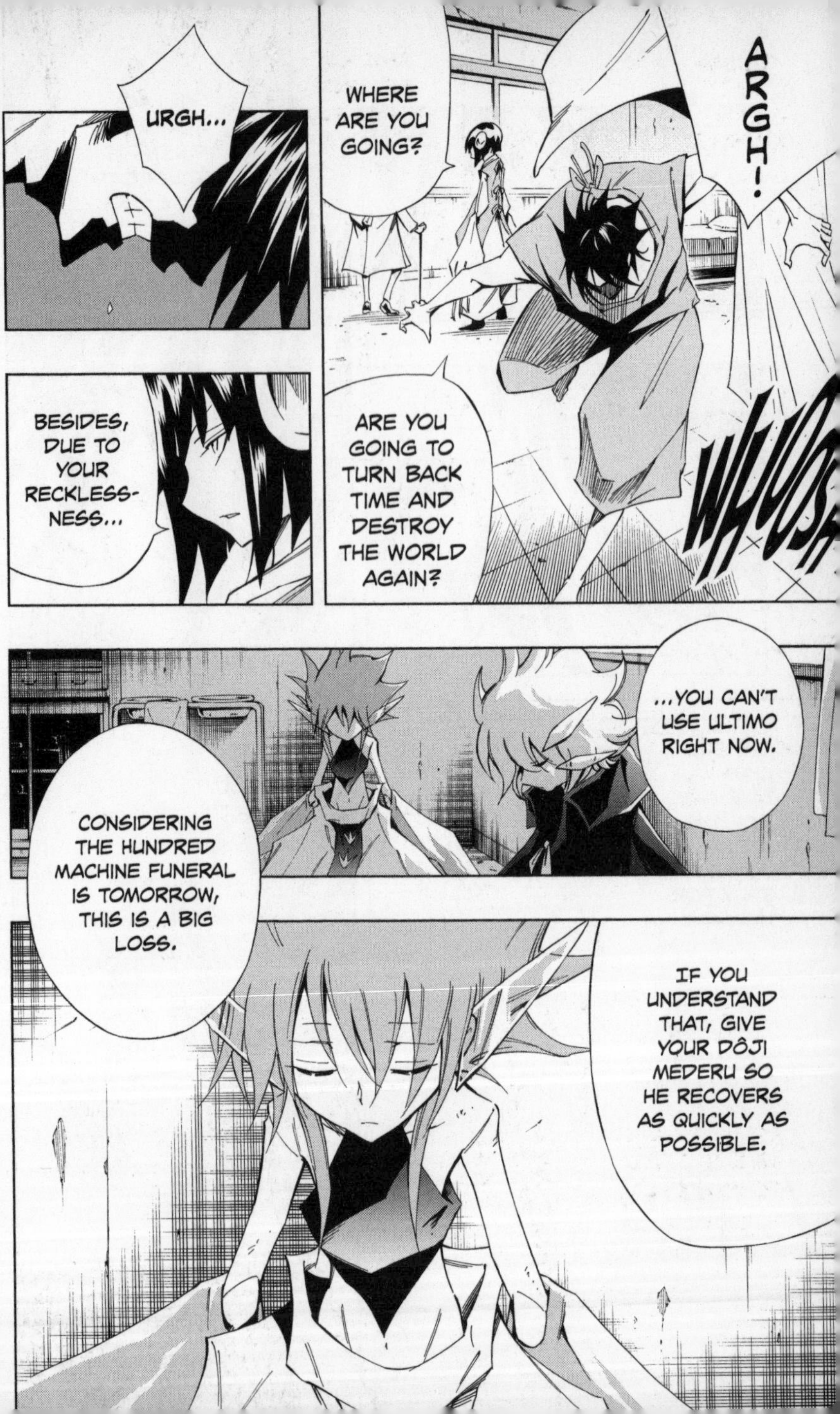
ARGH!
WHERE ARE YOU GOING?
WHOOSH
ARE YOU GOING TO TURN BACK TIME AND DESTROY THE WORLD AGAIN?
URGH...
BESIDES, DUE TO YOUR RECKLESS-NESS...
...YOU CAN'T USE ULTIMO RIGHT NOW.
CONSIDERING THE HUNDRED MACHINE FUNERAL IS TOMORROW, THIS IS A BIG LOSS.
IF YOU UNDERSTAND THAT, GIVE YOUR DÔJI MEDERU SO HE RECOVERS AS QUICKLY AS POSSIBLE.

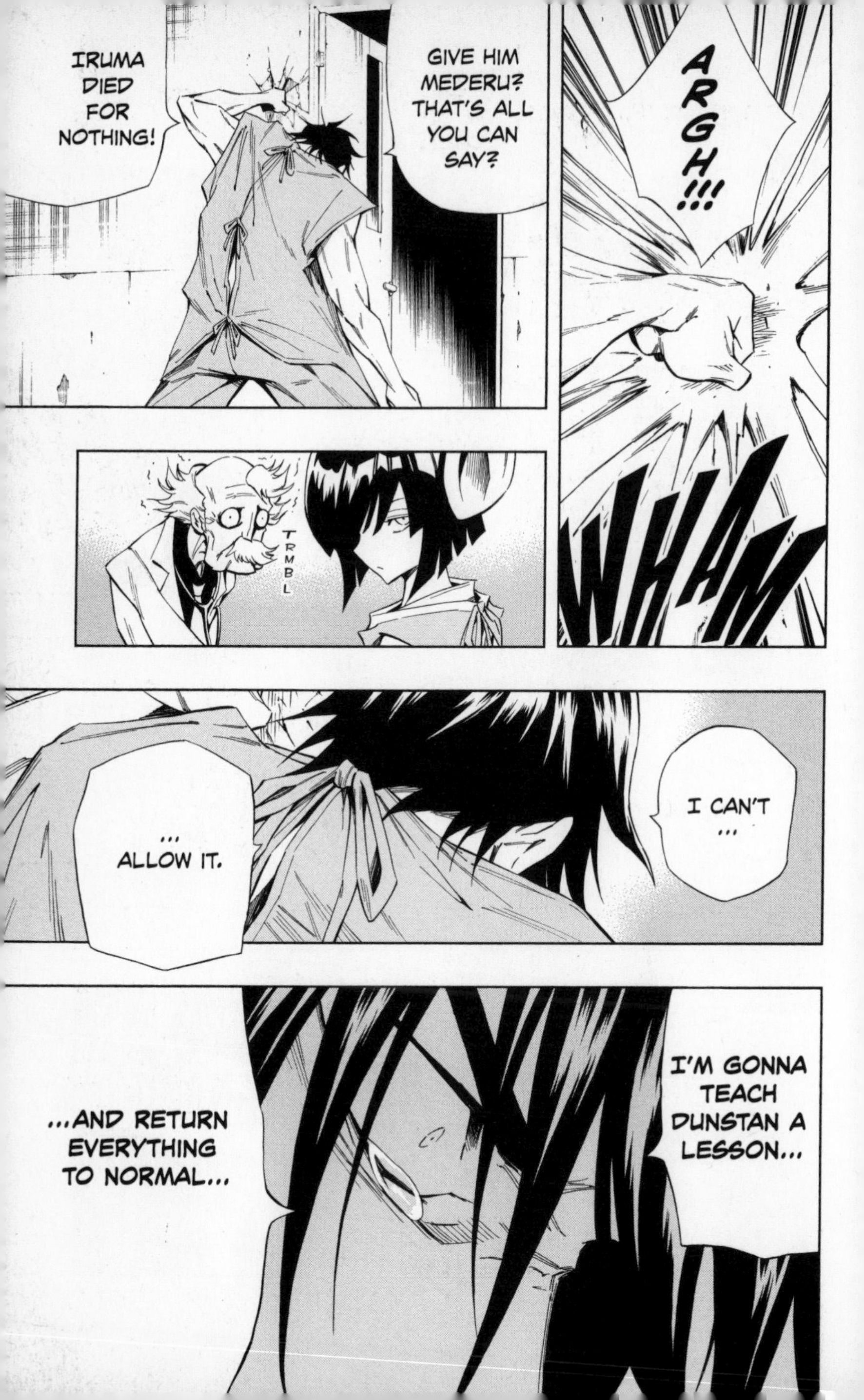
ARGH!!!
WHAM
GIVE HIM MEDERU? THAT'S ALL YOU CAN SAY?
IRUMA DIED FOR NOTHING!
TRMBL
I CAN'T ...
... ALLOW IT.
I'M GONNA TEACH DUNSTAN A LESSON...
...AND RETURN EVERYTHING TO NORMAL...

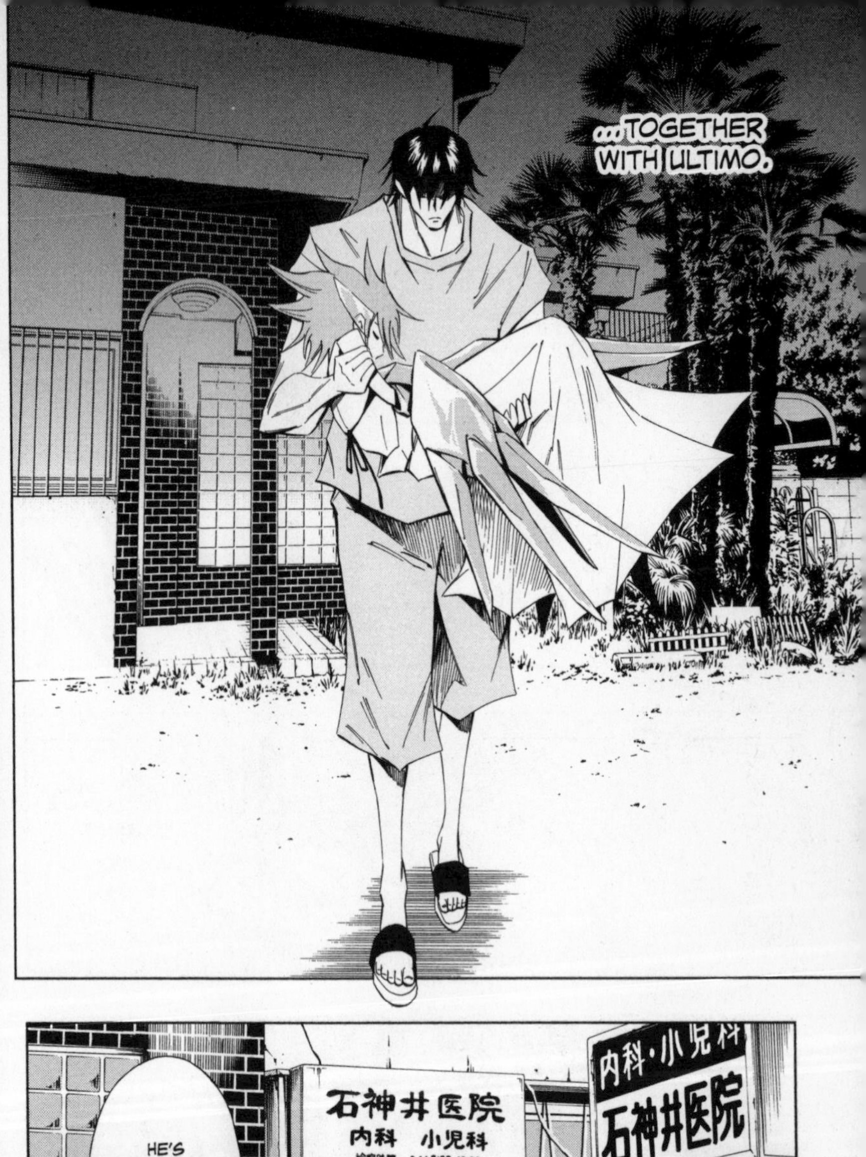
...TOGETHER WITH ULTIMO.

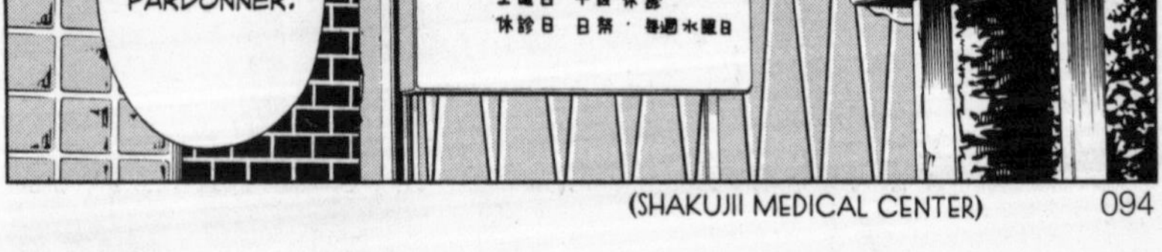
内科・小児科
石神井医院
石神井医院
内科 小児科
診療時間 AM 9:00~12:00
PM 3:00~6:00
土曜日 午後休診
休診日 日祭・毎週水曜日
HE'S INEXPERIENCED, PARDONNER.

(SHAKUJII MEDICAL CENTER)

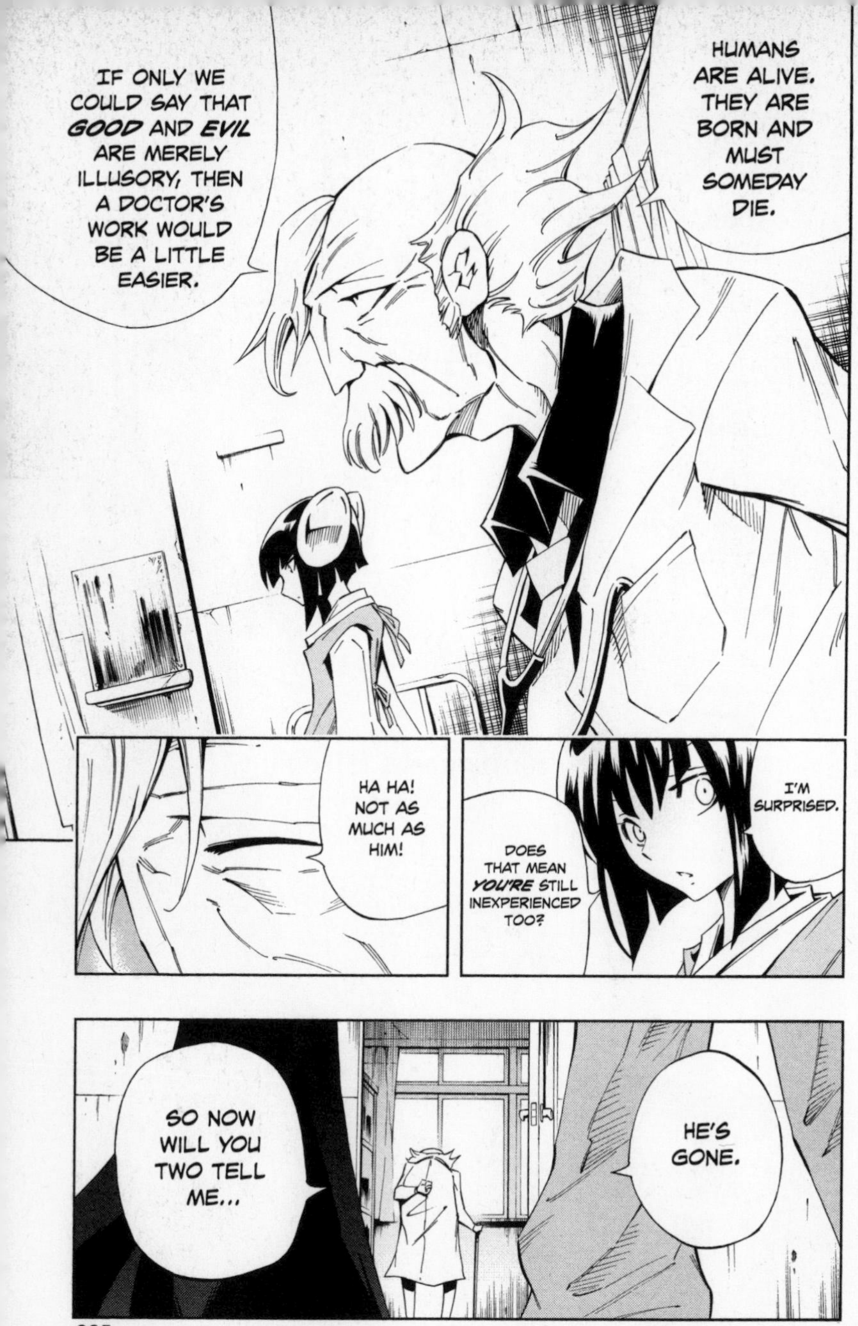
HUMANS ARE ALIVE. THEY ARE BORN AND MUST SOMEDAY DIE.
IF ONLY WE COULD SAY THAT ***GOOD*** AND ***EVIL*** ARE MERELY ILLUSORY, THEN A DOCTOR'S WORK WOULD BE A LITTLE EASIER.
I'M SURPRISED.
DOES THAT MEAN ***YOU'RE*** STILL INEXPERIENCED TOO?
HA HA! NOT AS MUCH AS HIM!
HE'S GONE.
SO NOW WILL YOU TWO TELL ME...

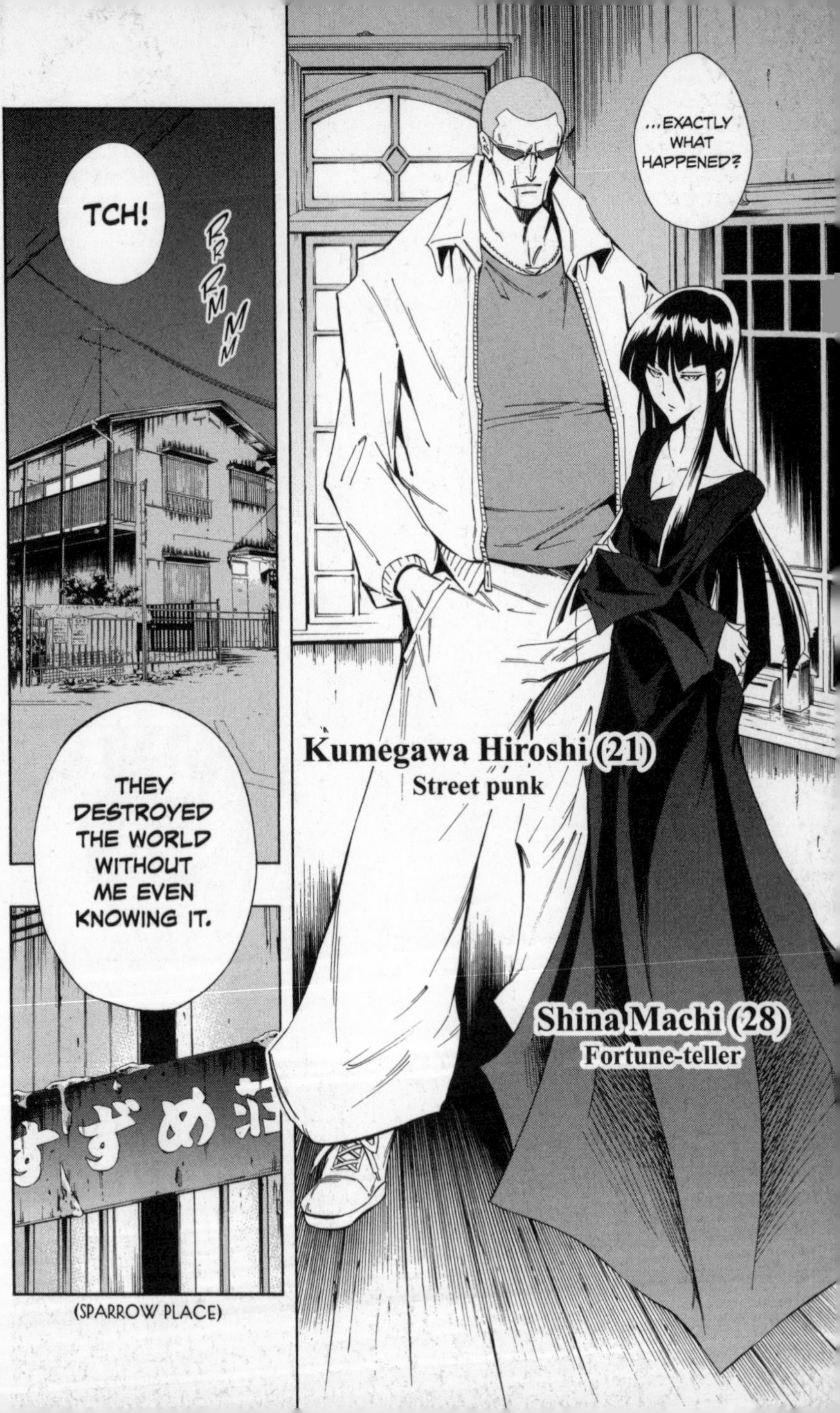
...EXACTLY WHAT HAPPENED?
Kumegawa Hiroshi (21)
Street punk
Shina Machi (28)
Fortune-teller
TCH!
RRRMMMM
THEY DESTROYED THE WORLD WITHOUT ME EVEN KNOWING IT.
すずめ荘
(SPARROW PLACE)

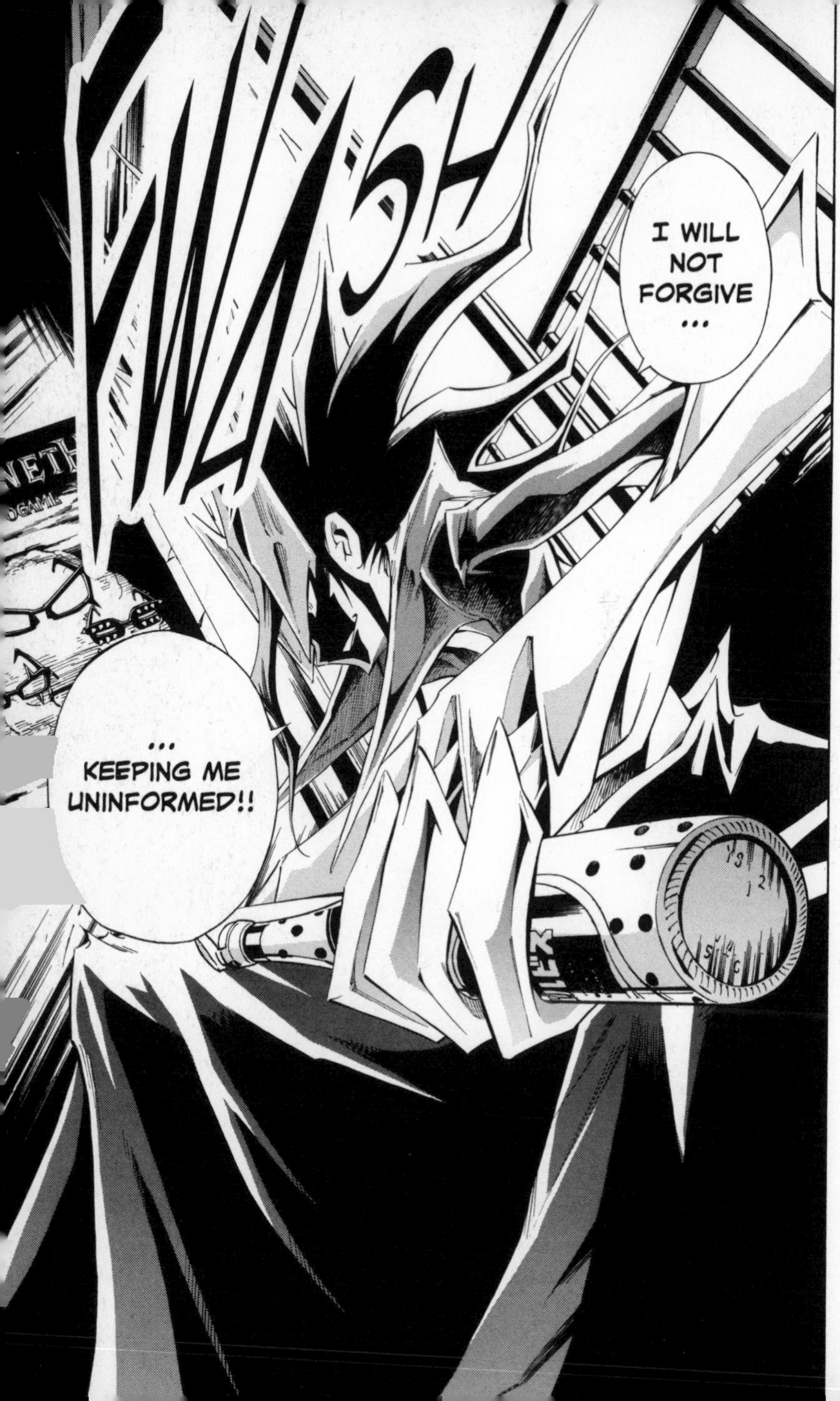
I WILL NOT FORGIVE ...
... KEEPING ME UNINFORMED!!

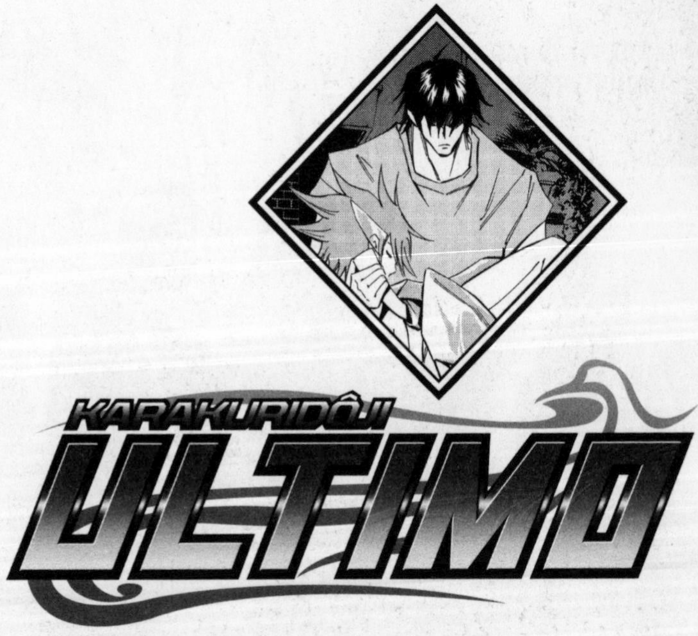

KARAKURIDÔJI
ULTIMO

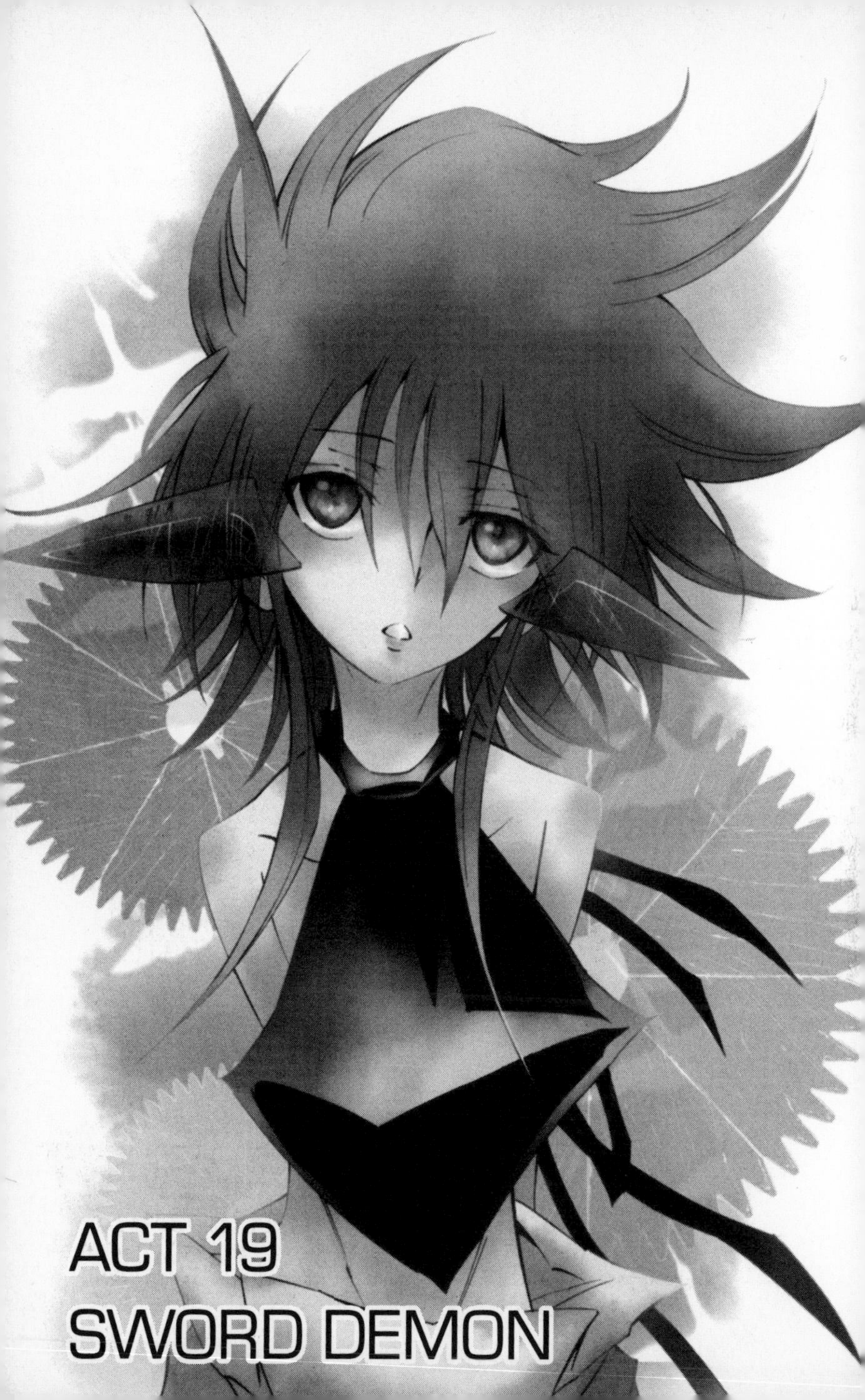
ACT 19
SWORD DEMON

KARAKURIDÔJI
ULTIMO

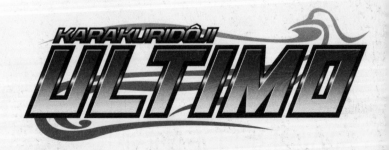

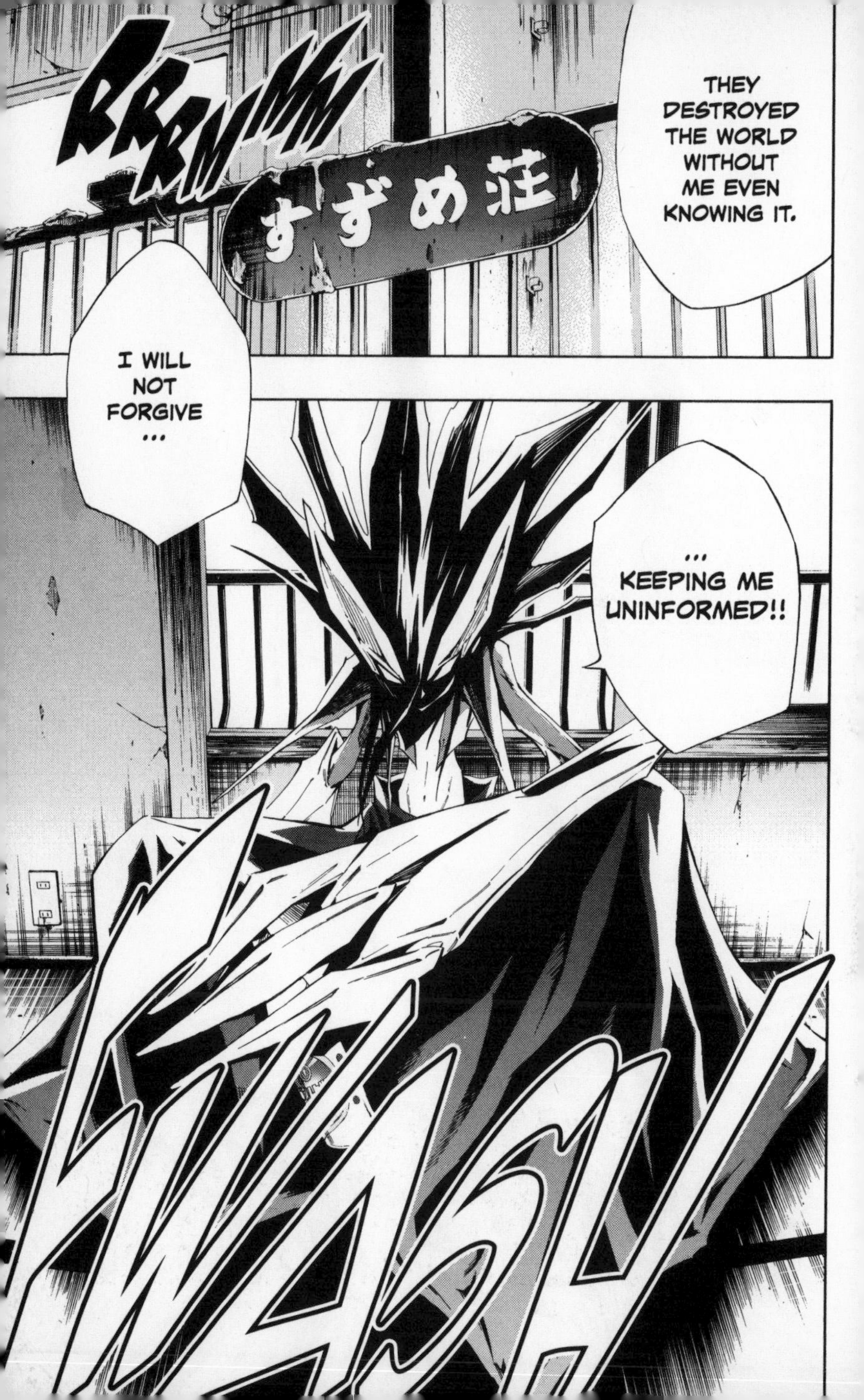
THEY DESTROYED THE WORLD WITHOUT ME EVEN KNOWING IT.
すずめ荘
BRRMMM
I WILL NOT FORGIVE ...
... KEEPING ME UNINFORMED!!
WHASH

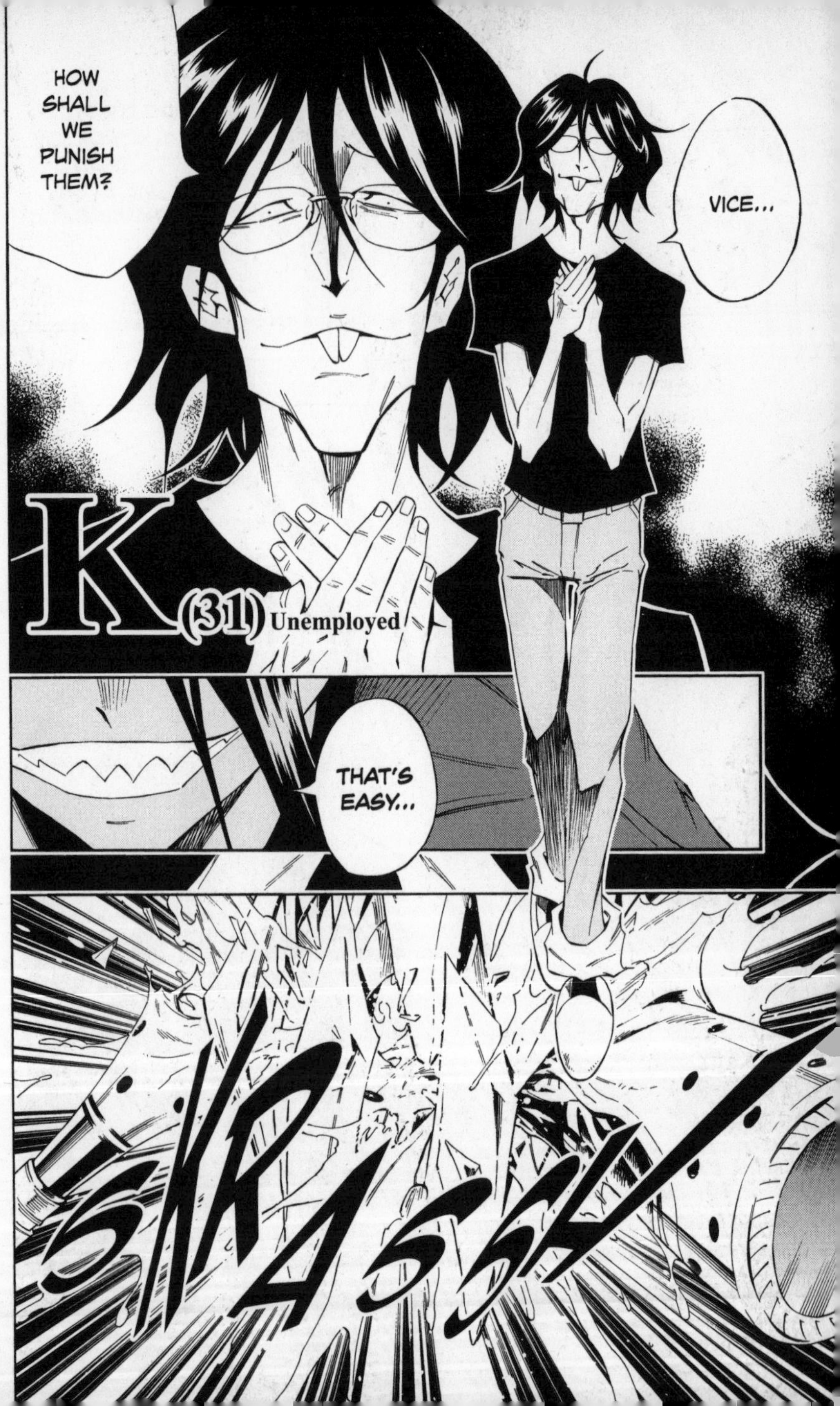
VICE...
HOW SHALL WE PUNISH THEM?
K (31) Unemployed
THAT'S EASY...
SKRASSH!

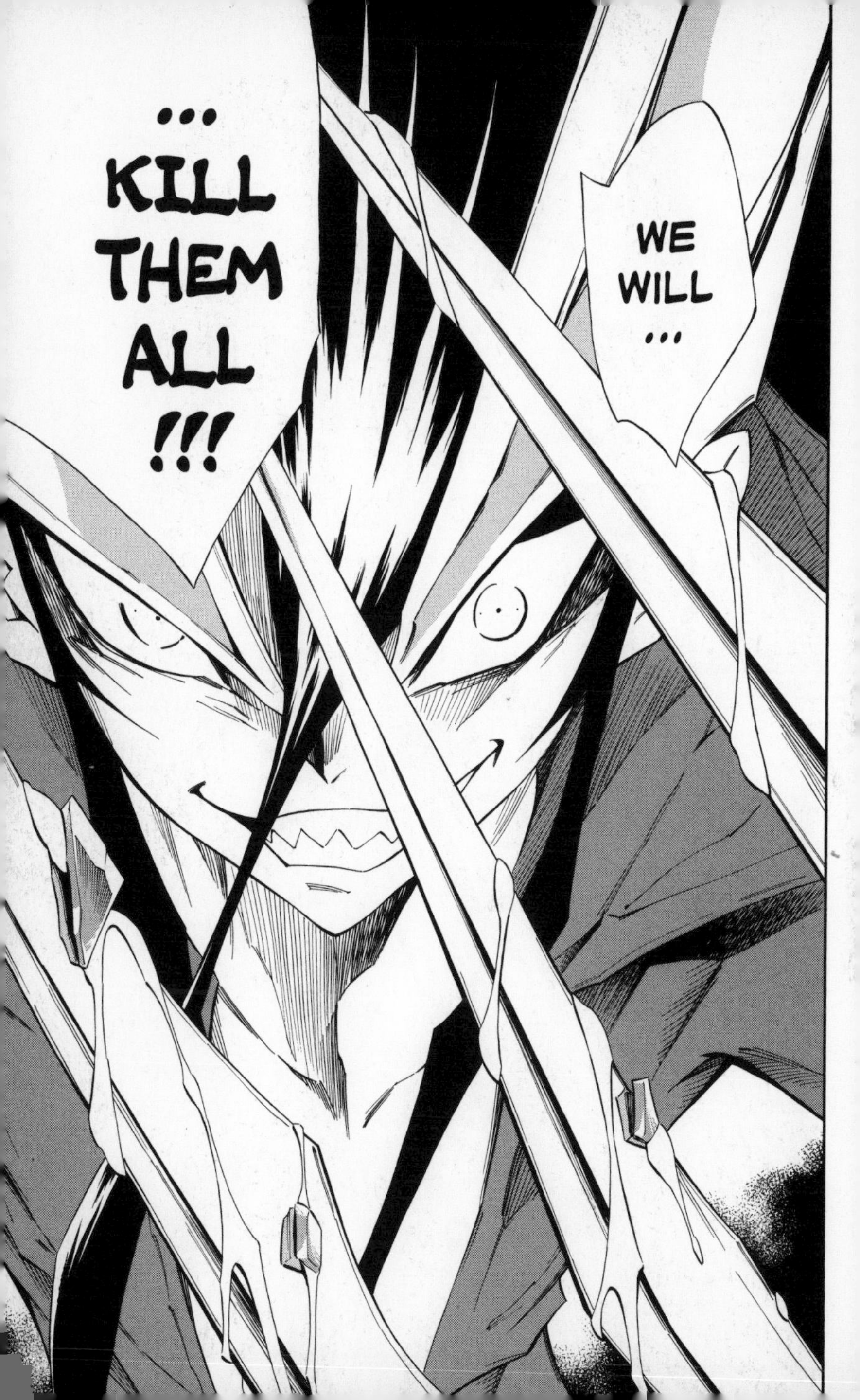
WE WILL ...
... KILL THEM ALL !!!

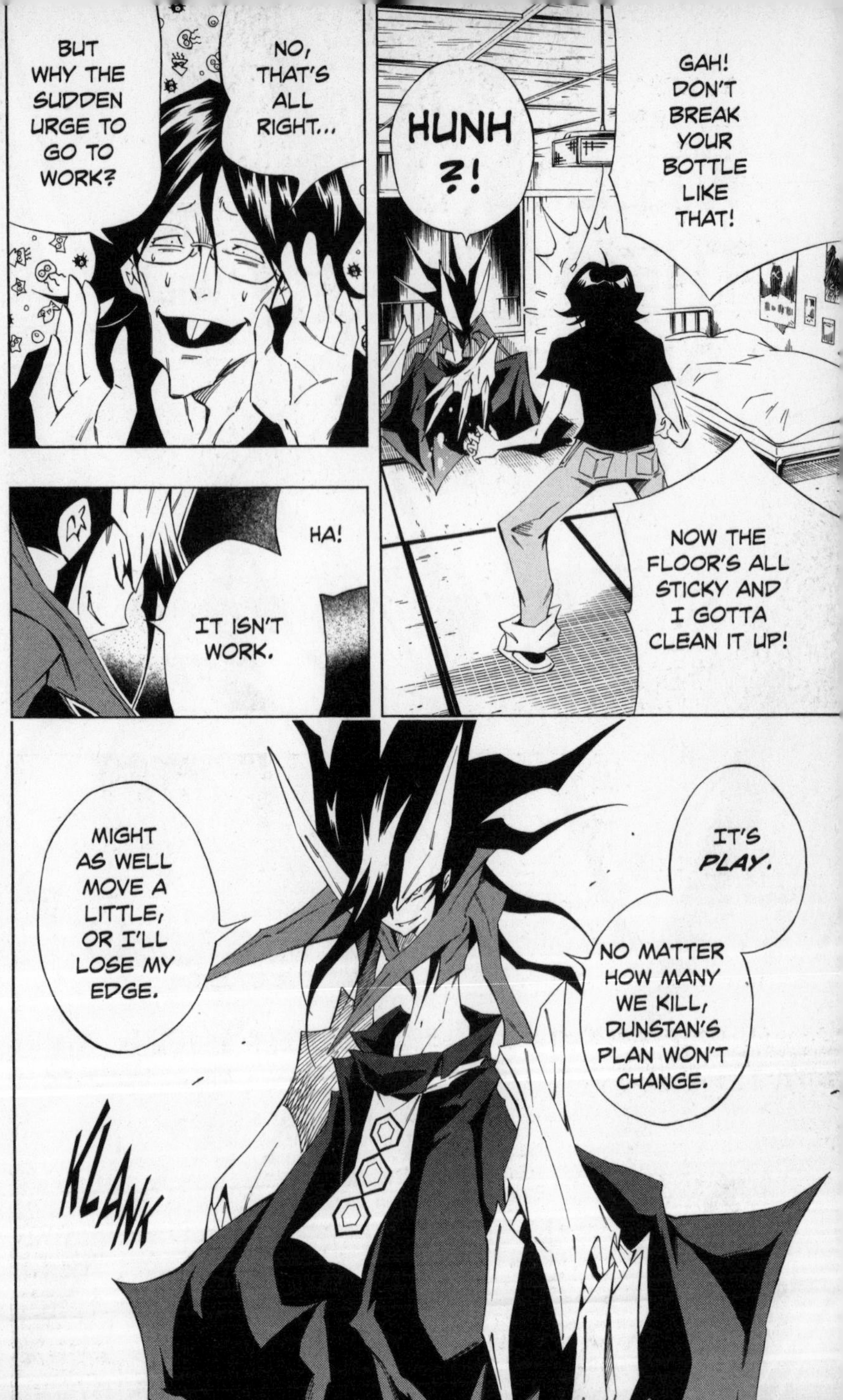
GAH! DON'T BREAK YOUR BOTTLE LIKE THAT!
HUNH ?!
NOW THE FLOOR'S ALL STICKY AND I GOTTA CLEAN IT UP!
NO, THAT'S ALL RIGHT...
BUT WHY THE SUDDEN URGE TO GO TO WORK?
HA!
IT ISN'T WORK.
IT'S *PLAY*.
NO MATTER HOW MANY WE KILL, DUNSTAN'S PLAN WON'T CHANGE.
MIGHT AS WELL MOVE A LITTLE, OR I'LL LOSE MY EDGE.
KLANK

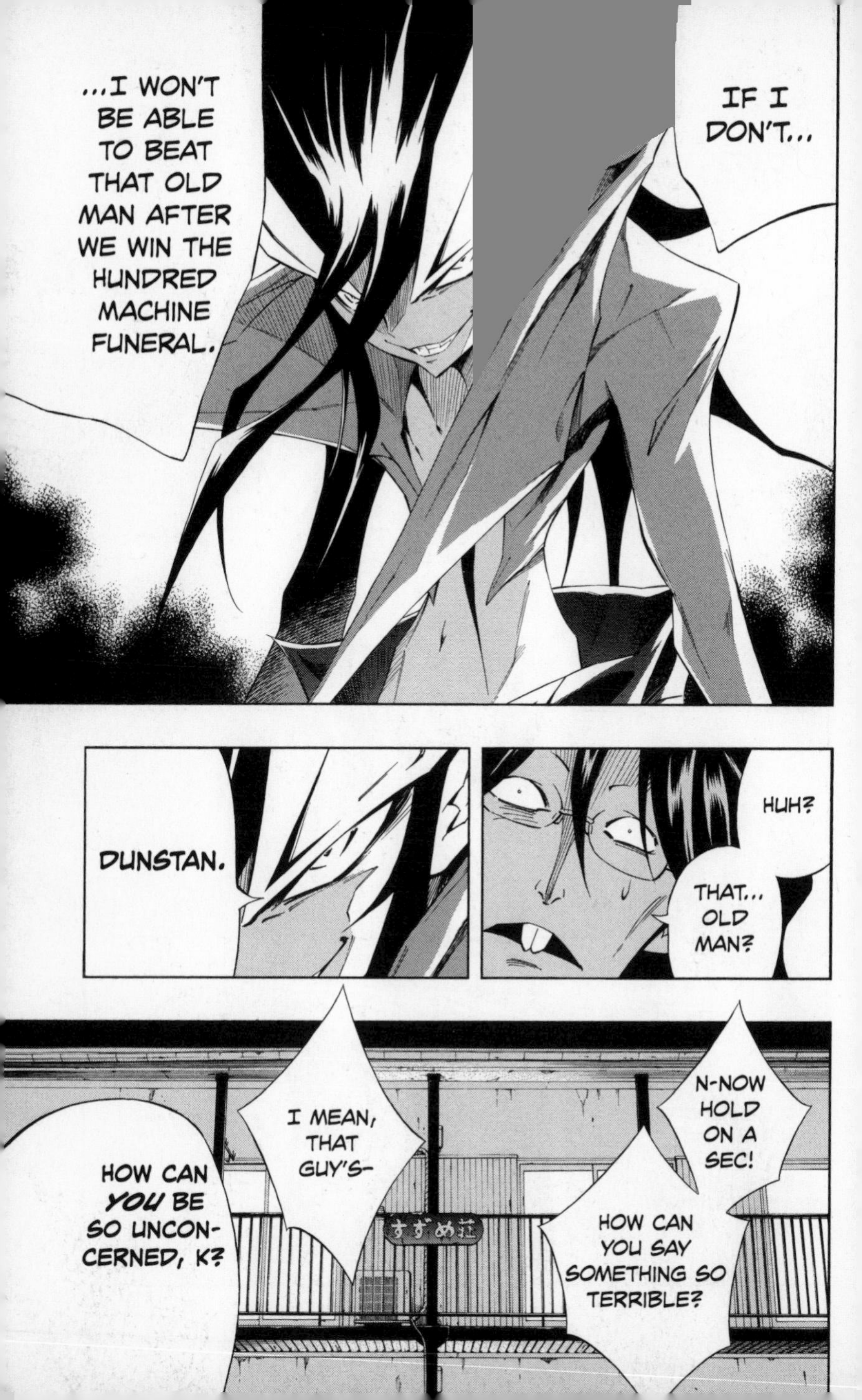
IF I DON'T...
...I WON'T BE ABLE TO BEAT THAT OLD MAN AFTER WE WIN THE HUNDRED MACHINE FUNERAL.
HUH?
THAT... OLD MAN?
DUNSTAN.
N-NOW HOLD ON A SEC!
HOW CAN YOU SAY SOMETHING SO TERRIBLE?
I MEAN, THAT GUY'S-
すずめ荘
HOW CAN *YOU* BE SO UNCON-CERNED, K?

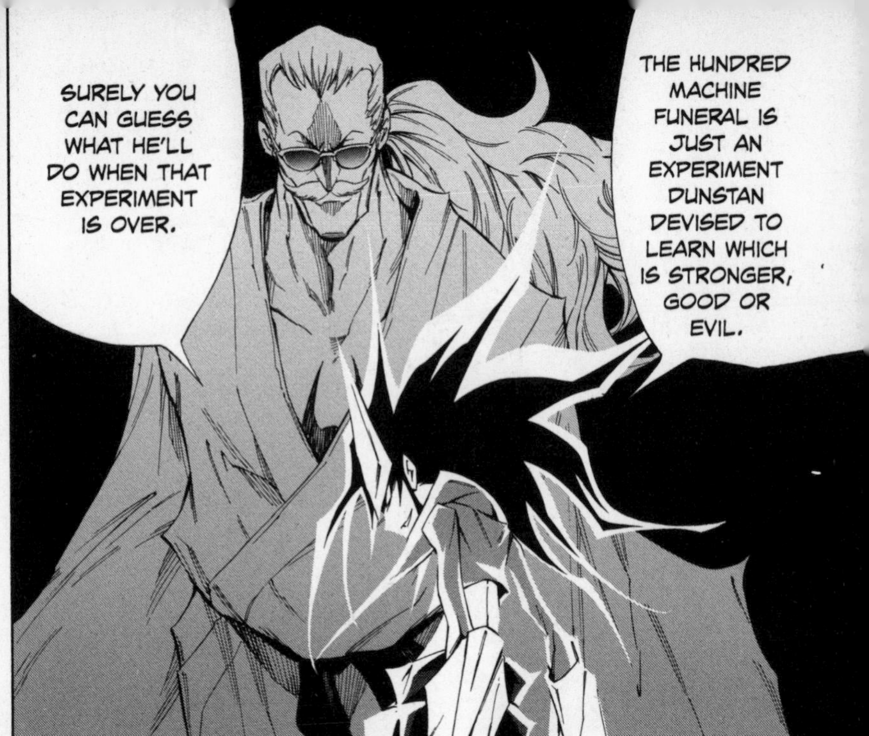
THE HUNDRED MACHINE FUNERAL IS JUST AN EXPERIMENT DUNSTAN DEVISED TO LEARN WHICH IS STRONGER, GOOD OR EVIL.
SURELY YOU CAN GUESS WHAT HE'LL DO WHEN THAT EXPERIMENT IS OVER.

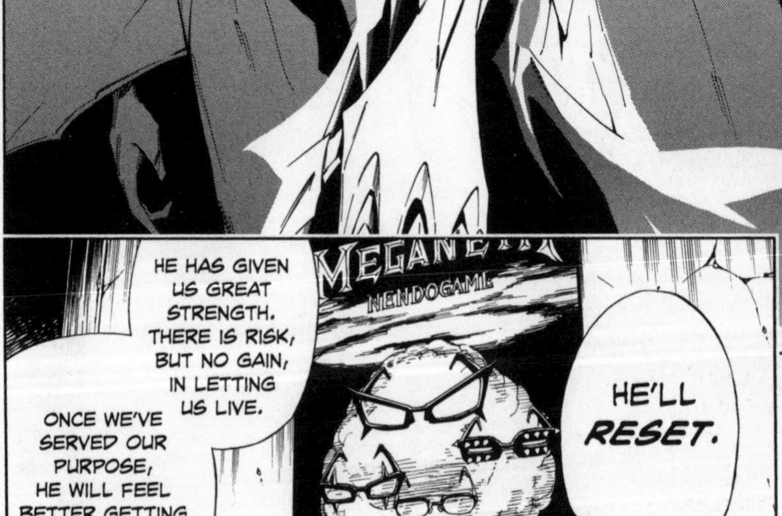
HE HAS GIVEN US GREAT STRENGTH. THERE IS RISK, BUT NO GAIN, IN LETTING US LIVE.
ONCE WE'VE SERVED OUR PURPOSE, HE WILL FEEL BETTER GETTING RID OF US.
NENDOGAMI
HE'LL *RESET*.

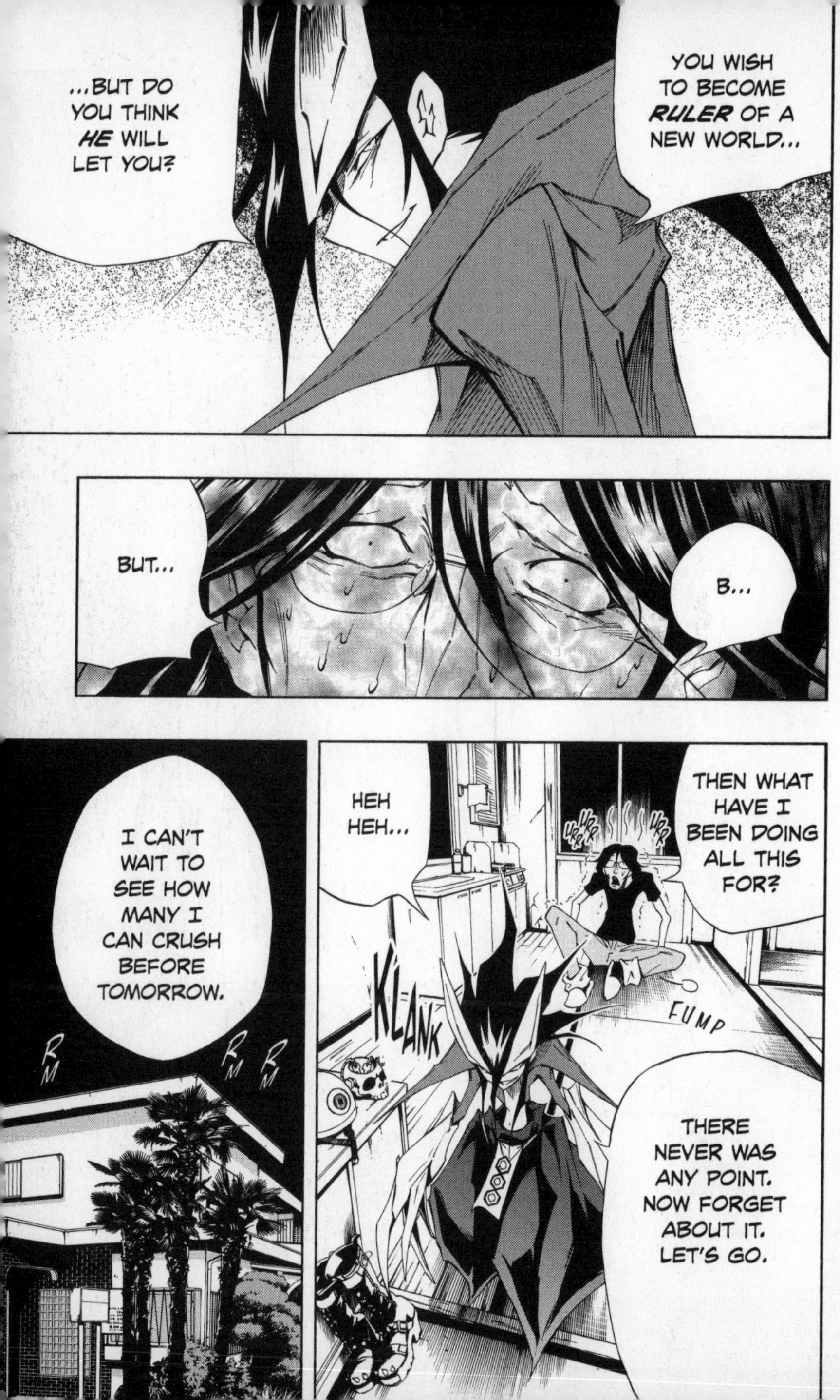
YOU WISH TO BECOME RULER OF A NEW WORLD...
...BUT DO YOU THINK HE WILL LET YOU?
B...
BUT...
THEN WHAT HAVE I BEEN DOING ALL THIS FOR?
URR URR URR
HEH HEH...
KLANK
FUMP
THERE NEVER WAS ANY POINT. NOW FORGET ABOUT IT. LET'S GO.
I CAN'T WAIT TO SEE HOW MANY I CAN CRUSH BEFORE TOMORROW.
RM RM RM

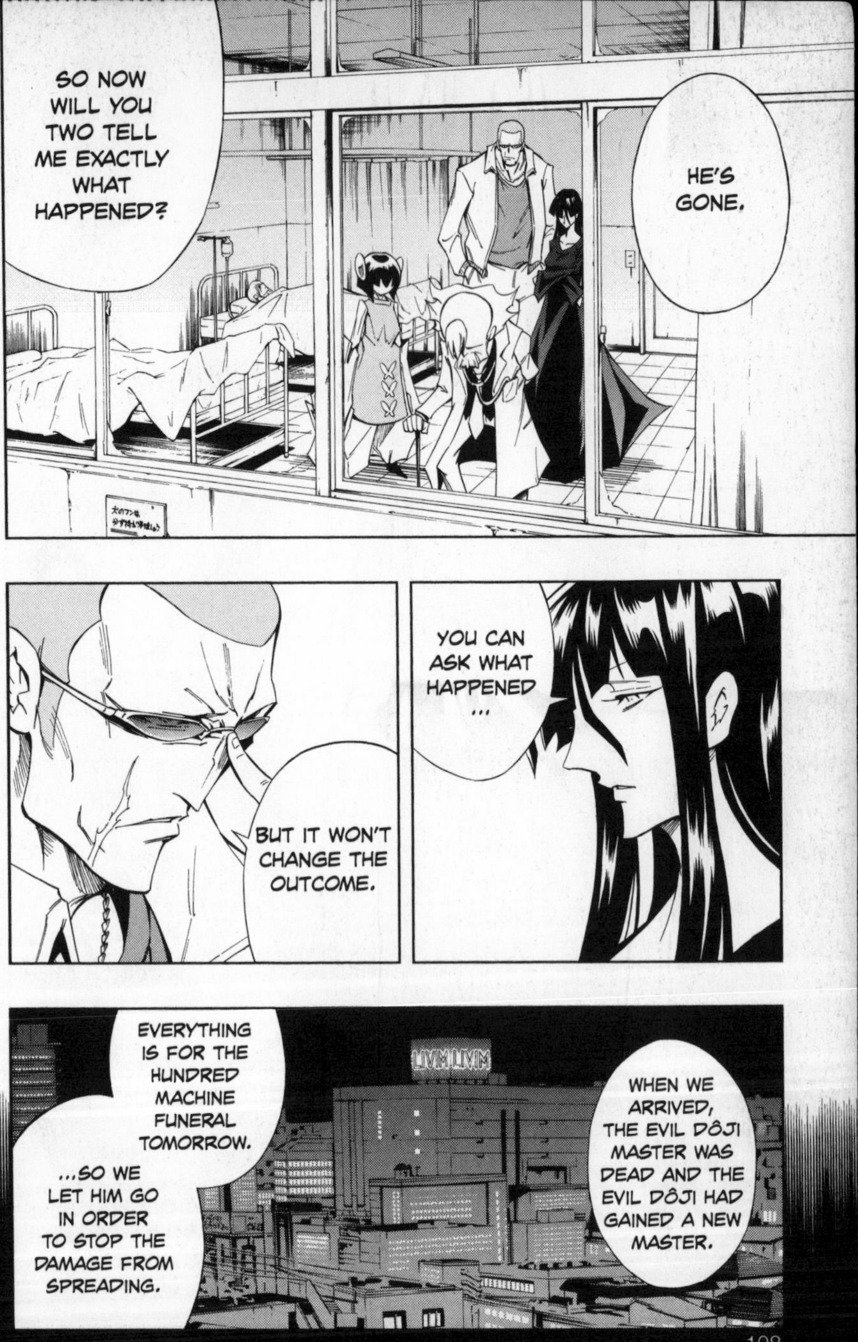
HE'S GONE.
SO NOW WILL YOU TWO TELL ME EXACTLY WHAT HAPPENED?
YOU CAN ASK WHAT HAPPENED ...
BUT IT WON'T CHANGE THE OUTCOME.
LIVIM LIVIM
WHEN WE ARRIVED, THE EVIL DÔJI MASTER WAS DEAD AND THE EVIL DÔJI HAD GAINED A NEW MASTER.
EVERYTHING IS FOR THE HUNDRED MACHINE FUNERAL TOMORROW.
...SO WE LET HIM GO IN ORDER TO STOP THE DAMAGE FROM SPREADING.

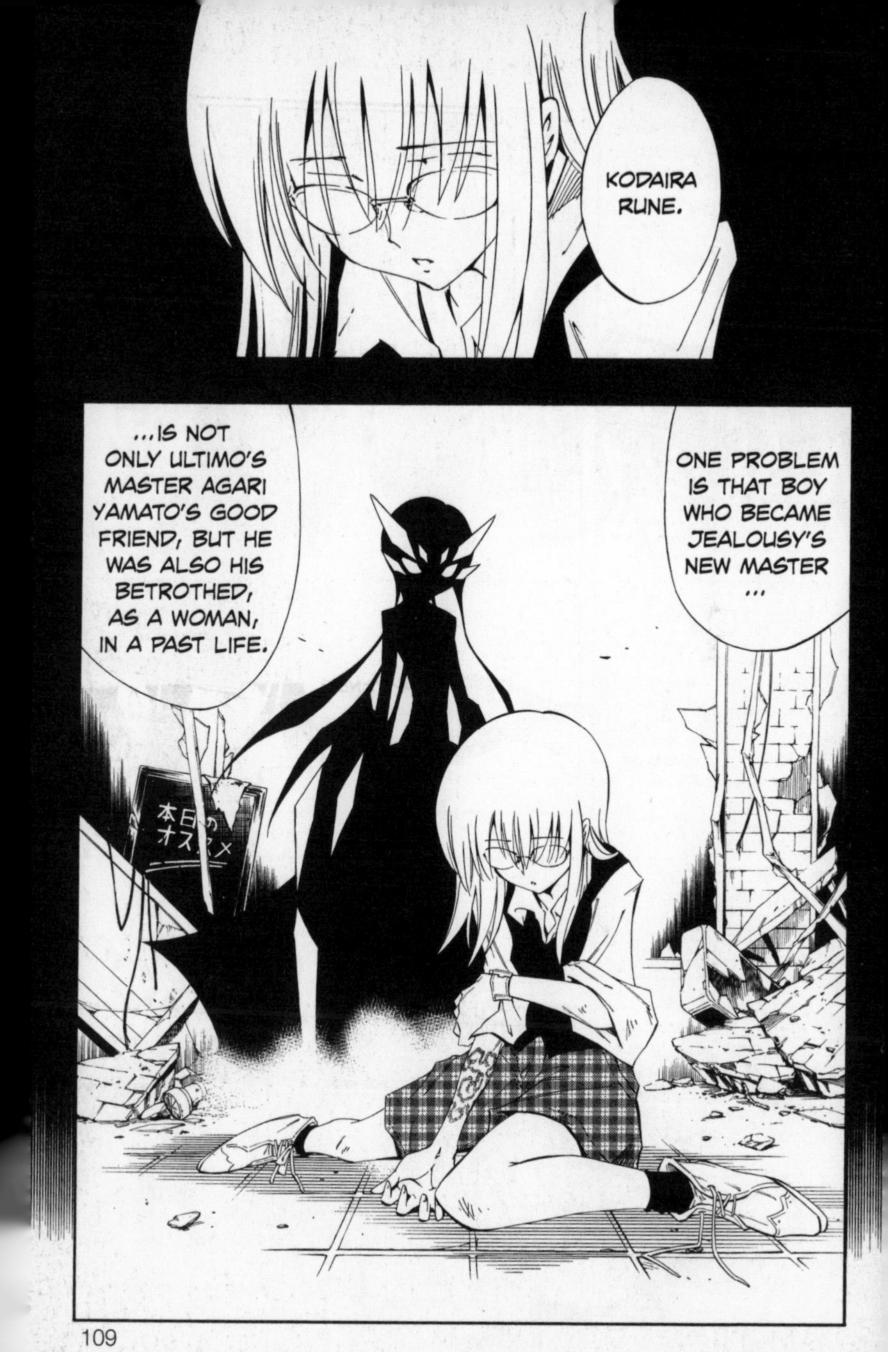
KODAIRA RUNE.
ONE PROBLEM IS THAT BOY WHO BECAME JEALOUSY'S NEW MASTER ...
...IS NOT ONLY ULTIMO'S MASTER AGARI YAMATO'S GOOD FRIEND, BUT HE WAS ALSO HIS BETROTHED, AS A WOMAN, IN A PAST LIFE.
本日のオススメ

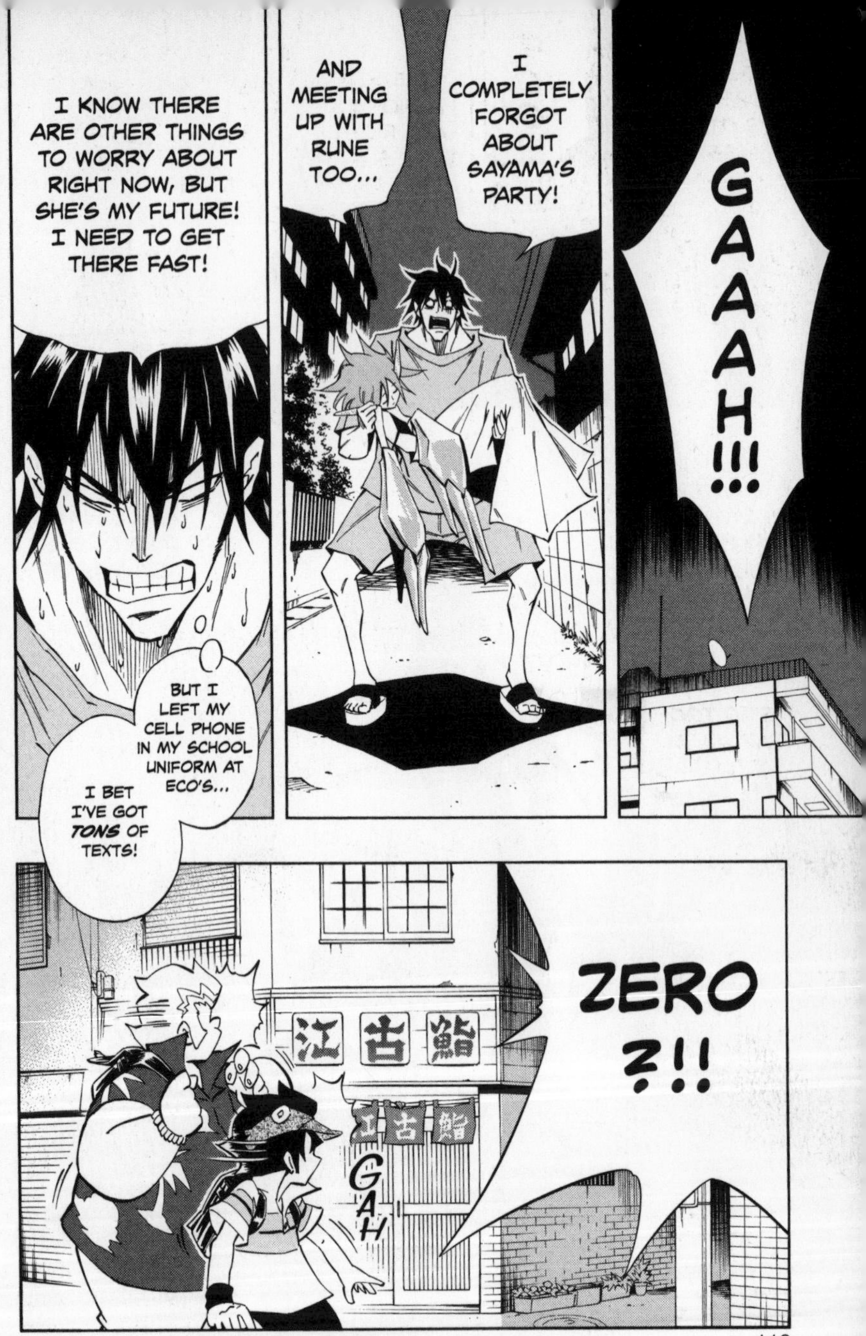
GAAAH!!!
I COMPLETELY FORGOT ABOUT SAYAMA'S PARTY!
AND MEETING UP WITH RUNE TOO...
I KNOW THERE ARE OTHER THINGS TO WORRY ABOUT RIGHT NOW, BUT SHE'S MY FUTURE! I NEED TO GET THERE FAST!
BUT I LEFT MY CELL PHONE IN MY SCHOOL UNIFORM AT ECO'S...
I BET I'VE GOT *TONS* OF TEXTS!
ZERO?!!
江古鮨
GAH
(ECO SUSHI)

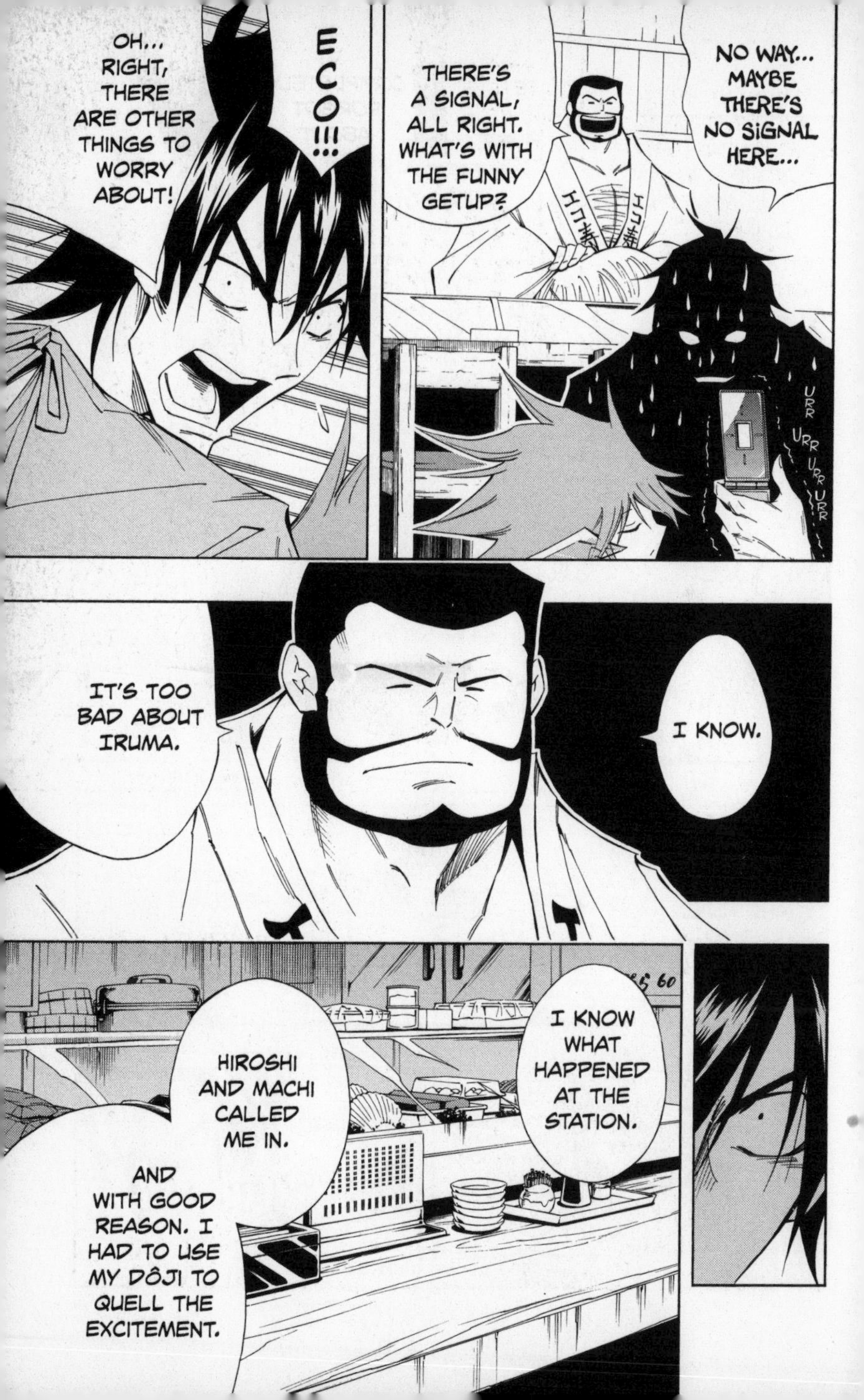
NO WAY... MAYBE THERE'S NO SIGNAL HERE...
THERE'S A SIGNAL, ALL RIGHT. WHAT'S WITH THE FUNNY GETUP?
URR URR URR URR
ECO!!!
OH... RIGHT, THERE ARE OTHER THINGS TO WORRY ABOUT!
I KNOW.
IT'S TOO BAD ABOUT IRUMA.
I KNOW WHAT HAPPENED AT THE STATION.
HIROSHI AND MACHI CALLED ME IN.
AND WITH GOOD REASON. I HAD TO USE MY DÔJI TO QUELL THE EXCITEMENT.

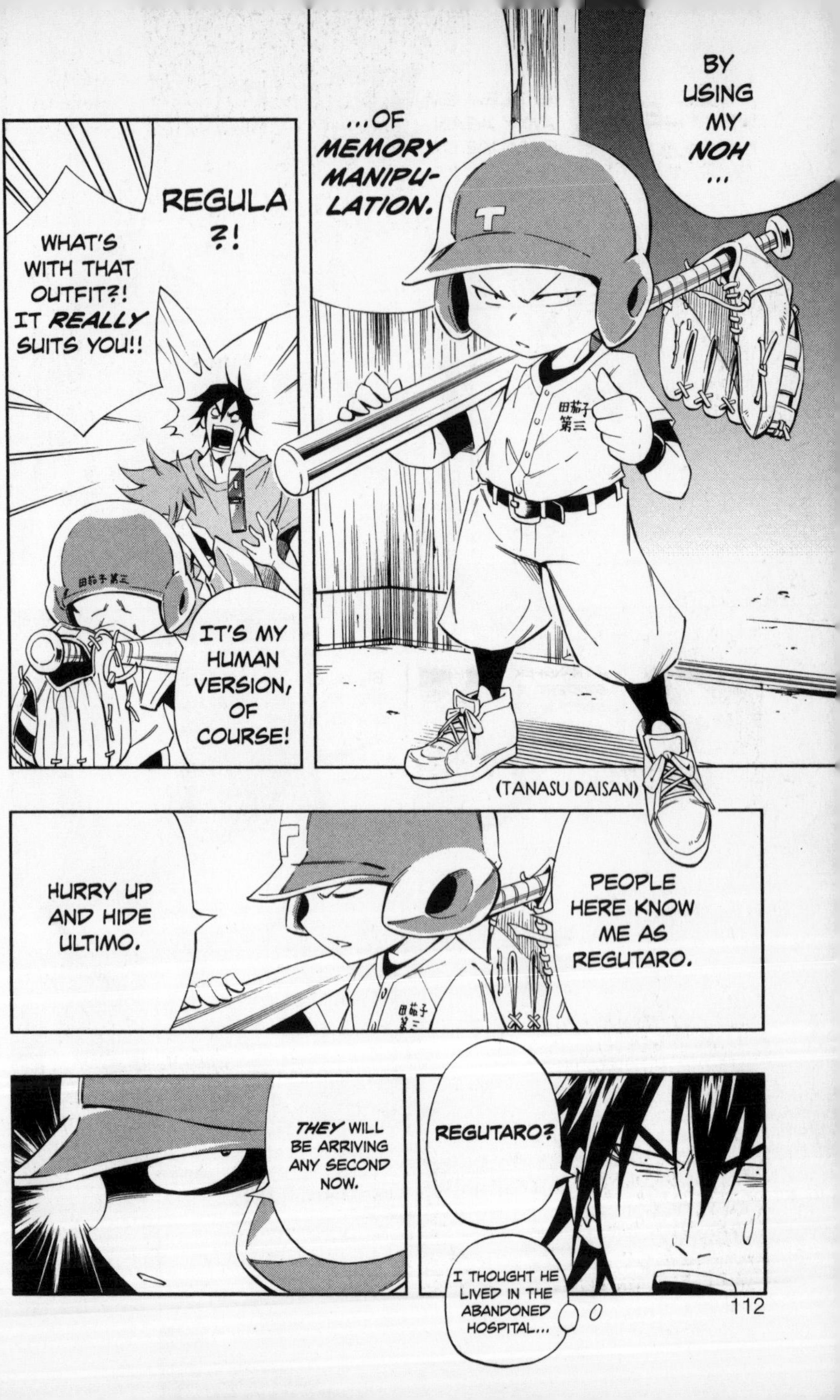
BY USING MY NOH...
...OF MEMORY MANIPULATION.
田茄子 第三
REGULA?!
WHAT'S WITH THAT OUTFIT?! IT REALLY SUITS YOU!!
IT'S MY HUMAN VERSION, OF COURSE!
(TANASU DAISAN)
PEOPLE HERE KNOW ME AS REGUTARO.
HURRY UP AND HIDE ULTIMO.
REGUTARO?
I THOUGHT HE LIVED IN THE ABANDONED HOSPITAL...
THEY WILL BE ARRIVING ANY SECOND NOW.

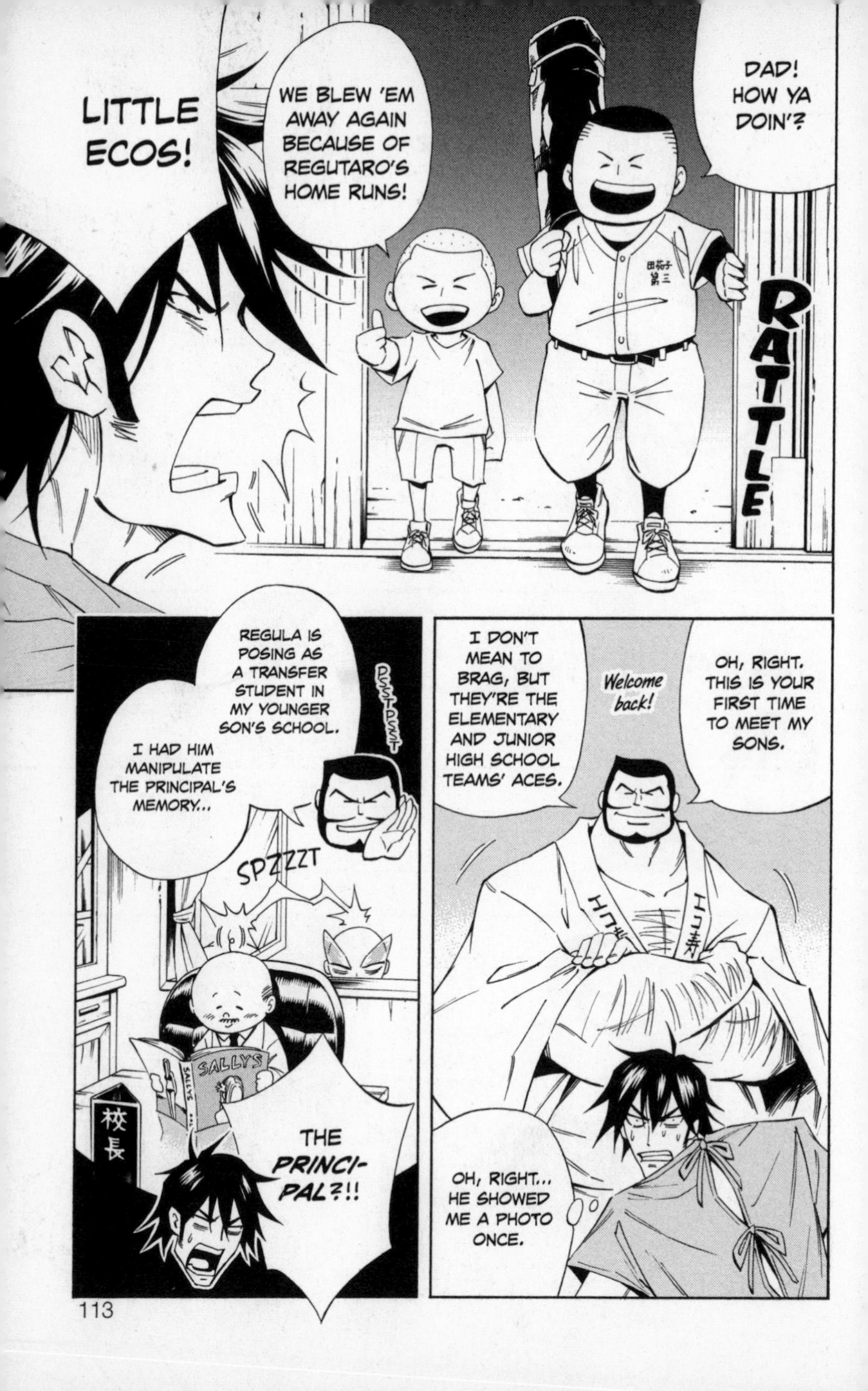
DAD! HOW YA DOIN'?
RATTLE
WE BLEW 'EM AWAY AGAIN BECAUSE OF REGUTARO'S HOME RUNS!
LITTLE ECOS!
OH, RIGHT. THIS IS YOUR FIRST TIME TO MEET MY SONS.
Welcome back!
I DON'T MEAN TO BRAG, BUT THEY'RE THE ELEMENTARY AND JUNIOR HIGH SCHOOL TEAMS' ACES.
OH, RIGHT... HE SHOWED ME A PHOTO ONCE.
PSSTPSST
REGULA IS POSING AS A TRANSFER STUDENT IN MY YOUNGER SON'S SCHOOL.
I HAD HIM MANIPULATE THE PRINCIPAL'S MEMORY...
SPZZZT
SALLY'S
校長
THE PRINCIPAL?!!

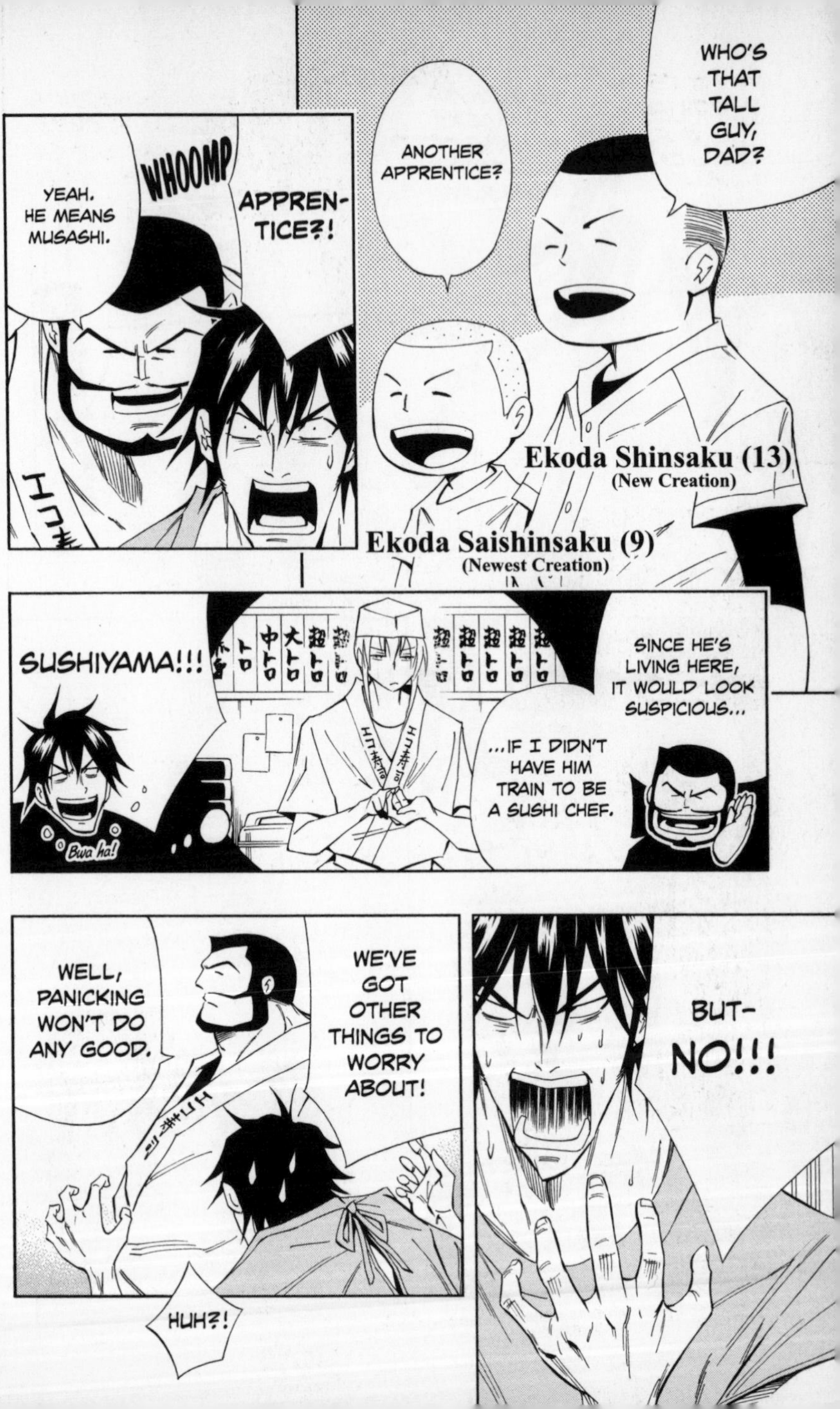
WHO'S THAT TALL GUY, DAD?
ANOTHER APPRENTICE?
Ekoda Shinsaku (13)
(New Creation)
Ekoda Saishinsaku (9)
(Newest Creation)
APPREN-TICE?!
WHOOMP
YEAH. HE MEANS MUSASHI.
SINCE HE'S LIVING HERE, IT WOULD LOOK SUSPICIOUS...
...IF I DIDN'T HAVE HIM TRAIN TO BE A SUSHI CHEF.
SUSHIYAMA!!!
Bwa ha!
BUT-
NO!!!
WE'VE GOT OTHER THINGS TO WORRY ABOUT!
WELL, PANICKING WON'T DO ANY GOOD.
HUH?!

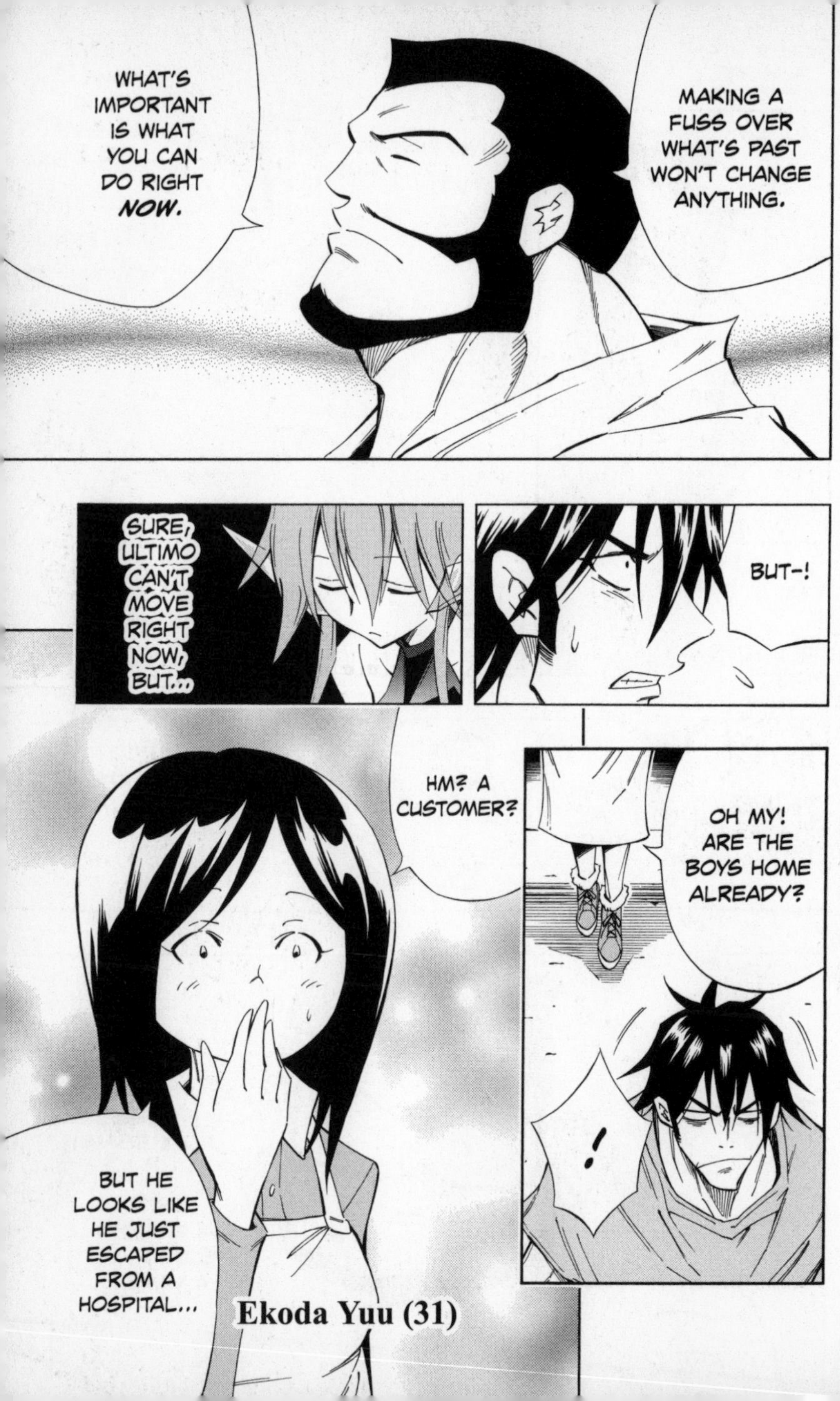
MAKING A FUSS OVER WHAT'S PAST WON'T CHANGE ANYTHING.
WHAT'S IMPORTANT IS WHAT YOU CAN DO RIGHT *NOW*.
BUT–!
SURE, ULTIMO CAN'T MOVE RIGHT NOW, BUT...
OH MY! ARE THE BOYS HOME ALREADY?
!
HM? A CUSTOMER?
BUT HE LOOKS LIKE HE JUST ESCAPED FROM A HOSPITAL...
Ekoda Yuu (31)

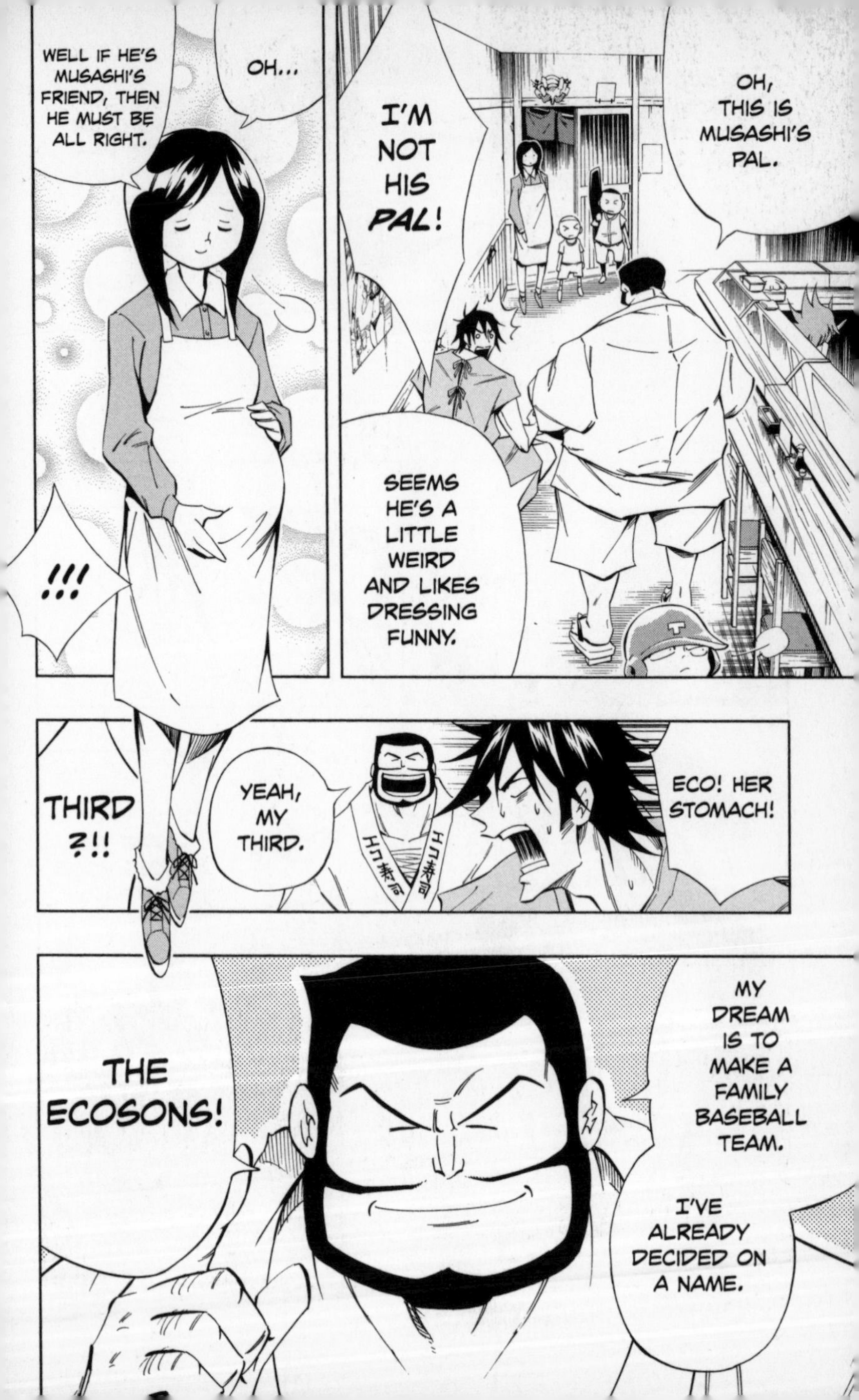
OH, THIS IS MUSASHI'S PAL.
I'M NOT HIS PAL!
SEEMS HE'S A LITTLE WEIRD AND LIKES DRESSING FUNNY.
OH...
WELL IF HE'S MUSASHI'S FRIEND, THEN HE MUST BE ALL RIGHT.
!!!
ECO! HER STOMACH!
YEAH, MY THIRD.
エコ寿司
エコ寿司
THIRD ?!!
MY DREAM IS TO MAKE A FAMILY BASEBALL TEAM.
I'VE ALREADY DECIDED ON A NAME.
THE ECOSONS!

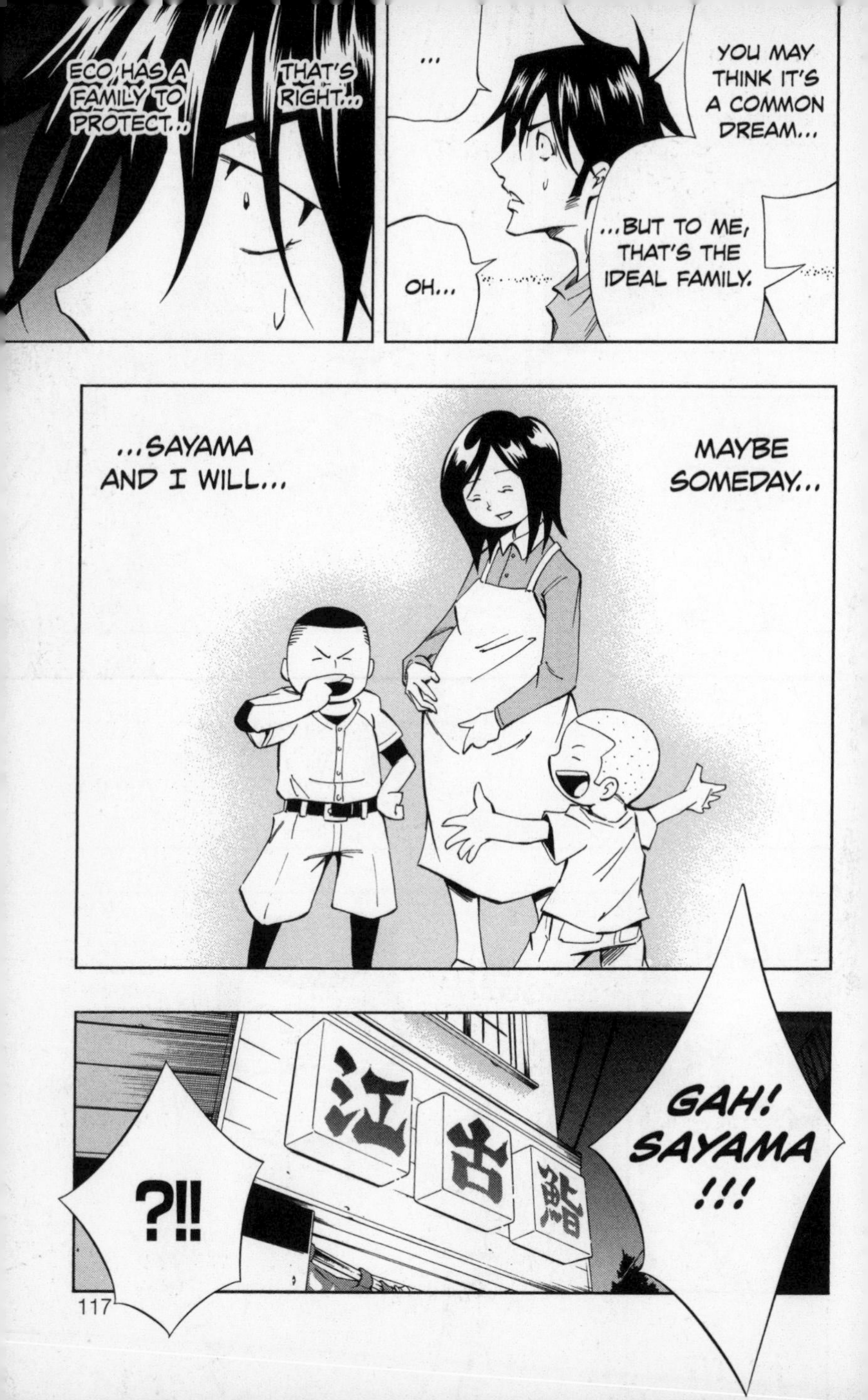
YOU MAY THINK IT'S A COMMON DREAM...
...BUT TO ME, THAT'S THE IDEAL FAMILY.
...
OH...
THAT'S RIGHT...
ECO HAS A FAMILY TO PROTECT...
MAYBE SOMEDAY...
...SAYAMA AND I WILL...
GAH! SAYAMA!!!
江古鮨
?!!

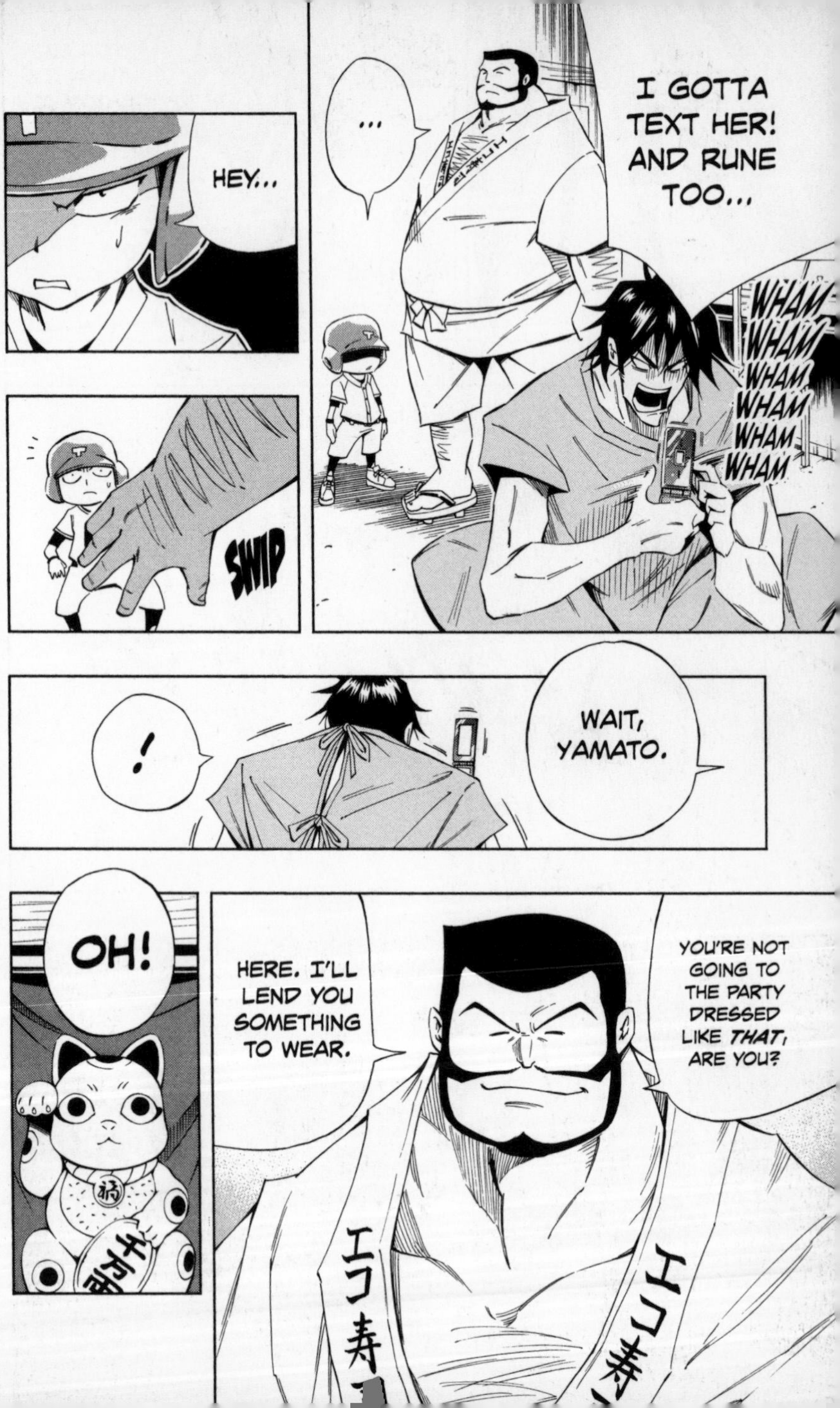
I GOTTA TEXT HER! AND RUNE TOO...
WHAM WHAM WHAM WHAM WHAM WHAM
...
HEY...
SWIP
WAIT, YAMATO.
!
YOU'RE NOT GOING TO THE PARTY DRESSED LIKE *THAT*, ARE YOU?
HERE. I'LL LEND YOU SOMETHING TO WEAR.
エコ寿
エコ寿
OH!

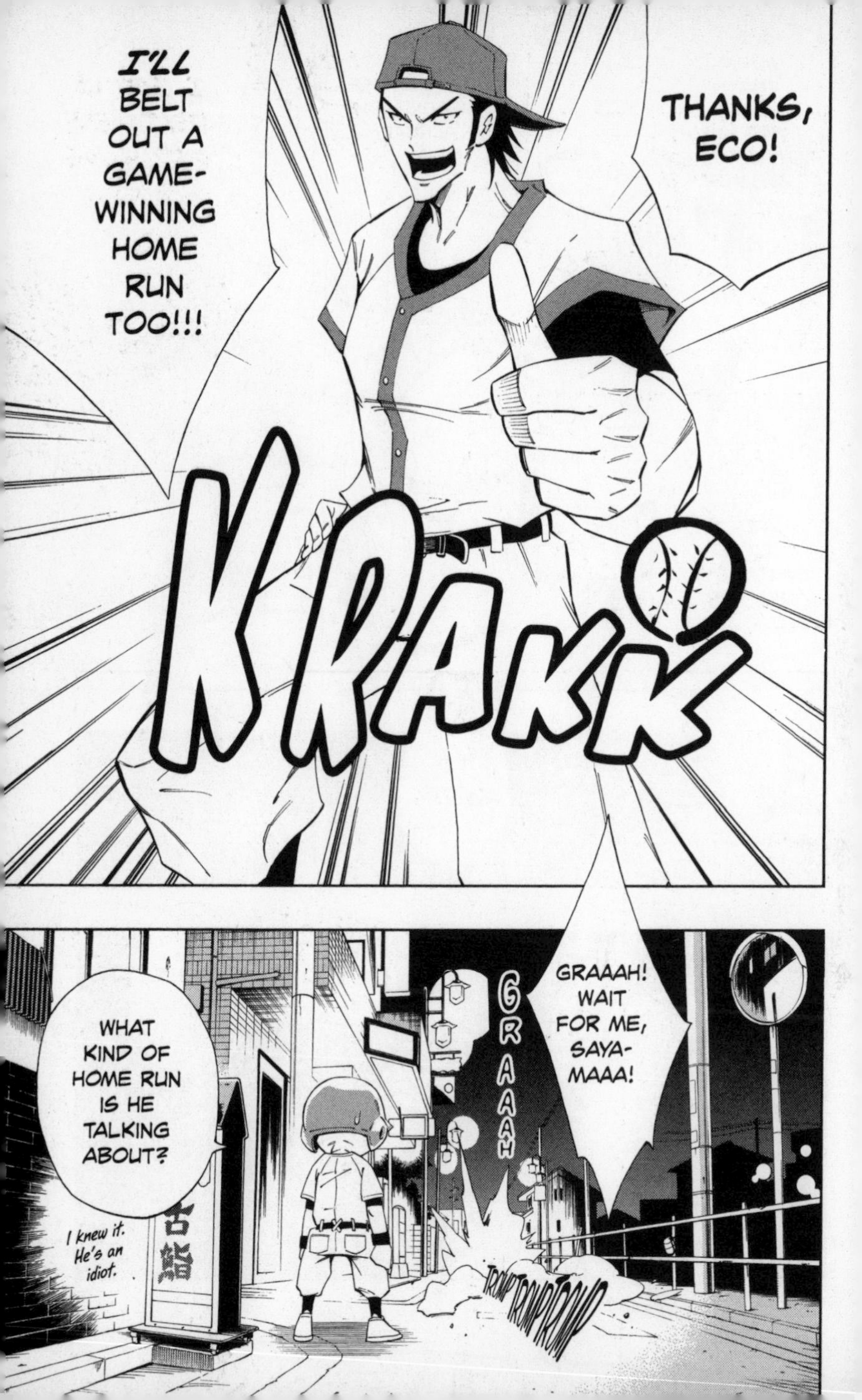
THANKS, ECO!
I'LL BELT OUT A GAME-WINNING HOME RUN TOO!!!
KRAKK
GRAAAH! WAIT FOR ME, SAYA-MAAA!
GRAAAAH
TROMP TROMP TROMP
WHAT KIND OF HOME RUN IS HE TALKING ABOUT?
I knew it. He's an idiot.

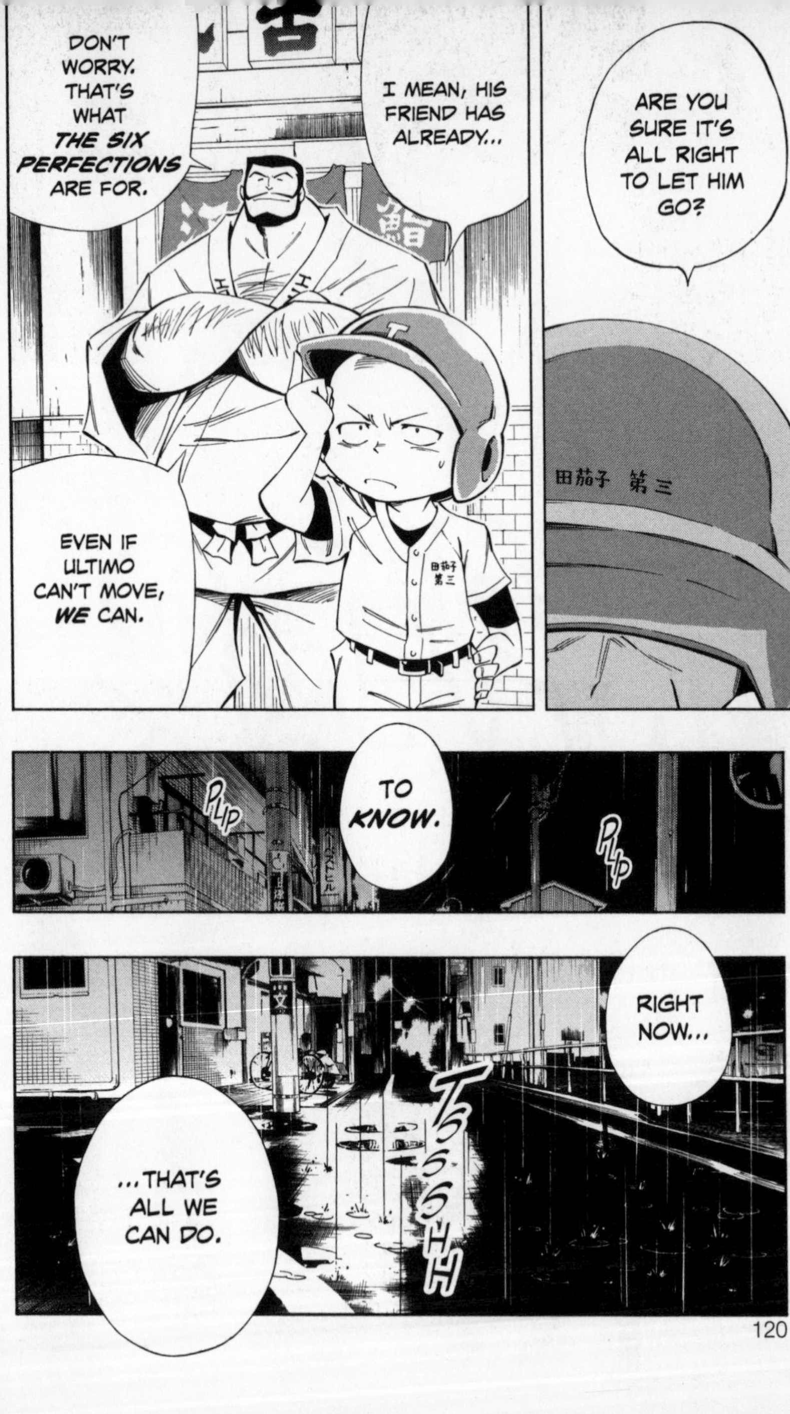
ARE YOU SURE IT'S ALL RIGHT TO LET HIM GO?
田茄子 第三
I MEAN, HIS FRIEND HAS ALREADY...
DON'T WORRY. THAT'S WHAT *THE SIX PERFECTIONS* ARE FOR.
EVEN IF ULTIMO CAN'T MOVE, *WE* CAN.
田茄子 第三
TO *KNOW.*
PLIP
PLIP
RIGHT NOW...
TSSSHH
...THAT'S ALL WE CAN DO.

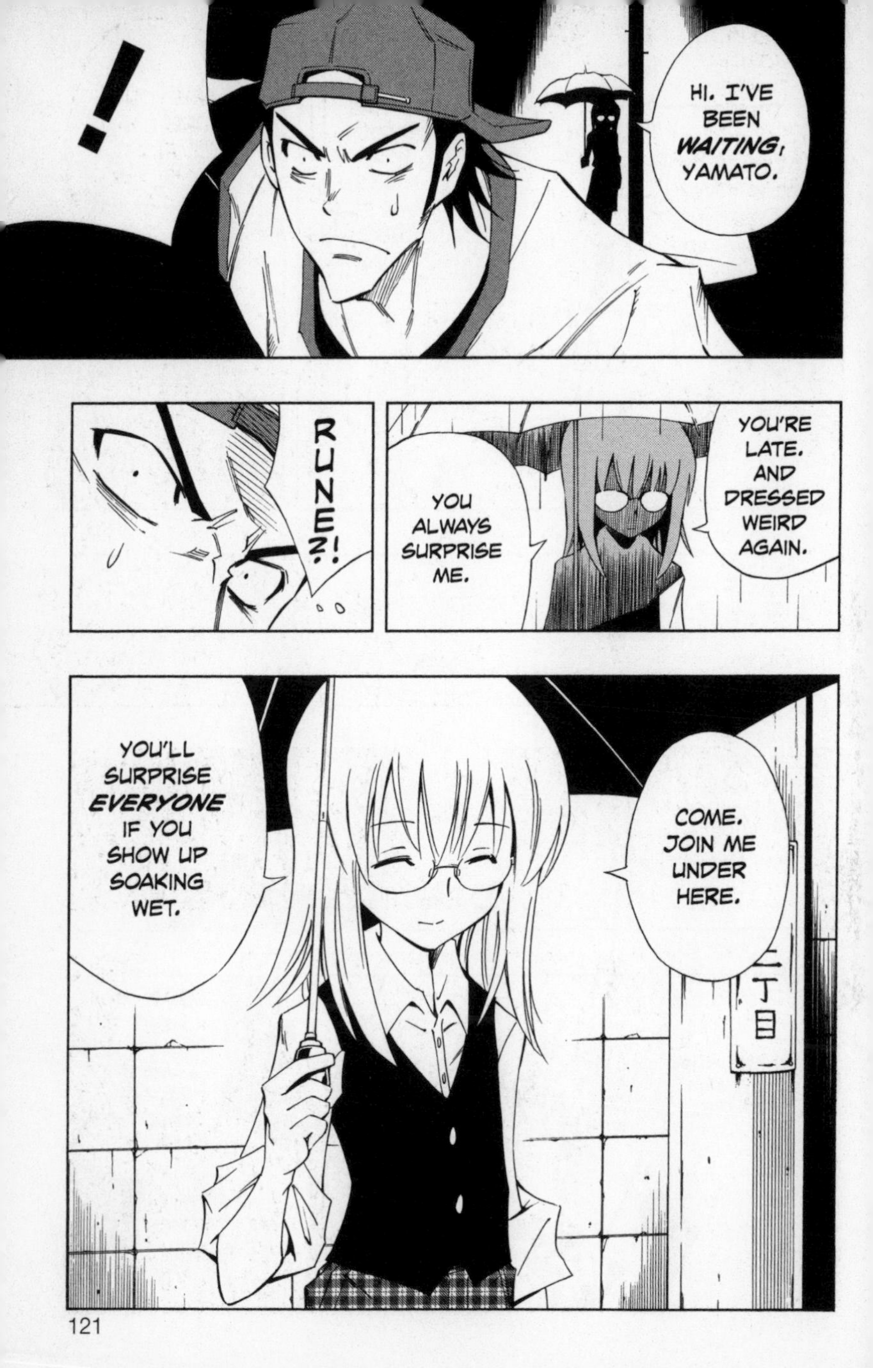
!
HI. I'VE BEEN *WAITING*, YAMATO.
YOU'RE LATE. AND DRESSED WEIRD AGAIN.
YOU ALWAYS SURPRISE ME.
RUNE?!
COME. JOIN ME UNDER HERE.
YOU'LL SURPRISE *EVERYONE* IF YOU SHOW UP SOAKING WET.
丁目

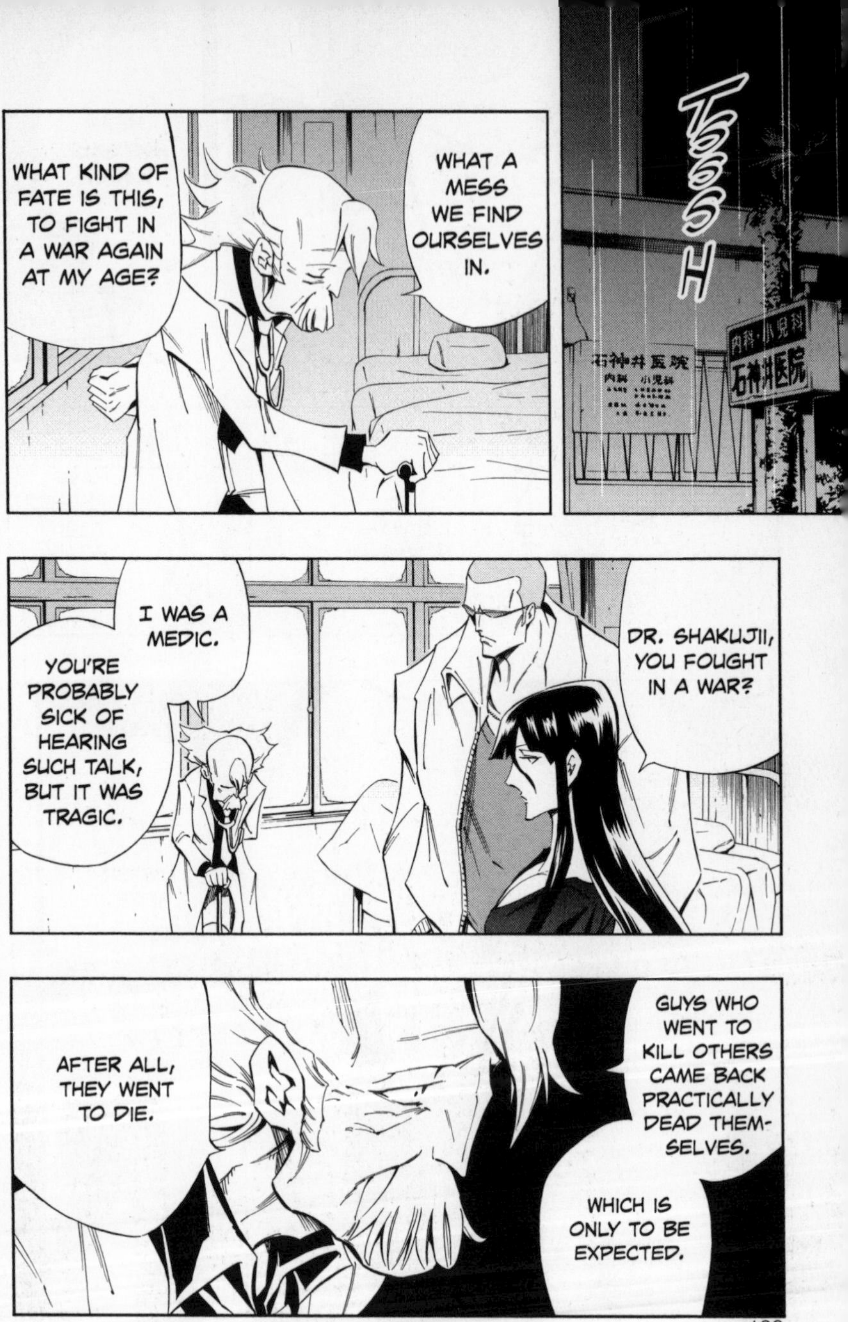
TSSSH
内科・小児科
石神井医院
WHAT A MESS WE FIND OURSELVES IN.
WHAT KIND OF FATE IS THIS, TO FIGHT IN A WAR AGAIN AT MY AGE?
DR. SHAKUJII, YOU FOUGHT IN A WAR?
I WAS A MEDIC.
YOU'RE PROBABLY SICK OF HEARING SUCH TALK, BUT IT WAS TRAGIC.
GUYS WHO WENT TO KILL OTHERS CAME BACK PRACTICALLY DEAD THEMSELVES.
WHICH IS ONLY TO BE EXPECTED.
AFTER ALL, THEY WENT TO DIE.

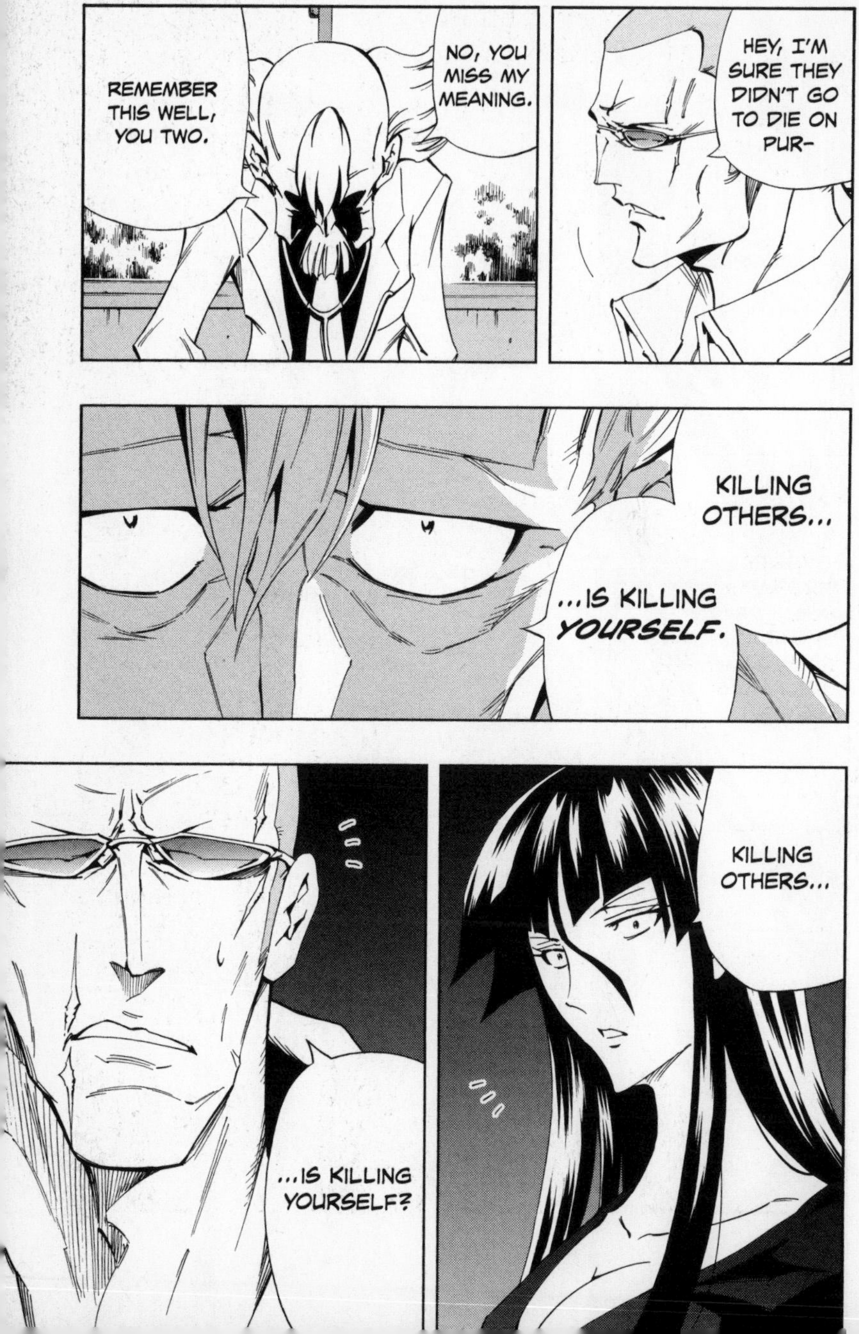
HEY, I'M SURE THEY DIDN'T GO TO DIE ON PUR-
NO, YOU MISS MY MEANING.
REMEMBER THIS WELL, YOU TWO.
KILLING OTHERS...
...IS KILLING *YOURSELF*.
KILLING OTHERS...
...IS KILLING YOURSELF?

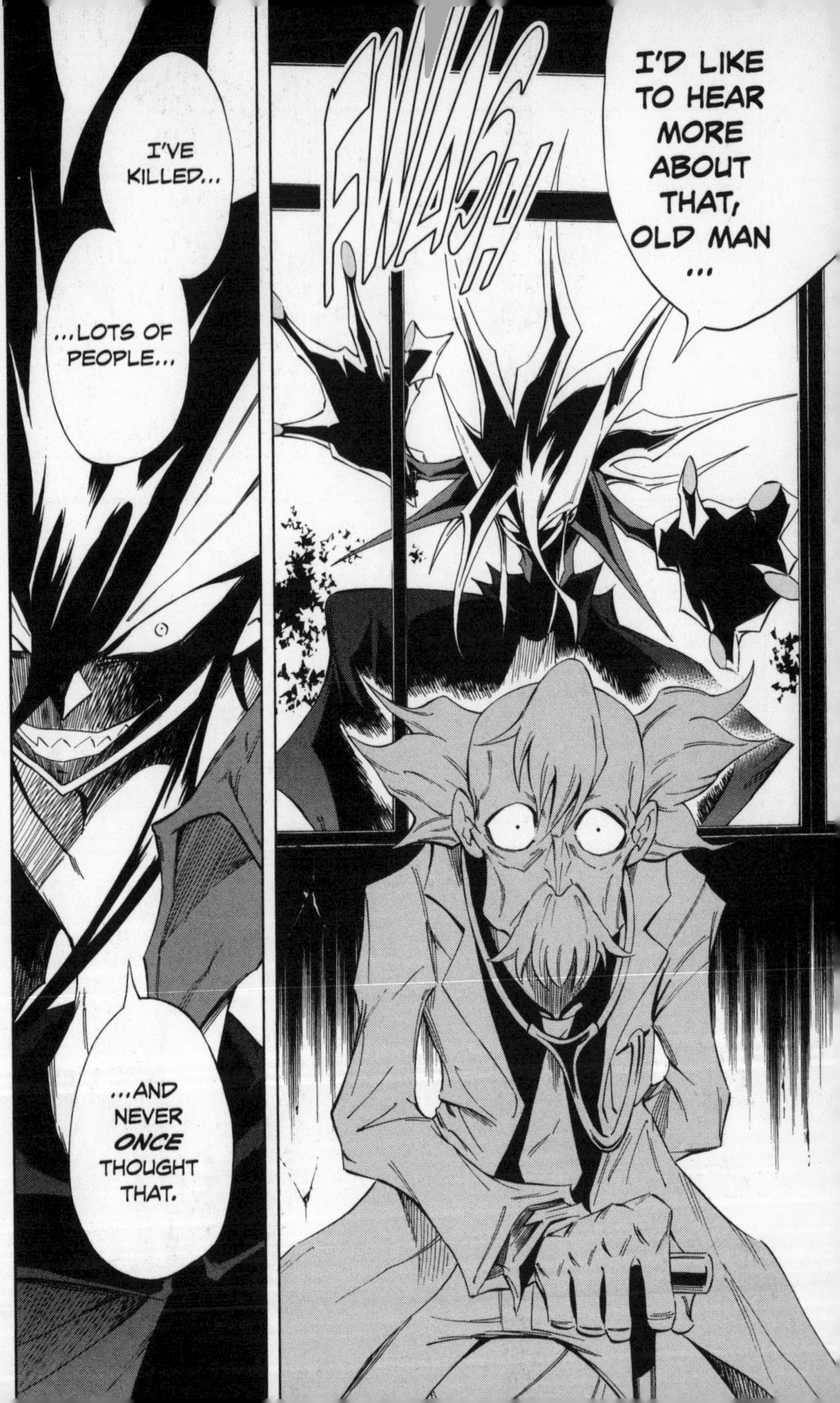
FWASH!
I'D LIKE TO HEAR MORE ABOUT THAT, OLD MAN ...
I'VE KILLED...
...LOTS OF PEOPLE...
...AND NEVER ONCE THOUGHT THAT.

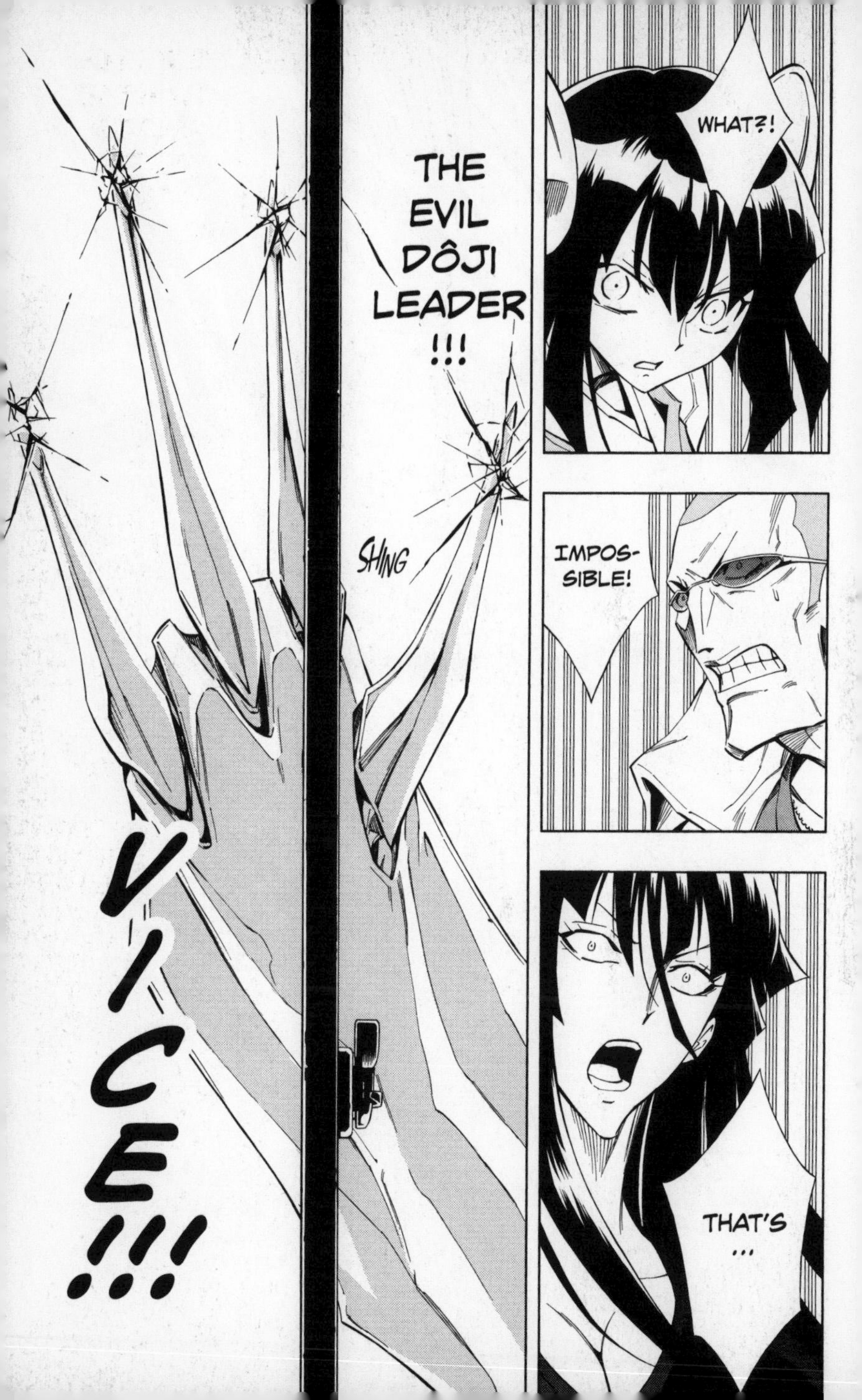
WHAT?!
IMPOS-
SIBLE!
THAT'S
...
THE EVIL DÔJI LEADER !!!
SHING
V-I-CE!!!

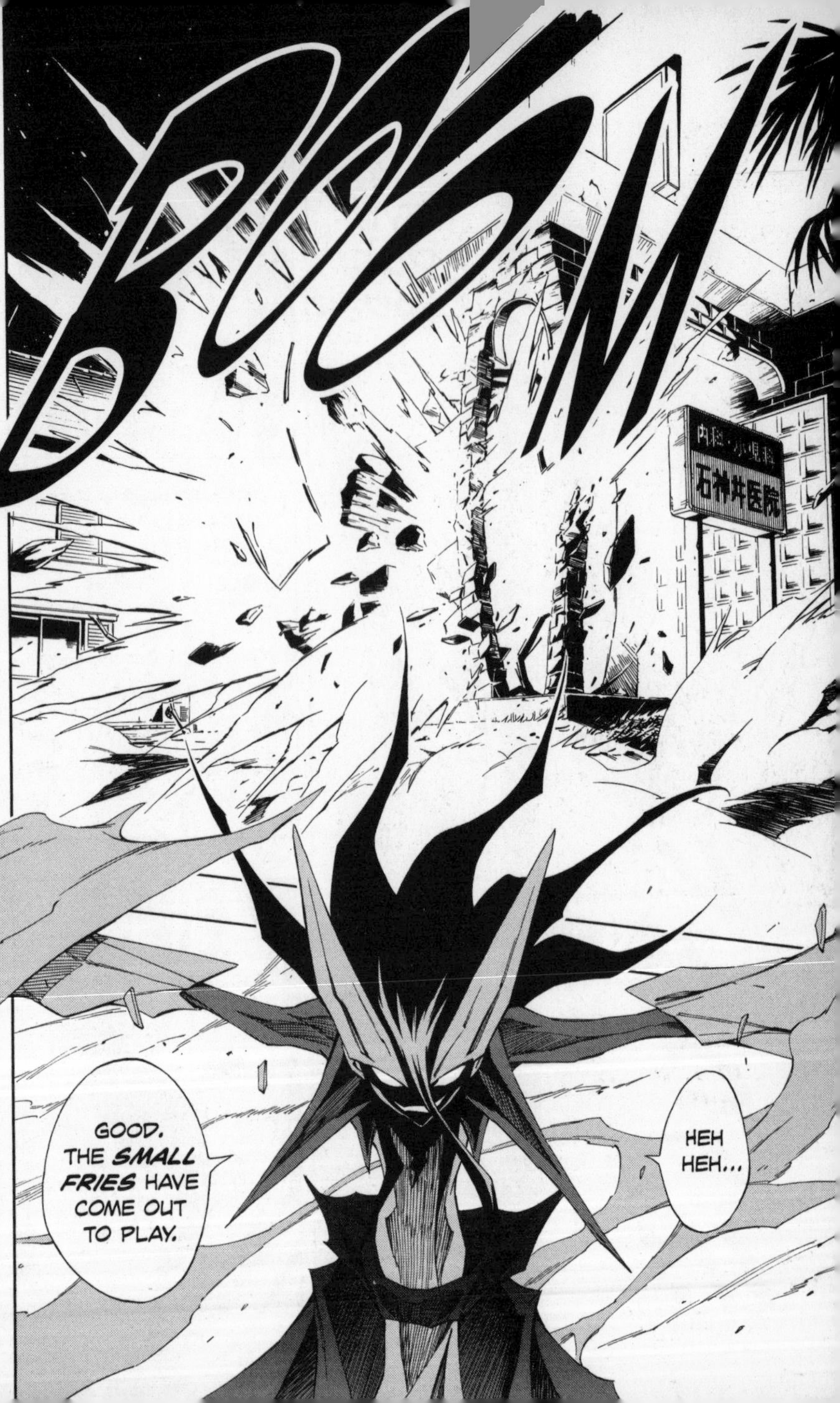
BOOM
内科・小児科
石神井医院
HEH HEH...
GOOD. THE *SMALL FRIES* HAVE COME OUT TO PLAY.

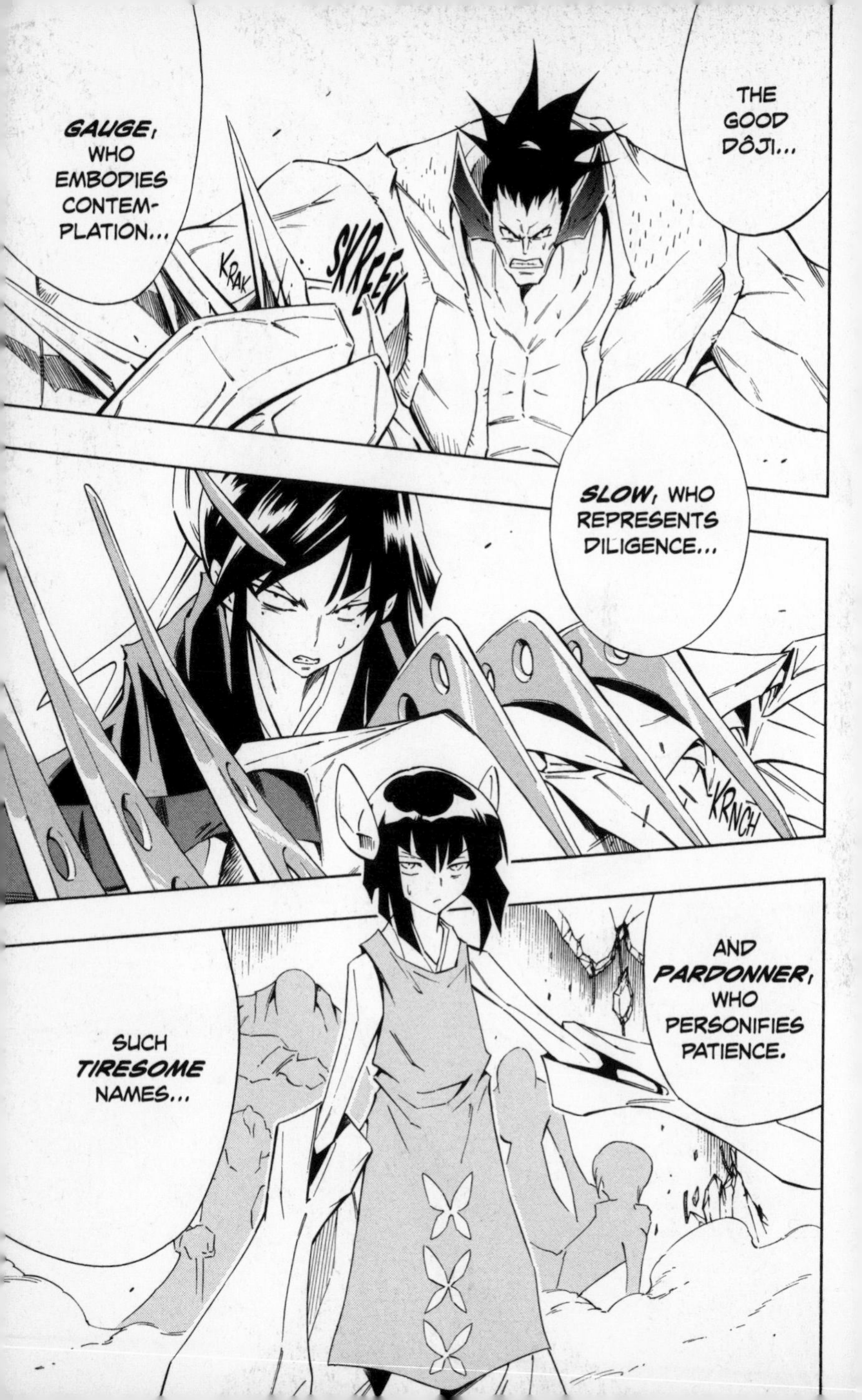
THE GOOD DÔJI...
GAUGE, WHO EMBODIES CONTEM-PLATION...
SKREEK
KRAK
SLOW, WHO REPRESENTS DILIGENCE...
KRNCH
AND PARDONNER, WHO PERSONIFIES PATIENCE.
SUCH TIRESOME NAMES...

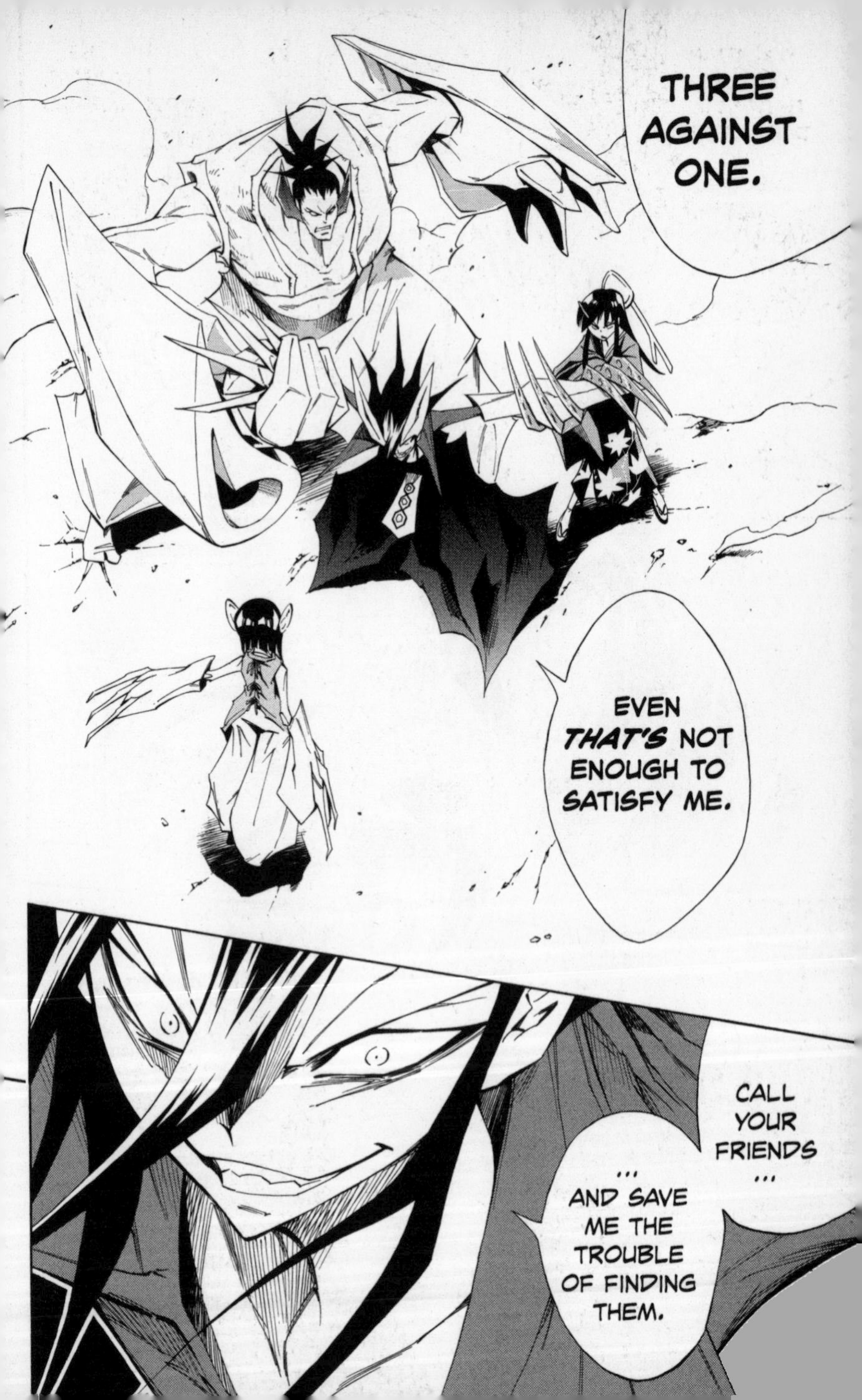
THREE AGAINST ONE.
EVEN *THAT'S* NOT ENOUGH TO SATISFY ME.
CALL YOUR FRIENDS ...
... AND SAVE ME THE TROUBLE OF FINDING THEM.

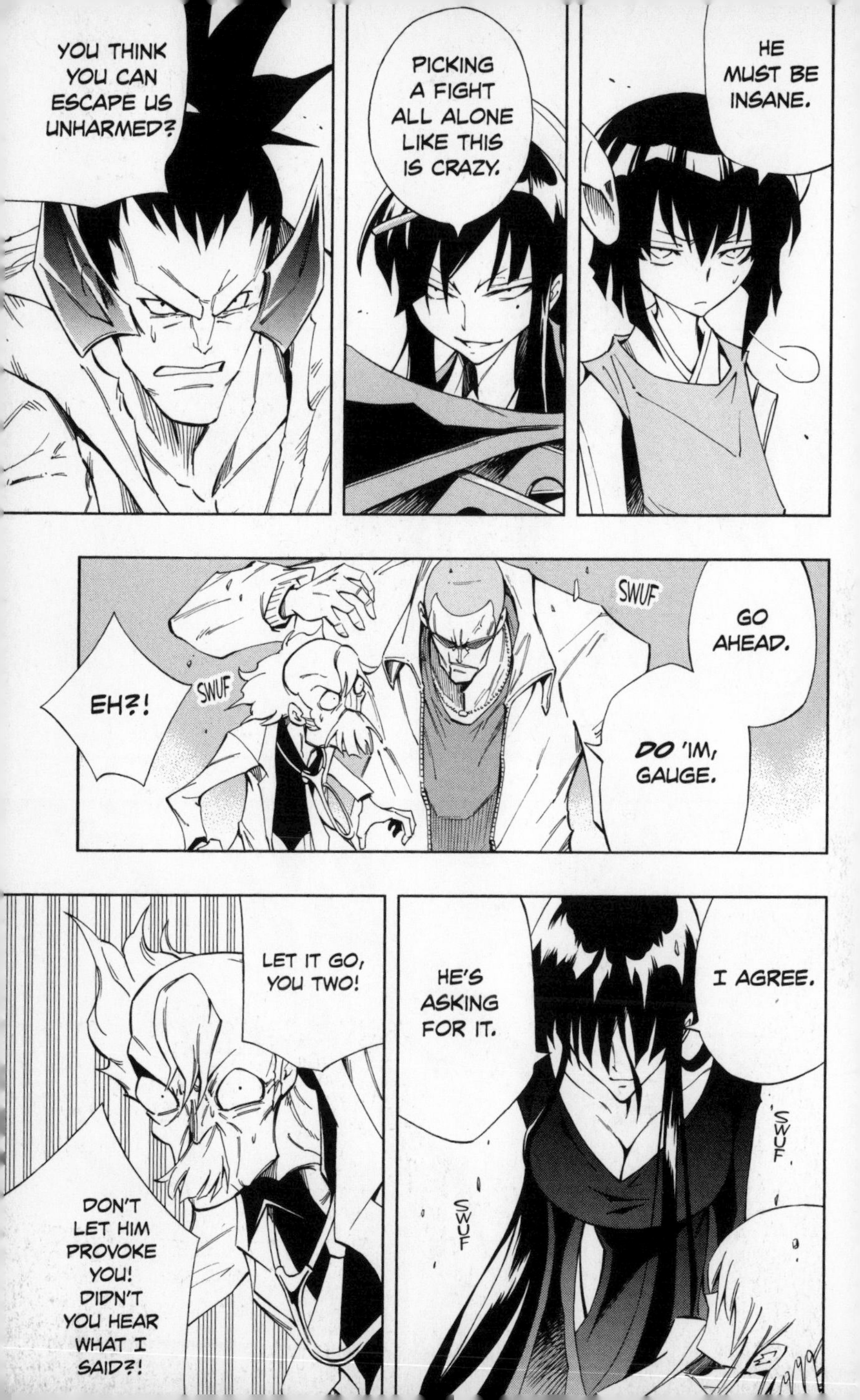
HE MUST BE INSANE.
PICKING A FIGHT ALL ALONE LIKE THIS IS CRAZY.
YOU THINK YOU CAN ESCAPE US UNHARMED?!
GO AHEAD.
DO 'IM, GAUGE.
SWUF
SWUF
EH?!
I AGREE.
HE'S ASKING FOR IT.
SWUF
SWUF
LET IT GO, YOU TWO!
DON'T LET HIM PROVOKE YOU! DIDN'T YOU HEAR WHAT I SAID?!

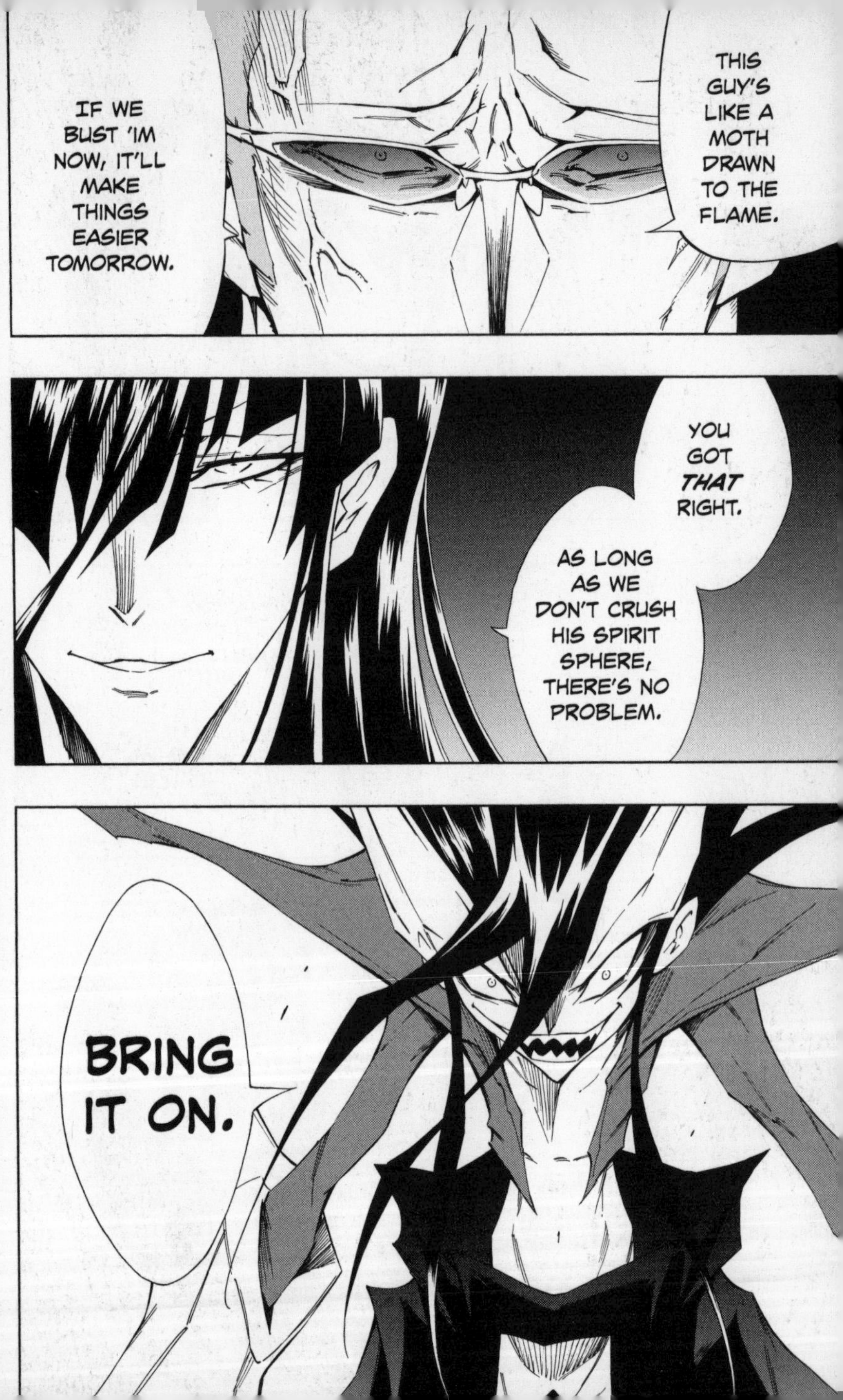
THIS GUY'S LIKE A MOTH DRAWN TO THE FLAME.
IF WE BUST 'IM NOW, IT'LL MAKE THINGS EASIER TOMORROW.
YOU GOT *THAT* RIGHT.
AS LONG AS WE DON'T CRUSH HIS SPIRIT SPHERE, THERE'S NO PROBLEM.
BRING IT ON.

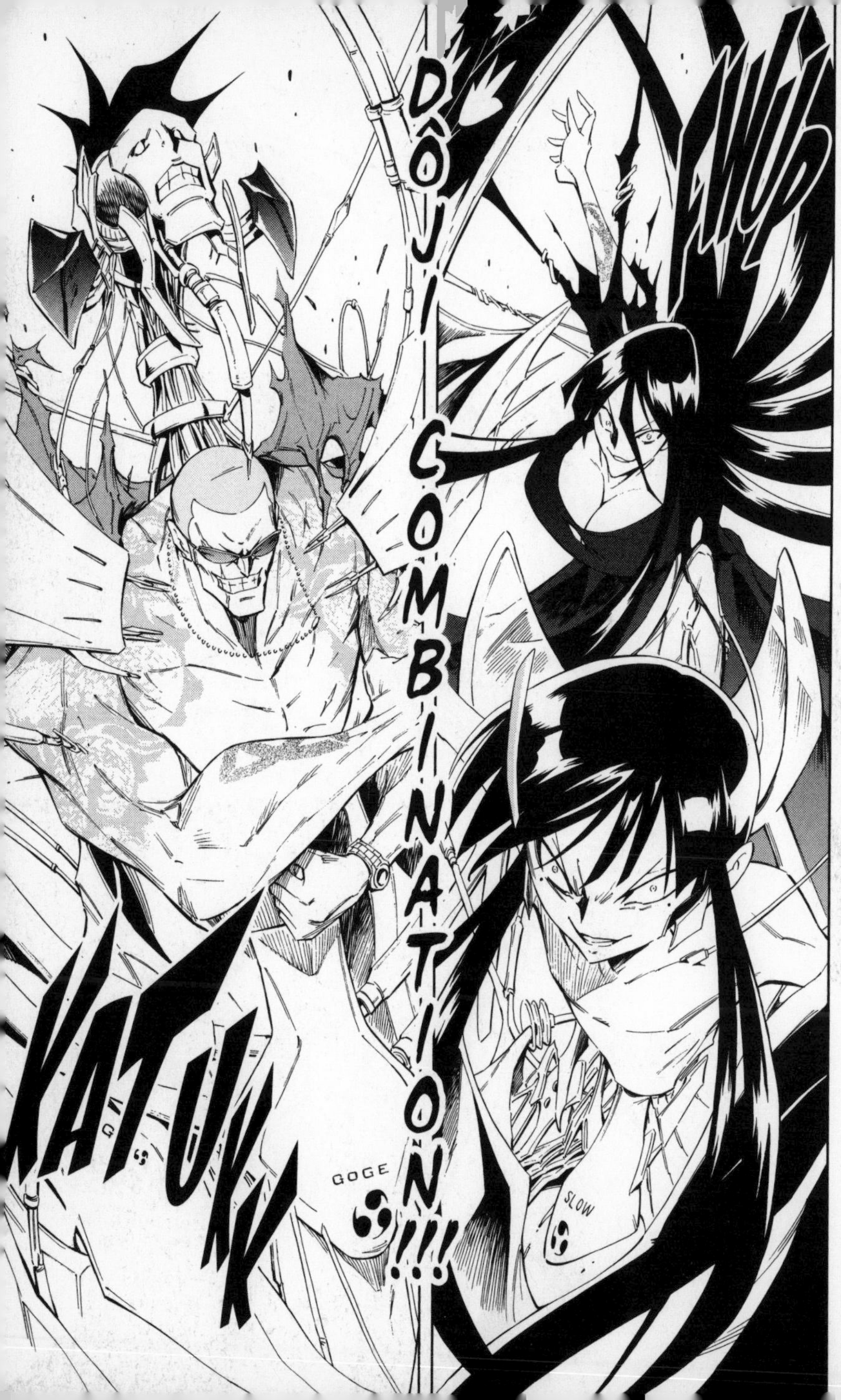
DÔJI COMBINATION!!!
KATUNK
GOGE
SLOW

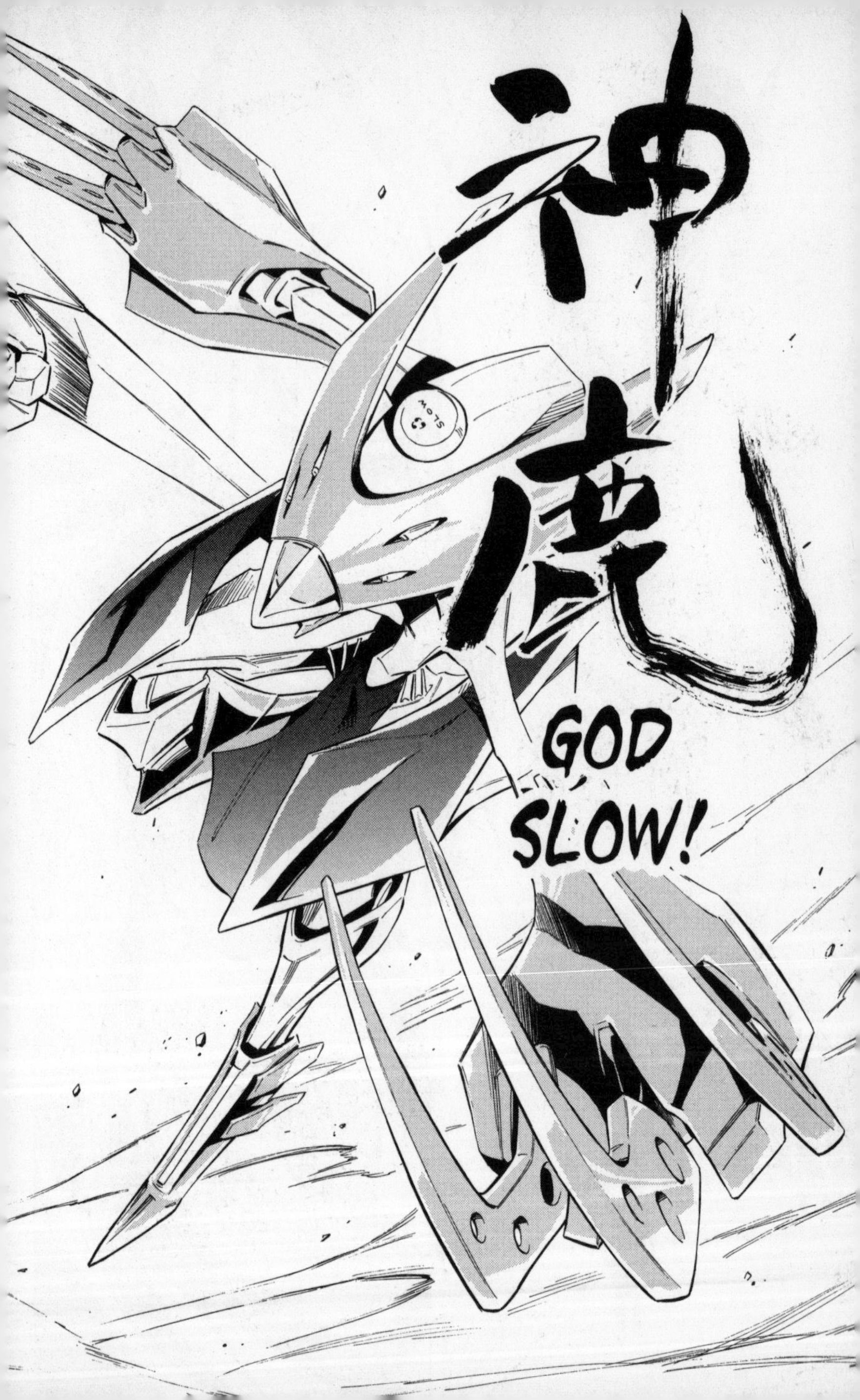
GOD SLOW!

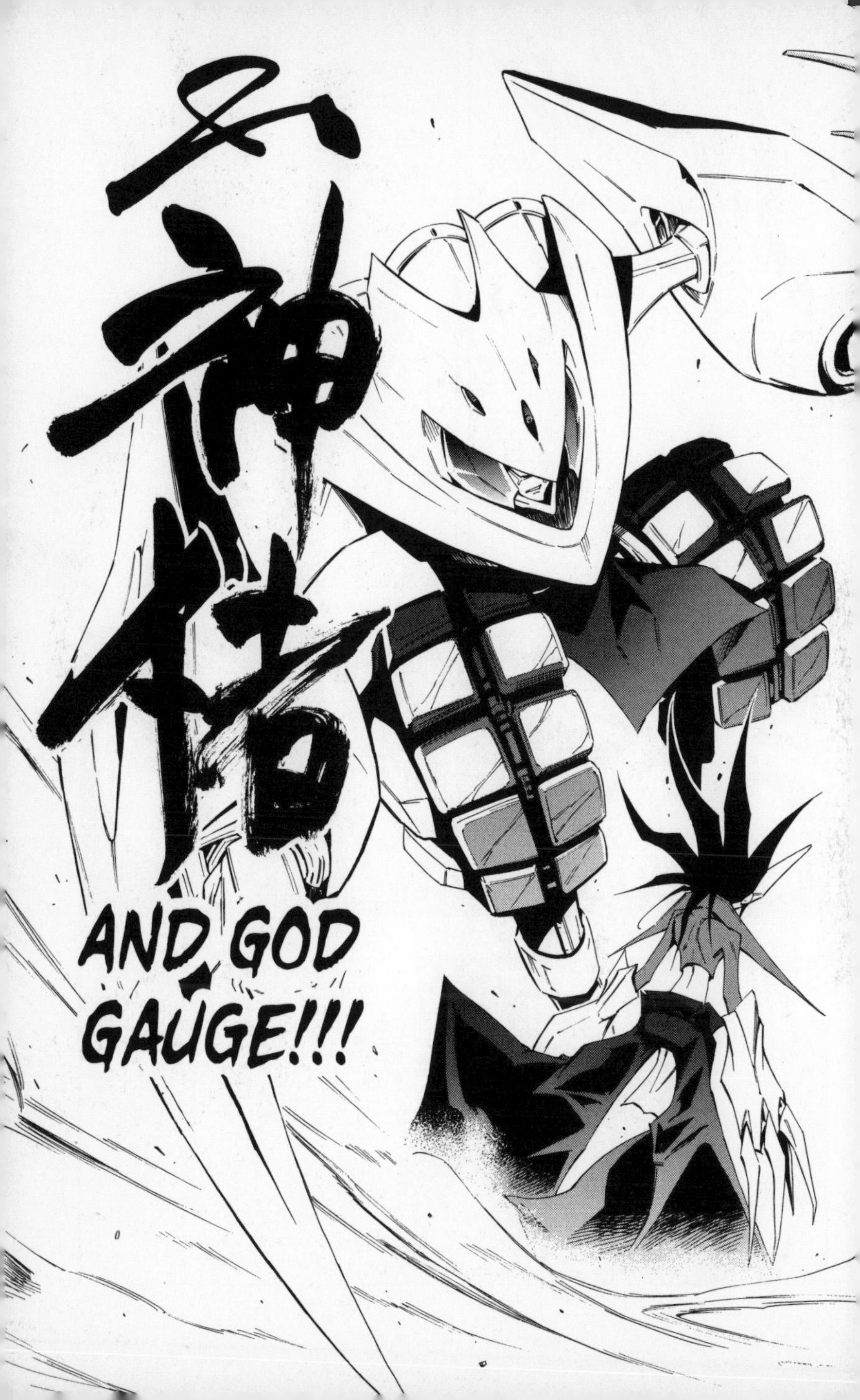
AND GOD GAUGE!!!

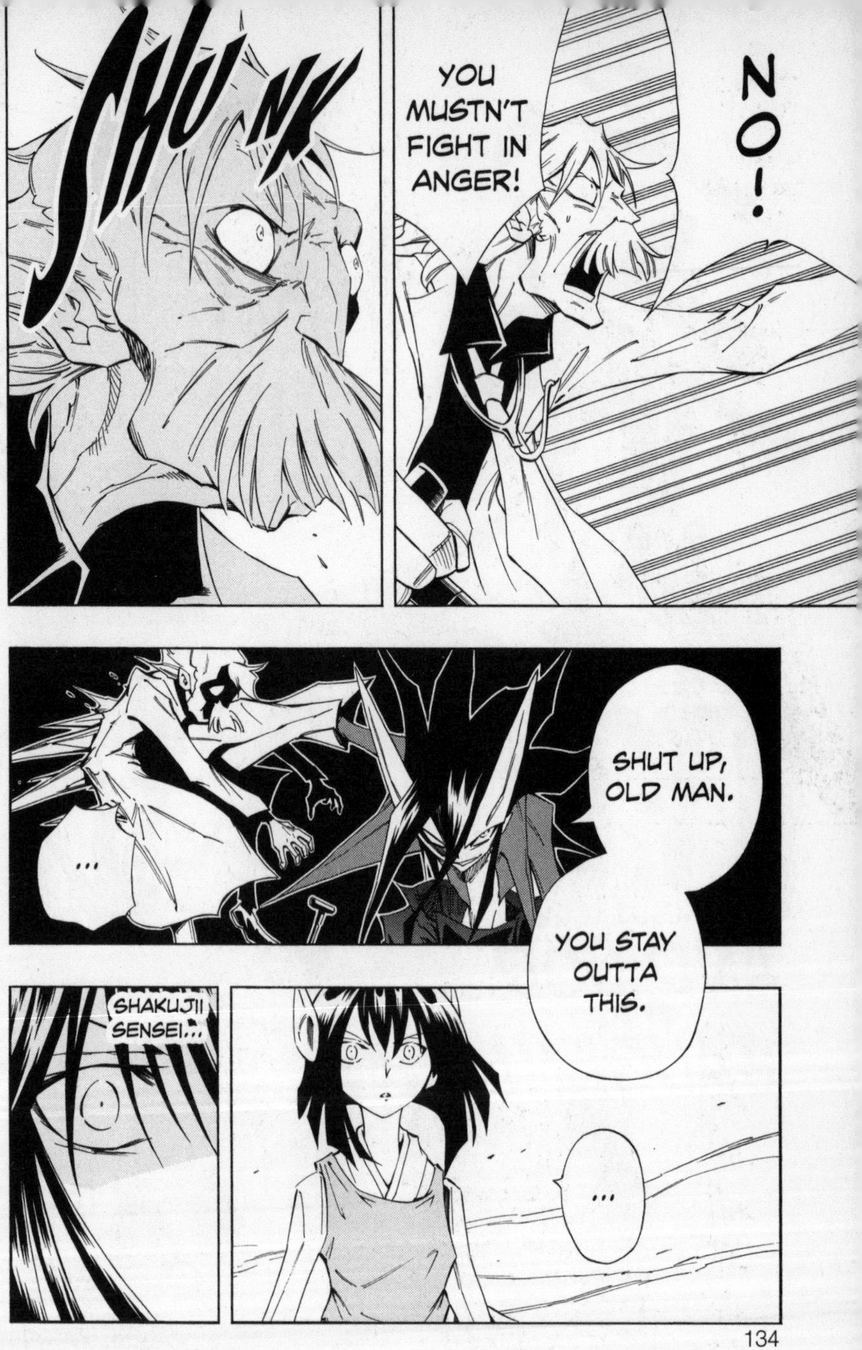
NO!
YOU MUSTN'T FIGHT IN ANGER!
SHUNK
SHUT UP, OLD MAN.
YOU STAY OUTTA THIS.
...
...
SHAKUJII SENSEI...

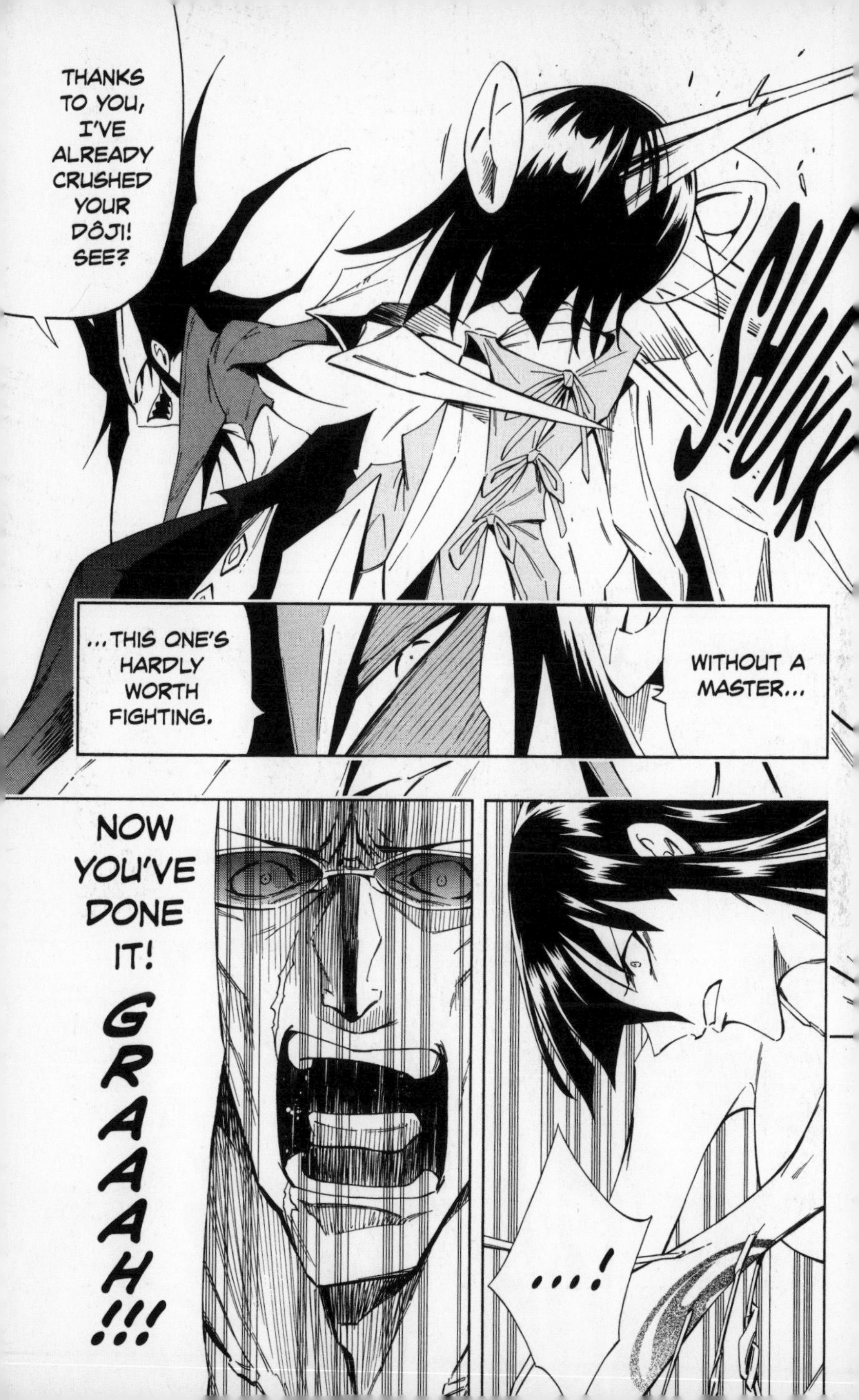
THANKS TO YOU, I'VE ALREADY CRUSHED YOUR DÔJI! SEE?
SHUKK
WITHOUT A MASTER...
...THIS ONE'S HARDLY WORTH FIGHTING.
...!
NOW YOU'VE DONE IT!
GRAAAAH!!!

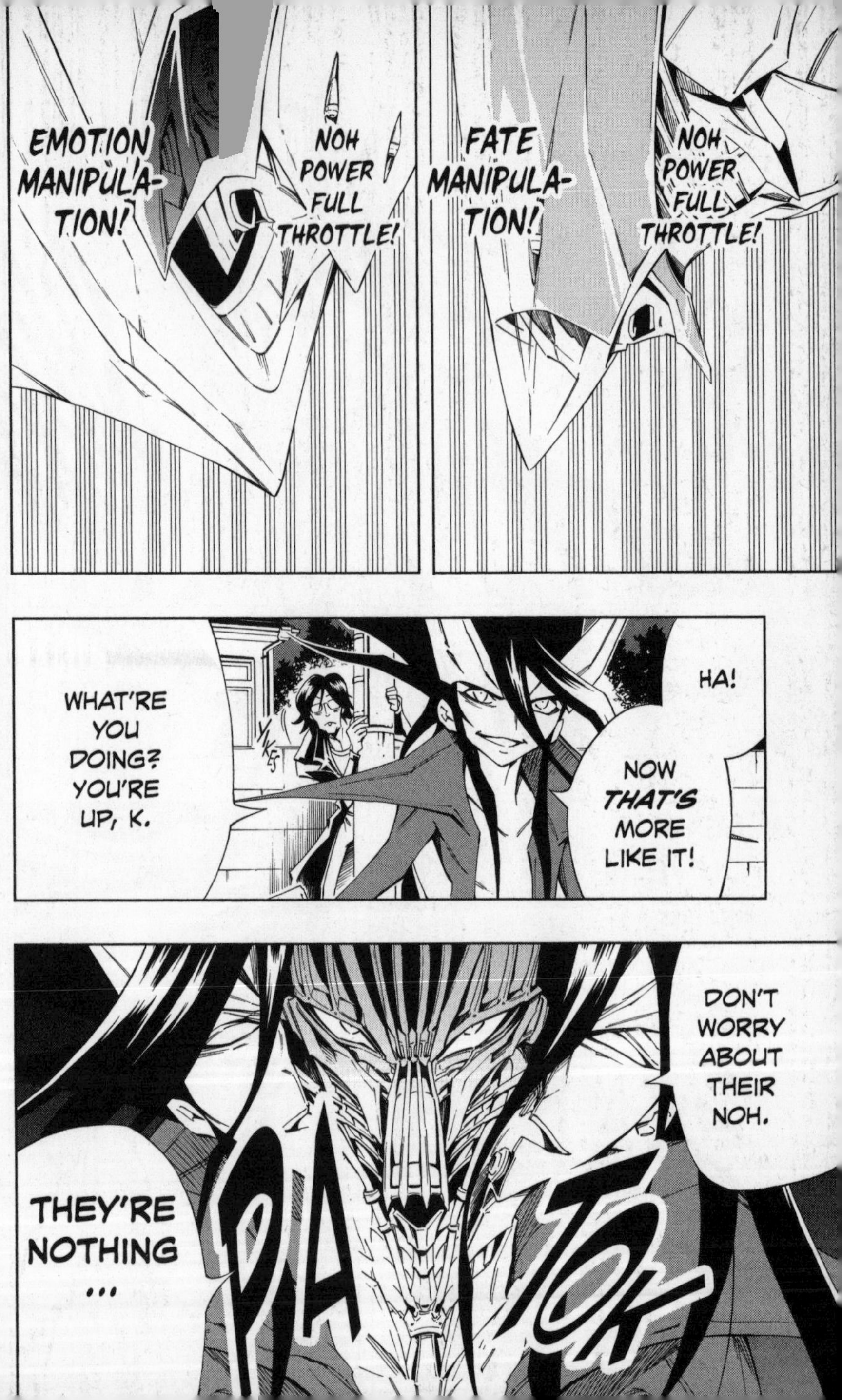
NOH POWER FULL THROTTLE!
FATE MANIPULA-TION!
NOH POWER FULL THROTTLE!
EMOTION MANIPULA-TION!
HA!
NOW *THAT'S* MORE LIKE IT!
YIKES
WHAT'RE YOU DOING? YOU'RE UP, K.
DON'T WORRY ABOUT THEIR NOH.
PA TOK
THEY'RE NOTHING ...

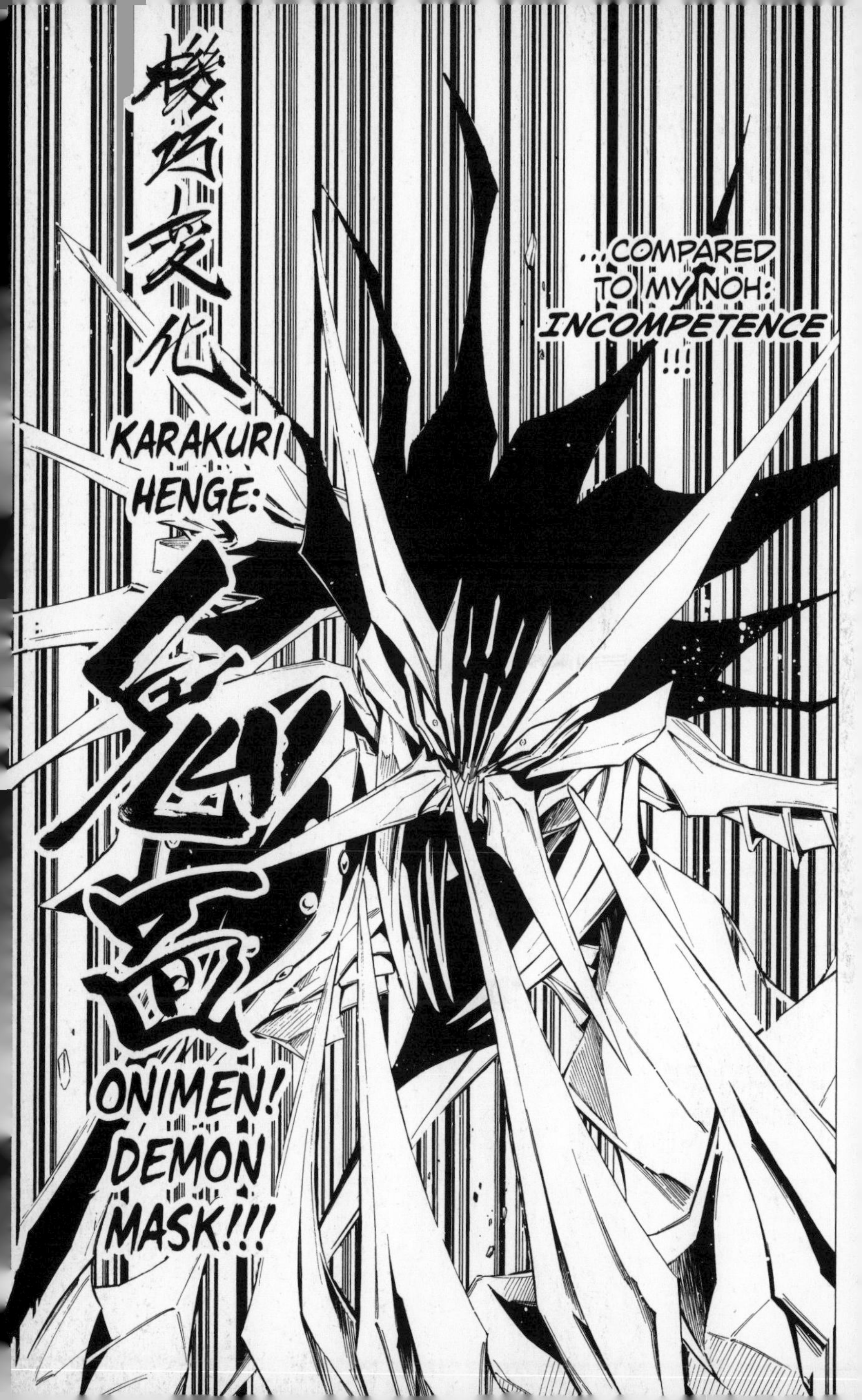
...COMPARED TO MY NOH: INCOMPETENCE !!!
機巧変化
KARAKURI HENGE:
鬼面
ONIMEN! DEMON MASK!!!

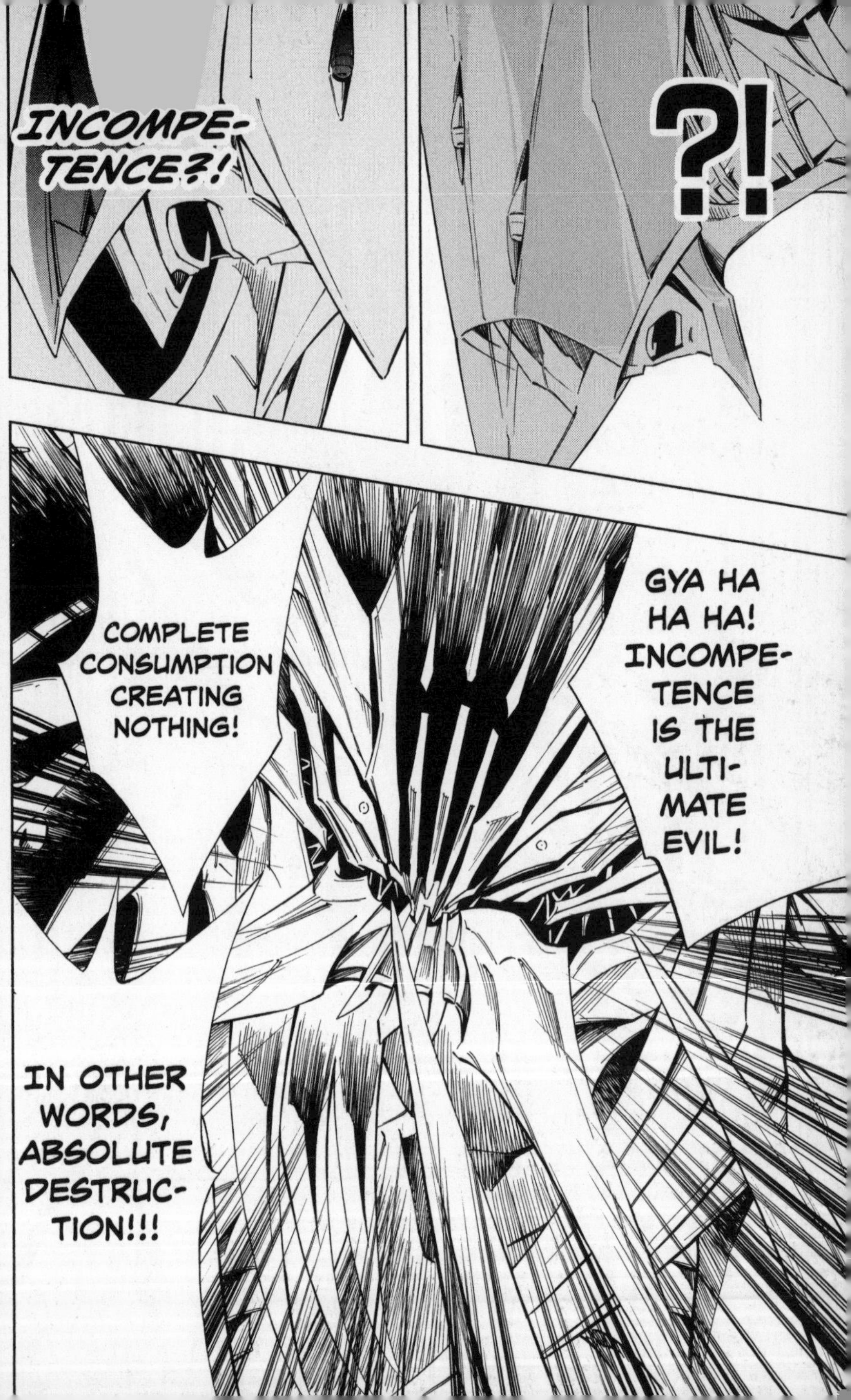
?!
INCOMPE-TENCE?!
GYA HA HA HA! INCOMPE-TENCE IS THE ULTI-MATE EVIL!
COMPLETE CONSUMPTION CREATING NOTHING!
IN OTHER WORDS, ABSOLUTE DESTRUC-TION!!!

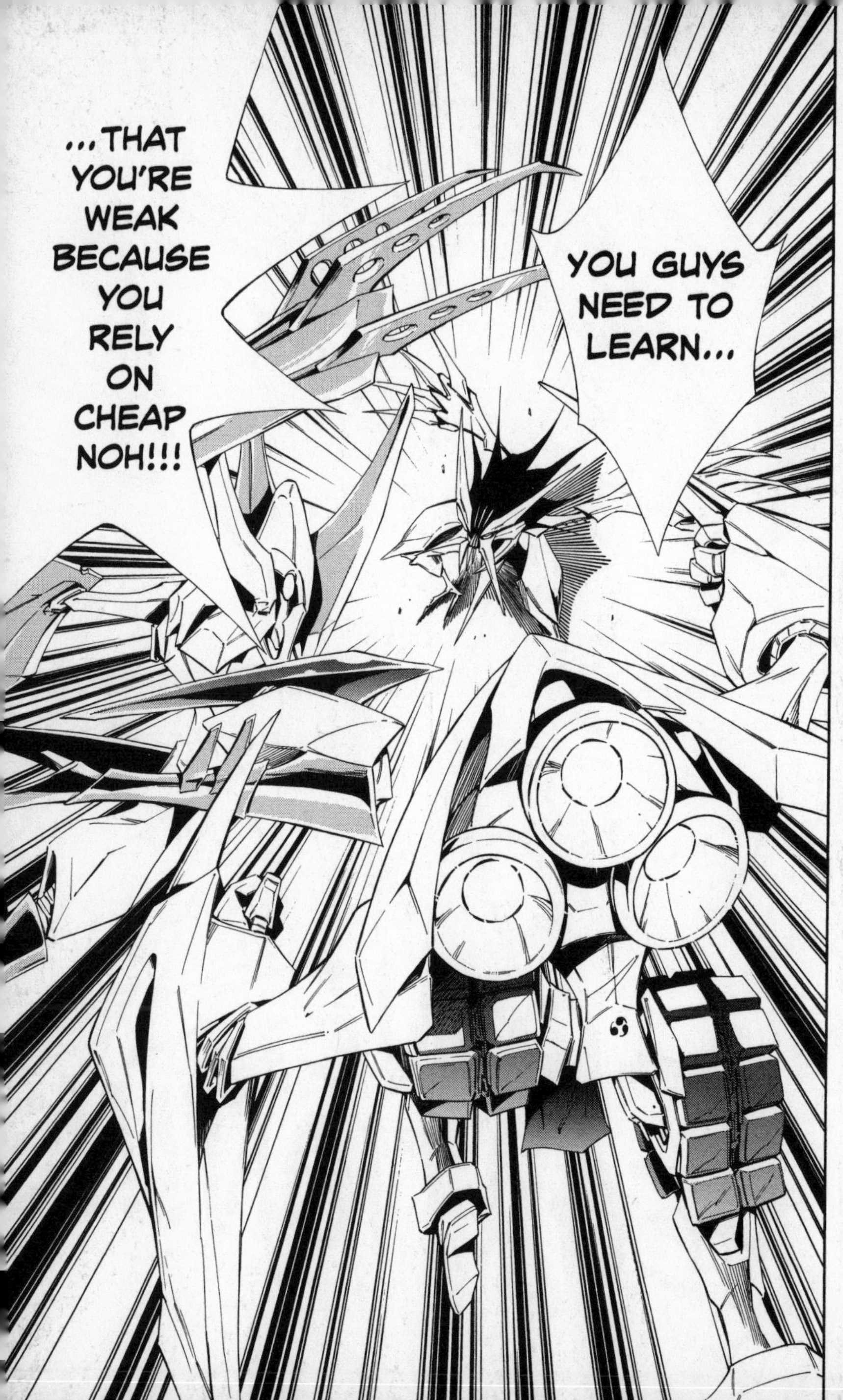
YOU GUYS NEED TO LEARN...
...THAT YOU'RE WEAK BECAUSE YOU RELY ON CHEAP NOH!!!

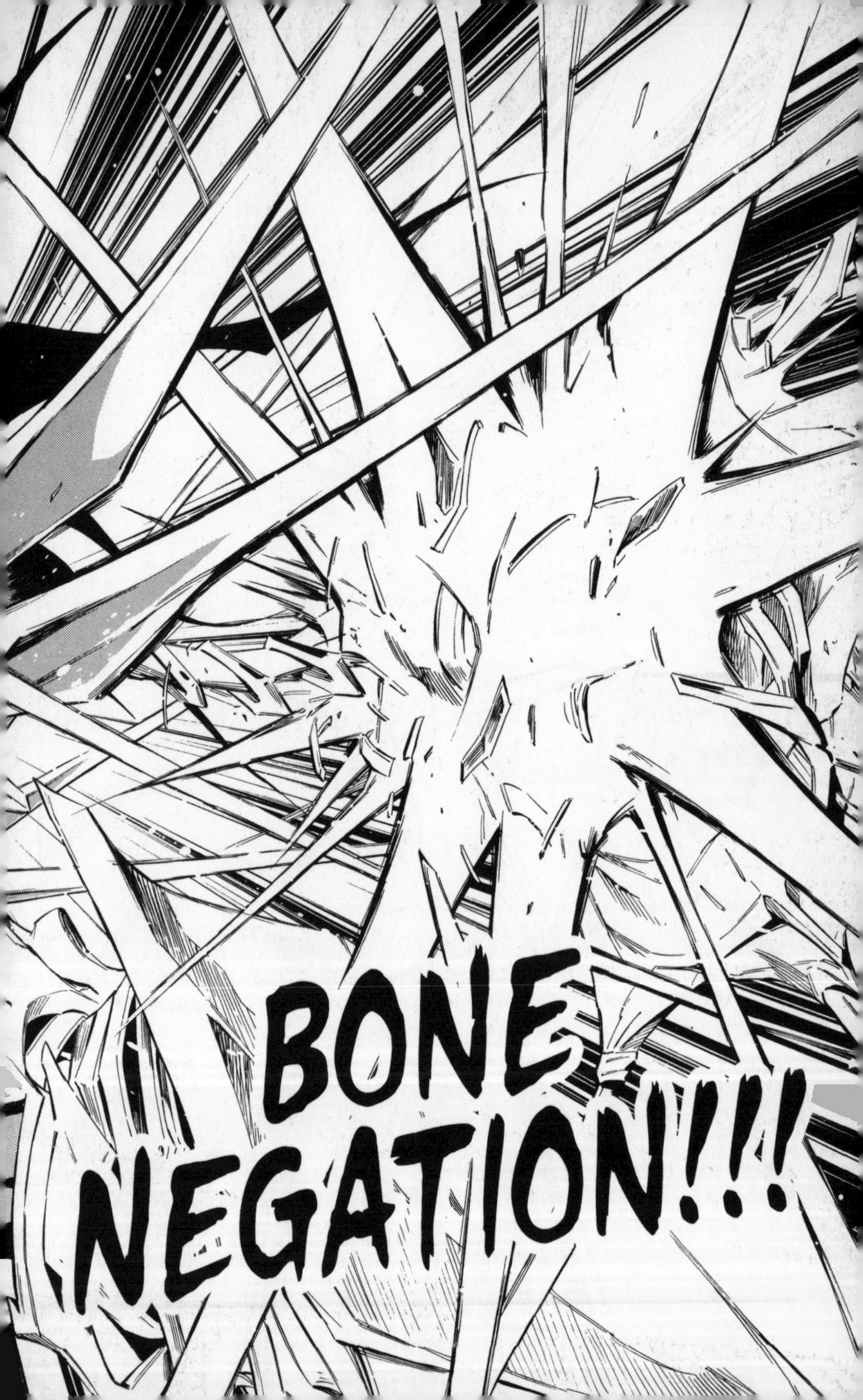
BONE NEGATION!!!

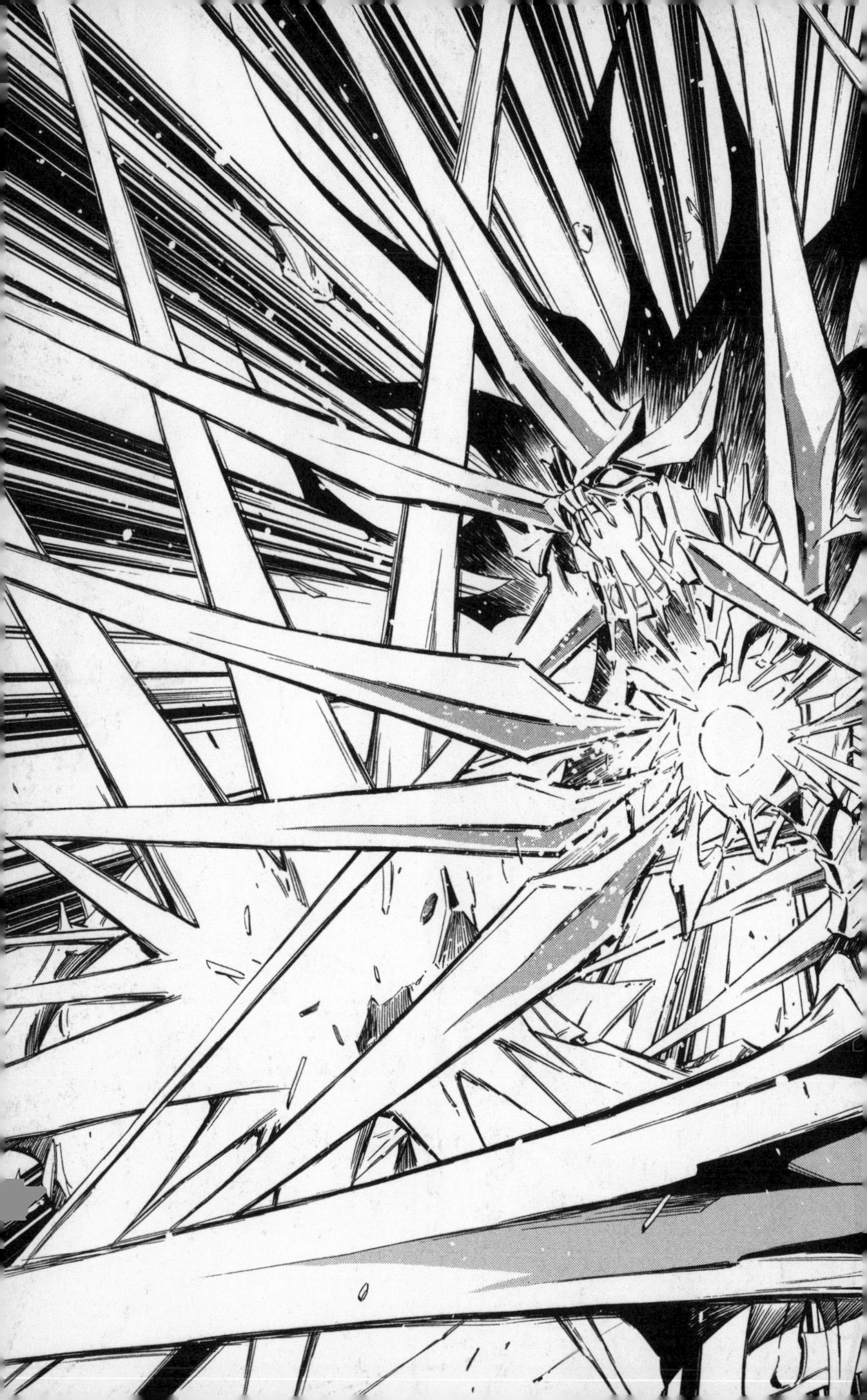

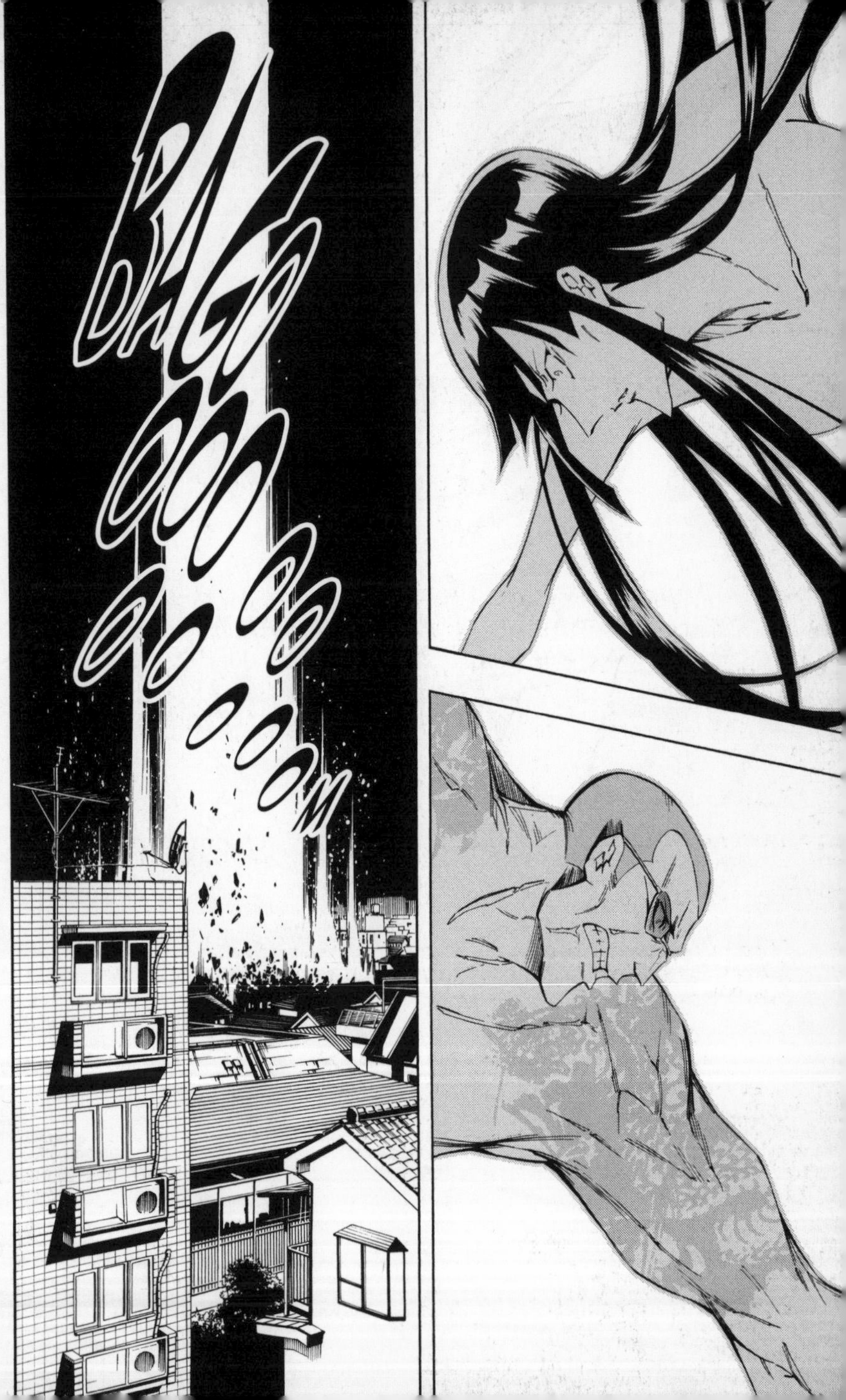
BAGOOOOOOOOOOM

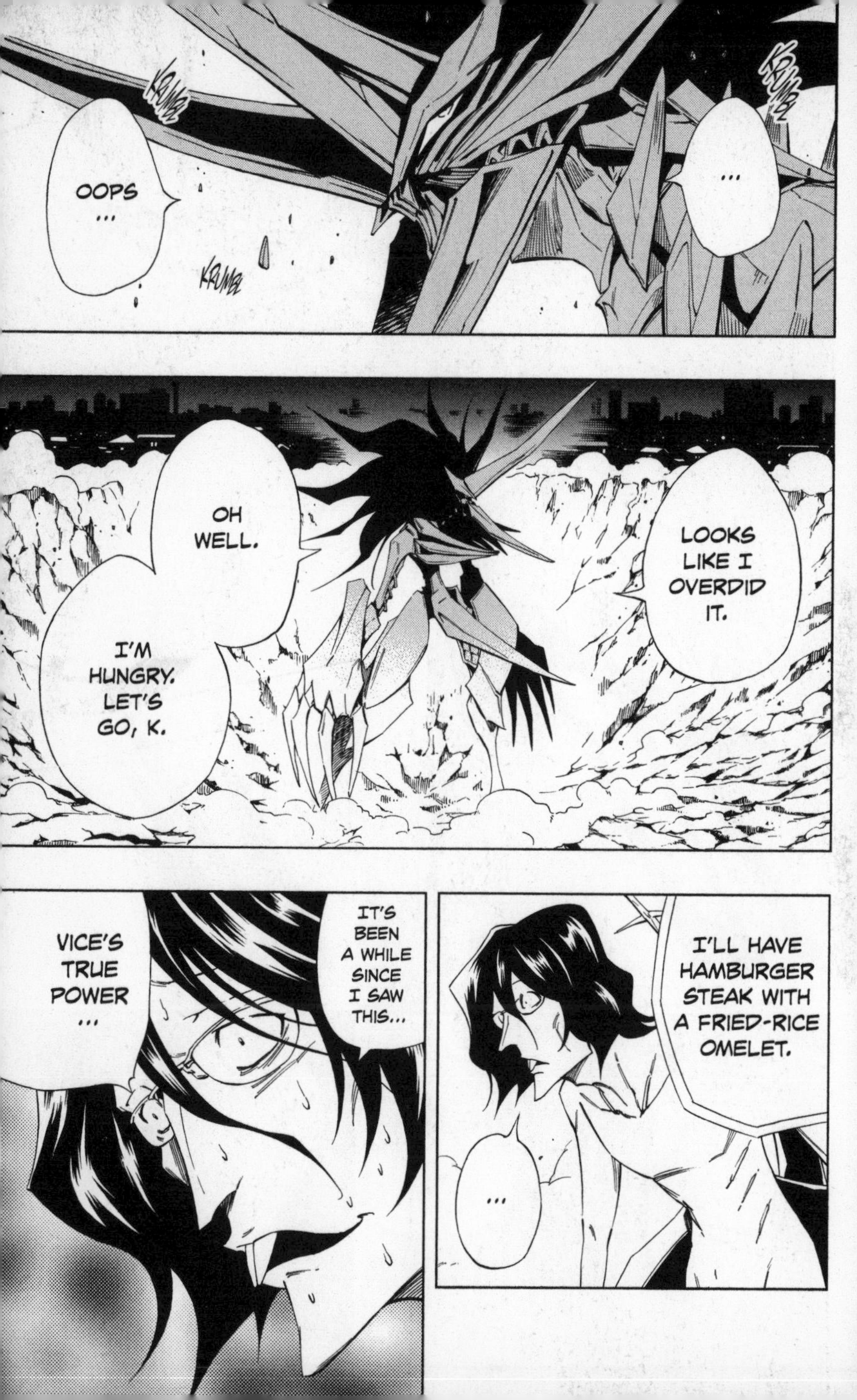
KRUMBL
...
KRUMBL
OOPS ...
KRUMBL
LOOKS LIKE I OVERDID IT.
OH WELL.
I'M HUNGRY. LET'S GO, K.
I'LL HAVE HAMBURGER STEAK WITH A FRIED-RICE OMELET.
...
IT'S BEEN A WHILE SINCE I SAW THIS...
VICE'S TRUE POWER ...

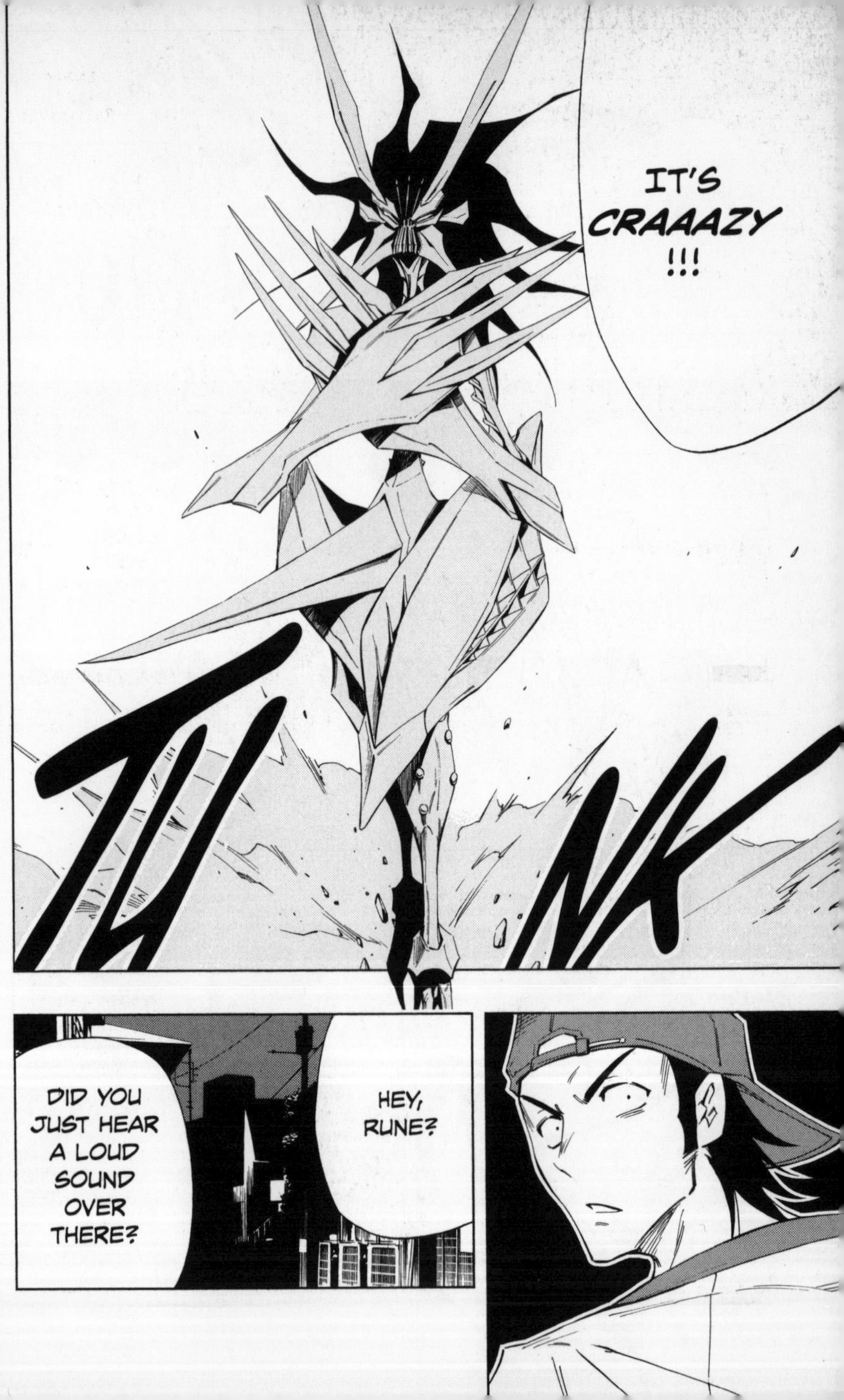
IT'S CRAAAZY!!!
TUNK
HEY, RUNE?
DID YOU JUST HEAR A LOUD SOUND OVER THERE?

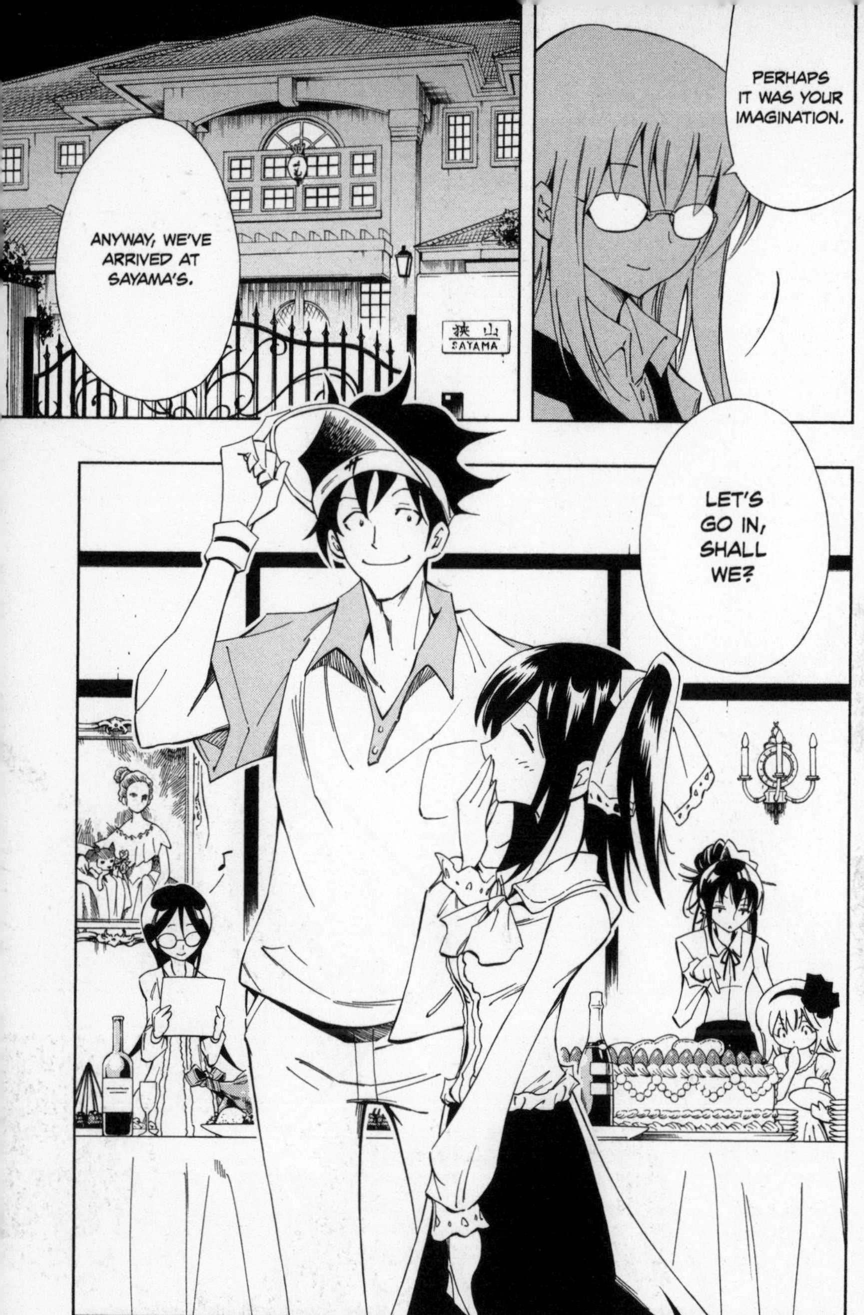
PERHAPS IT WAS YOUR IMAGINATION.
ANYWAY, WE'VE ARRIVED AT SAYAMA'S.
SAYAMA
LET'S GO IN, SHALL WE?

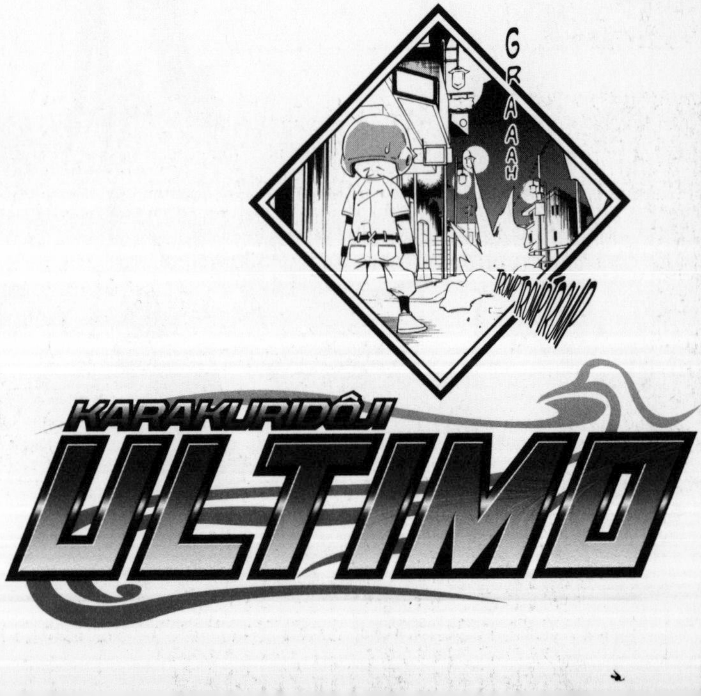
GRAAAAH
TROMP TROMP TROMP

KARAKURIDÔJI ULTIMO

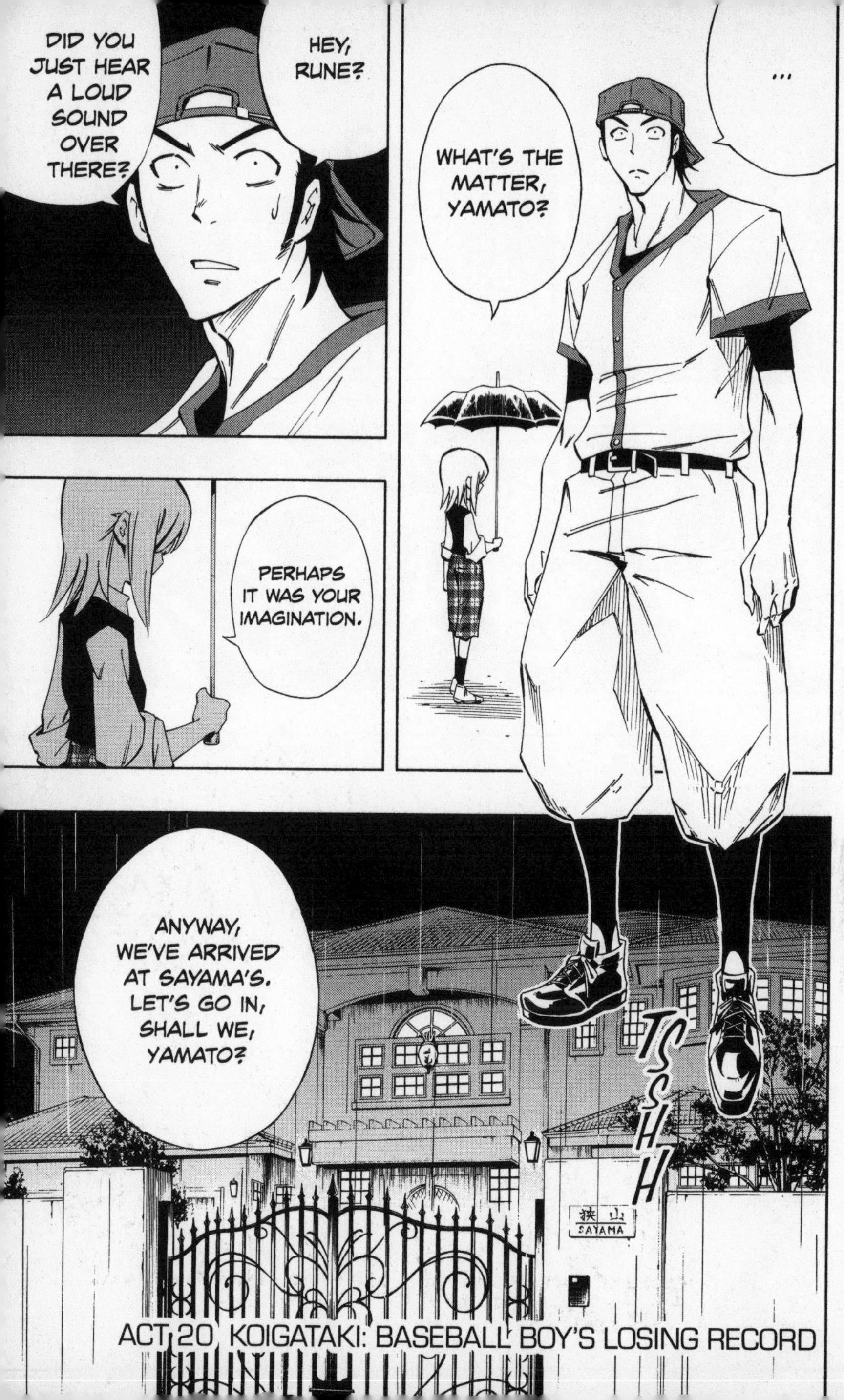
...
WHAT'S THE MATTER, YAMATO?
HEY, RUNE?
DID YOU JUST HEAR A LOUD SOUND OVER THERE?
PERHAPS IT WAS YOUR IMAGINATION.
TSSHH
ANYWAY, WE'VE ARRIVED AT SAYAMA'S. LET'S GO IN, SHALL WE, YAMATO?
狭山
SAYAMA
ACT 20 KOIGATAKI: BASEBALL BOY'S LOSING RECORD

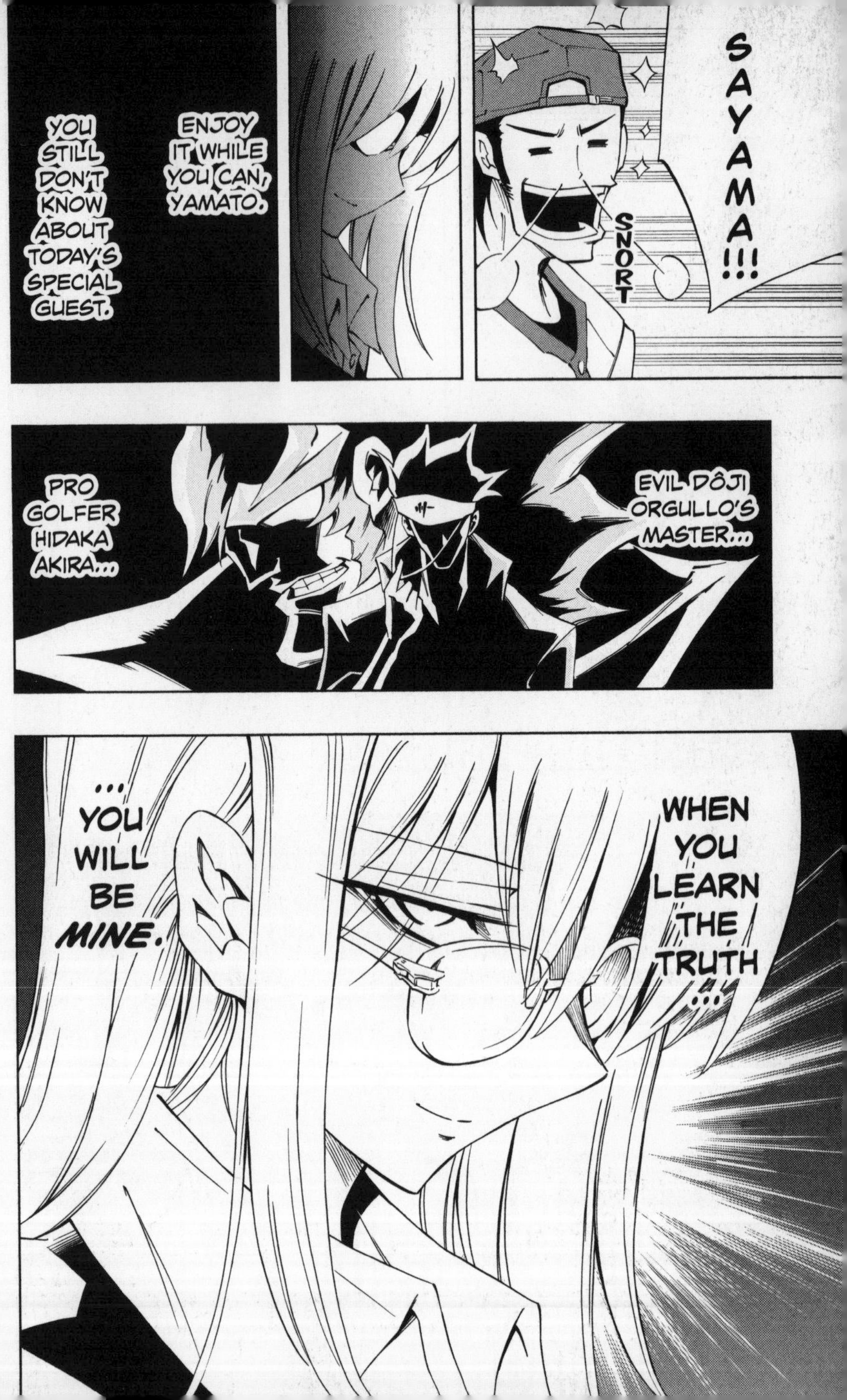
SAYAMA!!!
SNORT
ENJOY IT WHILE YOU CAN, YAMATO.
YOU STILL DON'T KNOW ABOUT TODAY'S SPECIAL GUEST.
EVIL DÔJI ORGULLO'S MASTER...
PRO GOLFER HIDAKA AKIRA...
WHEN YOU LEARN THE TRUTH...
...YOU WILL BE MINE.

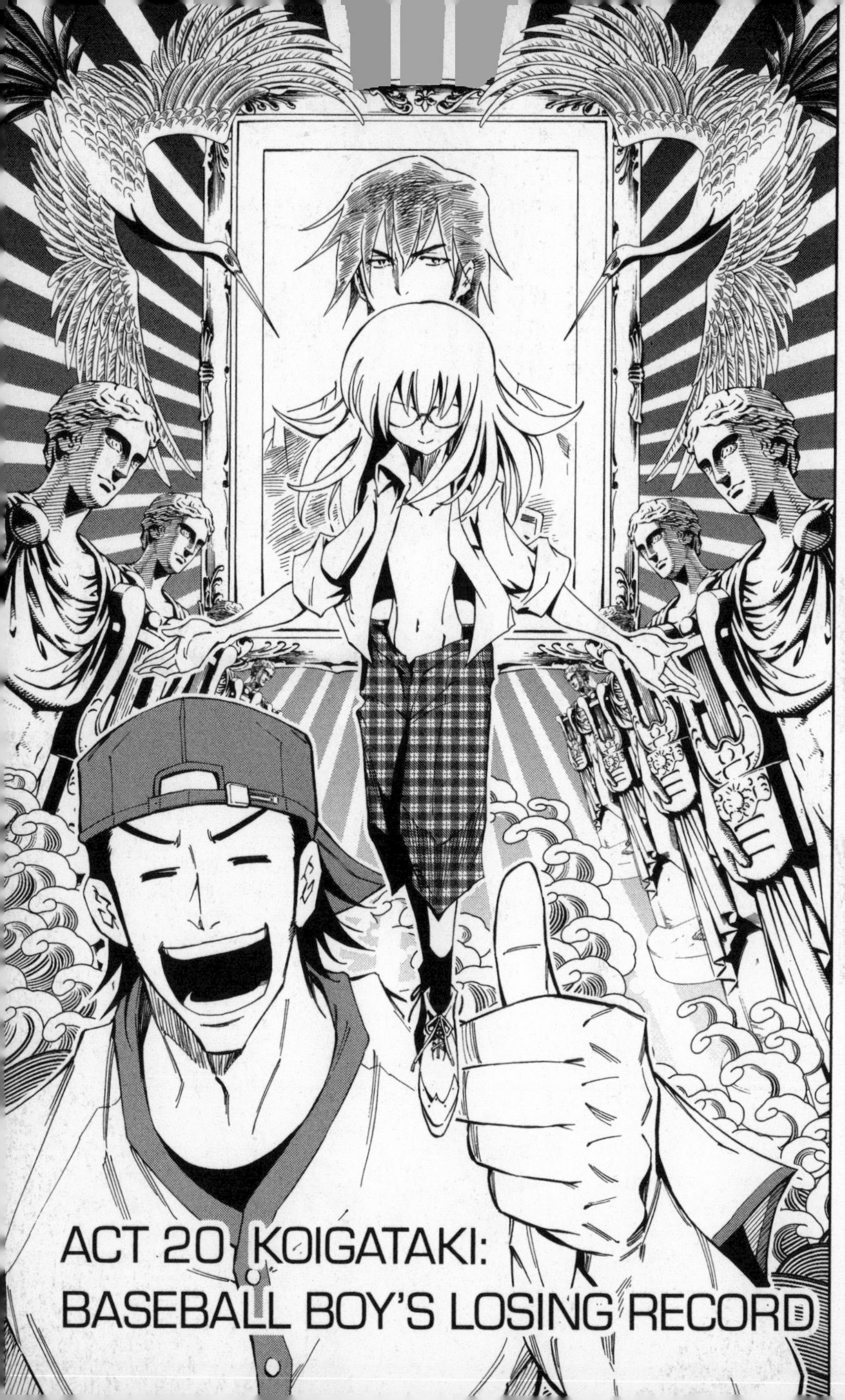

ACT 20 KOIGATAKI: BASEBALL BOY'S LOSING RECORD

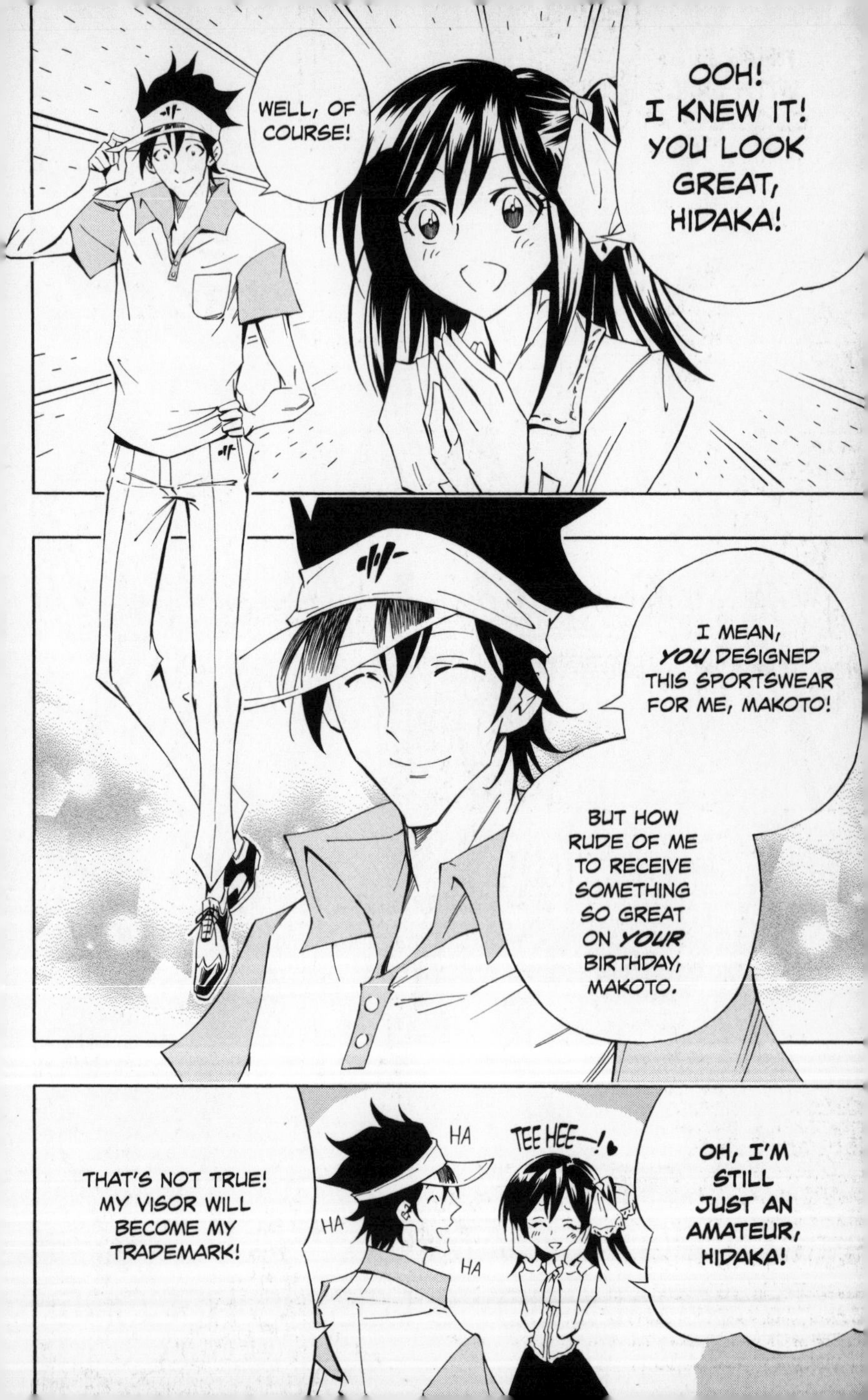
OOH! I KNEW IT! YOU LOOK GREAT, HIDAKA!
WELL, OF COURSE!
I MEAN, *YOU* DESIGNED THIS SPORTSWEAR FOR ME, MAKOTO!
BUT HOW RUDE OF ME TO RECEIVE SOMETHING SO GREAT ON *YOUR* BIRTHDAY, MAKOTO.
OH, I'M STILL JUST AN AMATEUR, HIDAKA!
TEE HEE—!♥
HA
HA
HA
THAT'S NOT TRUE! MY VISOR WILL BECOME MY TRADEMARK!

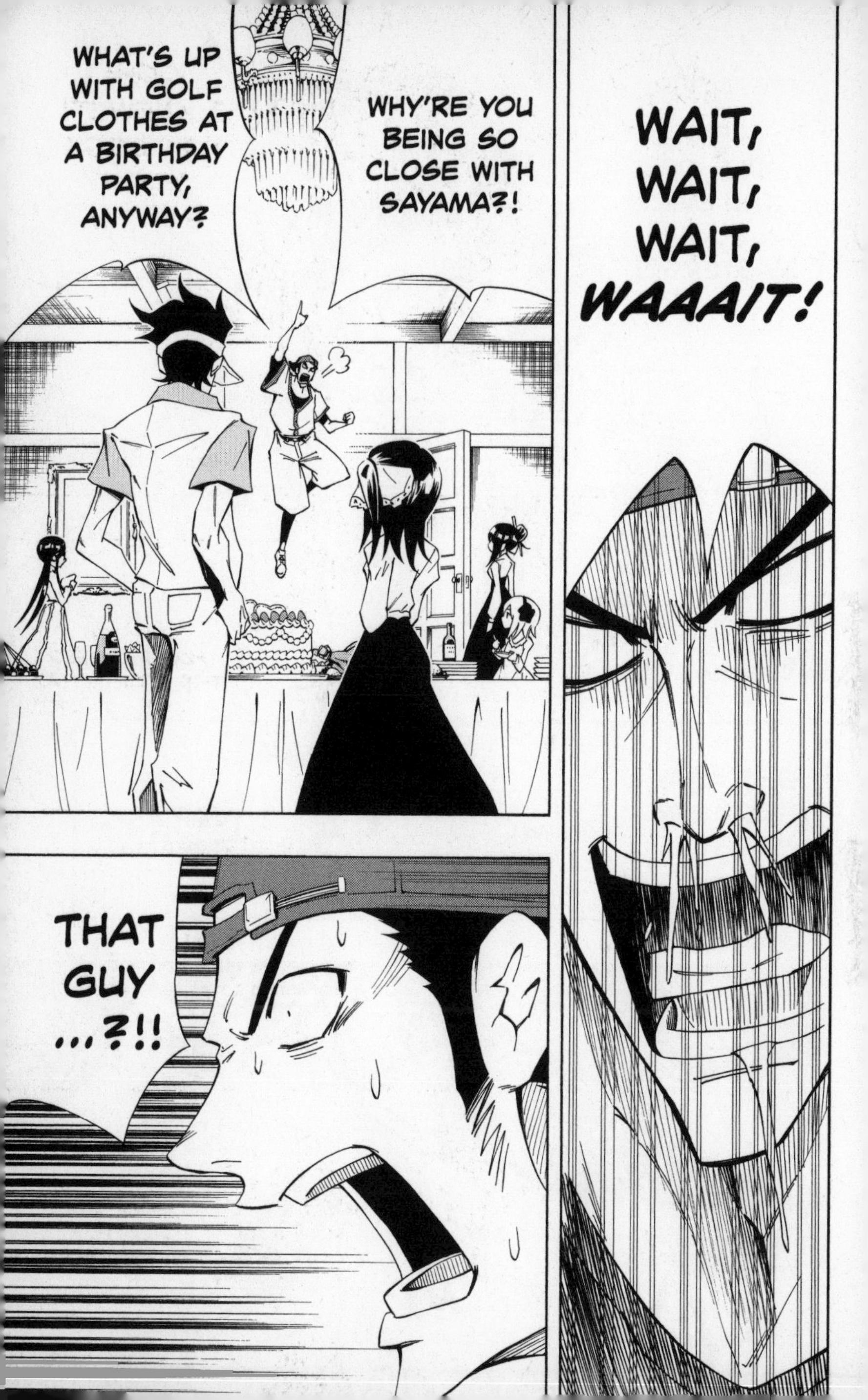
WAIT, WAIT, WAIT, WAAAIT!
WHY'RE YOU BEING SO CLOSE WITH SAYAMA?!
WHAT'S UP WITH GOLF CLOTHES AT A BIRTHDAY PARTY, ANYWAY?
THAT GUY ...?!!

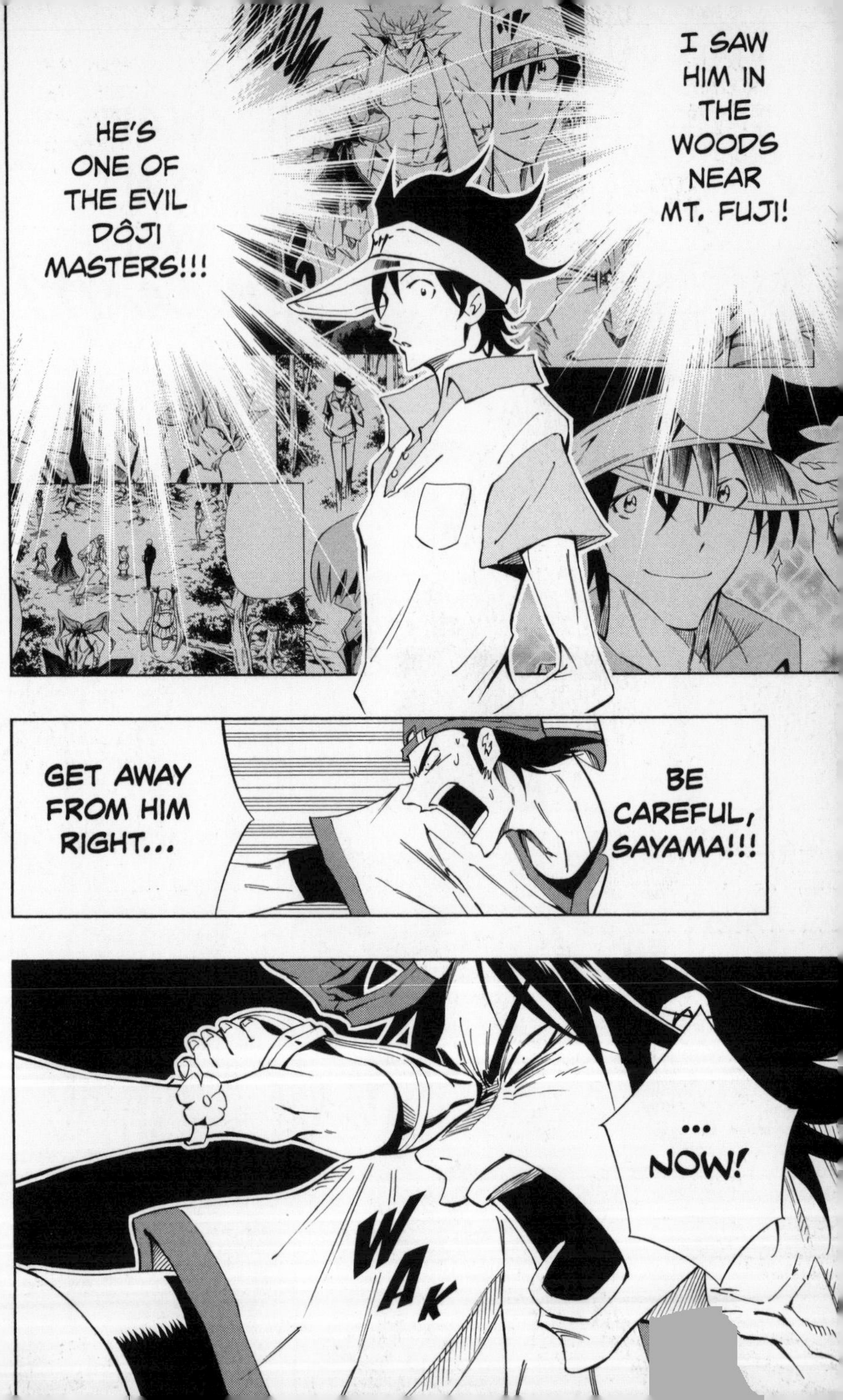
I SAW HIM IN THE WOODS NEAR MT. FUJI!
HE'S ONE OF THE EVIL DÔJI MASTERS!!!
BE CAREFUL, SAYAMA!!!
GET AWAY FROM HIM RIGHT...
...NOW!
WAK

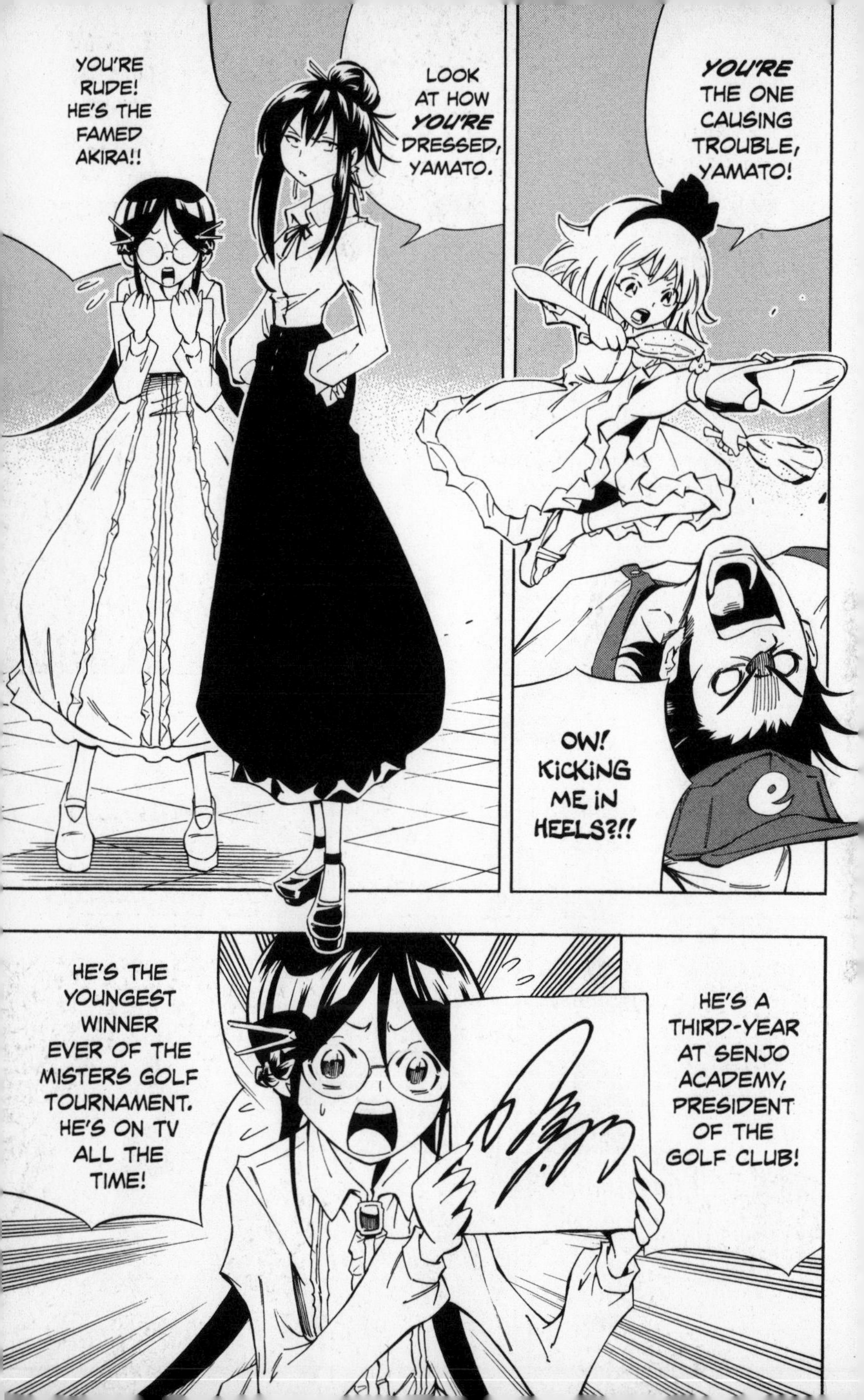

YOU'RE THE ONE CAUSING TROUBLE, YAMATO!
OW! KICKING ME IN HEELS?!!
LOOK AT HOW YOU'RE DRESSED, YAMATO.
YOU'RE RUDE! HE'S THE FAMED AKIRA!!
HE'S A THIRD-YEAR AT SENJO ACADEMY, PRESIDENT OF THE GOLF CLUB!
HE'S THE YOUNGEST WINNER EVER OF THE MISTERS GOLF TOURNAMENT. HE'S ON TV ALL THE TIME!

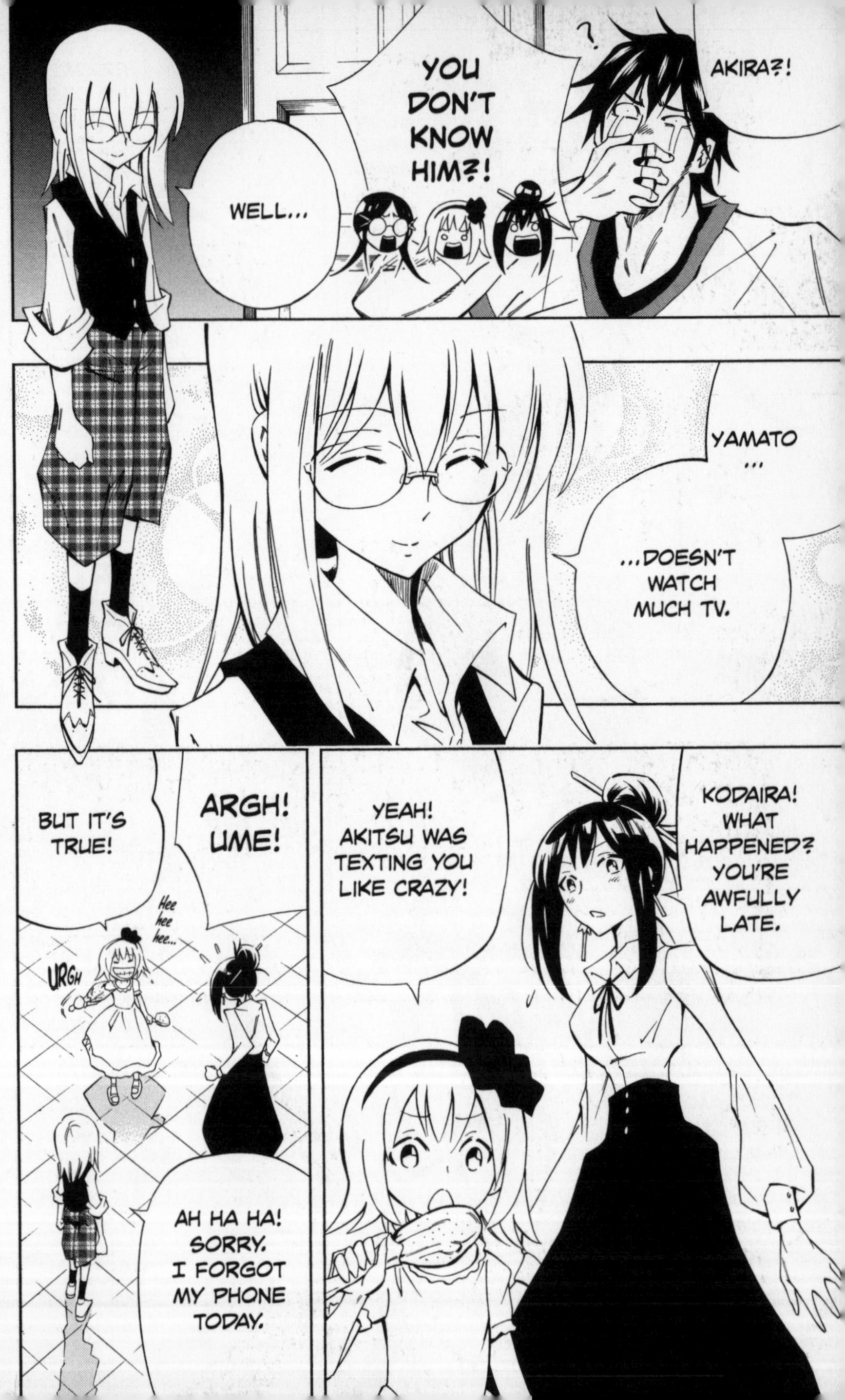
AKIRA?!
YOU DON'T KNOW HIM?!
WELL...
YAMATO ...
...DOESN'T WATCH MUCH TV.
KODAIRA! WHAT HAPPENED? YOU'RE AWFULLY LATE.
YEAH! AKITSU WAS TEXTING YOU LIKE CRAZY!
ARGH! UME!
BUT IT'S TRUE!
Hee hee hee...
URGH
AH HA HA! SORRY. I FORGOT MY PHONE TODAY.

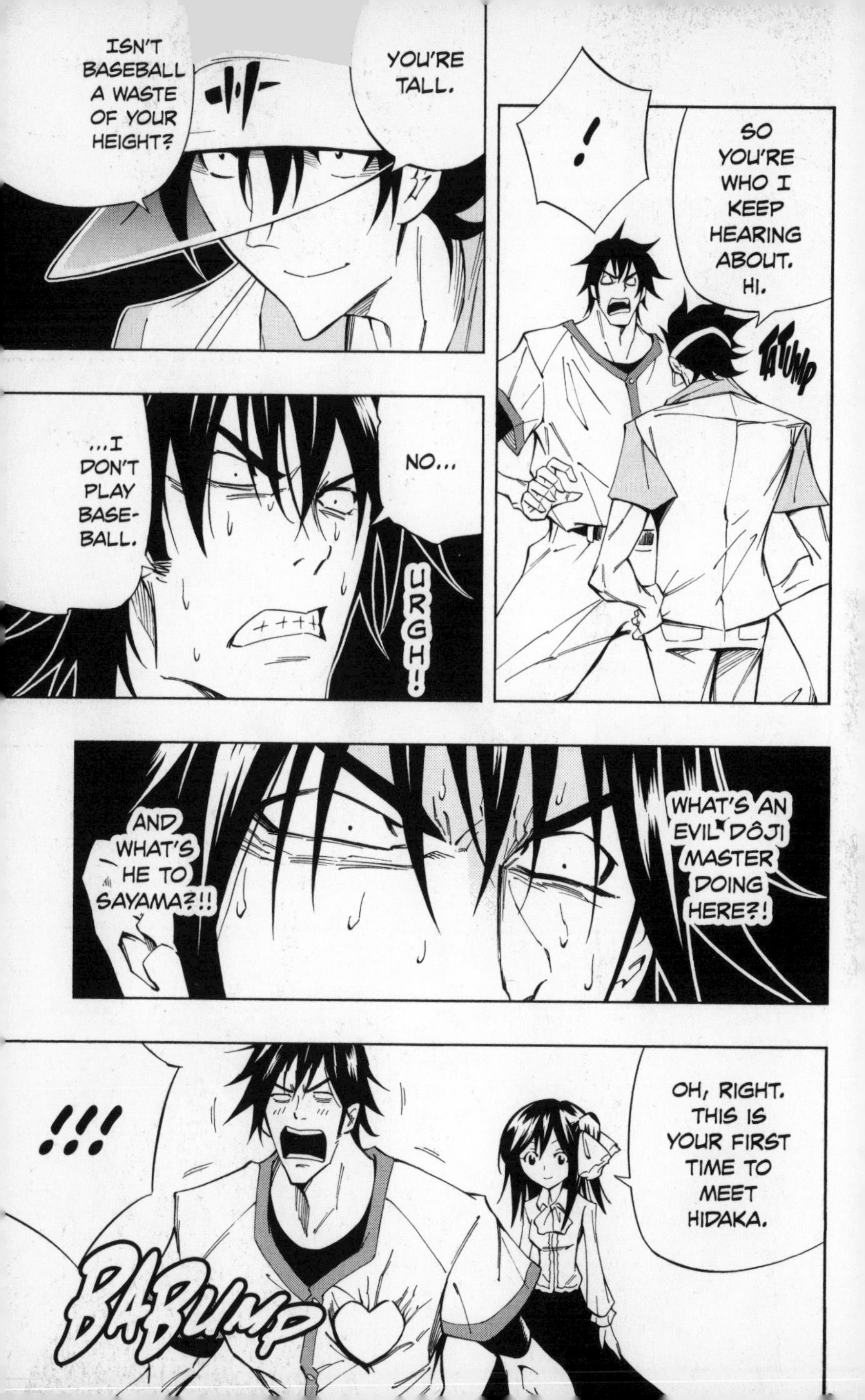
SO YOU'RE WHO I KEEP HEARING ABOUT. HI.
!
TATUMP
YOU'RE TALL.
ISN'T BASEBALL A WASTE OF YOUR HEIGHT?
NO...
...I DON'T PLAY BASE-BALL.
URGH!
WHAT'S AN EVIL DÔJI MASTER DOING HERE?!
AND WHAT'S HE TO SAYAMA?!!
OH, RIGHT. THIS IS YOUR FIRST TIME TO MEET HIDAKA.
!!!
BABUMP

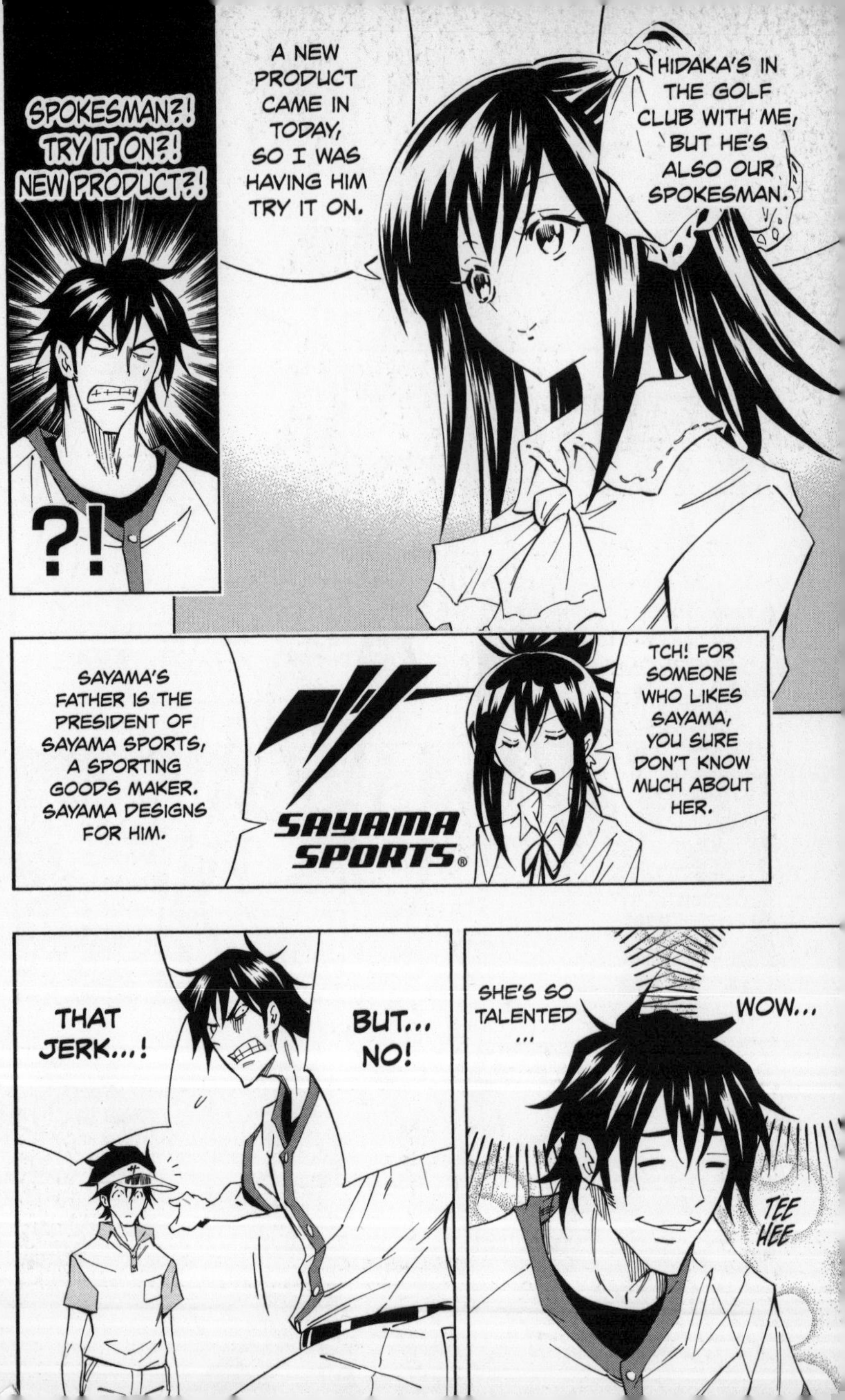
HIDAKA'S IN THE GOLF CLUB WITH ME, BUT HE'S ALSO OUR SPOKESMAN.
A NEW PRODUCT CAME IN TODAY, SO I WAS HAVING HIM TRY IT ON.
SPOKESMAN?! TRY IT ON?! NEW PRODUCT?!
?!
TCH! FOR SOMEONE WHO LIKES SAYAMA, YOU SURE DON'T KNOW MUCH ABOUT HER.
SAYAMA'S FATHER IS THE PRESIDENT OF SAYAMA SPORTS, A SPORTING GOODS MAKER. SAYAMA DESIGNS FOR HIM.
SAYAMA SPORTS®
WOW...
SHE'S SO TALENTED...
TEE HEE
BUT... NO!
THAT JERK...!

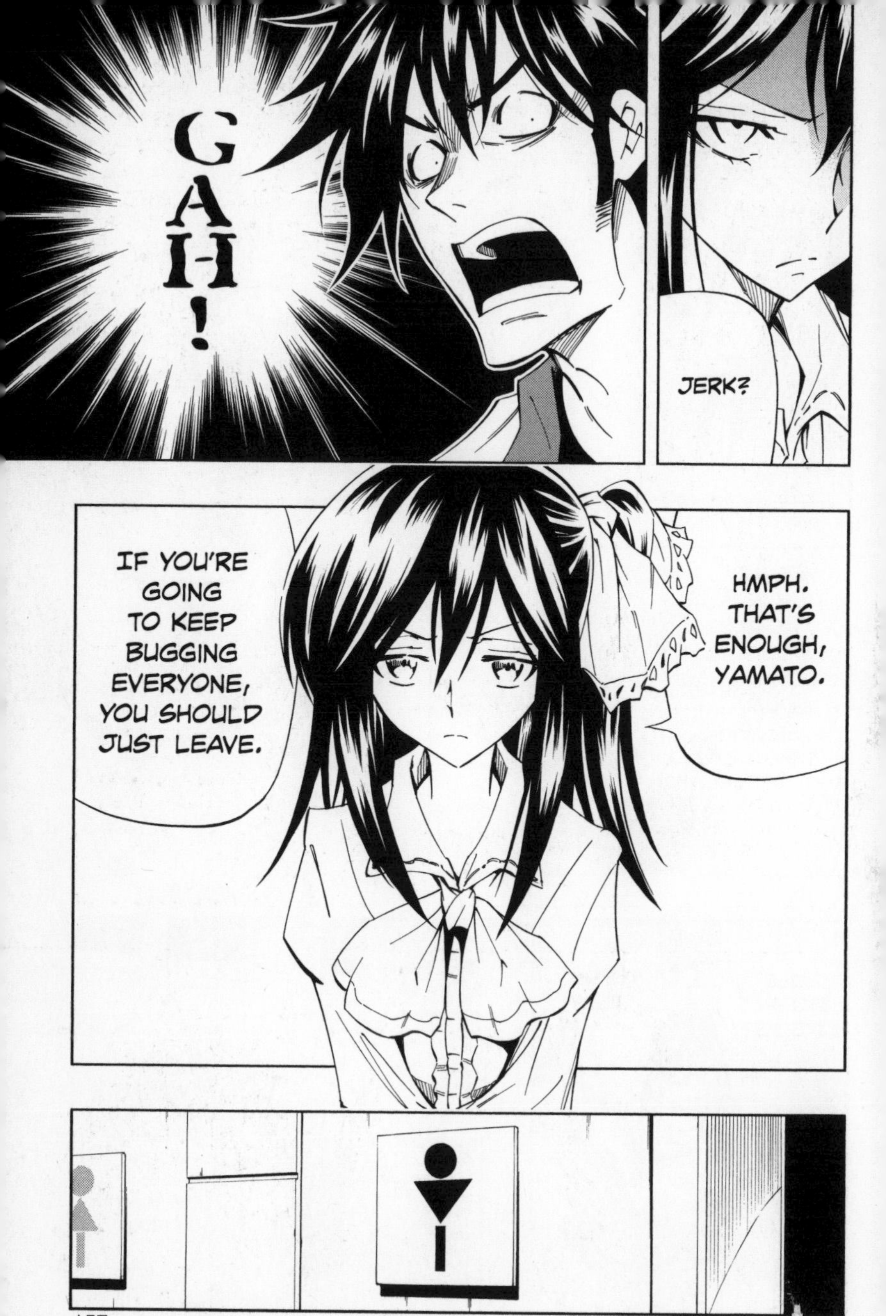
JERK?
GAH!
HMPH. THAT'S ENOUGH, YAMATO.
IF YOU'RE GOING TO KEEP BUGGING EVERYONE, YOU SHOULD JUST LEAVE.

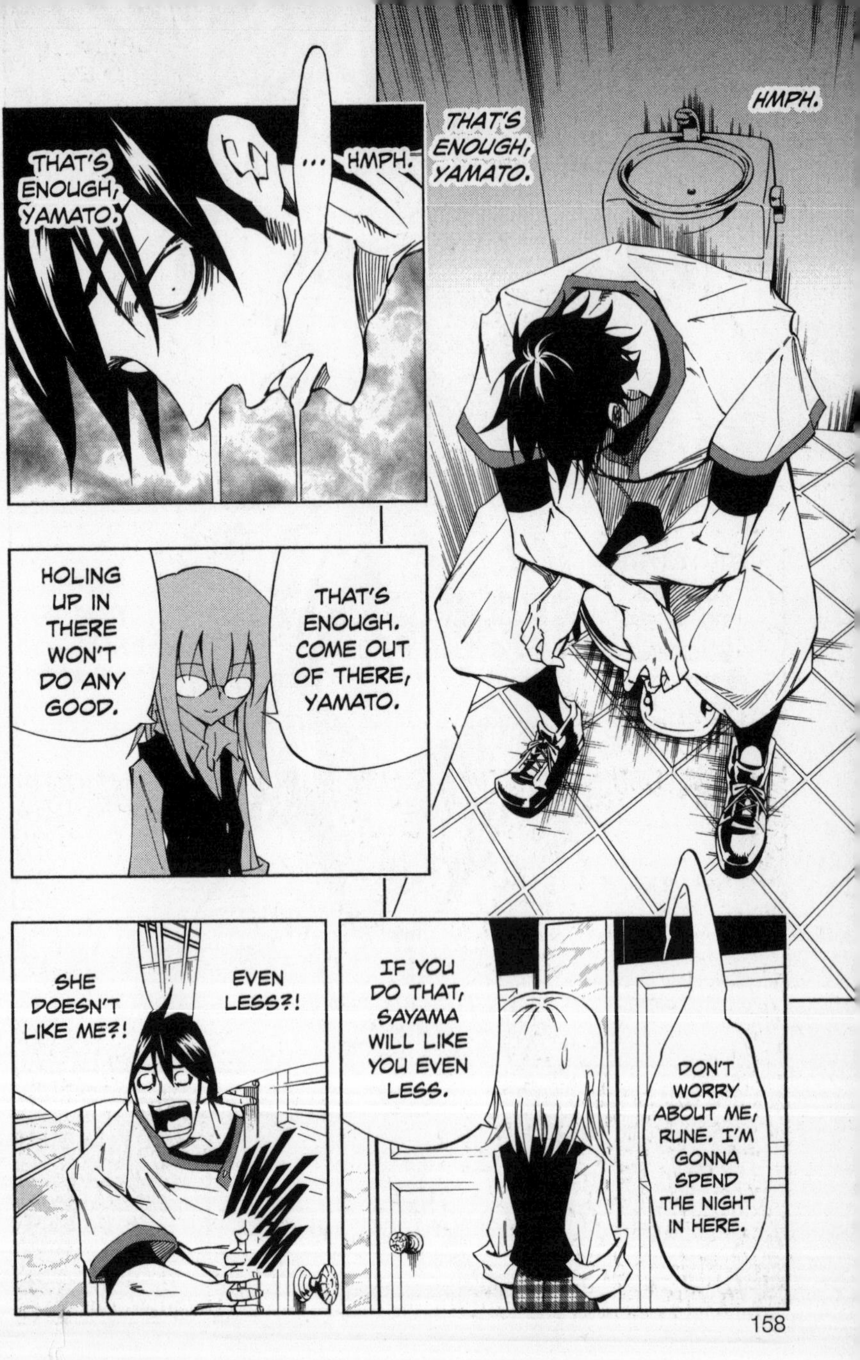
HMPH.
THAT'S ENOUGH, YAMATO.
... HMPH.
THAT'S ENOUGH, YAMATO.
THAT'S ENOUGH. COME OUT OF THERE, YAMATO.
HOLING UP IN THERE WON'T DO ANY GOOD.
DON'T WORRY ABOUT ME, RUNE. I'M GONNA SPEND THE NIGHT IN HERE.
IF YOU DO THAT, SAYAMA WILL LIKE YOU EVEN LESS.
EVEN LESS?!
SHE DOESN'T LIKE ME?!

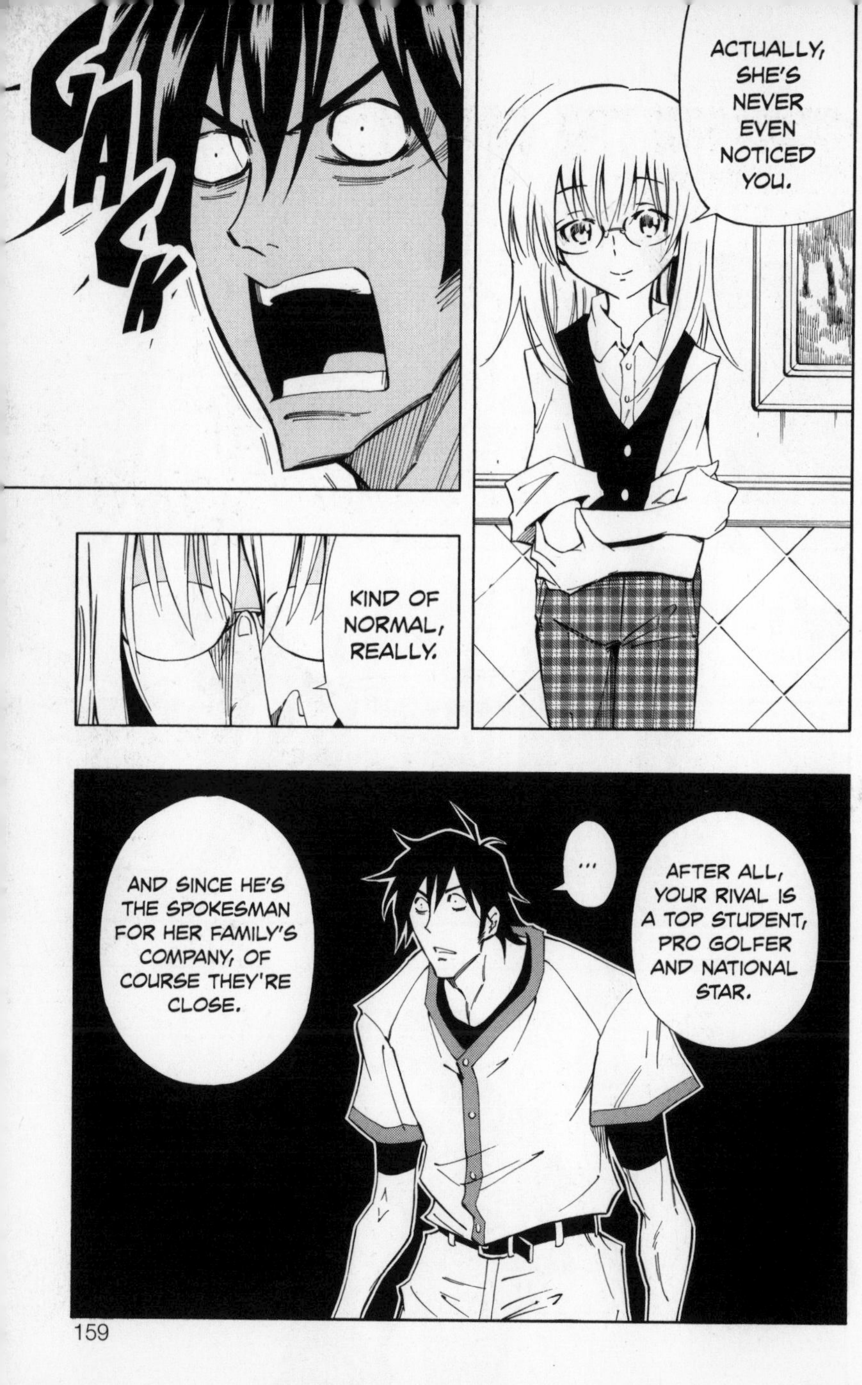
ACTUALLY, SHE'S NEVER EVEN NOTICED YOU.
GACK
KIND OF NORMAL, REALLY.
AFTER ALL, YOUR RIVAL IS A TOP STUDENT, PRO GOLFER AND NATIONAL STAR.
...
AND SINCE HE'S THE SPOKESMAN FOR HER FAMILY'S COMPANY, OF COURSE THEY'RE CLOSE.

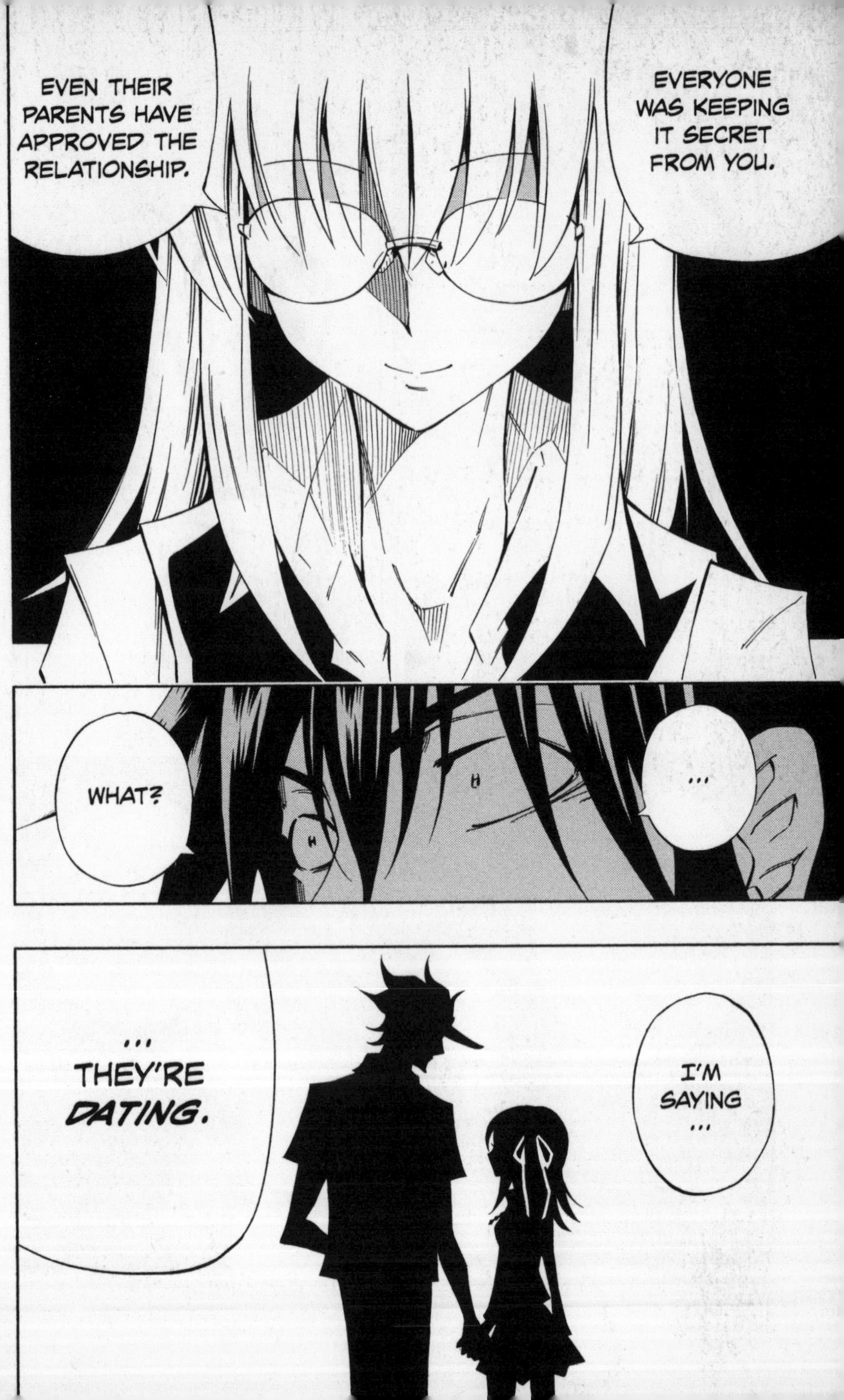
EVERYONE WAS KEEPING IT SECRET FROM YOU.
EVEN THEIR PARENTS HAVE APPROVED THE RELATIONSHIP.
...
WHAT?
I'M SAYING ...
... THEY'RE *DATING*.

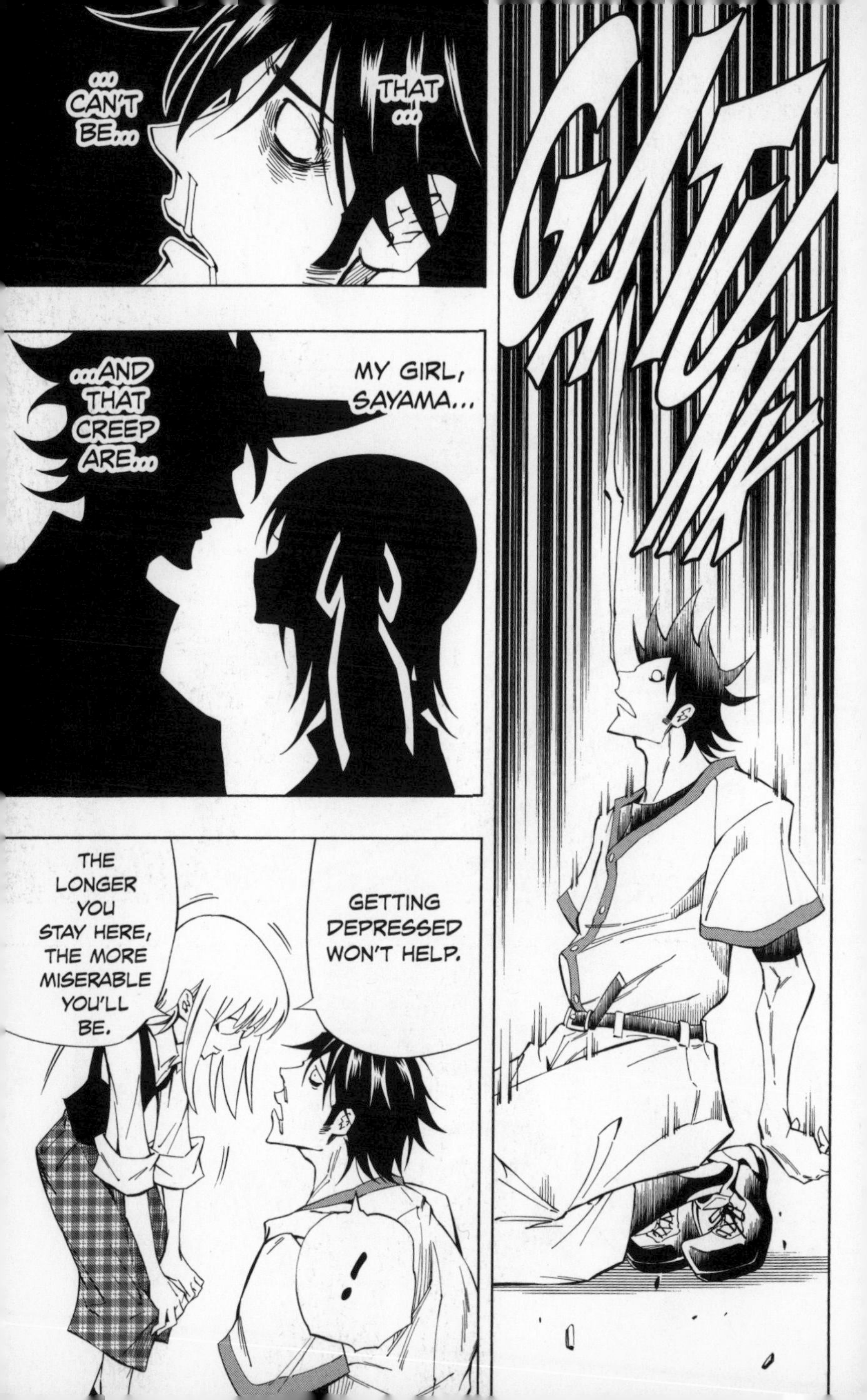
THAT ...
... CAN'T BE...
MY GIRL, SAYAMA...
...AND THAT CREEP ARE...
GETTING DEPRESSED WON'T HELP.
THE LONGER YOU STAY HERE, THE MORE MISERABLE YOU'LL BE.
!

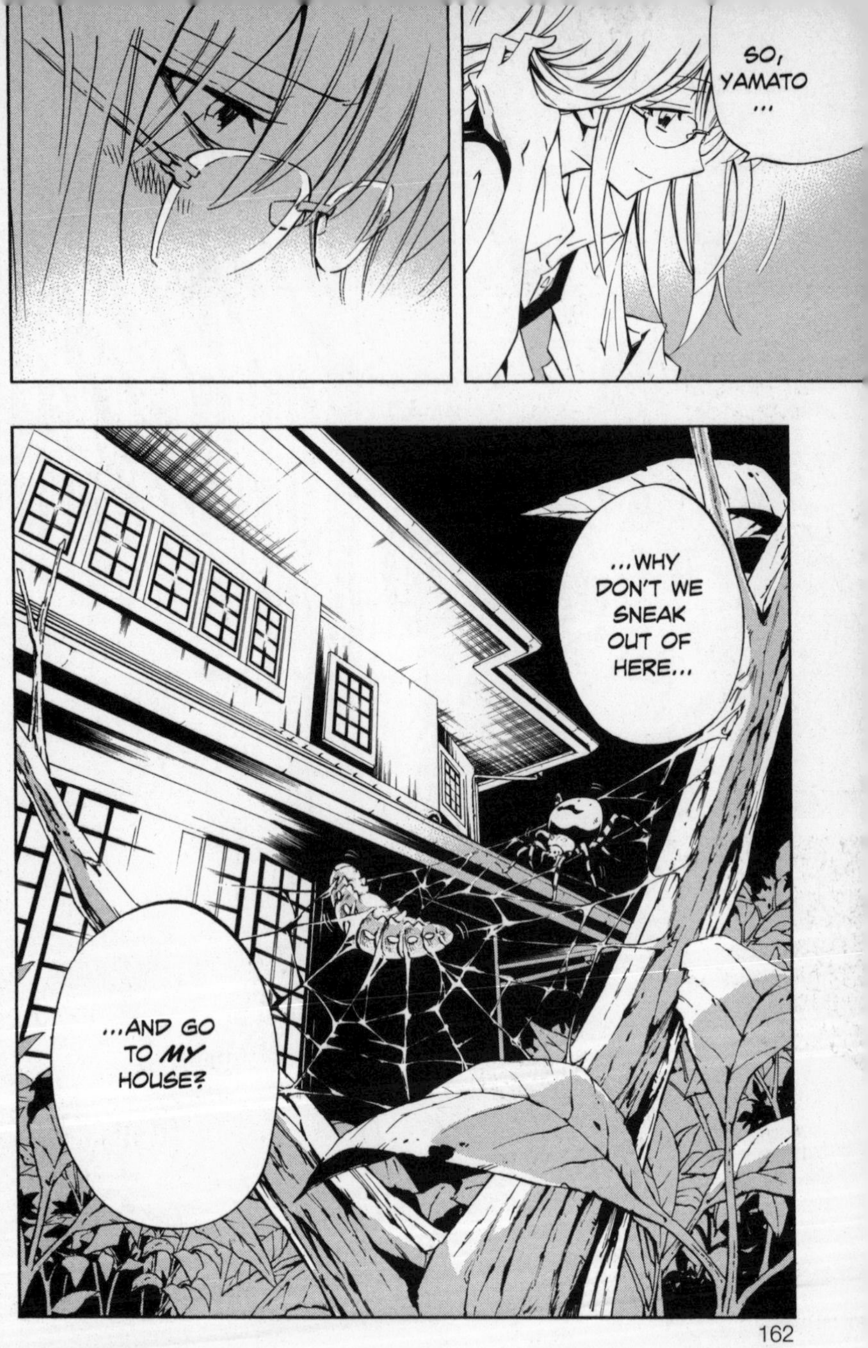
SO, YAMATO ...
...WHY DON'T WE SNEAK OUT OF HERE...
...AND GO TO *MY* HOUSE?

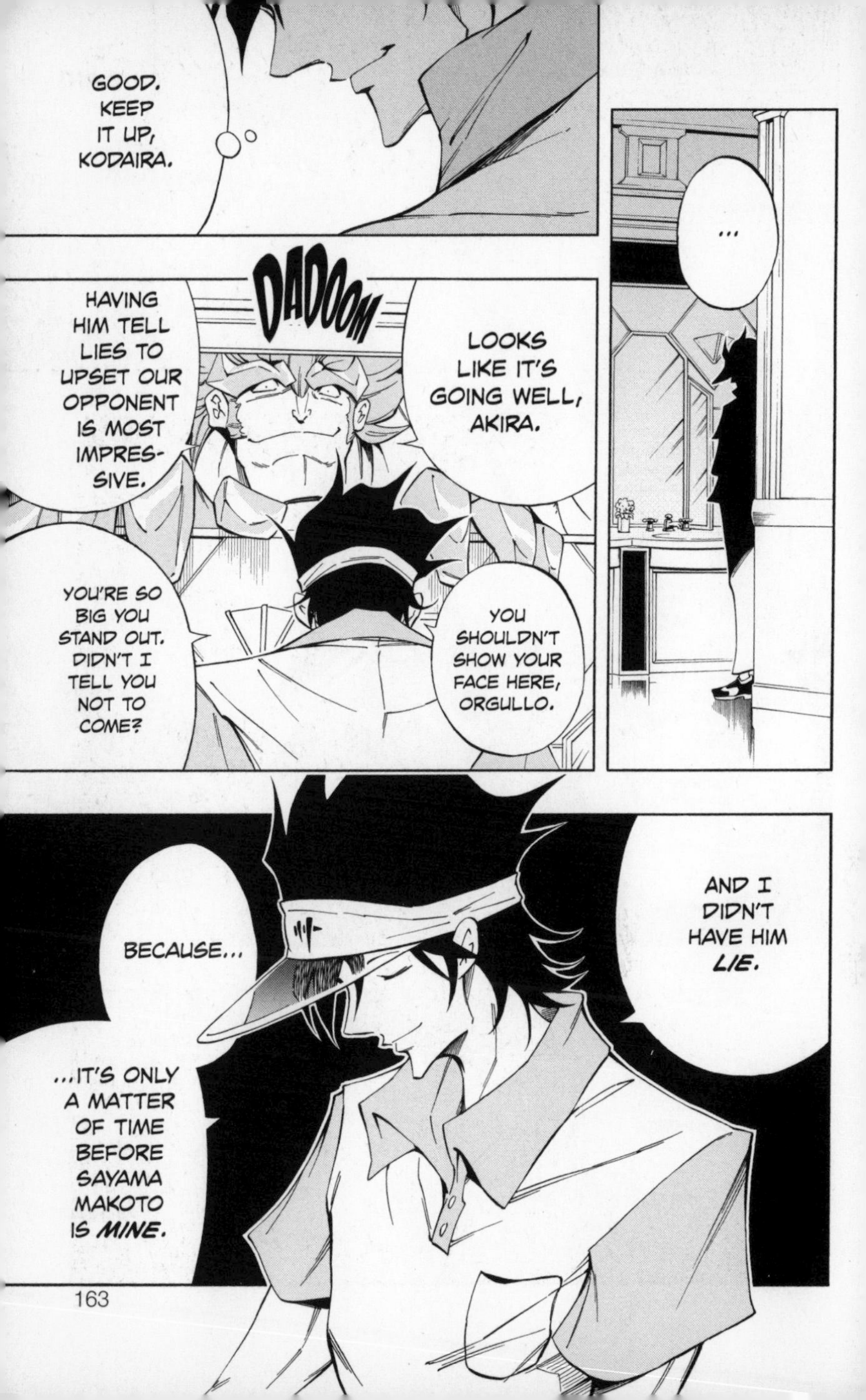
GOOD. KEEP IT UP, KODAIRA.
...
DADOOM
LOOKS LIKE IT'S GOING WELL, AKIRA.
HAVING HIM TELL LIES TO UPSET OUR OPPONENT IS MOST IMPRES-SIVE.
YOU SHOULDN'T SHOW YOUR FACE HERE, ORGULLO.
YOU'RE SO BIG YOU STAND OUT. DIDN'T I TELL YOU NOT TO COME?
AND I DIDN'T HAVE HIM *LIE*.
BECAUSE...
...IT'S ONLY A MATTER OF TIME BEFORE SAYAMA MAKOTO IS *MINE*.

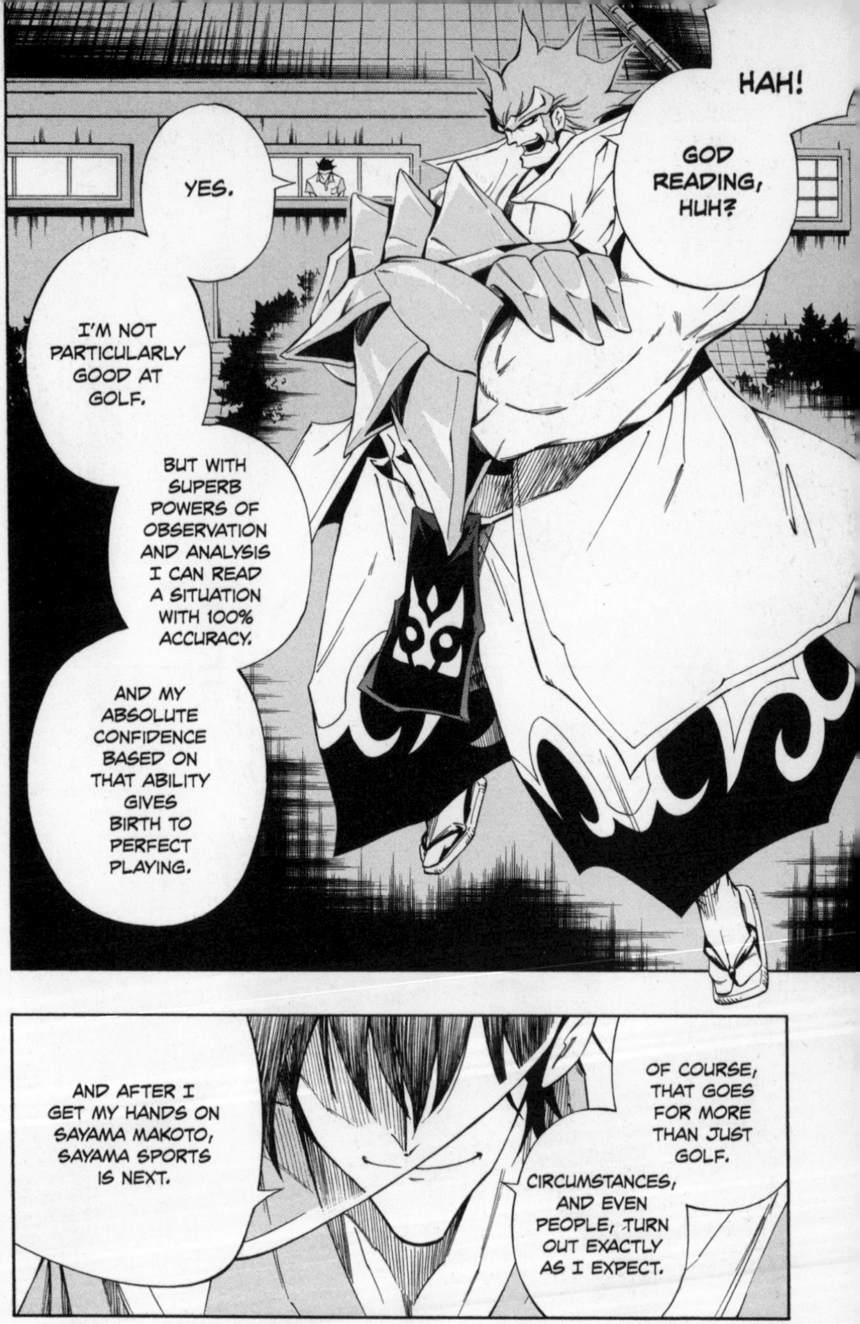
HAH!
GOD READING, HUH?
YES.
I'M NOT PARTICULARLY GOOD AT GOLF.
BUT WITH SUPERB POWERS OF OBSERVATION AND ANALYSIS I CAN READ A SITUATION WITH 100% ACCURACY.
AND MY ABSOLUTE CONFIDENCE BASED ON THAT ABILITY GIVES BIRTH TO PERFECT PLAYING.
OF COURSE, THAT GOES FOR MORE THAN JUST GOLF.
CIRCUMSTANCES, AND EVEN PEOPLE, TURN OUT EXACTLY AS I EXPECT.
AND AFTER I GET MY HANDS ON SAYAMA MAKOTO, SAYAMA SPORTS IS NEXT.

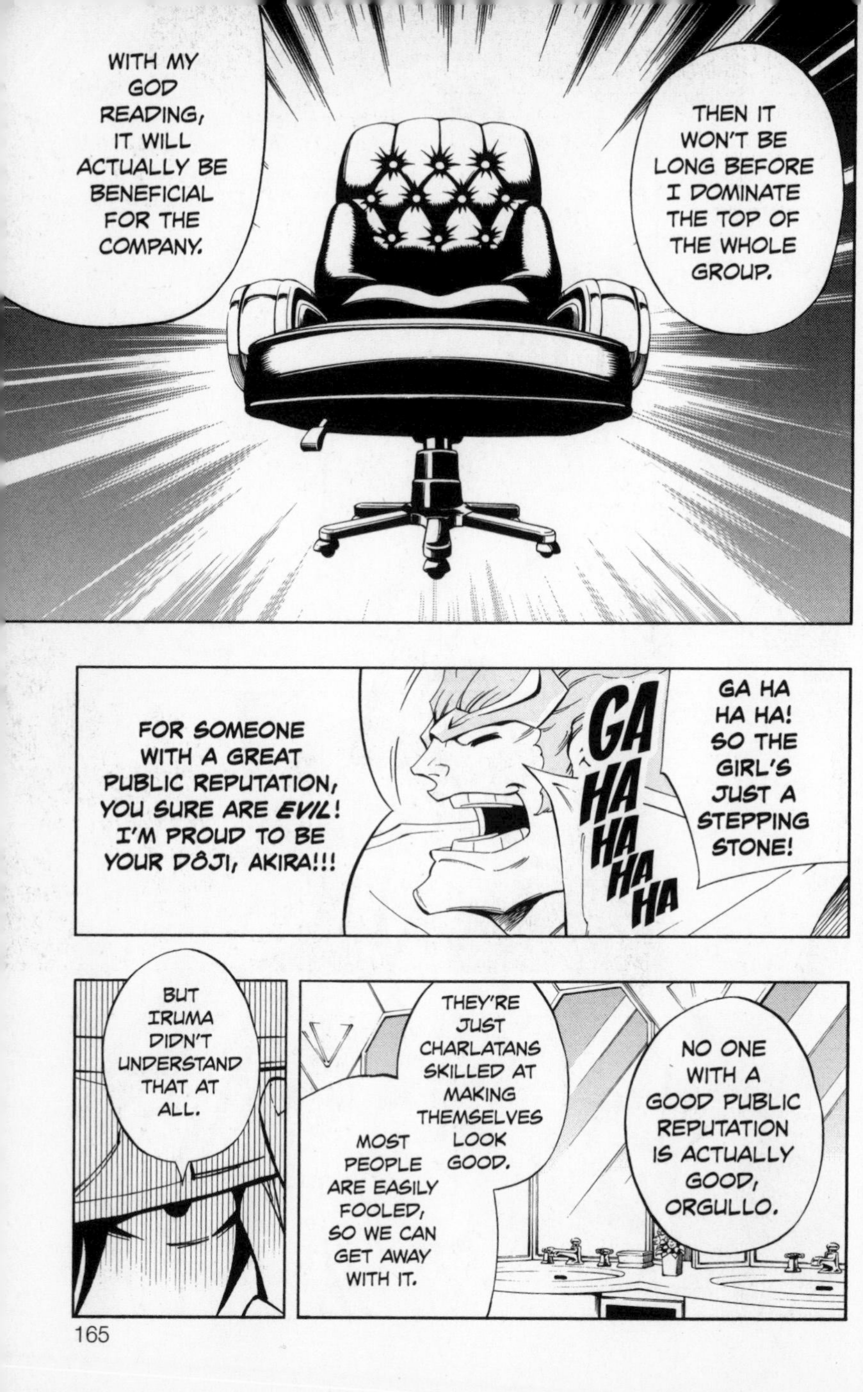
WITH MY GOD READING, IT WILL ACTUALLY BE BENEFICIAL FOR THE COMPANY.
THEN IT WON'T BE LONG BEFORE I DOMINATE THE TOP OF THE WHOLE GROUP.
GA HA HA HA! SO THE GIRL'S JUST A STEPPING STONE!
GA HA HA HA HA HA
FOR SOMEONE WITH A GREAT PUBLIC REPUTATION, YOU SURE ARE *EVIL*! I'M PROUD TO BE YOUR DÔJI, AKIRA!!!
NO ONE WITH A GOOD PUBLIC REPUTATION IS ACTUALLY GOOD, ORGULLO.
THEY'RE JUST CHARLATANS SKILLED AT MAKING THEMSELVES LOOK GOOD.
MOST PEOPLE ARE EASILY FOOLED, SO WE CAN GET AWAY WITH IT.
BUT IRUMA DIDN'T UNDERSTAND THAT AT ALL.

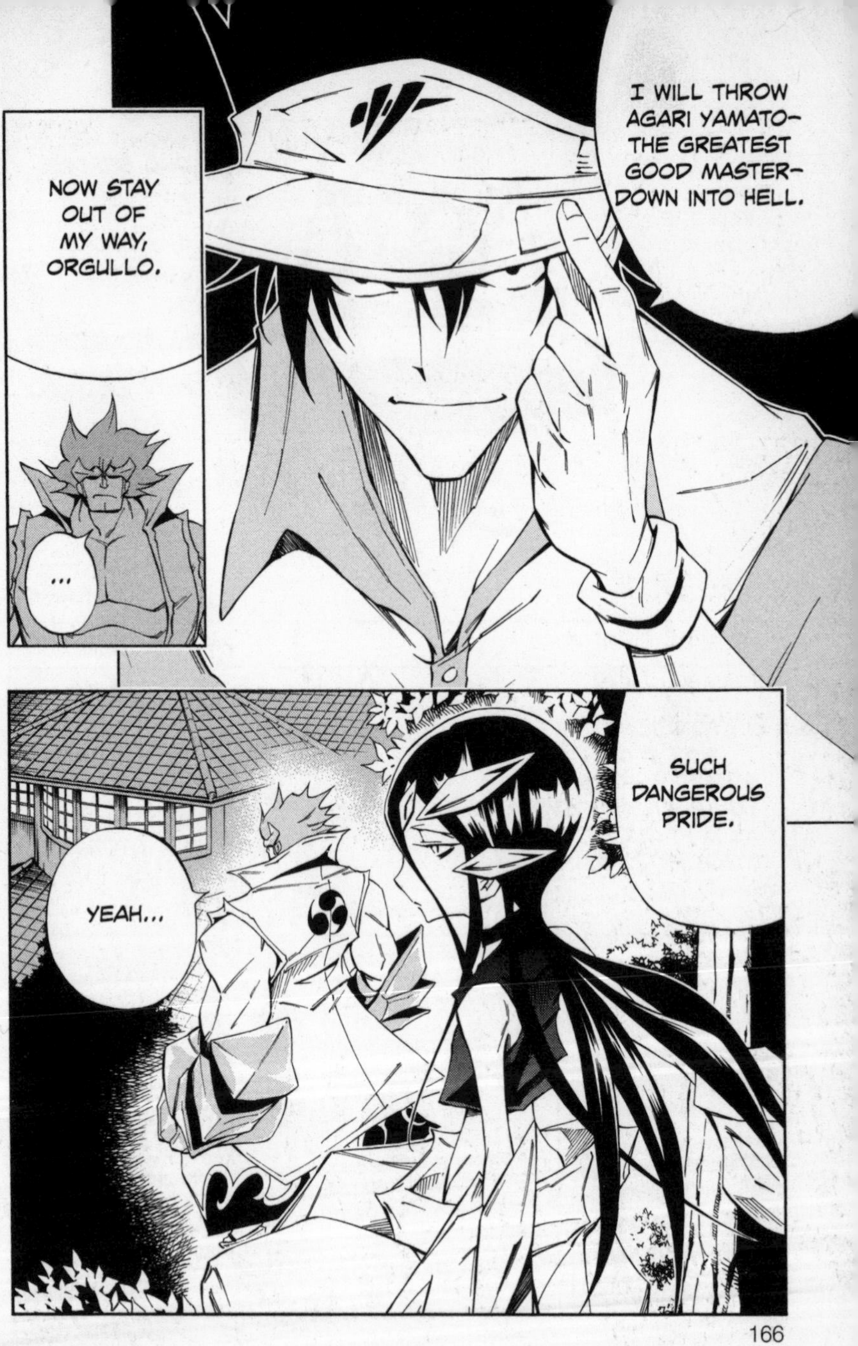
I WILL THROW AGARI YAMATO– THE GREATEST GOOD MASTER– DOWN INTO HELL.
NOW STAY OUT OF MY WAY, ORGULLO.
...
SUCH DANGEROUS PRIDE.
YEAH...

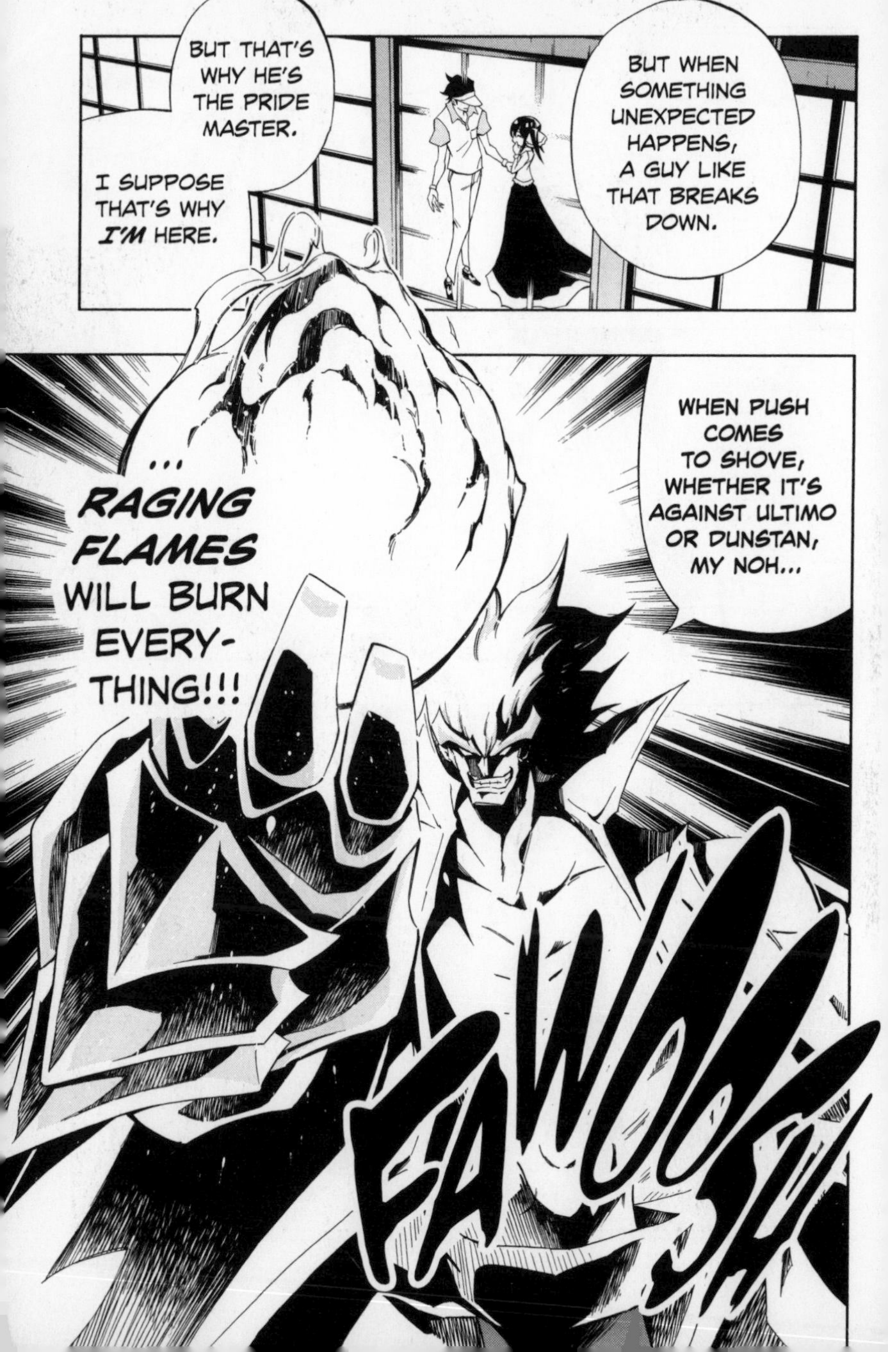

BUT WHEN SOMETHING UNEXPECTED HAPPENS, A GUY LIKE THAT BREAKS DOWN.
BUT THAT'S WHY HE'S THE PRIDE MASTER.
I SUPPOSE THAT'S WHY *I'M* HERE.
WHEN PUSH COMES TO SHOVE, WHETHER IT'S AGAINST ULTIMO OR DUNSTAN, MY NOH...
... *RAGING FLAMES* WILL BURN EVERY-THING!!!

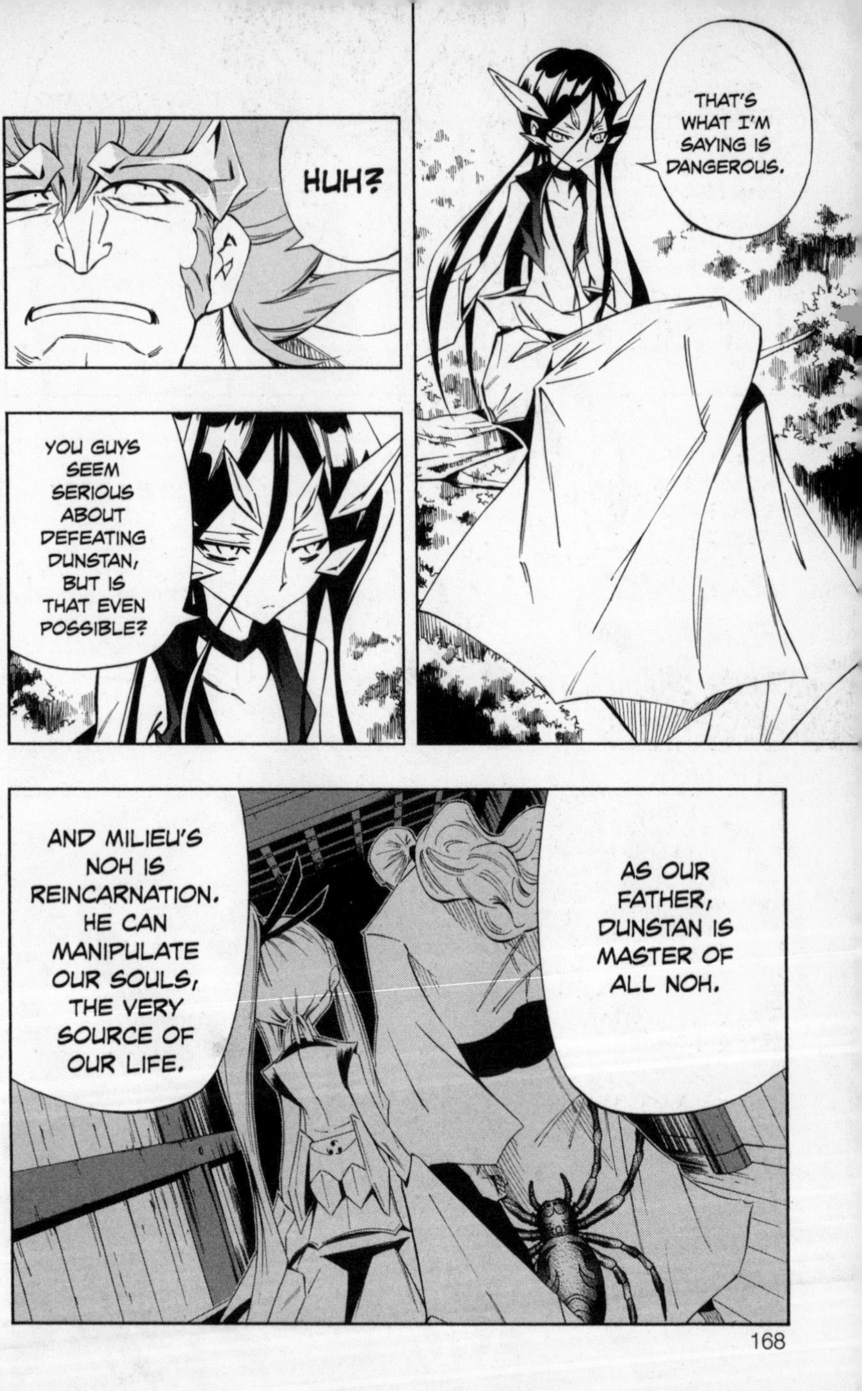
THAT'S WHAT I'M SAYING IS DANGEROUS.
HUH?
YOU GUYS SEEM SERIOUS ABOUT DEFEATING DUNSTAN, BUT IS THAT EVEN POSSIBLE?
AS OUR FATHER, DUNSTAN IS MASTER OF ALL NOH.
AND MILIEU'S NOH IS REINCARNATION. HE CAN MANIPULATE OUR SOULS, THE VERY SOURCE OF OUR LIFE.

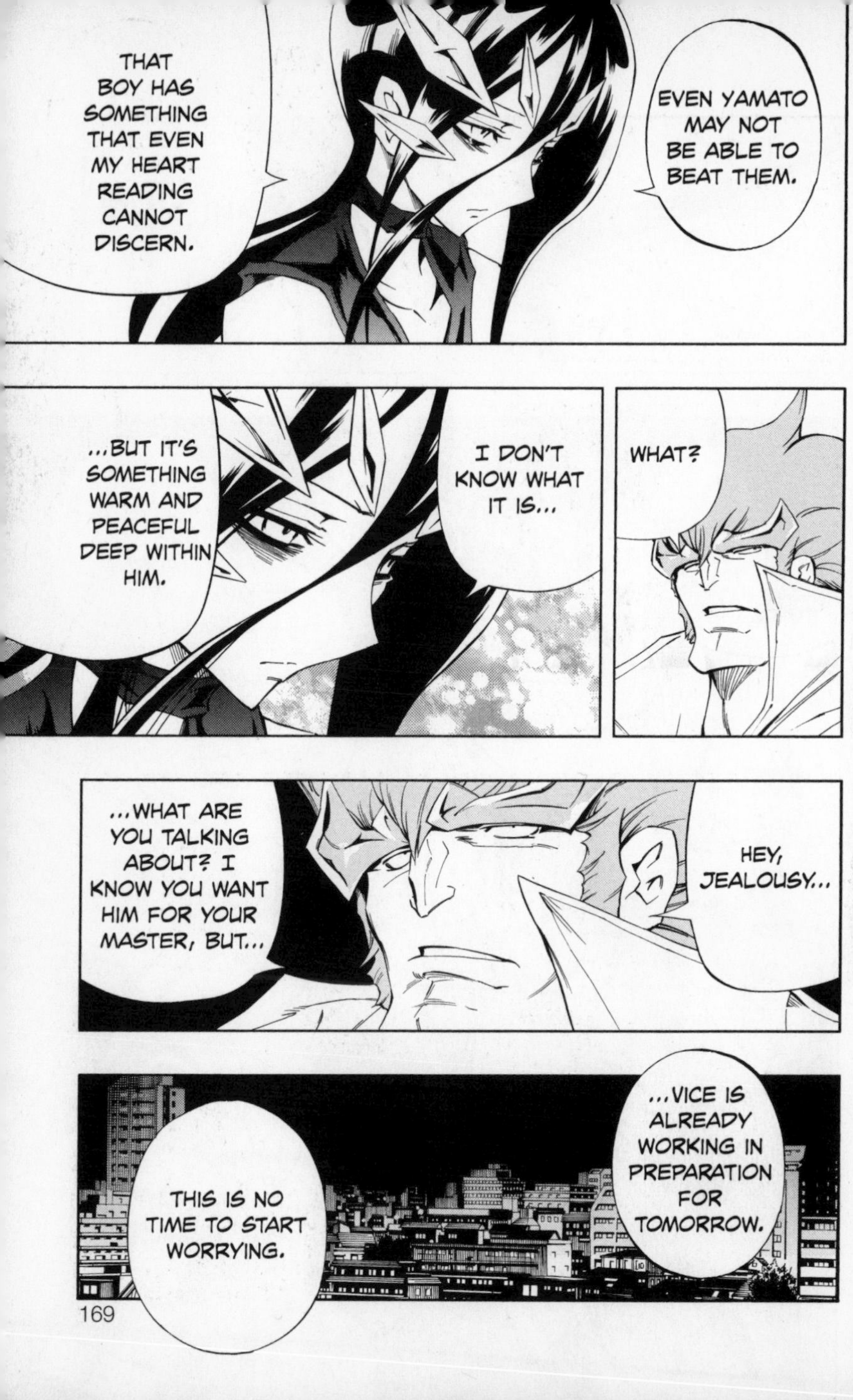
EVEN YAMATO MAY NOT BE ABLE TO BEAT THEM.
THAT BOY HAS SOMETHING THAT EVEN MY HEART READING CANNOT DISCERN.
WHAT?
I DON'T KNOW WHAT IT IS...
...BUT IT'S SOMETHING WARM AND PEACEFUL DEEP WITHIN HIM.
HEY, JEALOUSY...
...WHAT ARE YOU TALKING ABOUT? I KNOW YOU WANT HIM FOR YOUR MASTER, BUT...
...VICE IS ALREADY WORKING IN PREPARATION FOR TOMORROW.
THIS IS NO TIME TO START WORRYING.

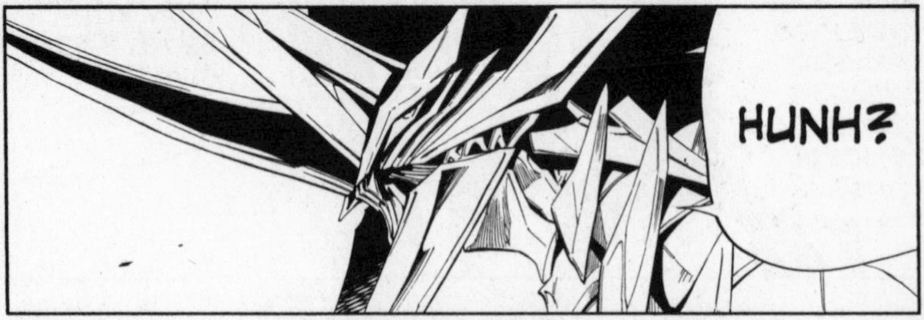
HUNH?
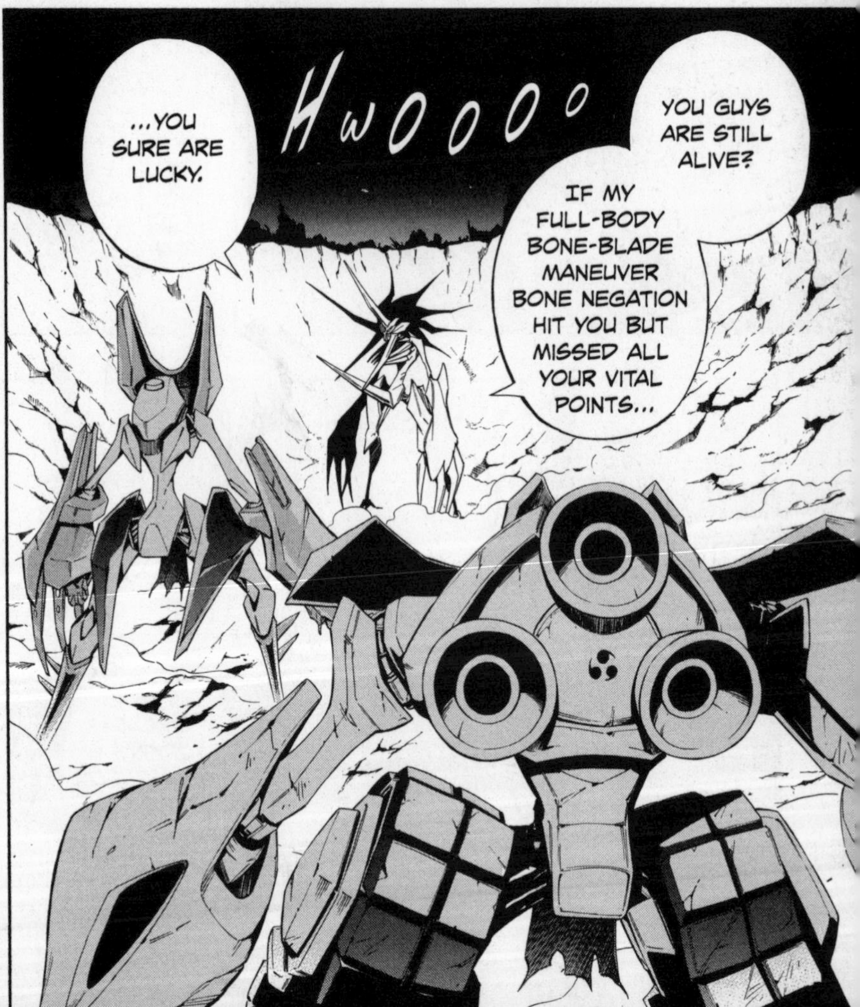
YOU GUYS ARE STILL ALIVE?
IF MY FULL-BODY BONE-BLADE MANEUVER BONE NEGATION HIT YOU BUT MISSED ALL YOUR VITAL POINTS...
HWOOOO
...YOU SURE ARE LUCKY.

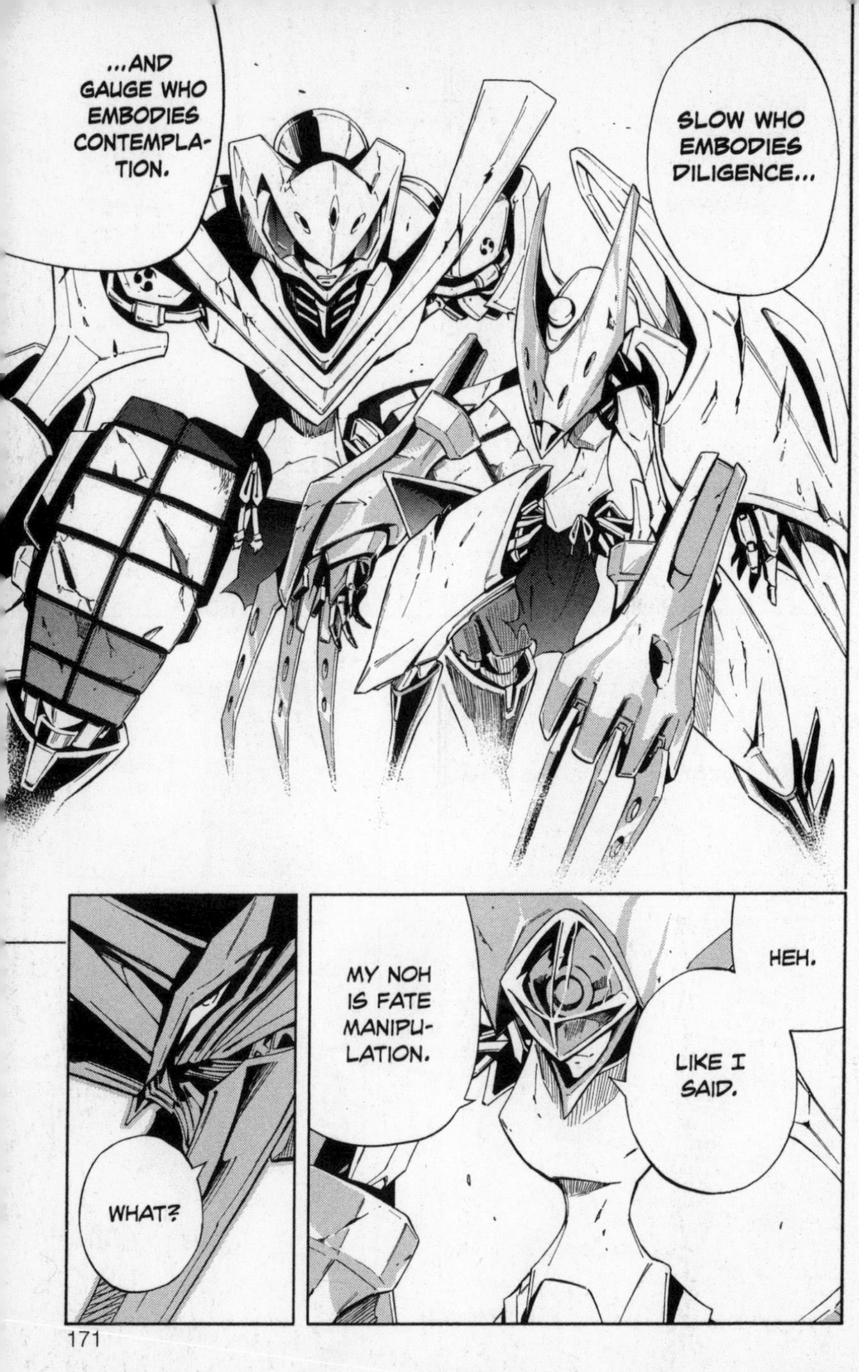
SLOW WHO EMBODIES DILIGENCE...
...AND GAUGE WHO EMBODIES CONTEMPLA-TION.
HEH.
LIKE I SAID.
MY NOH IS FATE MANIPU-LATION.
WHAT?

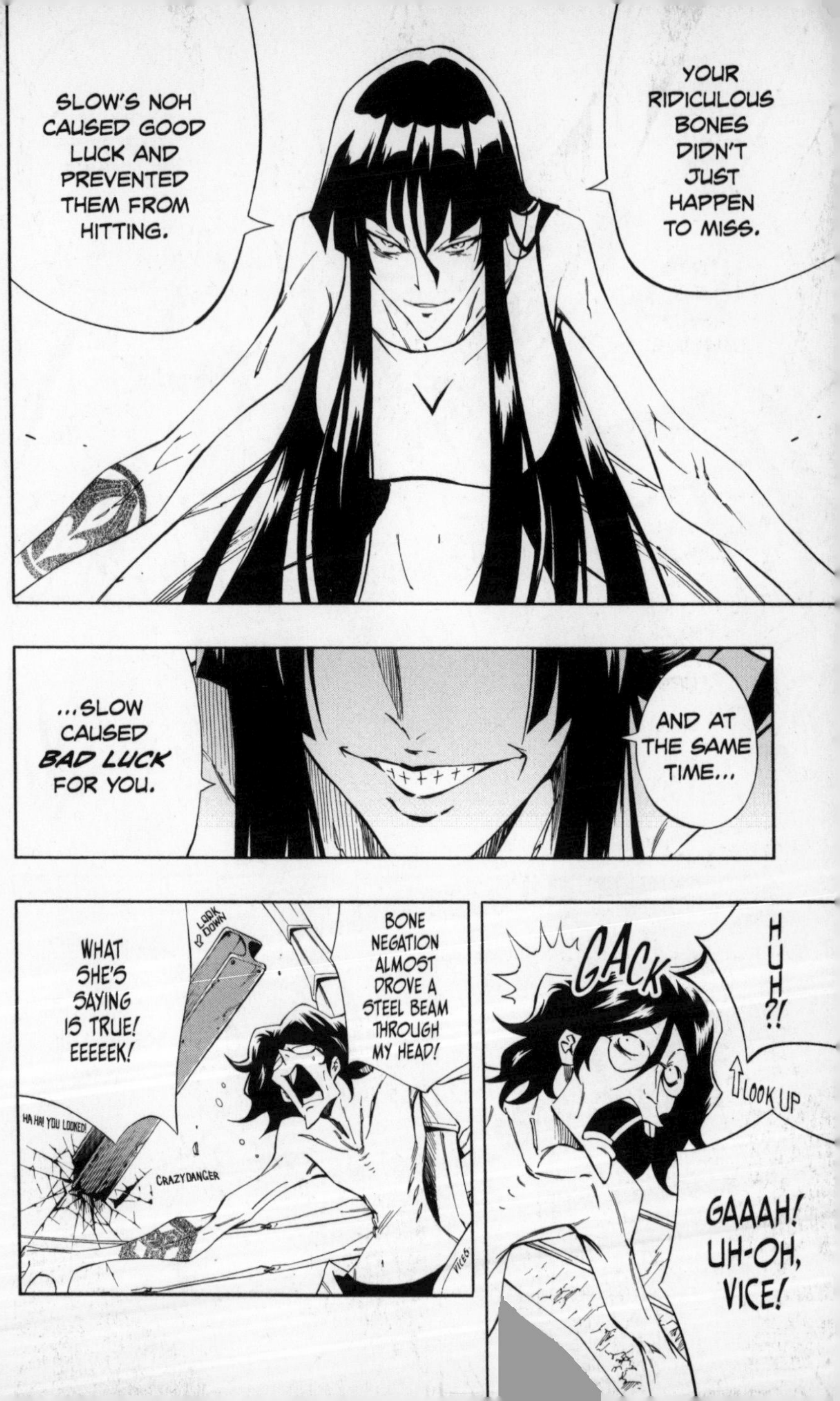
YOUR RIDICULOUS BONES DIDN'T JUST HAPPEN TO MISS.
SLOW'S NOH CAUSED GOOD LUCK AND PREVENTED THEM FROM HITTING.
AND AT THE SAME TIME...
...SLOW CAUSED BAD LUCK FOR YOU.
HUH?!
GACK
LOOK UP
GAAAH! UH-OH, VICE!
BONE NEGATION ALMOST DROVE A STEEL BEAM THROUGH MY HEAD!
LOOK DOWN
WHAT SHE'S SAYING IS TRUE! EEEEEK!
HA HA! YOU LOOKED!
CRAZYDANGER
VICES

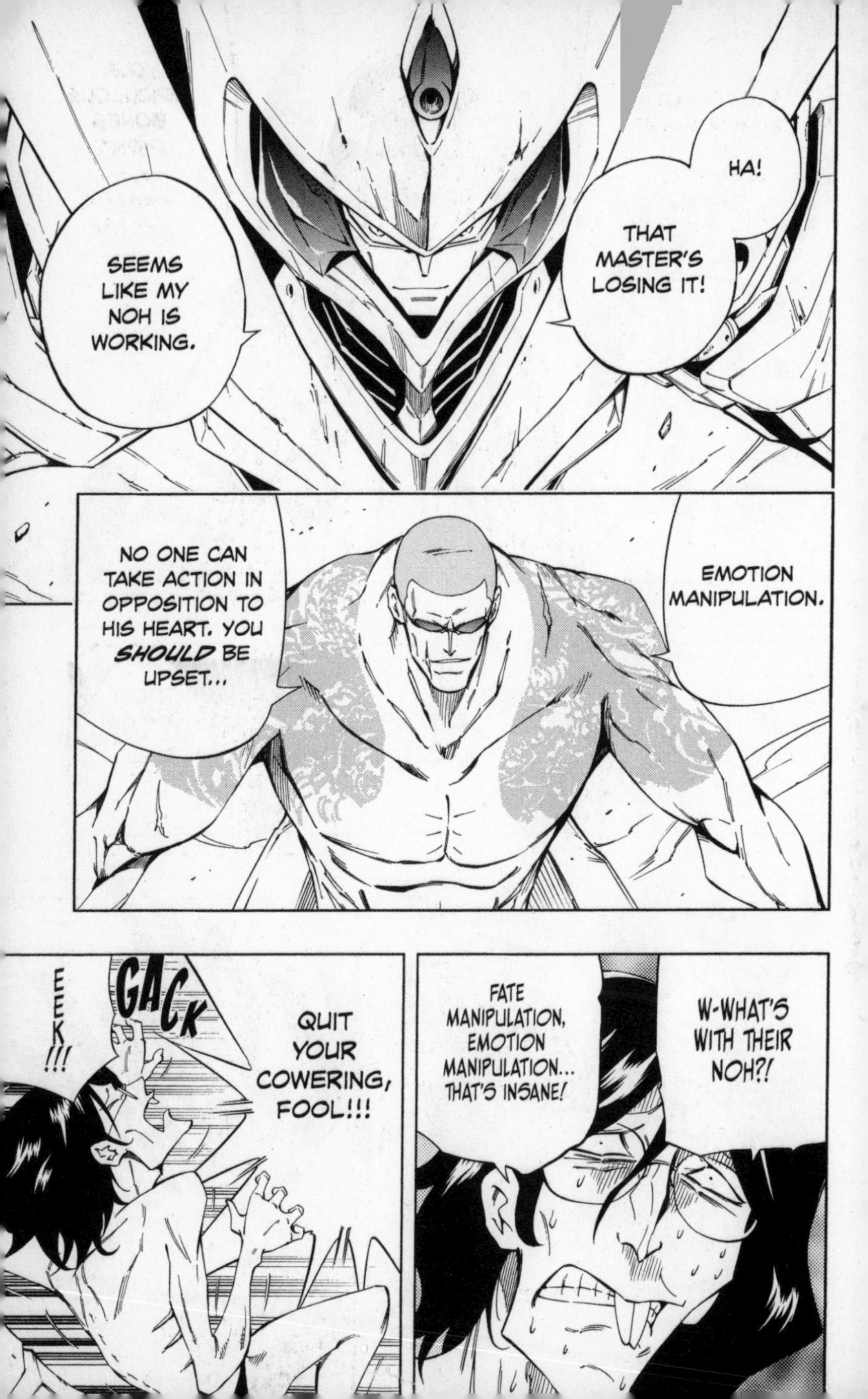
HA!
THAT MASTER'S LOSING IT!
SEEMS LIKE MY NOH IS WORKING.
EMOTION MANIPULATION.
NO ONE CAN TAKE ACTION IN OPPOSITION TO HIS HEART. YOU *SHOULD* BE UPSET...
W-WHAT'S WITH THEIR NOH?!
FATE MANIPULATION, EMOTION MANIPULATION... THAT'S INSANE!
QUIT YOUR COWERING, FOOL!!!
GACK
EEK!!!

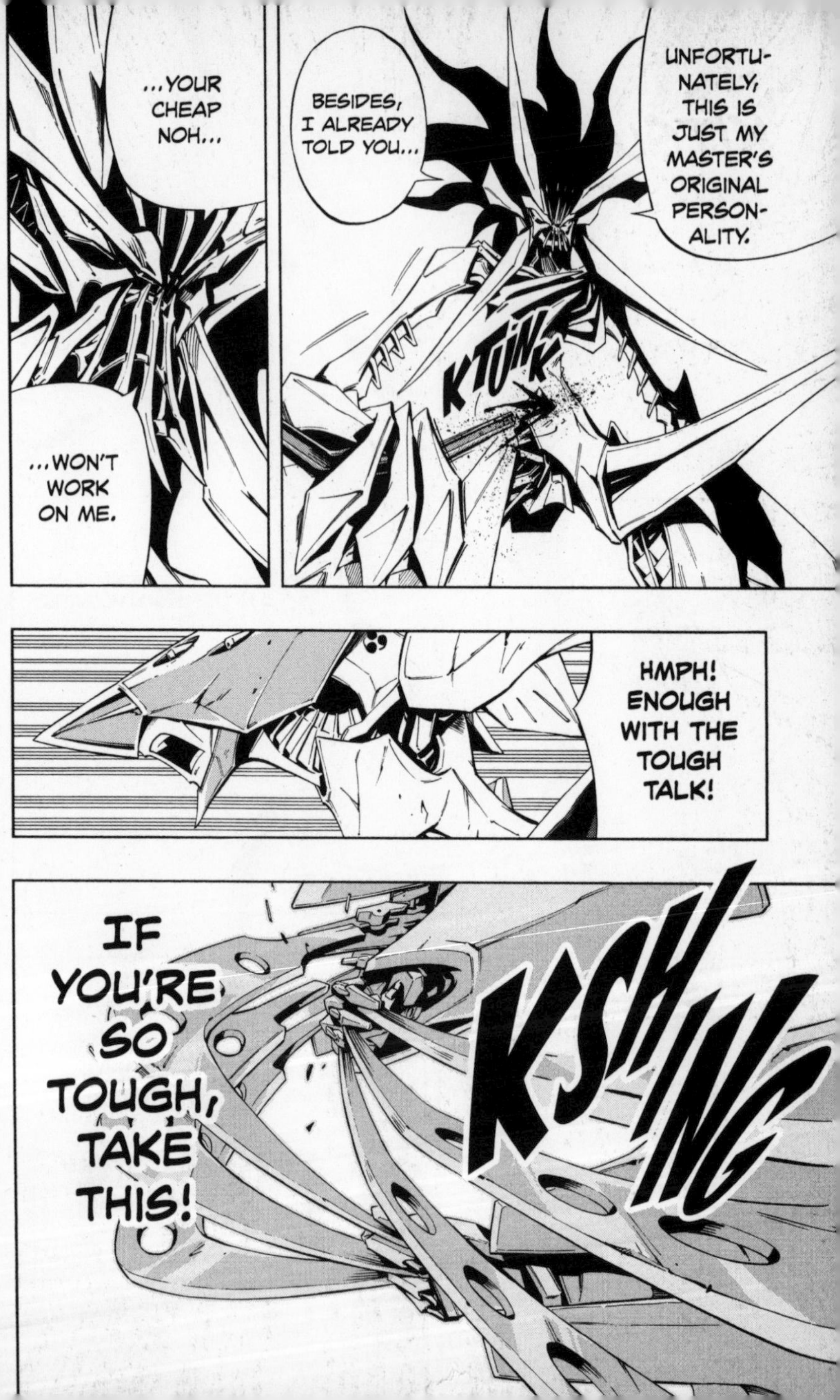
UNFORTU-NATELY, THIS IS JUST MY MASTER'S ORIGINAL PERSON-ALITY.
BESIDES, I ALREADY TOLD YOU...
KTUNK
...YOUR CHEAP NOH...
...WON'T WORK ON ME.
HMPH! ENOUGH WITH THE TOUGH TALK!
IF YOU'RE SO TOUGH, TAKE THIS!
KSHING

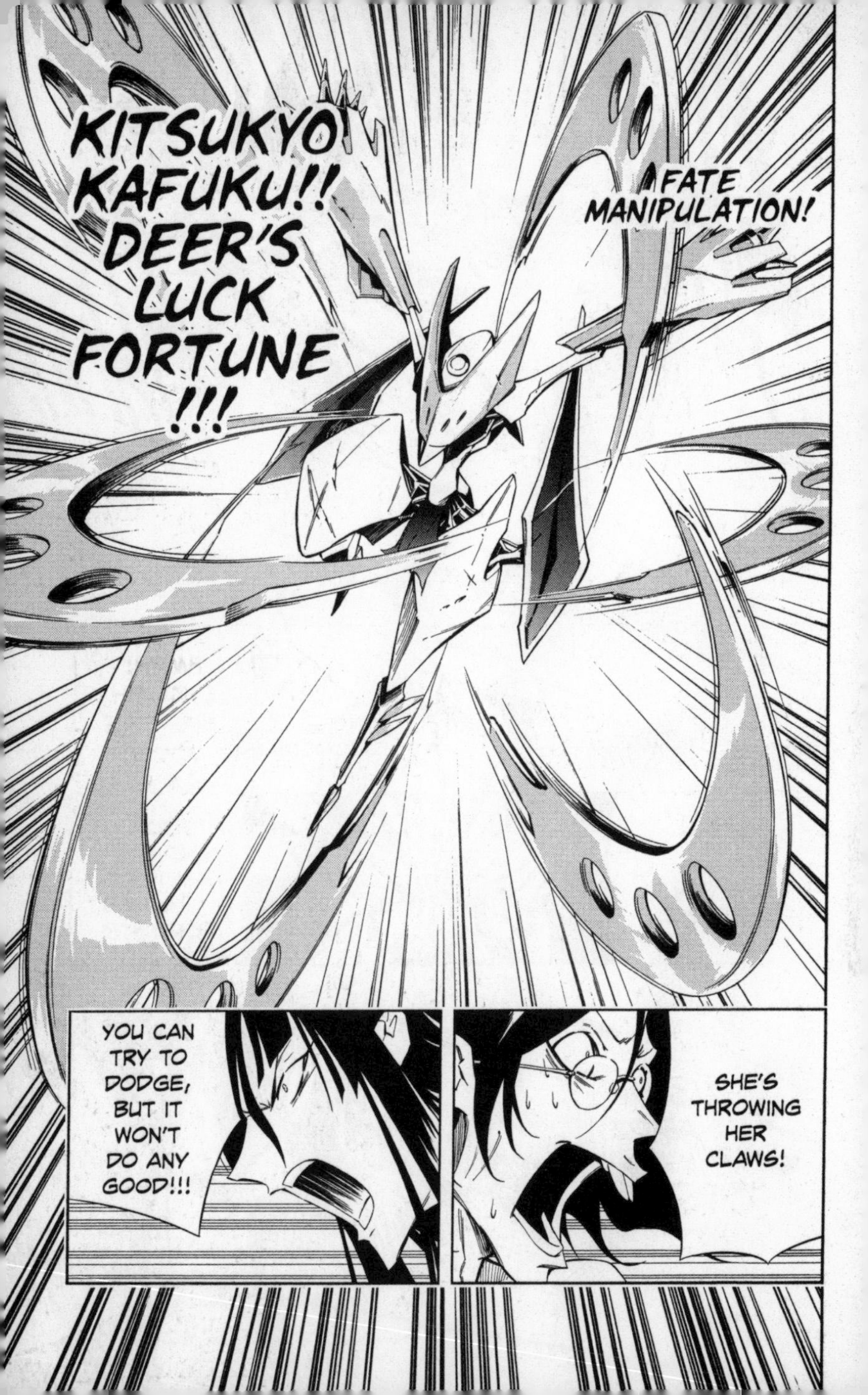
FATE MANIPULATION!
KITSUKYO KAFUKU!! DEER'S LUCK FORTUNE !!!
SHE'S THROWING HER CLAWS!
YOU CAN TRY TO DODGE, BUT IT WON'T DO ANY GOOD!!!

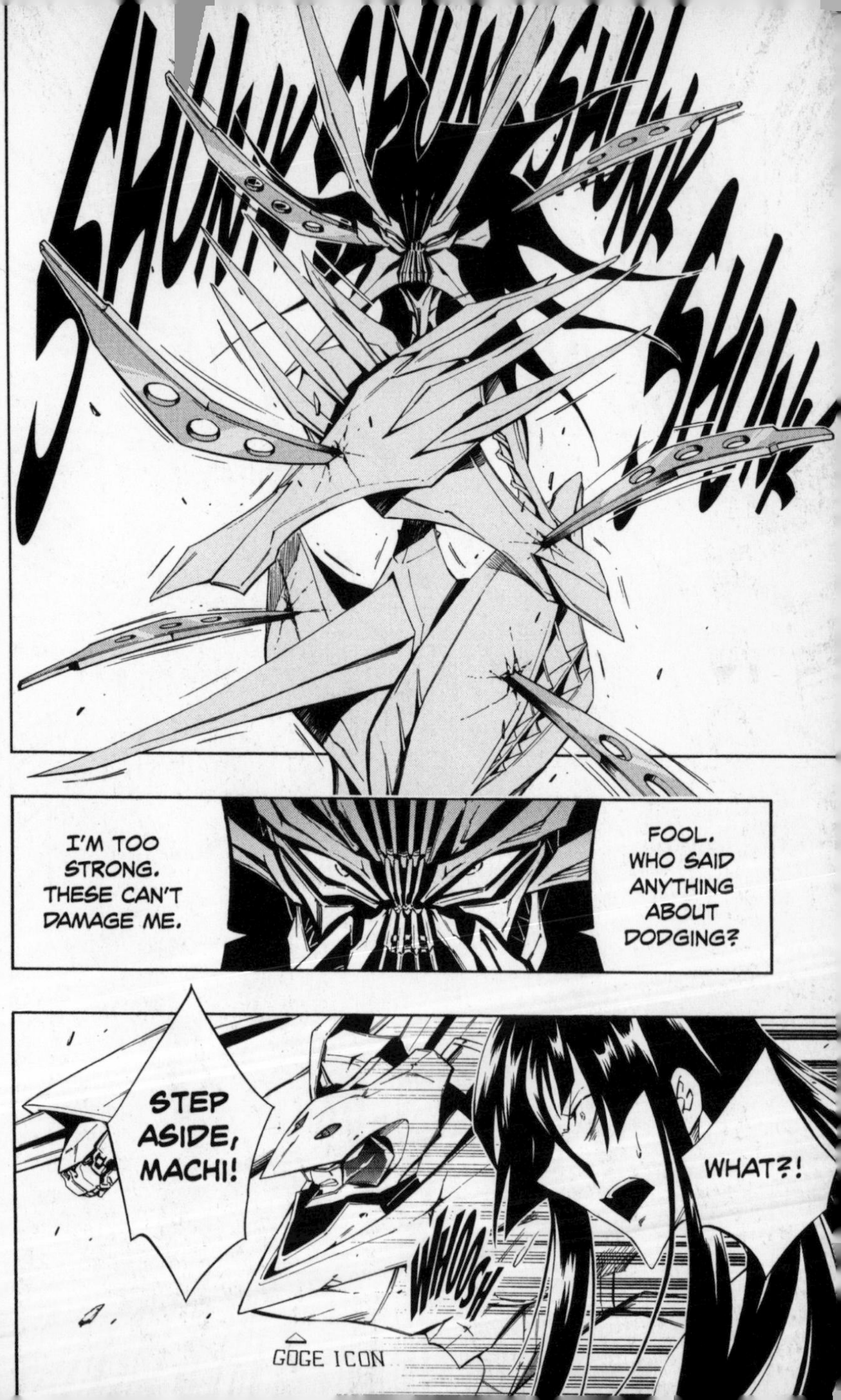
SHUNK
SHUNK
SHUNK
SHUNK
FOOL. WHO SAID ANYTHING ABOUT DODGING?
I'M TOO STRONG. THESE CAN'T DAMAGE ME.
WHAT?!
WHOOSH
STEP ASIDE, MACHI!
GOGE ICON

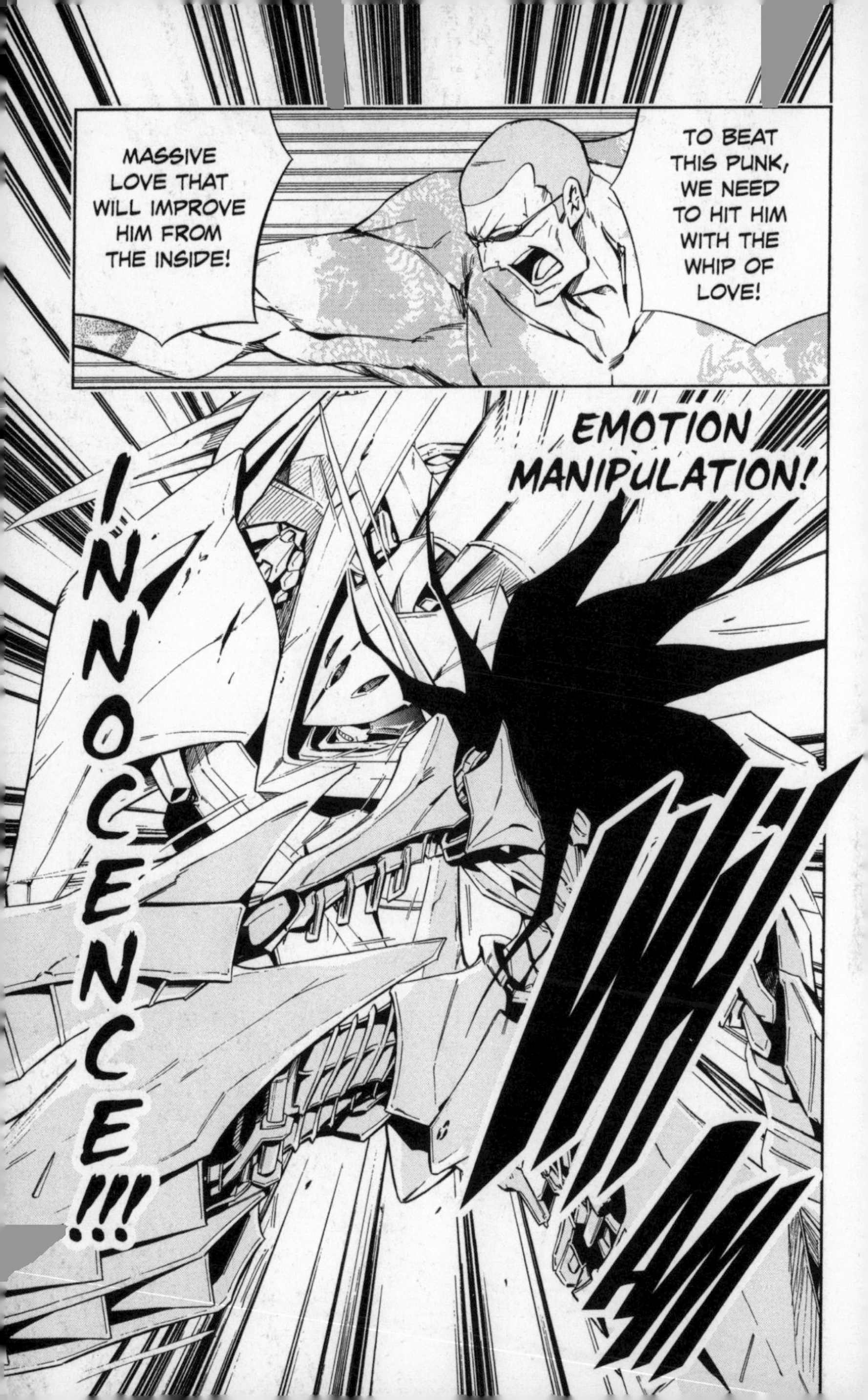
TO BEAT THIS PUNK, WE NEED TO HIT HIM WITH THE WHIP OF LOVE!
MASSIVE LOVE THAT WILL IMPROVE HIM FROM THE INSIDE!
EMOTION MANIPULATION!
INNOCENCE!!!

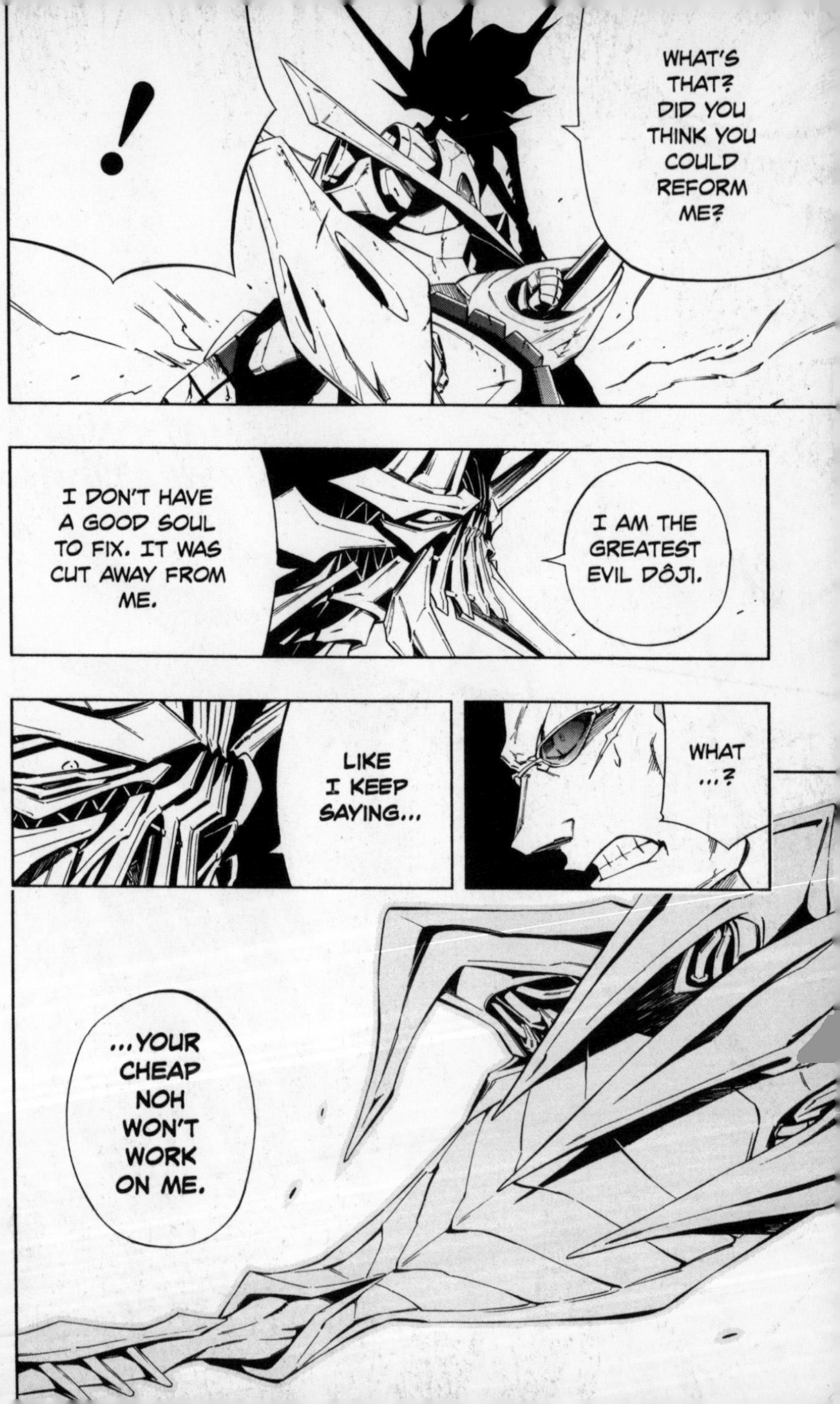
WHAT'S THAT? DID YOU THINK YOU COULD REFORM ME?
!
I AM THE GREATEST EVIL DÔJI.
I DON'T HAVE A GOOD SOUL TO FIX. IT WAS CUT AWAY FROM ME.
WHAT ...?
LIKE I KEEP SAYING...
...YOUR CHEAP NOH WON'T WORK ON ME.

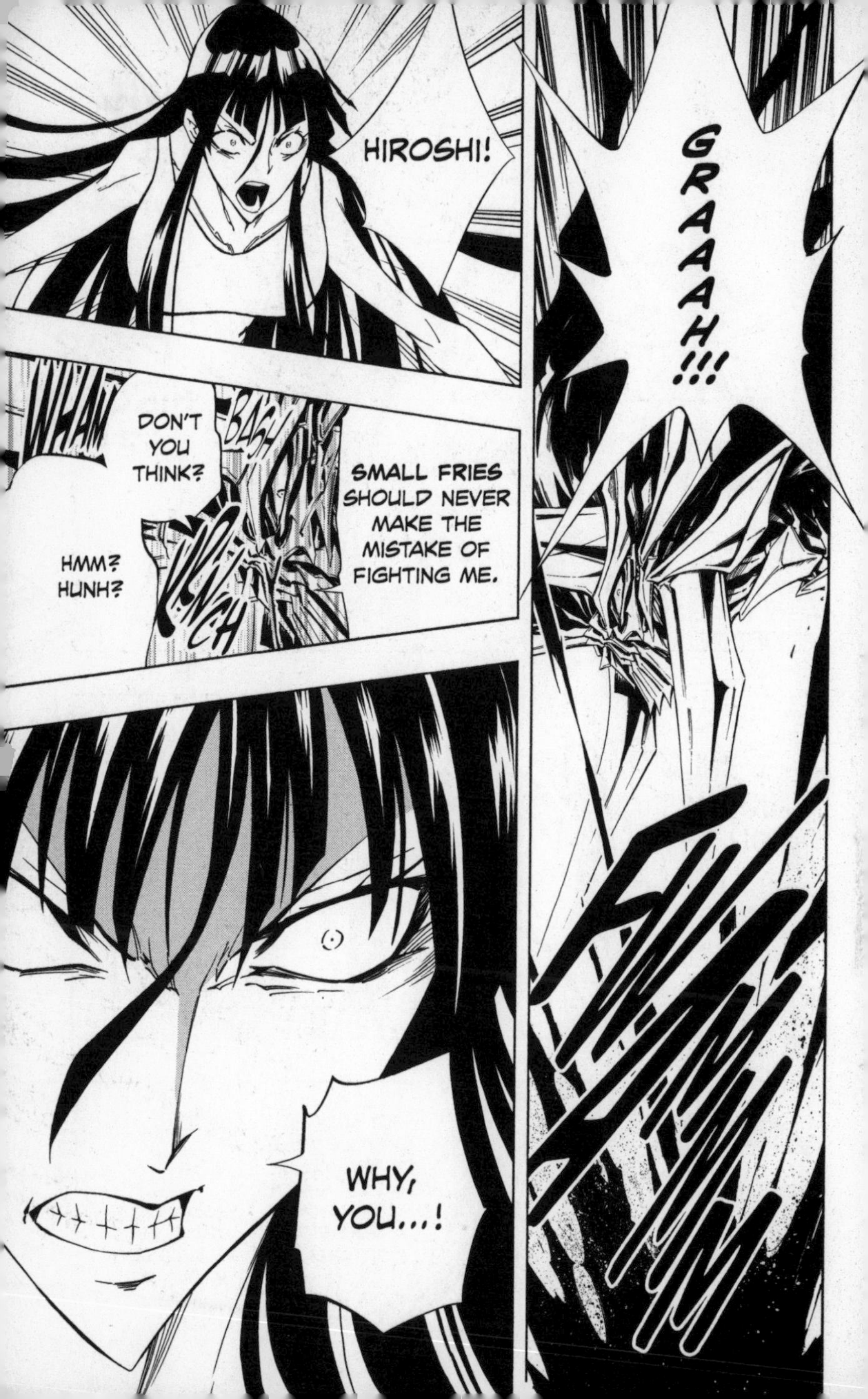
GRAAAAH!!!
HIROSHI!
SMALL FRIES SHOULD NEVER MAKE THE MISTAKE OF FIGHTING ME.
BASH
DON'T YOU THINK?
WHAM
HMM? HUNH?
WHY, YOU...!

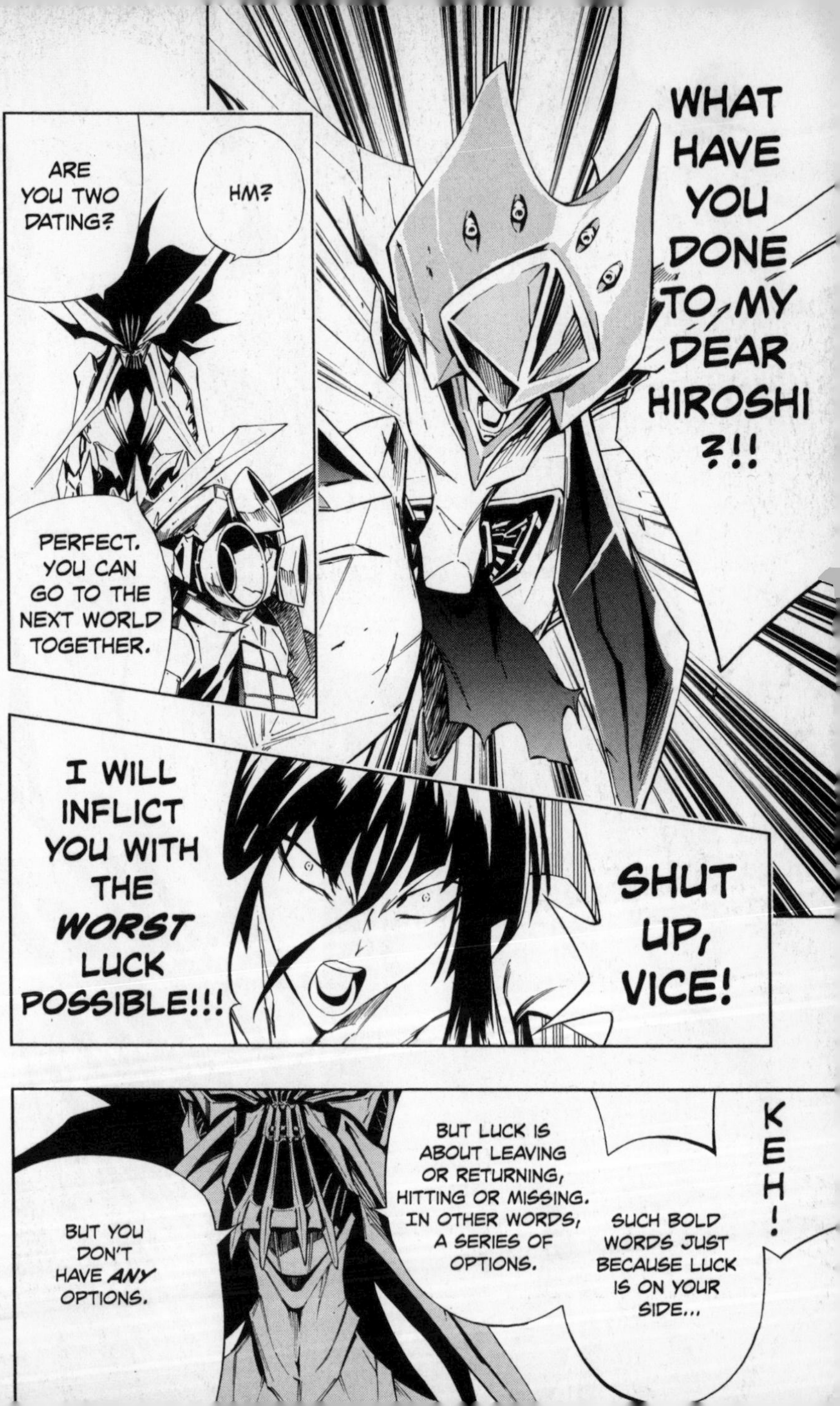
WHAT HAVE YOU DONE TO MY DEAR HIROSHI ?!!
HM?
ARE YOU TWO DATING?
PERFECT. YOU CAN GO TO THE NEXT WORLD TOGETHER.
SHUT UP, VICE!
I WILL INFLICT YOU WITH THE *WORST* LUCK POSSIBLE!!!
KEH!
SUCH BOLD WORDS JUST BECAUSE LUCK IS ON YOUR SIDE...
BUT LUCK IS ABOUT LEAVING OR RETURNING, HITTING OR MISSING. IN OTHER WORDS, A SERIES OF OPTIONS.
BUT YOU DON'T HAVE *ANY* OPTIONS.

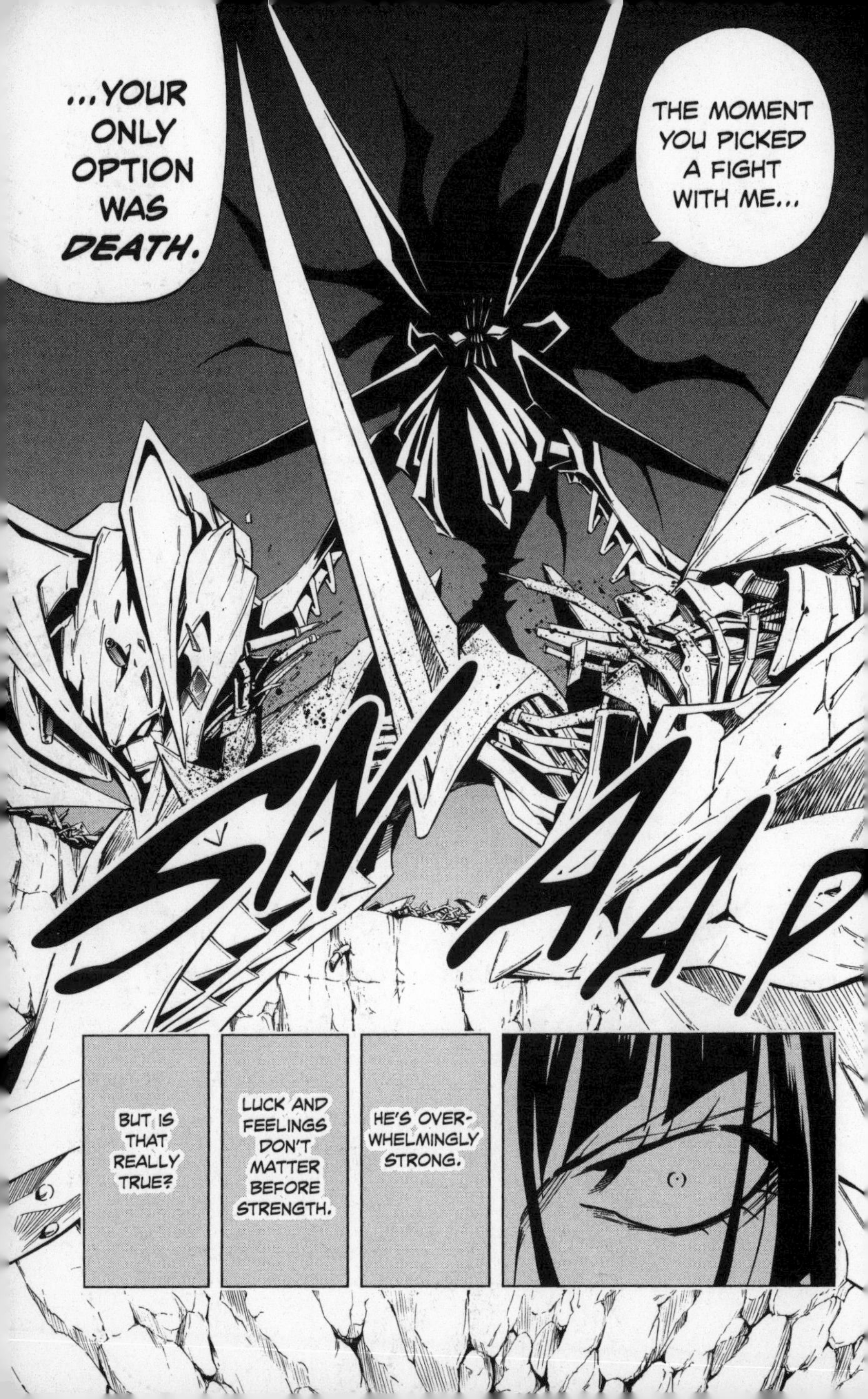
THE MOMENT YOU PICKED A FIGHT WITH ME...
...YOUR ONLY OPTION WAS DEATH.
SNAAP
HE'S OVER-WHELMINGLY STRONG.
LUCK AND FEELINGS DON'T MATTER BEFORE STRENGTH.
BUT IS THAT REALLY TRUE?

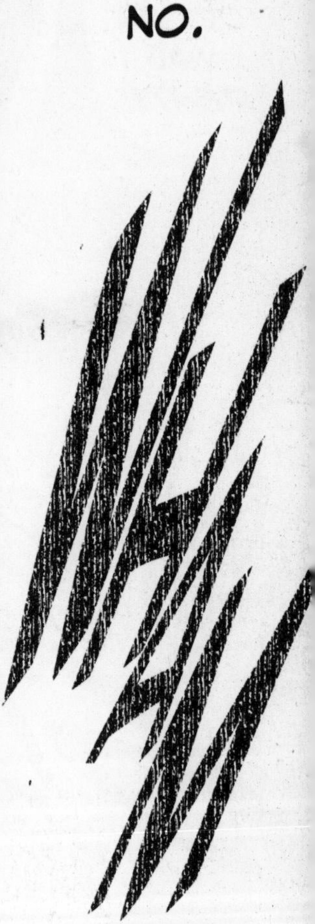
NO.
I'M JUST TOO WEAK.
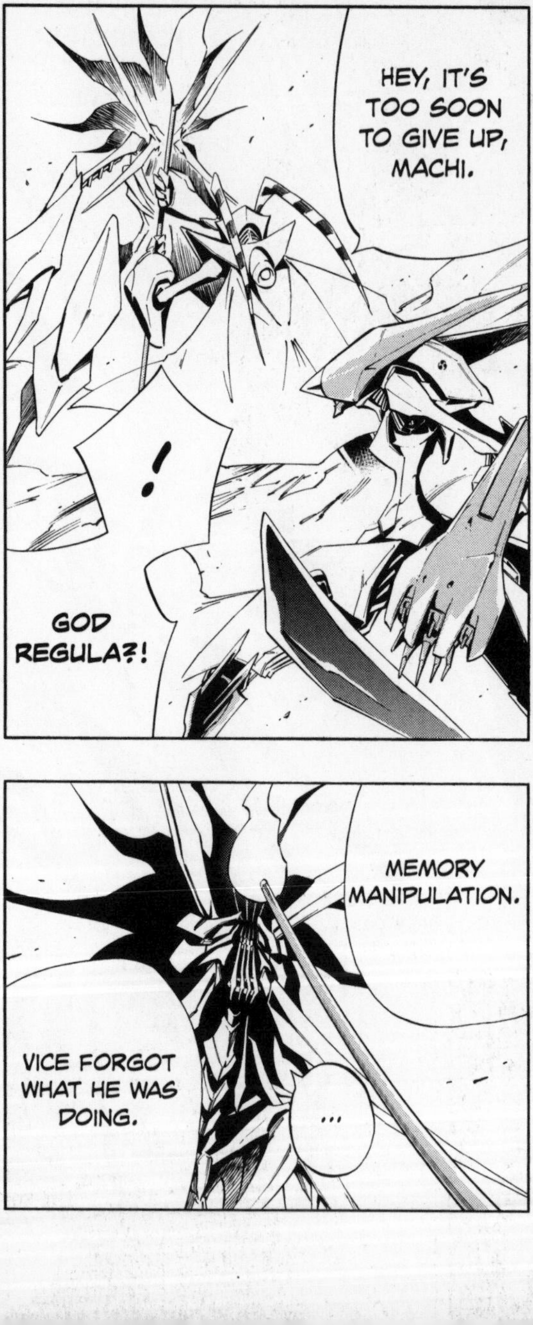
HEY, IT'S TOO SOON TO GIVE UP, MACHI.
!
GOD REGULA?!
MEMORY MANIPULATION.
VICE FORGOT WHAT HE WAS DOING.
...

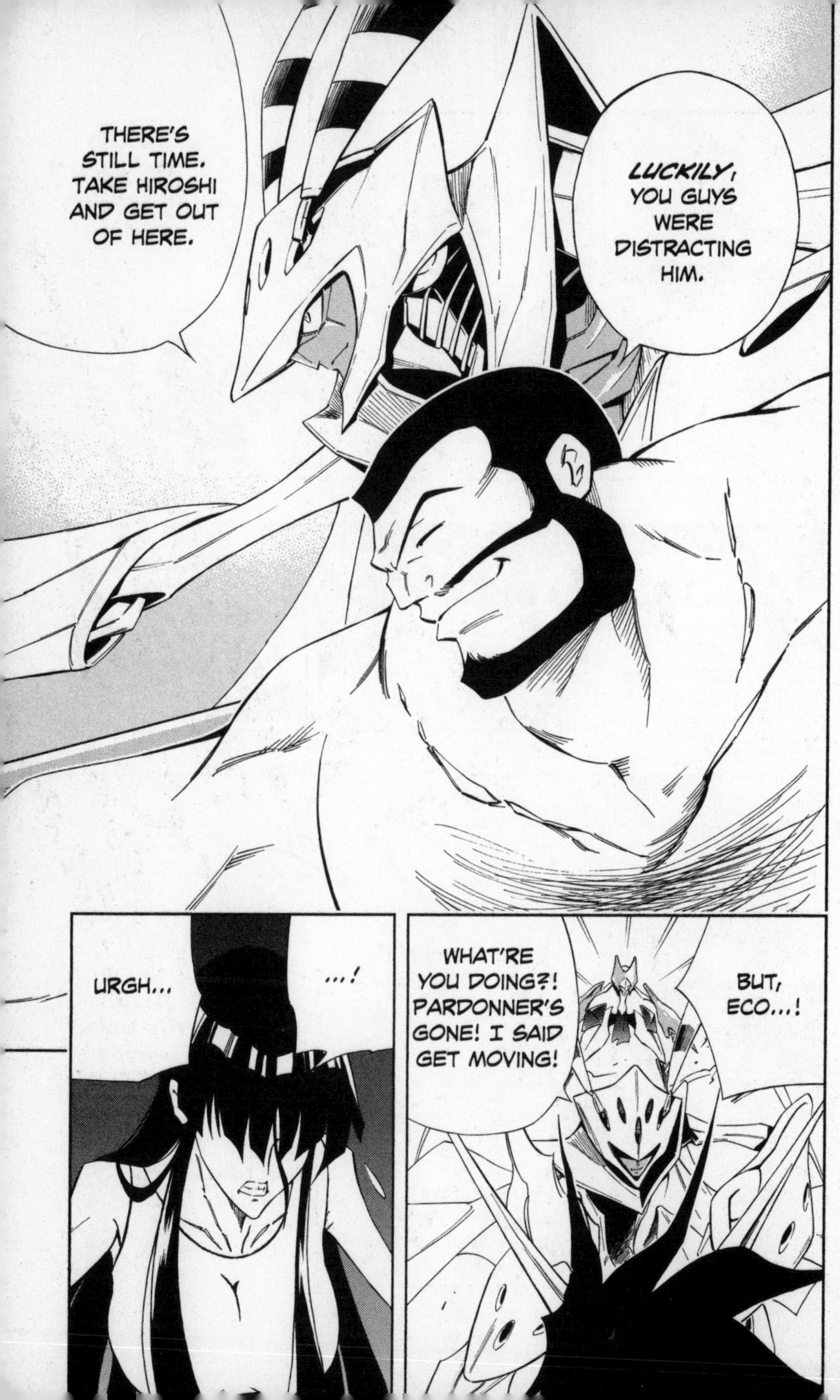
LUCKILY, YOU GUYS WERE DISTRACTING HIM.
THERE'S STILL TIME. TAKE HIROSHI AND GET OUT OF HERE.
BUT, ECO...!
WHAT'RE YOU DOING?! PARDONNER'S GONE! I SAID GET MOVING!
...!
URGH...

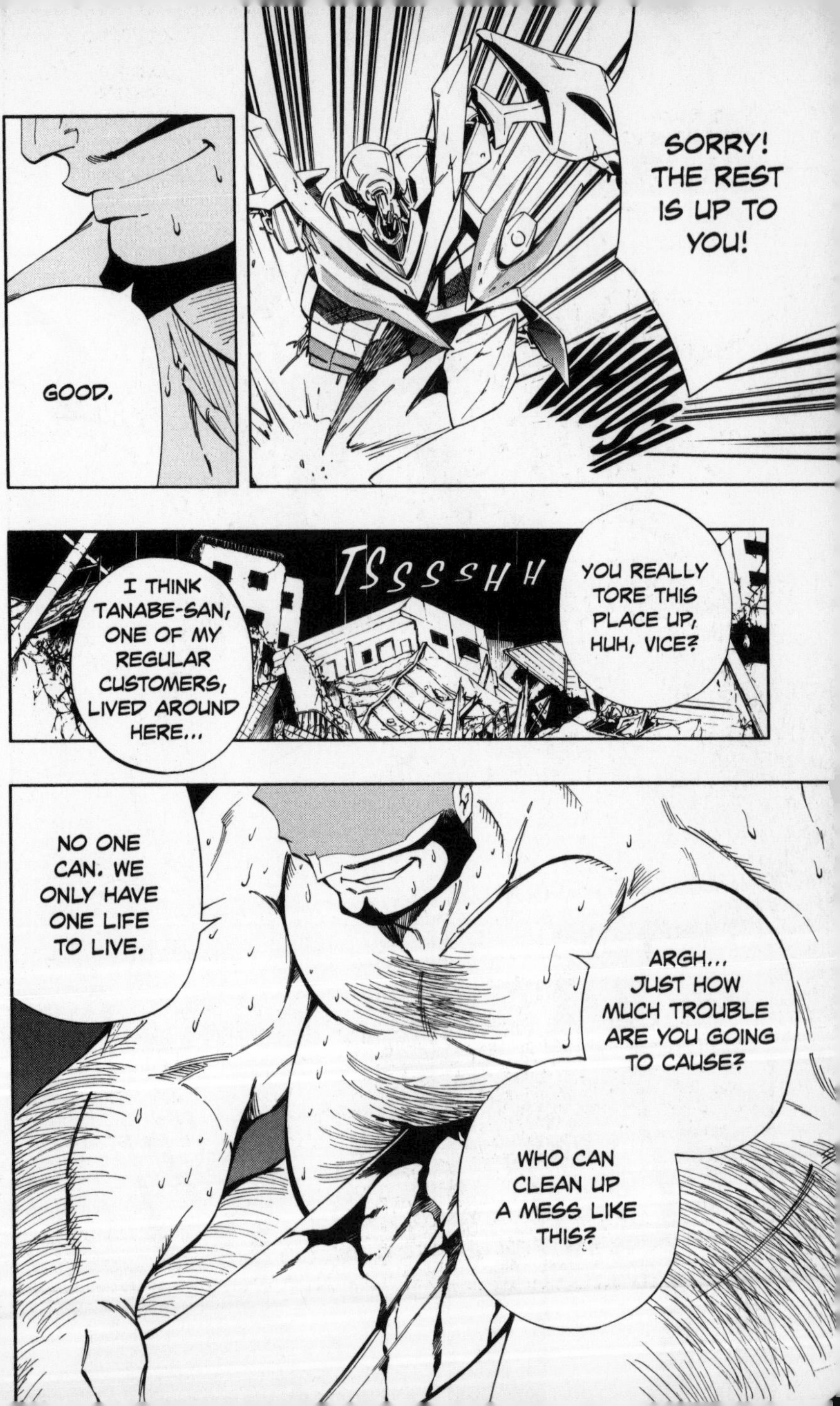
SORRY! THE REST IS UP TO YOU!
GOOD.
YOU REALLY TORE THIS PLACE UP, HUH, VICE?
TSSSSHH
I THINK TANABE-SAN, ONE OF MY REGULAR CUSTOMERS, LIVED AROUND HERE...
ARGH... JUST HOW MUCH TROUBLE ARE YOU GOING TO CAUSE?
WHO CAN CLEAN UP A MESS LIKE THIS?
NO ONE CAN. WE ONLY HAVE ONE LIFE TO LIVE.

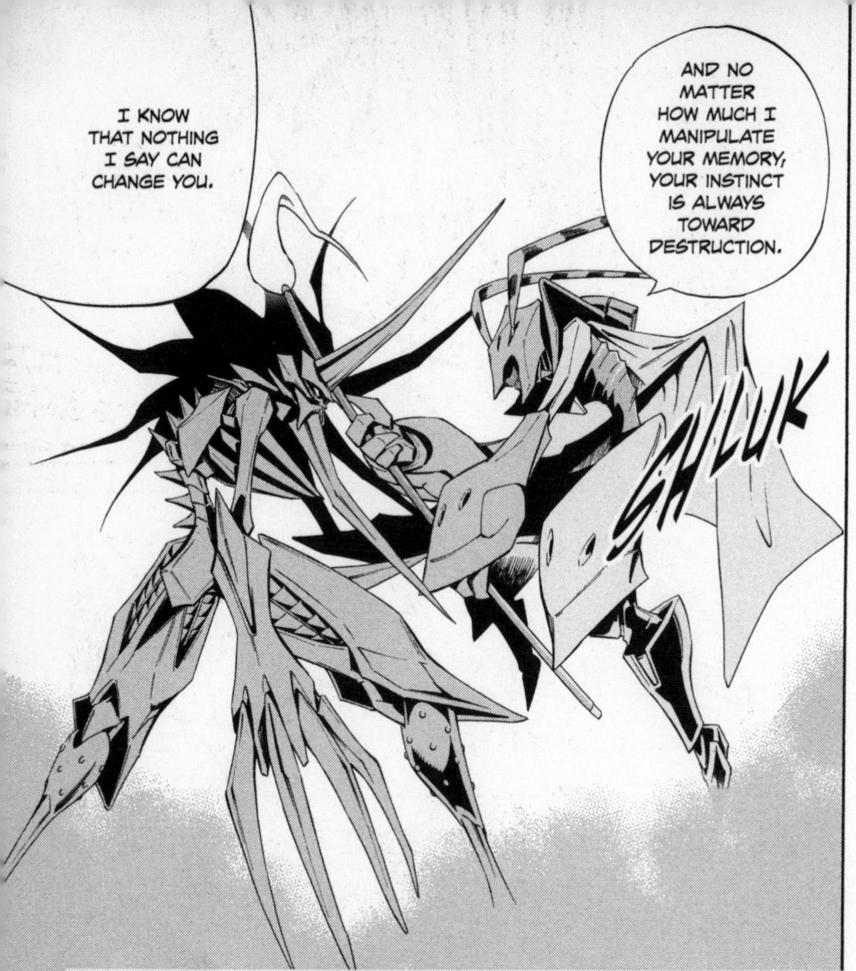
AND NO MATTER HOW MUCH I MANIPULATE YOUR MEMORY, YOUR INSTINCT IS ALWAYS TOWARD DESTRUCTION.
I KNOW THAT NOTHING I SAY CAN CHANGE YOU.
SHLUK

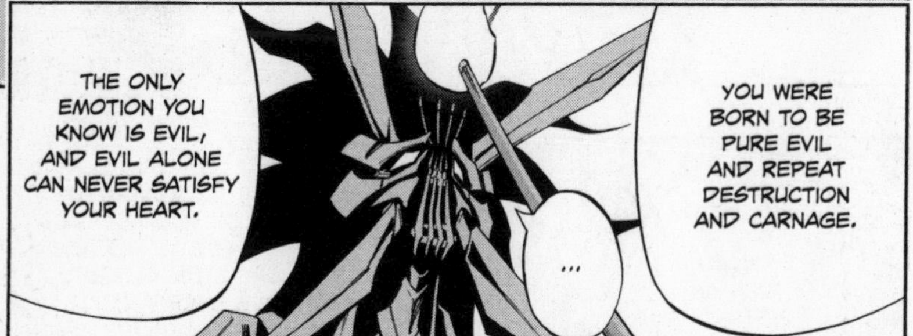
YOU WERE BORN TO BE PURE EVIL AND REPEAT DESTRUCTION AND CARNAGE.
...
THE ONLY EMOTION YOU KNOW IS EVIL, AND EVIL ALONE CAN NEVER SATISFY YOUR HEART.

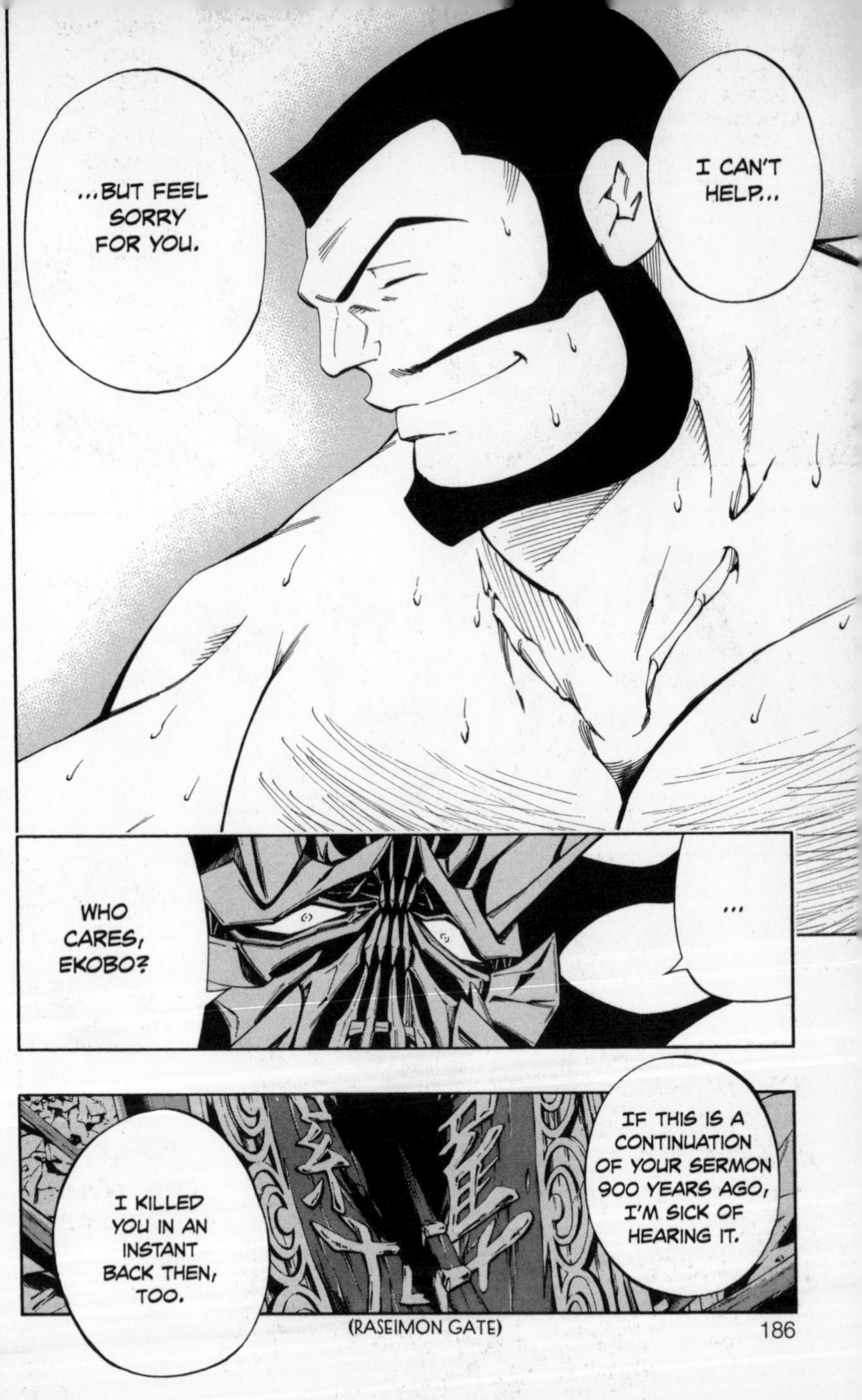
I CAN'T HELP...
...BUT FEEL SORRY FOR YOU.
...
WHO CARES, EKOBO?
IF THIS IS A CONTINUATION OF YOUR SERMON 900 YEARS AGO, I'M SICK OF HEARING IT.
I KILLED YOU IN AN INSTANT BACK THEN, TOO.

(RASEIMON GATE)

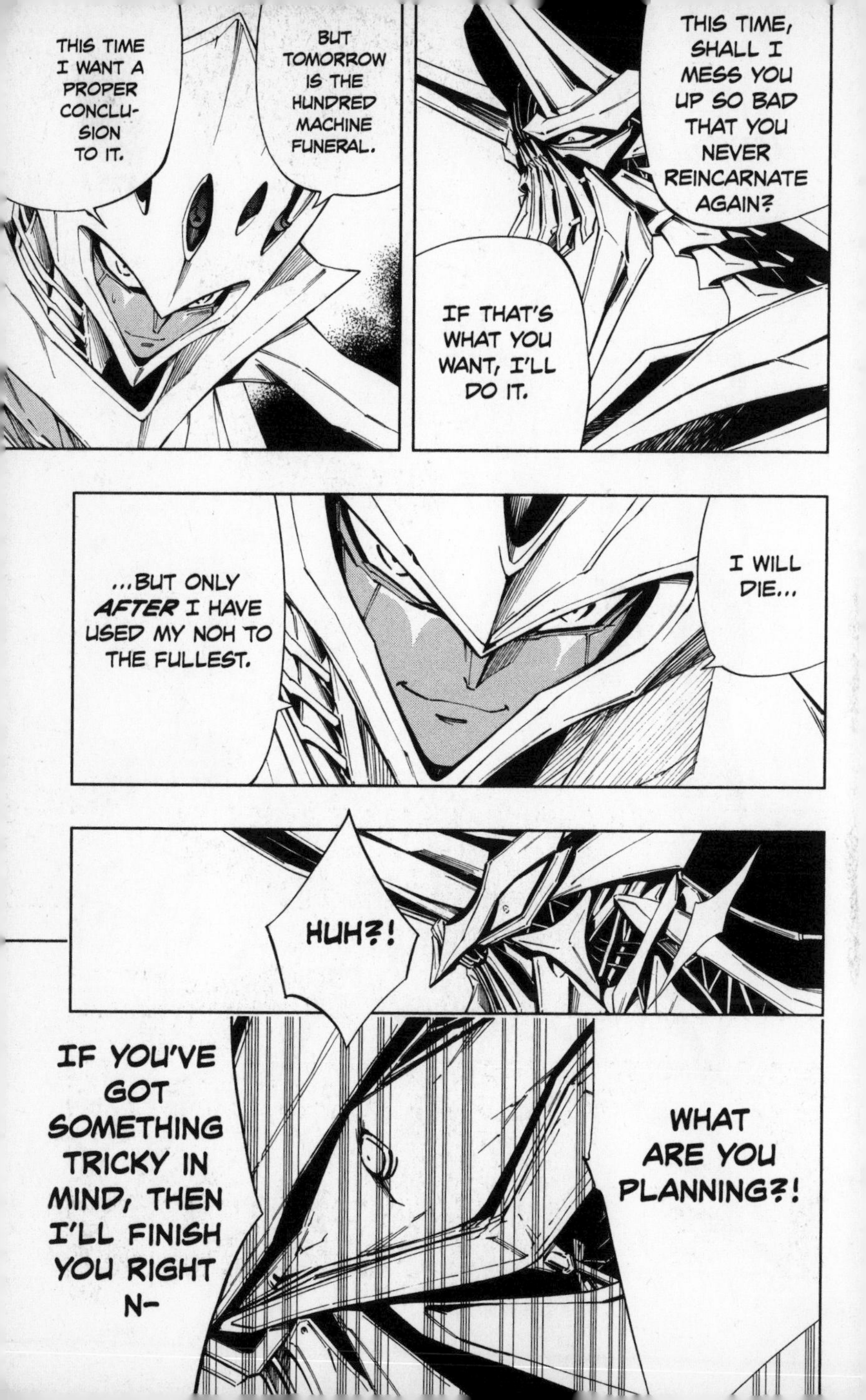
THIS TIME, SHALL I MESS YOU UP SO BAD THAT YOU NEVER REINCARNATE AGAIN?
IF THAT'S WHAT YOU WANT, I'LL DO IT.
BUT TOMORROW IS THE HUNDRED MACHINE FUNERAL.
THIS TIME I WANT A PROPER CONCLU-SION TO IT.
I WILL DIE...
...BUT ONLY *AFTER* I HAVE USED MY NOH TO THE FULLEST.
HUH?!
WHAT ARE YOU PLANNING?!
IF YOU'VE GOT SOMETHING TRICKY IN MIND, THEN I'LL FINISH YOU RIGHT N-

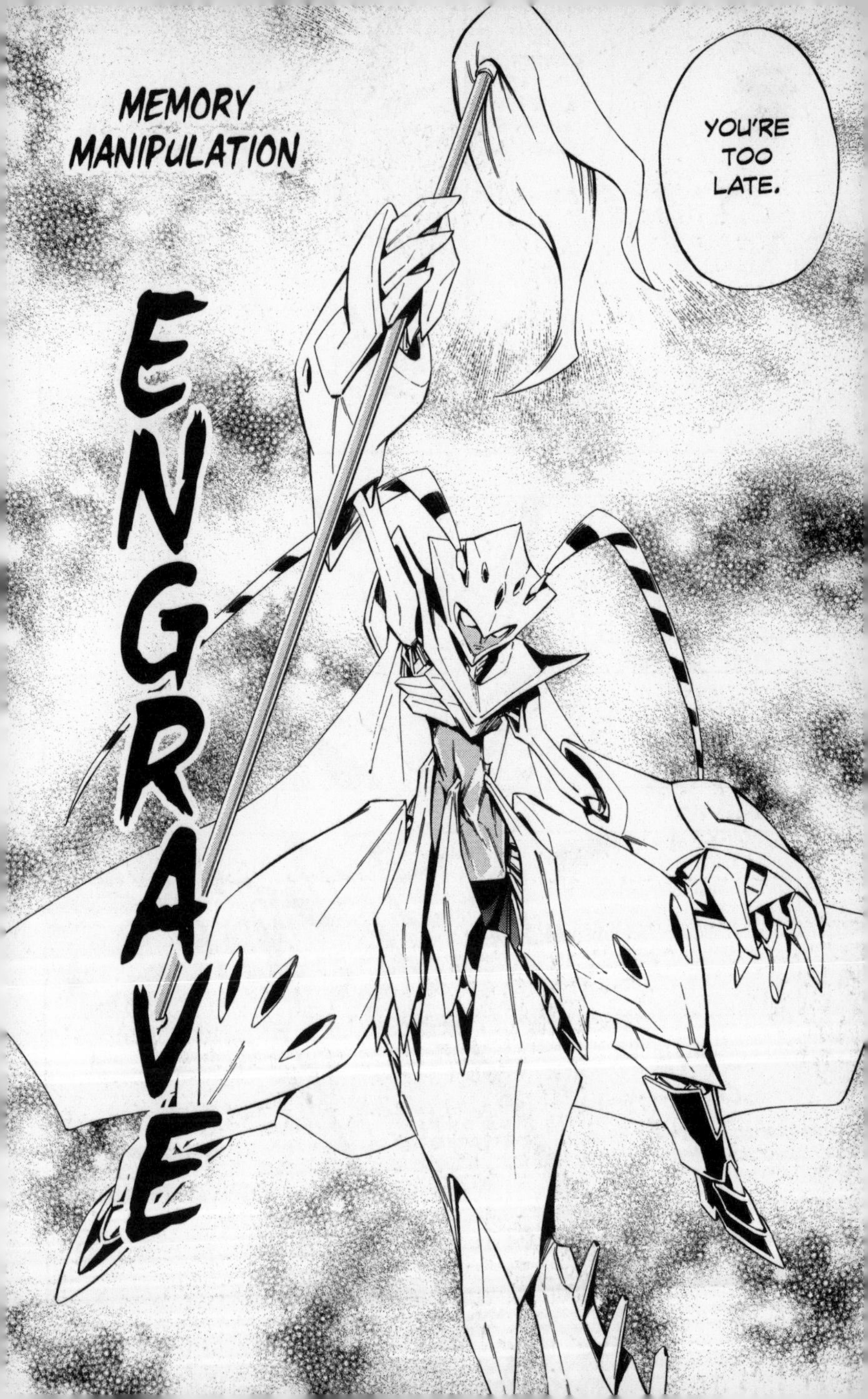
YOU'RE TOO LATE.
MEMORY MANIPULATION
ENGRAVE

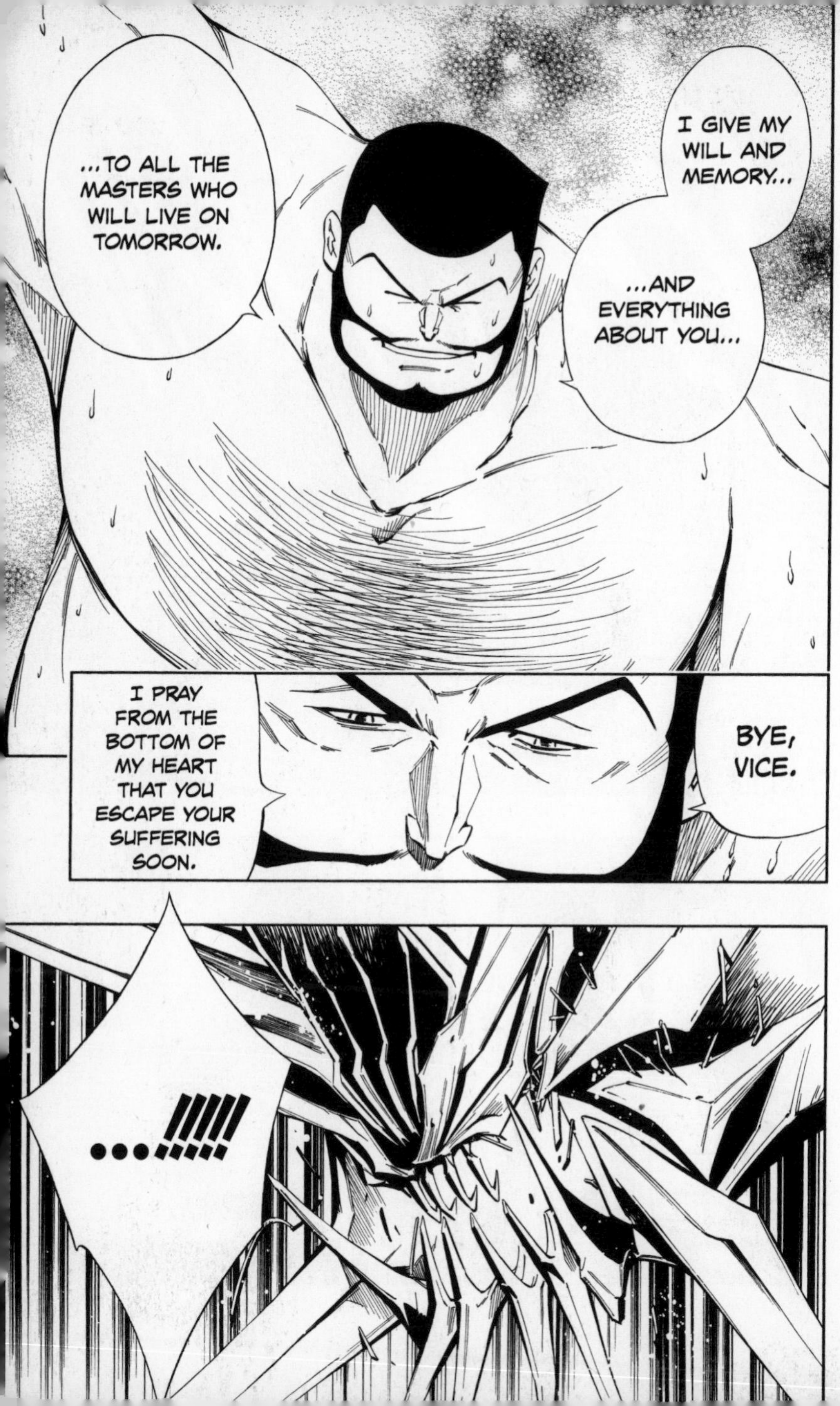
I GIVE MY WILL AND MEMORY...
...AND EVERYTHING ABOUT YOU...
...TO ALL THE MASTERS WHO WILL LIVE ON TOMORROW.
BYE, VICE.
I PRAY FROM THE BOTTOM OF MY HEART THAT YOU ESCAPE YOUR SUFFERING SOON.
...!!!!!!

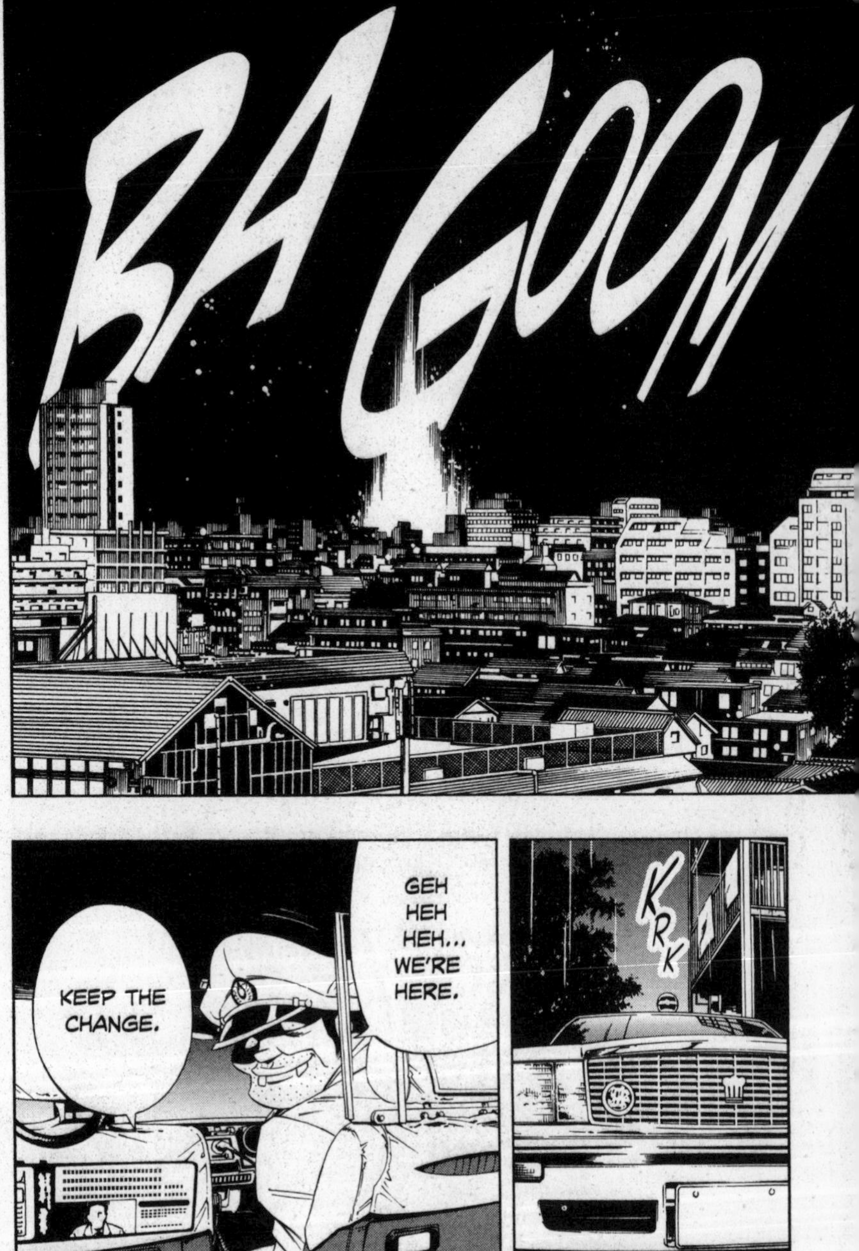
BA GOOM
KRK
GEH HEH HEH... WE'RE HERE.
KEEP THE CHANGE.

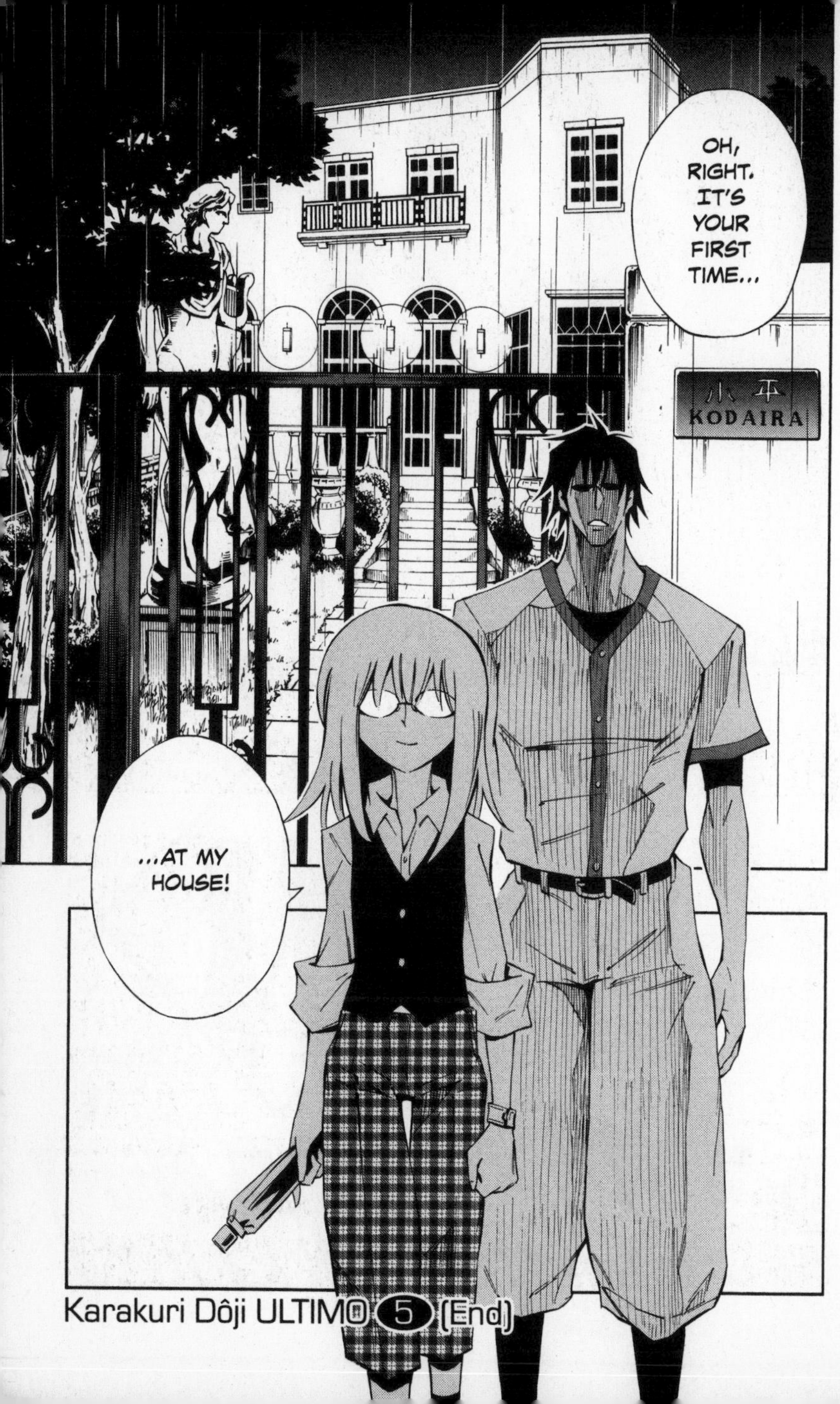
OH, RIGHT. IT'S YOUR FIRST TIME...
小平
KODAIRA
...AT MY HOUSE!
Karakuri Dôji ULTIMO 5 (End)

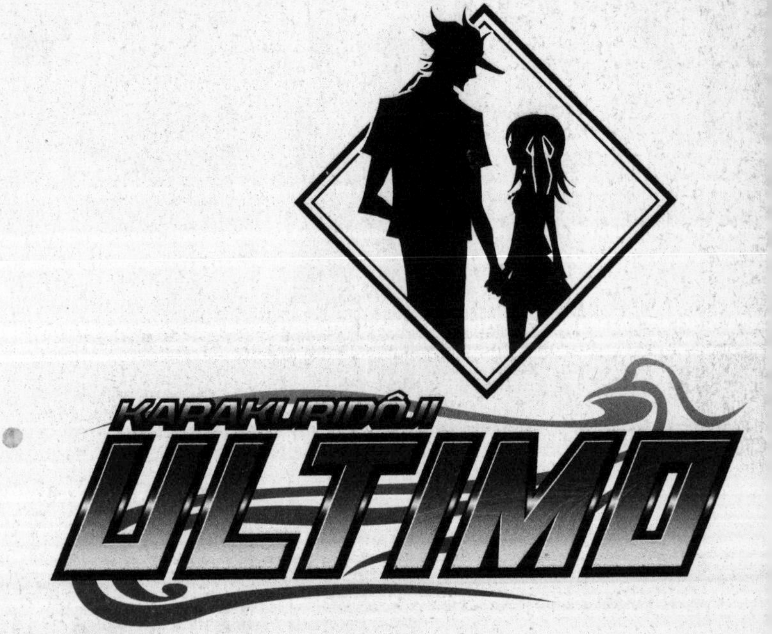

KARAKURIDÔJI

ULTIMO

ULTIMO

Volume 5

Original Concept: Stan Lee
Story and Art by: Hiroyuki Takei

SHONEN JUMP Manga Edition

This graphic novel contains material that was originally published in English in SHONEN JUMP #95–98. Artwork in the magazine may have been slightly altered from that presented here.

Translation | John Werry
Series Touch-up Art & Lettering | James Gaubatz
Design | Fawn Lau
Series Editor | Joel Enos
Graphic Novel Editor | Megan Bates

Printed in the U.S.A.

Published by VIZ Media, LLC
P.O. Box 77010
San Francisco, CA 94107

10 9 8 7 6 5 4 3 2 1
First printing, June 2011

RATED T

PARENTAL ADVISORY
ULTIMO is rated T for Teen and is recommended for ages 13 and up. This volume contains fantasy

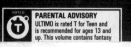

STAN LEE

As a kid, Stanley Martin Lieber spent a lot of time dreaming up wild adventures. By the time he got to high school, he was putting his imagination to work writing stories at Timely, a publishing company that went on to become the legendary Marvel Comics. Starting with the *Fantastic Four*, Lee and his partner Jack Kirby created just about every superhero you can think of, including *Spider-Man*, the *X-Men*, the *Hulk*, *Iron Man*, *Daredevil* and *Thor*. Along the way, he wrote under many pen names, but the one that stuck was Stan Lee.

HIROYUKI TAKEI

Unconventional author/artist Hiroyuki Takei began his career by winning the coveted Hop Step Award (for new manga artists) and the Osamu Tezuka Cultural Prize (named after the famous artist of the same name). After working as an assistant to famed artist Nobuhiro Watsuki, Takei debuted in *Weekly Shonen Jump* in 1997 with *Butsu Zone*, an action series based on Buddhist mythology. His multicultural adventure manga *Shaman King*, which debuted in 1998, became a hit and was adapted into an anime TV series. Takei lists Osamu Tezuka, American comics and robot anime among his many influences.

...WE'LL *CRUSH* HIM BEFORE HE RETURNS TO NORMAL.

IN THE NEXT VOLUME...
THE HOUSE OF AWAKENING

ust when Jealousy and Rune get Yamato in their nasty clutches, his ancient self awakens to save the day. But does the bandit Yamato from 900 years ago have the same priorities and desires as our modern-day unlikely hero Yamato? And even if he can keep his mind on the business of stopping the Hundred Machine Funeral, Désir—now with a comely human accomplice—has a plan to sidetrack him yet again!

AVAILABLE SEPTEMBER 2011!

The World's Greatest Manga
Now available on your iPad

**Full of FREE previews and tons of
new manga for you to explore**

From legendary manga like *Dragon Ball*
to *Bakuman₀*, the newest series from the
creators of *Death Note*, the best manga
in the world is now available on the iPad
through the official VIZ Manga app.

- **Free App**
- **New content weekly**
- **Free chapter 1 previews**

BAKUMAN。

STORY BY TSUGUMI OHBA
ART BY TAKESHI OBATA

From the creators of *Death Note*

The mystery
behind manga making
REVEALED!

Average student Moritaka Mashiro enjoys drawing for fun. When his classmate and aspiring writer Akito Takagi discovers his talent, he begs to team up. But what exactly does it take to make it in the manga-publishing world?

Bakuman。, Vol. 1
ISBN: 978-1-4215-3513-5
$9.99 US / $12.99 CAN *

Manga on sale at store.viz.com
Also available at your local bookstore or comic store

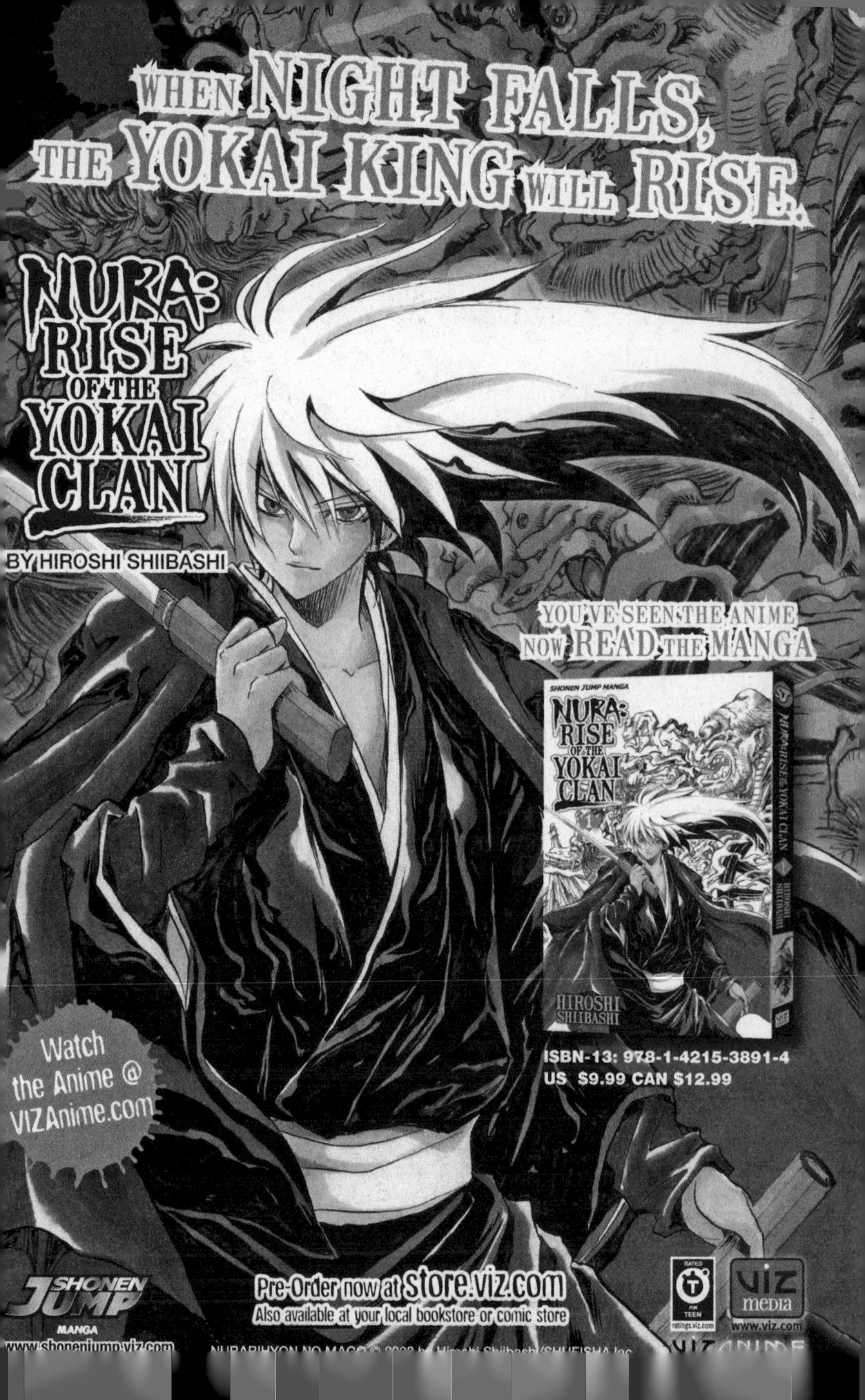

WHEN NIGHT FALLS, THE YOKAI KING WILL RISE.
NURA: RISE OF THE YOKAI CLAN
BY HIROSHI SHIIBASHI
YOU'VE SEEN THE ANIME
NOW READ THE MANGA
SHONEN JUMP MANGA
NURA: RISE OF THE YOKAI CLAN
HIROSHI SHIIBASHI
ISBN-13: 978-1-4215-3891-4
US $9.99 CAN $12.99
Watch the Anime @ VIZAnime.com
SHONEN JUMP MANGA
www.shonenjump.viz.com
Pre-Order now at store.viz.com
Also available at your local bookstore or comic store
RATED T FOR TEEN
ratings.viz.com
VIZ media
www.viz.com

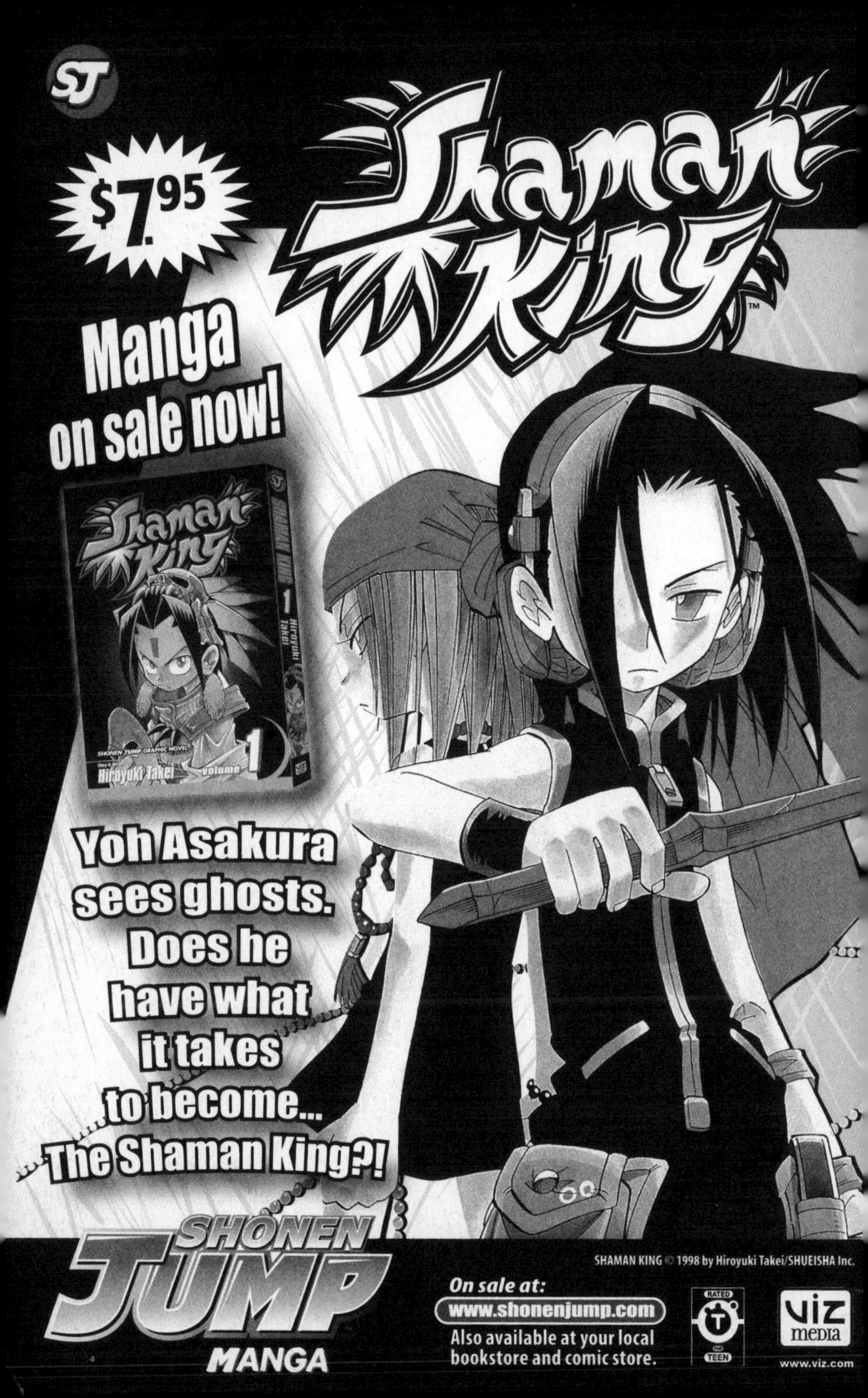
SJ
$7.95
Shaman King™
Manga on sale now!
Shaman King
SHONEN JUMP GRAPHIC NOVEL
Hiroyuki Takei
volume 1
Yoh Asakura sees ghosts. Does he have what it takes to become... The Shaman King?!
SHONEN JUMP MANGA
SHAMAN KING © 1998 by Hiroyuki Takei/SHUEISHA Inc.
On sale at:
www.shonenjump.com
Also available at your local bookstore and comic store.
RATED T TEEN
VIZ media
www.viz.com

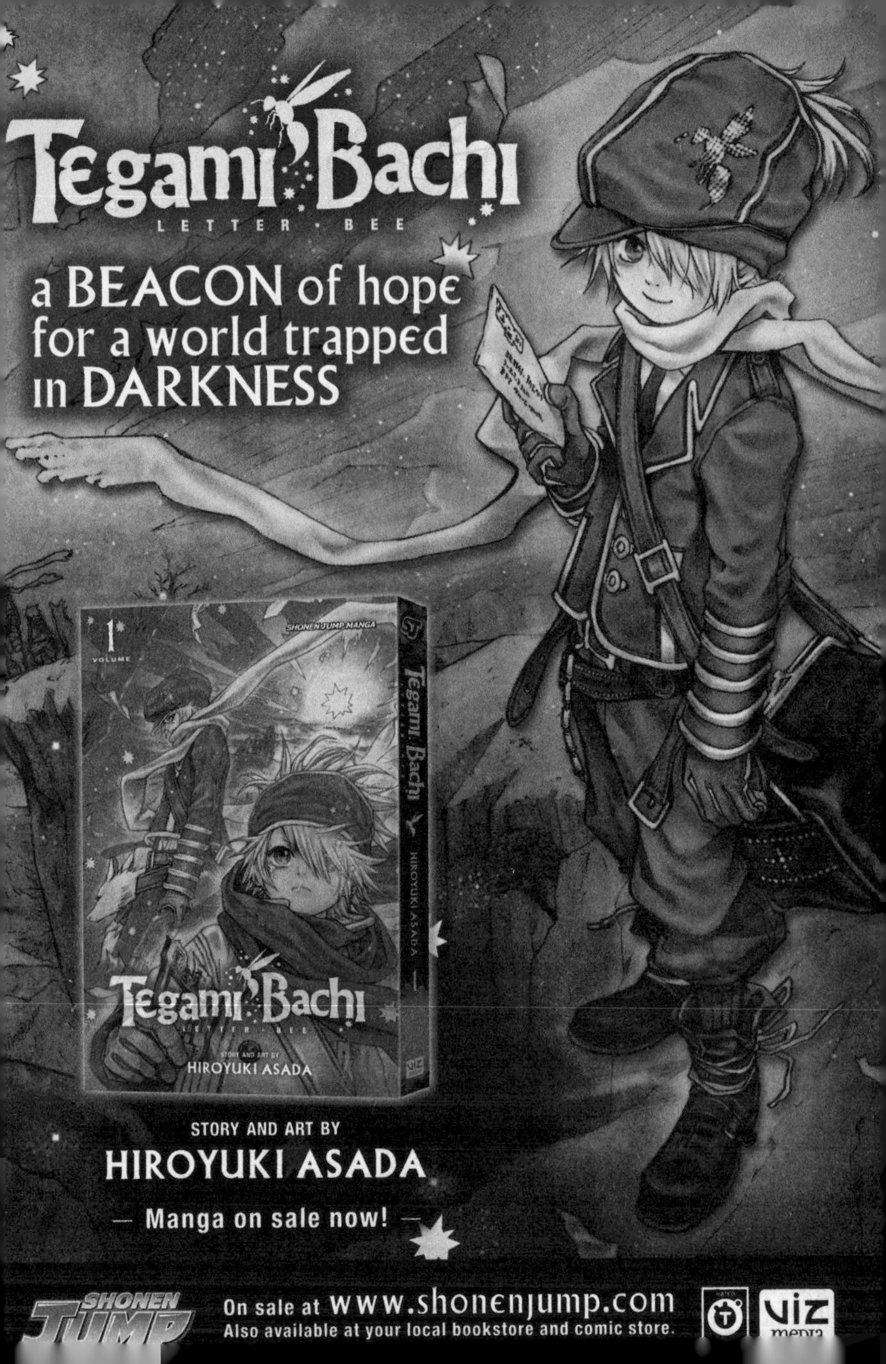
Tegami Bachi
LETTER • BEE
a BEACON of hope for a world trapped in DARKNESS
1 VOLUME
SHONEN JUMP MANGA
Tegami Bachi
HIROYUKI ASADA
Tegami Bachi
LETTER BEE
STORY AND ART BY
HIROYUKI ASADA
STORY AND ART BY
HIROYUKI ASADA
— Manga on sale now! —
SHONEN JUMP
On sale at www.shonenjump.com
Also available at your local bookstore and comic store.
VIZ media

SHONEN JUMP

THE WORLD'S MOST POPULAR MANGA

**STORY AND ART BY
TITE KUBO**

**STORY AND ART BY
EIICHIRO ODA**

**STORY AND ART BY
HIROYUKI ASADA**

JUMP INTO THE ACTION BY TELLING US WHAT YOU LOVE (AND WHAT YOU DON'T)

LET YOUR VOICE BE HEARD!

SHONENJUMP.VIZ.COM/MANGASURVEY

HELP US MAKE MORE OF THE WORLD'S MOST POPULAR MANGA!